T0211846

IFIP Advances in Information and Communication Technology 457

Editor-in-Chief

Kai Rannenberg, Goethe University, Frankfurt, Germany

IFIP – The International Federation for Information Processing

IFIP was founded in 1960 under the auspices of UNESCO, following the First World Computer Congress held in Paris the previous year. An umbrella organization for societies working in information processing, IFIP's aim is two-fold: to support information processing within its member countries and to encourage technology transfer to developing nations. As its mission statement clearly states,

> IFIP's mission is to be the leading, truly international, apolitical organization which encourages and assists in the development, exploitation and application of information technology for the benefit of all people.

IFIP is a non-profitmaking organization, run almost solely by 2500 volunteers. It operates through a number of technical committees, which organize events and publications. IFIP's events range from an international congress to local seminars, but the most important are:

- The IFIP World Computer Congress, held every second year;
- Open conferences;
- Working conferences.

The flagship event is the IFIP World Computer Congress, at which both invited and contributed papers are presented. Contributed papers are rigorously refereed and the rejection rate is high.

As with the Congress, participation in the open conferences is open to all and papers may be invited or submitted. Again, submitted papers are stringently refereed.

The working conferences are structured differently. They are usually run by a working group and attendance is small and by invitation only. Their purpose is to create an atmosphere conducive to innovation and development. Refereeing is also rigorous and papers are subjected to extensive group discussion.

Publications arising from IFIP events vary. The papers presented at the IFIP World Computer Congress and at open conferences are published as conference proceedings, while the results of the working conferences are often published as collections of selected and edited papers.

Any national society whose primary activity is about information processing may apply to become a full member of IFIP, although full membership is restricted to one society per country. Full members are entitled to vote at the annual General Assembly. National societies preferring a less committed involvement may apply for associate or corresponding membership. Associate members enjoy the same benefits as full members, but without voting rights. Corresponding members are not represented in IFIP bodies. Affiliated membership is open to non-national societies, and individual and honorary membership schemes are also offered.

More information about this series at http://www.springer.com/series/6102

Jan Camenisch · Simone Fischer-Hübner
Marit Hansen (Eds.)

Privacy and Identity Management for the Future Internet in the Age of Globalisation

9th IFIP WG 9.2, 9.5, 9.6/11.7, 11.4, 11.6/SIG 9.2.2
International Summer School
Patras, Greece, September 7–12, 2014
Revised Selected Papers

Springer

Editors
Jan Camenisch
IBM Research Zurich
Rüschlikon
Switzerland

Simone Fischer-Hübner
Karlstad University
Karlstad
Sweden

Marit Hansen
Unabhängiges Landeszentrum
    für Datenschutz Schleswig-Holstein
    (ULD)
Kiel
Germany

ISSN 1868-4238   ISSN 1868-422X (electronic)
IFIP Advances in Information and Communication Technology
ISBN 978-3-319-37009-5   ISBN 978-3-319-18621-4 (eBook)
DOI 10.1007/978-3-319-18621-4

Springer Cham Heidelberg New York Dordrecht London
© IFIP International Federation for Information Processing 2015
Softcover reprint of the hardcover 1st edition 2015

Printed on acid-free paper

Springer International Publishing AG Switzerland is part of Springer Science+Business Media
(www.springer.com)

Preface

New technologies such as social media, cloud computing, big data, and ubiquitous and ambient technologies operate on a global scale, their use not only touches the countries where they originate (in many cases, the USA), but individuals and groups around the globe. The recent revelations regarding the surveillance practices further prove that personal data is communicated, collected, and processed on a global scale. Privacy and identity management issues have hence become global issues requiring the attention of multiple disciplines, both technical (computer science, cryptography) and non-technical (law, ethics, social sciences, philosophy), and the need to look beyond national borders.

Now, how can the individuals' privacy rights be achieved effectively in a globalizing information society in which both states and private enterprises exhibit great data hunger? What technologies, frameworks, and tools do we need to gain, regain, and maintain informational self-determination and lifelong privacy? Do we have to advance the concepts of privacy and identity management in this quickly evolving world?

These questions and many others were addressed by the IFIP Summer School 2014 on Privacy and Identity Management for the Future Internet in the Age of Globalization. The Summer School organization was a joint effsort of IFIP (International Federation for Information Processing, Working Groups 9.2, 9.5, 9.6/11.7, 11.4, 11.6, Special Interest Group 9.2.2), the University of Patras, Kritiki, and the EU research projects ABC4Trust, A4Cloud, AU2EU, PRISMS, and FutureID.

The aim of the IFIP Summer School is traditionally manifold: to increase the research community in privacy and identity management, to further research, and to enable the update of privacy-enhancing technologies. To address this, the school has invited a number of keynote speakers and held sessions with contributed papers and workshops dedicated to the discussion of particular topics.

This time, the summer school was honored to have keynote presentations by Rehab Alnemr, Kim Cameron, Michael Friedewald, Zoi Kolitsi, George Metakides, Marit Hansen, Joachim Meyer, Gregory Neven, Christine O'Keefe, Bart Preneel, Nadya Purtova, Kai Rannenberg, Marc van Lieshout, and Aimee van Wynsberghe. Thank you all for your great talks!

Complementing the keynotes, the summer school featured a number of parallel workshop sessions. Eleven of these were dedicated to the presentation and discussion of the papers selected from the submissions. In addition to this, there were a number of other workshops where topics were discussed.

The ABC4Trust project arranged for four workshop sessions discussing different aspects of attributed-based credentials supporting privacy (Privacy-ABCs). The first workshop session focused on new application scenarios and storage devices for credentials such as mobile devices and smart cards. The second one discussed the practical use of inspection and revocation in the context of anonymous credentials. The third workshop session was concerned with data protection and privacy requirements as well as the legal context for Privacy-ABCs. In the fourth session, the participants could get their hands on the Privacy-ABCs: it was explained how to download and install the code available from the ABC4Trust repository and how to build applications on top of it.

The A4Cloud project gave a tutorial on accountability metrics and tools that have been developed within the A4Cloud project.

Finally, a Smart Society Project workshop was held on ethical aspects, privacy risks, and technical privacy solutions in relation to Peer Profiling in Collective Adaptive Systems.

This book contains the thoroughly refereed post-conference proceedings of the summer school. In particular, it contains revised papers selected from numerous submissions. In the first round, submitted papers were reviewed and selected for presentation at the summer school. Most of these papers were revised based on the comments and discussions at the summer school and have undergone a second thorough round of review (by 2 to 5 reviewers), selection, and revision to be included in the present proceedings.

In addition to these papers, the proceedings contain four keynote papers: "Privacy and Security Perceptions of European Citizens: A Test of the Trade-off Model" by Michael Friedewald, Marc van Lieshout, Sven Rung, Merel Ooms, and Jelmer Ypma, "Towards an Engineering Model of Privacy-Related Decisions" by Joachim Meyer, "Privacy and Confidentiality in Service Science and Big Data Analytics" by Christine O'Keefe, and "ABC4Trust: Protecting Privacy in Identity Management by Bringing Privacy-ABCs into Real-life" by Ahmad Sabouri and Kai Rannenberg.

Finally, the Program Committee Chairs selected the paper entitled "Event Invitations in Decentralized Online Social Networks: Formalization and Protocol Design" by Guillermo Rodríguez-Cano et al. for the Best Student Paper Award. Congratulations Guillermo!

We express our gratitude to the numerous people who made the summer school such a success: all the authors who submitted papers, the keynote speakers, the participants, and, last but clearly not least, the members of the organizing and the Program and Steering Committees as well as the additional reviewers. In particular, we owe special thanks to the Local Organizers from the University of Patras, Panagiota Panagopoulou, Vasia Liagkou, and Yannis Stamatiou, for their great hospitality and support.

Thank you!

March 2015

Jan Camenisch
Simone Fischer-Hübner
Marit Hansen

Organization

Program Committee

Karin Bernsmed	SINTEF, Norway
Franziska Boehm	Münster University, Germany
Katrin Borcea-Pfitzmann	Technische Universität Dresden, Germany
Caspar Bowden	Privacy Advocate, UK
Ian Brown	Oxford University, UK
Sonja Buchegger	Royal Institute of Technology (KTH), Sweden
Jan Camenisch	IBM Research, Switzerland
Bart De Decker	Katholieke Universiteit Leuven, Belgium
Penny Duquenoy	Middlesex University, UK
David Erdos	University of Cambridge, UK
Simone Fischer-Hübner	Karlstad University, Sweden
Sara Foresti	University of Milan, Italy
Michael Friedewald	Fraunhofer Institute for Systems and Innovation Research (ISI), Germany
Lothar Fritsch	Norwegian Computer Center, Norway
Thomas Gross	Newcastle University, UK
Marit Hansen	Unabhängiges Landeszentrum für Datenschutz Schleswig-Holstein (ULD), Germany
Jaap-Henk Hoepman	Radboud University, The Netherlands
Bert-Jaap Koops	Tilburg University, The Netherlands
Eleni Kosta	Tilburg University, The Netherlands
Ioannis Krontiris	Huawei Technologies Co. Ltd., Germany
Louise Leenen	CSIR, South Africa
Ronald Leenes	Tilburg University, The Netherlands
Vasiliki Liagkou	University of Patras, Greece
Refik Molva	Eurecom, France
Maartje Niezen	Tilburg University, The Netherlands
Norberto Patrignani	Politecnico di Torino, Italy
Siani Pearson	HP Labs, UK
Charles Raab	Edinburgh University, UK
Johanneke Siljee	TNO, The Netherlands
Einar Snekkenes	Gjøvik University College, Norway
Bibi Van Den Berg	Leiden University, The Netherlands
Jozef Vyskoc	VaF, Slovak Republic
Diane Whitehouse	The Castlegate Consultancy, UK
David Wright	Trilateral Research & Consulting, UK
Erik Wästlund	Karlstad University, Sweden

Tal Zarsky	Haifa University, Israel
Rose-Mharie Åhlfeldt	University of Skövde, Sweden
Melek Önen	Eurecom, France

Additional Reviewers

Milutinovic, Milica
Put, Andreas

Contents

Privacy Technologies and Protocols

Project Workshops and Tutorial Papers

Invited Keynote Papers

ABC4Trust: Protecting Privacy in Identity Management by Bringing Privacy-ABCs into Real-Life

Ahmad Sabouri[✉] and Kai Rannenberg

Deutsche Telekom Chair of Mobile Business and Multilateral Security,
Goethe University Frankfurt, Theodor-W.-Adorno-Platz 4, 60323 Frankfurt, Germany
{Ahmad.Sabouri,Kai.Rannenberg}@m-chair.de
https://www.abc4trust.eu

Abstract. Security of the Identity Management system or privacy of the users? Why not both? Privacy-preserving Attribute-based Credentials (Privacy-ABCs) can cope with this dilemma and offer a basis for privacy-respecting Identity Management systems.

This paper explains the distinct features of Privacy-ABCs as implemented in the EU-sponsored ABC4Trust project via example usage scenarios from the ABC4Trust pilot trials. In particular, it aims for a deeper insight from the application perspective on how Privacy-ABCs can support addressing real-life Identity Management requirements while users' privacy is protected.

1 Introduction

As using online services penetrates deeper in our everyday life, lots of trust-sensitive transactions such as banking and shopping are carried out online and many users would prefer to perform their transactions online rather than follow the traditional procedures. In this regard, the biggest challenges are to deal with proper user authentication and access control, without threatening users' privacy.

The currently employed Identity Management systems have limitations when it comes to users' privacy. Nevertheless, new promising techniques, known as Privacy-ABCs, have emerged to enable privacy-respecting Identity Management solutions. In this regard, the ABC4Trust EU Project[1] put considerable effort to foster adoption of such technologies by designing an architectural framework for Privacy-ABCs, implementing it, and trialling it in two pilots.

In this paper, we aim to elaborate on the most important features provided by Privacy-ABCs via real-life example usage scenarios from the ABC4Trust trials. The rest of this paper is organized as follows. Section 2 describes the issues of the existing Identity Management systems. In Sect. 3, we introduce Privacy-ABCs and explain how they work. Later we describe the ABC4Trust pilots in Sect. 4.

---

[1] https://abc4trust.eu.

© IFIP International Federation for Information Processing 2015
J. Camenisch et al. (Eds.): Privacy and Identity 2014, IFIP AICT 457, pp. 3–16, 2015.
DOI: 10.1007/978-3-319-18621-4_1

Section 5 focuses on the most important features of Privacy-ABCs and there we elaborate how these features help to deal with the requirements of the pilots. Later in Sect. 6, we briefly describe the ABC4Trust architecture for Privacy-ABCs and then conclude the paper in Sect. 7.

2   Privacy Issues in Identity Management

This chapter describes the privacy issues in nowadays digital identity management systems. Although most of the commonly used strong authentication techniques offer a suitable level of security, they are not appropriately designed to protect the privacy of the users. For instance, use of X.509 [1] certificates causes "Over-identification" by mandating the users to reveal all the attested attributes in the certificate to preserve the validity of the digital signature even if only a subset of attributes is required for the authentication purpose. Apart from this, the online users also have to be able to compartmentalize their activities in different domains and prevent profiling by both Service Providers and Identity Service Providers (IdSP). Evidently, the static representation of X.509 certificates fails to address the problem and makes it possible to trace users' online activities.

Using online authentication and authorization techniques such as OpenID [2], SAML [3], Facebook Connect [4], and OAuth [5] could support the minimal disclosure principle, as they enable the user to provide the Service Provider with only the requested information rather than the whole user's profile stored at the IdSP. However, all these protocols suffer from a so-called "Calling Home" problem, meaning that for every authentication transaction the user is required to contact the IdSP (e.g., Facebook, OpenID Provider). This introduces privacy risks to both users and Service Providers. More specifically, it would not be difficult for the IdSP to trace the user and profile her online activities due to the knowledge it gains about the Service Providers she visits. Moreover, the IdSP can collect a considerable amount of information about a Service Provider by analysing the profile of the users who request to authenticate to that specific service.

In summary, when designing identity management and access control systems inspired by the paradigm of Privacy by Design, the following concepts related to data thriftiness shall be of direct or indirect interest for bodies working on privacy-friendly ecosystems:

– Partial Identities and Partial Identifiers: More and more public and private parties are trying to overcome the natural borders between domains of activities, making users ever more transparent from ever more perspectives, e.g. for many Service Providers offering services that relate to different parts of users' lives. Partial Identities and Partial Identifiers become more and more important for users to retain these borders by reducing the dangers of unwanted linkability across domains. Therefore the definition of Identity as a "set of attributes related to an entity", that has been globally standardized in the Part 1 of the framework for identity management [6] developed by ISO/IEC

JTC 1/SC 27/WG 5 "Identity Management and Privacy Technologies", is useful for designing privacy-respecting identity management.

- Unlinkability: Unlinkability is related to Partial Identities and Identifiers, but in this context focusses on multiple uses of services within one domain. It ensures that a user may make multiple uses of resources or services without others being able to profile these activities.
- Minimal Disclosure: It is a common practice that Service Providers rely on the information about users provided by other entities that have an authentic profile of users' attributes. However, these entities typically possess a richer collection of information than is needed by the respective Service Provider. In this regard, the users should have the possibility to calibrate the amount of disclosed information to the requested set only. Therefore on the side of the Service Providers risk management processes compatible with the minimal disclosure need to be established.

3 Privacy-Preserving Attribute-Based Credentials (Privacy-ABCs)

Privacy-ABCs can offer strong authentication and a high level of security to Service Providers with user privacy preserved, so that it follows the paradigm of Multilateral Security [7]. Users can obtain certified attributes in the form of Privacy-ABCs, and later derive unlinkable tokens that only reveal the necessary subset of information needed by the Service Providers. Prominent instantiations of such Privacy-ABC technologies are Microsoft U-Prove[2] [8] and IBM Idemix[3] [9].

A Credential is defined to be "a certified container of attributes issued by an Issuer to a User" [10]. An Issuer vouches for the correctness of the attribute values for a User when issuing a credential for her. For example, a school can issue an "Enrolment Credential" for a pupil, which contains several attested attributes such as first name, last name, student id and the enrolment year.

Fig. 1. A sample presentation scenario

A typical authentication scenario using Privacy-ABCs is shown in Fig. 1 where a User seeks to access an online service offered by a Service Provider. The Service Provider performs a so-called Verifier role and expresses its requirement for granting access to the service in the form of a Presentation Policy. In

---

[2] http://www.microsoft.com/uprove.

[3] http://www.zurich.ibm.com/idemix/.

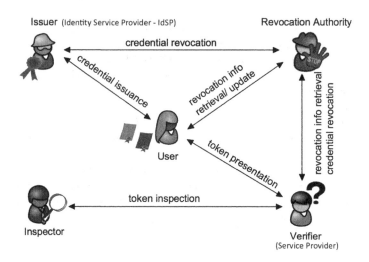

Fig. 2. Entities and relations in the Privacy-ABC's architecture [10]

the next step, the User needs to come up with a combination of her credentials to derive an acceptable authentication token that satisfies the given policy. After the Verifier confirms the authenticity and credibility of the Presentation Token, the User gains access to the corresponding service. It is worth noting that the human User is represented by her UserAgent, a software component running either on a local device (e.g., on the User's computer or mobile phone) or remotely on a trusted cloud service. In addition, the User may also bind credentials to special hardware tokens, e.g. smart cards, to improve security.

As Fig. 2 shows, in addition to *User*, *Issuer*, and *Verifier*, two other (optional) entities are involved during the life-cycle of Privacy-ABCs [10]. The Revocation Authority is responsible for revoking issued credentials. Both the User and the Verifier must obtain the most recent revocation information from the Revocation Authority to generate presentation tokens and respectively, verify them. The Inspector is an entity who can de-anonymize presentation tokens under specific circumstances. To make use of this feature, the Verifier must specify in the presentation policy the conditions, i.e., which Inspector should be able to recover which attribute(s) and under which circumstances. The User is informed about the de-anonymization options at the time that the presentation token is generated and she has to be involved actively to make this possible.

The EC funded project Attribute-based Credentials for Trust (ABC4Trust)[4] brought all the common features of the existing Privacy-ABC technologies together and provided a framework abstracting from the concrete cryptographic realization of the modules underneath. This gives software developers the flexibility to build Privacy-ABC enabled systems without concern about what cryptographic schemes will be employed at the bottom layer. As a direct result, the

---

[4] https://abc4trust.eu.

Service Providers are free to choose from those concrete cryptographic libraries that implement the ABC4Trust required interfaces, and plug them into their software solutions. This helps to avoid a lock-in with a specific technology, as the threat of a lock-in reduces the trust into an infrastructure.

4   Trialling Privacy-ABCs in Real Life Applications

The ABC4Trust project realized the first ever implementation of Privacy-ABC systems in production environments and gathered experiences on operation, interoperability, user acceptance, and so forth in two specific trials. Having these two pilots gave the opportunity to test Privacy-ABCs use and performance with two user groups of differing skills and needs. One user group were were students at a Greek university, whereas the other group were pupils at a school in Sweden. The trials were designed quite different in order to cover a broad variety of requirements and thus as well credentials.

4.1   Online Course Evaluation

A standard practice in most universities is to collect the opinions of the students who have taken a course and to evaluate different aspects of that course to further improve the quality of education. However, both the students and the professors have legitimate concerns about the process of course evaluation. The students may be worried about their identities being linked to their evaluation forms, resulting in negative impacts on their grades or education records. Meanwhile, professors consider a minimum level of participation in the lectures to be necessary for the students to get the real experience of the course and therefore to be eligible to evaluate it. The scenario becomes even more complex in terms of security, privacy, and trust, when electronic evaluation is desired.

Privacy-ABCs could help to address the aforementioned requirements in an online course evaluation system. In this regard, ABC4Trust executed two rounds of trials in Fall 2012 and Fall 2013 at the Patras University in Greece to realize such a system. Whilst the identity and privacy of the students were protected, the opinions of the students, who had attended more than a certain number of lectures, were collected via an evaluation portal.

At the beginning of the semester, the pilot participants were provided with their start-up kit including smart cards and necessary login information enabling the participants to bootstrap their access to the pilot system, register their smart cards and obtain their Privacy-ABCs from the identity management system.

After the initialization actions were taken at the beginning of the semester, the students could record their participation in the lectures on their smart cards. Upon entering the lecture room, every student had to swipe her card in front of the device installed in the room in order to collect attendance units for that specific lecture. It is important to mention that these units were collected anonymously, meaning that no identifiable information was transferred to the system, which otherwise might have led to privacy breaches. Therefore, the attendance records were only stored on the smart cards of the students and not anywhere else.

During the evaluation period, the student could access the evaluation form online and submit their opinion if they could prove that:

1. they are a student of the university,
2. they are registered in the course,
3. they have attended at least a minimum number of the lectures from the course.

If all these conditions were met, the smart card could produce a Privacy-ABCs presentation proof that attested the student's eligibility to evaluate the course. While it was not possible to link the evaluations to the identity of the participants, the authentication step was designed in a way that the evaluation portal could prevent the same users from submitting multiple evaluations.

The second round of the trial aimed to further test the Privacy-ABCs' features developed in ABC4Trust in an actual deployment environment. New features such as revocation of credentials, advance issuance, and inspection of tokens (de-anonymization) were implemented and introduced into the pilot. The scenarios of the first round were extended in order to best integrate these new features. More specifically, after the students submitted their evaluations, they could receive a new credential allowing them to later take part in a privacy-friendly tombola. When the winner was selected, her identity was revealed through the inspection of her presentation token. In this phase, there was no privacy risk for the winner with regard to the evaluation she provided, as the only information one could learn was that the winner had submitted an evaluation form.

4.2   School Community Interaction Platform

The Norrtullskolan school in Söderhamn, Sweden, hosted the second pilot of ABC4Trust, where a privacy-friendly communication platform, built upon Privacy-ABCs, was deployed to encourage communication between pupils, their parents and school personnel. The pupils were able to authenticate themselves in order to access restricted online activities and restricted information. Moreover, they were able to remain anonymous when they asked private and sensitive questions to school personnel, while simultaneously assuring the school personnel that they were communicating with the authorised pupils of the respective school or class.

The platform was developed as a web-based application to be used for chat communication, counselling, political discussions, and exchange of sensitive and personal data between pupils, parents, and school personnel such as teachers, administrators, coaches, and nurses. This pilot specially helped to gather information on the usability of the Privacy-ABC systems under especially challenging usability conditions posed by children users. Due to the wide range of activities in this trial, the pilot was operated in two rounds where the first round was on a smaller scale to investigate the scalability of the platform and thus be able to address its shortcomings before a larger scale deployment.

All the pilot participants were equipped with the necessary hardware so that they could use the platform from their personal computers as well as the computers in the school. The smart cards were preloaded with a set of credentials that specified the participants' basic information such as first name, last name, and birth-date, their roles (i.e. pupil, parent, teacher, nurse, etc.), the classes and courses that the pupils were enrolled in, consequently giving the chance to define the access policies based on these attributes in the credentials.

The community interaction platform used an abstract model called "Restricted Area" (RA) that provided the virtual environment for the aforementioned communication activities. Every user could initiate such a private space and define access policies in order to restrict the participation to her desired target group. For example, a teacher could create an RA with "Chat" functionality to collect the opinions of the pupils about her teaching methods and limit the access to this chat room to participants of a specific class. In this case, the pupils of that class could join the discussion without being identified, while the other students from the school were prohibited to enter this chat room.

5 Privacy-ABCs Features

In this section we introduce some of the most important features of Privacy-ABCs along with examples of their usage in the real scenarios of our trials. In summary, we talk about pseudonyms and their relation to partial identities, minimal disclosure, untraceability and unlinkability, advance credential issuance techniques, Inspection process, and security mechanisms.

5.1 Multiple Pseudonyms

Using X.509 certificates, a user is identified by her public key, which is associated with her secret key. The issue here is that for every secret key there is only one public key. As a result, the user will be linkable across different domains where the public key is used, unless she accepts the hassle of managing multiple key pairs. The concept of "pseudonyms" in Privacy-ABC system can be considered as equivalent to public keys. However, the major difference is that "many" different unlinkable pseudonyms can be derived from a single secret key, allowing the user to establish partial identities in different domains that are not possible to correlate.

The Söderhamn pilot of ABC4Trust heavily benefited from pseudonyms to realize the concept of "Alias" in their School Community Interaction Platform. Every pupil has the possibility to appear in the online community under various human friendly nicknames (aliases) representing partial identities. These aliases are bound to Privacy-ABC pseudonyms behind the scenes. Once a user requests a new alias, the system checks the database to ensure that the alias is not already registered. When there is no conflict, the user submits a pseudonym bound to the selected alias name to be registered in the database. Afterwards, whenever the user desires to login under that alias, the system requires to produce and prove ownership of the same related pseudonym. As a result, no impersonation is possible and nobody can figure out whether two aliases belong to the same person.

5.2   Identifying Returning Users

Even though unlinkable Privacy-ABC pseudonyms are very attractive to support users' privacy, sometimes a system may fail delivering its service if a certain level of linkability is not provided. To elaborate more on such cases, we take the example of the ABC4Trust Patras pilot, where an online course evaluation system was implemented.

A privacy-respecting course evaluation system must allow the students to fill the questionnaire and express their opinion without being identified. However, the result could be manipulated if the students have the possibility to establish multiple partial identities to submit multiple evaluations under different pseudonyms, and therefore positively or negatively influence the aggregated results. Thus, for a correct and accurate delivery of the service, the course evaluation system must be able to link the users to their previous visits of the system and only allow them to "update" their evaluations, instead of submitting a new entry. At the same time, there should not be a way to learn about the identity of the students.

"Scope-exclusive" pseudonyms are special types of Privacy-ABC pseudonyms that enable the Service Provider to force the users to show the same pseudonym given the same "scope" string. Therefore, whenever the users visit the course evaluation portal, they face a policy requiring a scope exclusive pseudonym for a fixed scope. As a result, they are obliged to produce the same pseudonym value every time, allowing the system to recognize a returning user.

5.3   Minimal, Untraceable, and Unlinkable Presentation of Credentials

In a Privacy-ABC system, users can receive certified claims about their attributes in the form of credentials. For example, a Civil Registration Authority is entitled to issue authentic credentials attesting name, last name, birth-date, etc., representing an ID card.

Privacy-ABCs provide three distinct features to their users. Let's take the School Credential of the Söderhamn pilot as the basis for our examples here. The School Credential (also called CredSchool) is equivalent to a membership card and contains the first name, last name, birth-date, and the school name. As mentioned earlier, the pupils could login to the system using a human friendly nickname, called alias, which is not linkable to their real identities. In order to participate in a school-bound activity, such as a political discussion, a sample access policy would require a proof that they are from the same school (i.e. Norrtullskolan).

X.509 certificates require users to present their certificate as it is needed to preserve the integrity of the signature. This urges the users to disclose their first name, last name, and the birth-date even though only the school name was needed. Conversely, Privacy-ABCs support minimal disclosure allowing the users to selectively disclose a subset of the attributes from their credentials. In the example of the Söderhamn pilot, the pupils could use their CredSchool to reveal only the school name whilst keeping the other attributes hidden. In this way the system did not learn any further information than needed. Moreover, Privacy-ABCs support "predicates over attributes" enabling the users to prove some facts about their attributes without actually revealing them. For instance, the pupils could prove that their birth-date from the CredSchool is before a given date and therefore they are older than a certain age, and still keep their actual birth-date hidden.

Another advantage of Privacy-ABCs can be better explained when focusing on the static representation of X.509 certificates. An X.509 user could be immediately identified when the Service Provider and the certificate issuer collude. In another word, the use of the credentials is traceable by the issuer due to the static representation of the certificates during the issuance and the presentation steps. Despite, Privacy-ABCs experience some transformations between the issuance and presentation phase so there is no way to trace their usage, unless the revealed attributes give such an opportunity. In our example, the pupils could use their CredSchool to prove that they are part of the Norrtullskolan, and this piece of information would not allow a colluding credential issuer to identify the users.

Similarly, the same static nature of X.509 certificates enables another privacy threat to the users. It would allow the Service Providers to link different transactions of the same users and build a profile. This would not be possible with Privacy-ABCs as the users are able to produce unlinkable tokens from their credentials for each transaction. In our example scenarios, a pupil could use the same CredSchool to make presentations about their school name when appearing under different aliases in the system and ensure that this would not introduce any linkability between their aliases.

5.4   Blind Transfer of Attributes

Let's introduce an example scenario from the ABC4Trust Patras pilot to better elaborate on the feature of blind transfer of attributes. To encourage the pilot participants to continue to the last step, we announced a tombola to take place at the end of the trial for those who submitted their evaluation of the course. The approach was to issue to the students a Tombola Credential after submission of their evaluation. However, the new credential had to contain the matriculation number of the student. This looks challenging as the students were not identified when interacting with the portal.

Advanced credential issuance techniques of Privacy-ABCs support a feature called "carried-over attribute" that allows an issuer to issue a credential containing an attribute value transferred from another credential that the user holds, without learning the attribute value. Therefore, in the Patras trial, after submitting the evaluation form, the Tombola Credential Issuer could issue credentials to the users and transfer the matriculation number from their University Credential into it without getting to know what the matriculation number is.

5.5   Recovering the Identity via Inspection

On the first look, the Inspection feature of Privacy-ABCs may be misinterpreted as a back door to the provided anonymity. Thus explaining and using this concept and its processes requires extra care. The first important point to mention about the Inspection is that it would not be possible always, meaning that before anybody would be able to recover the identity of the user behind a transaction, the user should have gone into some agreements and delivered extra information that would make the Inspection technically possible.

When requesting access to a resource protected by Inspection, the users would get informed about the terms and conditions (called Inspection Grounds). If the user accepts the agreement, some additional information, such as a unique identifier in the domain, must be "verifiably" encrypted under the public key of a trusted third party, called Inspector, and has to be embedded in the presentation token delivered to the Service Provider. In case of a misuse, the Service Provider has the possibility to forward this token to the Inspector along with an evidence for the violation of the agreements. The Inspector is responsible for investigating the case and checking whether the claim of violation by the Service Provider holds. Upon confirmation, the Inspector could decrypt the token and recover the identifier.

Inspection is mainly used to achieve accountability. For instance, in the Söderhamn pilot, the school is legally responsible for every infrastructure it provides to the pupils and it must be able to deal with any case that introduces threats to the pupils, such as mobbing. Therefore, a process was designed to allow the pupils report inappropriate contents in the discussion forum. If a forum is protected by Inspection, the "Inspection Board", comprising of the school principal, some teachers and representatives of the pupils, receives the case to judge. If the content is against the terms of use, they send the corresponding token to the Inspector to recover the unique identifier of the pupil.

Inspection can be helpful in other types of scenarios as well. For example, in an online payment process, the credit card number of the customer can be delivered in an inspectable token encrypted under the public key of the bank. In this way, the online shop can ensure that the customer is providing a valid credit card number without actually seeing it. The shop can forward this to the bank to perform the corresponding transfer of credit. A similar scenario is implemented in the ABC4Trust "Hotel Booking" demo[5].

Another example for a different usage of Inspection was demonstrated in the Patras pilot. As we mentioned earlier, the students would receive a Tombola Credential containing their matriculation number after submitting their evaluation forms. Using this credential they could participate in a tombola. However, this could have caused the threat to identify whoever submitted an evaluation

---

[5] https://abc4trust.eu/demo/hotelbooking.

of the course. To make the process privacy-friendly the tombola system required the participants to disclose their matriculation number in an inspectable form and not in clear text. In the end, the Inspector could extract the identity of the winner only and the other students could stay unknown to the system.

5.6   Securing Privacy-ABCs

A typical misuse case is when the users share their credentials in order to let the others benefit from the resources that they normally do not have the necessary credentials to access. Privacy-ABCs try to overcome this problem by offering the "key-binding" feature, which essentially binds a credential to the secret key of the user. Thus, when the users want to lend their credentials, the have to give out their secret key as well. In a Privacy-ABC system, a Service Provider can require a combination of credentials (e.g. a credit card together with a passport) for a presentation and it can enforce that both credentials must be bound to the "same secret key". The "same key as" policy can be applied on pseudonyms as well, meaning that a presentation policy can ask for a credential that is bound to the same secret key as the one used to generate a pseudonym.

Using smart cards as the key/credential storage improves security and portability of Privacy-ABCs. One could rely on the tamper-resistance of smart cards and enhance the security via on-board computation of the operations requiring the secret key. In this way, the secret key never has to leave the card and stays protected as long as the smart card is not tampered with. ABC4Trust also benefited from smart cards in its both pilots and released its smart card firmware on Github[6] to be publicly available.

6   ABC4Trust Layered Architecture

The ABC4Trust architecture has been designed to decompose future implementations of Privacy-ABC technologies into sets of modules and specify the abstract functionality of these components in such a way that they are independent from algorithms or cryptographic components used underneath. The functional decomposition foresees possible architectural extensions to additional functional modules that may be desirable and feasible using future Privacy-ABC technologies or extensions of existing ones.

The interchangeability of Privacy-ABC techniques in the ABC4Trust framework is the outcome of its layered architecture design. Figure 3 depicts part of the high level ABC4Trust architecture where two of the main actors, namely User and Verifier, interact in a typical service request scenario. The core of the architecture is called ABCE (ABC Engine) layer; it provides the necessary APIs to the application layer residing on the top and utilizes the interfaces offered by the bottom layer called CE (Crypto Engine). To complete the picture an XML-based language framework has been designed so that ABCE peers from

---

[6] https://github.com/p2abcengine/.

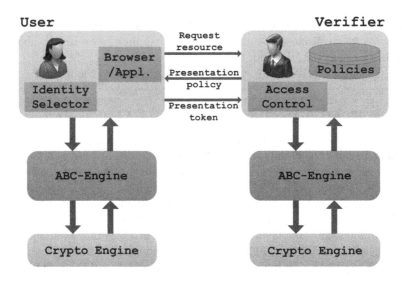

Fig. 3. ABC4Trust layerd architecture, User-Verifier interaction

different entities of the system, e.g. the User and the Verifier, can communicate in a technology-agnostic manner. Putting all the pieces together, the application layer follows the corresponding steps defined in the protocol specification [10], calls the appropriate ABCE APIs, and exchanges messages with the other parties. Further down in the layers, upon receiving an API call, the ABCE performs technology-agnostic operations, such as matching the given access policy with the user's credentials, interacting with the user in case it is needed, and invoking crypto APIs from the CE in order to accomplish cryptographic operations. Finally the bottom layer CE is where the different realizations of Privacy-ABC technologies appear and provide their implementations for the required features.

ABC4Trust also presents a modular model for the crypto layer [10]. The main responsibilities of the Cryptographic Engine are to generate cryptographic key material, issue new credentials by means of a two-party protocol, generate the cryptographic evidence for a Presentation Token to prove that a user satisfies a Presentation Policy, and verify such a proof. This crypto architecture defines the building blocks of Privacy-ABC technologies and their interfaces allowing implementation of additional features and extending the functionalities.

7   Conclusion and Outlook

This paper has documented the features and the usage of Privacy-ABCs for privacy-respecting identity management considering the interests of the respective stakeholders. Especially users are enabled to manage their identities and IDs. The examples in Sect. 5 document privacy-friendly applications in different phases of the businesses process of the two trials, that ABC4Trust conducted.

In some cases identity information flows have been channeled and restricted according to heritage separations of domains, e.g. when enabling users to manage multiple pseudonyms without having to manage multiple key pairs. In some cases new types of channeling and restricting of information flows were enabled by the cryptographic features used in Privacy-ABCs, e.g. the blind transfer of attributes.

In any case it turned out that the definition of Identity as a "set of attributes related to an entity" as globally standardized in the Part 1 of the framework for identity management [6] developed by ISO/IEC JTC 1/SC 27/WG 5 "Identity Management and Privacy Technologies" is useful for designing privacy-respecting identity management.

There are open challenges in the area of assurance tokens which are needed to carry the credentials and process the calculation of presentation tokens. Their design needs to follow several principles

- Enabling the assurance token holder to influence
  - the character and the degree of identification and
  - the amount of identification information;
- Enabling the assurance token to protect itself by e.g. the following features:
  - Ability to verify the controller by e.g. an extra channel to avoid, that an attacker impersonates a controller, e.g. establishes an illegitimate smart card reader to exploit information from the token;
  - A portfolio of communication mechanisms for redundancy to ensure, that any controller, that wishes to access the token, can be verified via an an additional communication channel beyond the channel offered by the controller;
  - Sufficient access control towards relevant data, e.g. a magnet stripe or unprotected chip would not be enough;
  - Enough processing power for complex operations such as cryptographic operations;
- Enabling communication
  - between assurance token holder and assurance token, so that the user can control, what the assurance token is processing and how it is interacting with other entities.

Smart cards are usually able to protect themselves, but their limited user interfaces (even considering a secure reader) makes it challenging for the user to influence the character and degree of identification and the amount of identification information. Moreover the communication between the user as assurance token holder and the assurance token is limited.

Smartphones offer many more options for the interaction between user and assurance token, but they are not as good to protect themselves and the keys stored within them. Reason for this are the complexity of nowadays smartphones or similar devices and the lack of operating system security. Mobiles phones with more robust protection are urgently needed. Mobile phones with a trusted execution environment (TEE) are a step into the right direction, but the TEE must be securely connected to the user interface making sure, that users' confidential input for the TEE is not misdirected and that output from the TEE is correctly displayed.

References

1. X.509: information technology - open systems interconnection - the directory: public/key and attribute certificate frameworks. http://www.itu.int/rec/T-REC-X.509/en
2. Openid authentication 2.0, December 2007. http://openid.net/specs/openid-authentication-2_0.html
3. Assertions and protocols for the OASIS security assertion markup language (saml) v2.0, March 2005. http://docs.oasis-open.org/security/saml/v2.0/saml-core-2.0-os.pdf
4. Facebook login. https://developers.facebook.com/products/login/
5. Hardt, D.: Oauth 2.0 authorization protocol, October 2012. http://tools.ietf.org/html/rfc6749
6. ISO/IEC 2011: ISO/IEC 24760–1:2011 information technology - security techniques - a framework for identity management - part 1: terminology and concepts, 1st edn. 15–12-2011. http://standards.iso.org/ittf/PubliclyAvailableStandards/index.html
7. Rannenberg, K.: Multilateral security - a concept and examples for balanced security. In: Proceedings of the 9th ACM New Security Paradigms Workshop 2000 (NSPW 2000), pp. 151–162. ACM, New York (2000) [Online]. Available: http://doi.acm.org/10.1145/366173.366208
8. Brands, S.: Rethinking Public Key Infrastructures and Digital Certificates: Building in Privacy. MIT Press (2000)
9. Camenisch, J., Van Herreweghen, E.: Design and implementation of the idemix anonymous credential system. In: Proceedings of the 9th ACM Conference on Computer and Communications Security, pp. 21–30. ACM (2002)
10. Bichsel, P., Camenisch, J., Dubovitskaya, M., Enderlein, R.R., Krenn, S., Krontiris, I., Lehmann, A., Neven, G., Dam Nielsen, J., Paquin, C., Preiss, F.-S., Rannenberg, K., Sabouri, A., Stausholm, M.: Architecture for attribute-based credential technologies - final version. In: The ABC4Trust EU Project, Deliverable D2.2 (2014). Available at https://abc4trust.eu/download/Deliverable_D2.2.pdf. Last accessed on 08–11–2014

Towards an Engineering Model of Privacy-Related Decisions

Joachim Meyer[✉]

Department of Industrial Engineering,
Tel Aviv University, Tel Aviv-Yafo, Israel
jmeyer@tau.ac.il

Abstract. People make numerous decisions that affect their own or others' privacy, including the decisions to engage in certain activities, to reveal and share information or to allow access to information. These decisions depend on properties of the information to be revealed, the situation in which the decision is made, the possible recipients of the information, and characteristics of the individual person. System design should ideally protect users from unwanted consequences by allowing them to make informed decisions, at times blocking users' ability to perform certain actions (e.g., when the user is a minor). The development of alerting and blocking mechanisms should be based on predictive models of user behavior, similar to engineering models in other domains. These models can be used to evaluate different design alternatives and to assess the required system specifications. Predictive models of privacy decisions will have to combine elements from normative decision making and from behavioral, descriptive research on decision making. Some major issues in the development and validation of such models are presented.

Keywords: Privacy · Decision making · Models · Cognitive engineering

1 Introduction

Privacy has become a major concern in people's interaction with technologies. The storing of vast amounts of information and the possible access to this information by other people, by governmental agencies, or by companies and other organizations expose people to the threat of others gaining information about them on almost all aspects of their lifes. The people who access the information are usually unknown to the individual, may use the information against the individual's interest, and the individual generally has no way to redress the issue.

At the same time, people also gain benefits from revealing information. They receive personalized services, such as adapted product offerings on websites, they may have access to location-related recommendations, they can get emergency support when they are in an accident (if they are connected to a system that monitors their status and location), etc. The rapidly blooming field of social networks is based entirely on people's willingness, and even desire, to share personal information. Thus sharing information and having others access one's information are not necessarily bad, nor are they necessarily good. Rather, as is usually the case, they have both positive and negative sides.

© IFIP International Federation for Information Processing 2015
J. Camenisch et al. (Eds.): Privacy and Identity 2014, IFIP AICT 457, pp. 17–25, 2015.
DOI: 10.1007/978-3-319-18621-4_2

1.1 Privacy Decision Making

The notion that providing access to one's personal information can have advantages and disadvantages for a person has been known for a long time. It implies that people may want to weigh the advantages and disadvantages and choose whether to reveal information. This idea is central in the definition of privacy, proposed by Westin (1967), as "the claim of individuals, groups or institutions to determine for themselves when, how, and to what extent information about them is communicated to others." He recognizes the dynamic nature of these choices by also stating that "… each individual is continually engaged in a personal adjustment process in which he balances the desire for privacy with the desire for disclosure and communication …"

Thus one can analyze a person's privacy related actions as the result of decision processes. The active sharing of information, the engagement in activities that generate information, or the failure to prevent private information from becoming public, can all be seen as results of decision processes. According to economic normative models of decision making (such as the Expected Utility Model), the decisions should be made, based on the expected outcomes when information is revealed and when it is not. However, for privacy decisions, as for decisions in most other domains, people's actual decision making deviates from the prescriptions of classic economic models (e.g., Acquisti and Grossklags 2005). Furthermore, privacy-related decisions are inherently difficult to analyze, even with simple economic models, since the consequences (costs and benefits) occur at different points in the future, they occur with some (largely unknown) probabilities, and they are in most cases not directly translatable into monetary values.

Privacy-related decisions have a variety of outcomes that have very different importance and meaning for different people. Basically, there are three major categories of outcomes (see Table 1):

Social. Privacy-related decisions can affect the relations a person has with other people. Communicating with others, by, for instance, posting on social networks, can provide various benefits. These include communicating about a person's status, creating and managing the impressions others might have about the person, maintaining relationships with others, etc. These actions may also have negative consequences, such as offending certain people, or information reaching people who were not supposed to see it (e.g., the boss seeing an employee intoxicated).

Economic. Sharing of information may be motivated by economic benefits a person receives when agreeing to share the information. Examples are people joining customer loyalty programs, where they receive minor benefits for agreeing to reveal their identity (e.g., swipe their card) whenever they perform a purchase. Revealing information may also have negative economic implications. For instance, if an insurance company obtains information showing that a person is at an increased risk for some chronic disease, the company may raise the person's insurance rates.

Functional. Sharing of information may provide functional benefits. For instance, one must share location information to receive location-dependent services or recommendations. Sharing one's identity with a website allows the site to customize the information to the individual's characteristics, etc. However, the shared information may also be misused, as happens in the most extreme case when it is used by a criminal, for instance to perform identity theft.

Ideally people should make privacy-related decisions after considering all possible consequences. This is obviously problematic, and it is unrealistic to expect that people explicitly evaluate and weigh each of the consequences (and there may be very many), their probability, and their utility in some common measure. However, it may be possible to predict to some extent which possible consequences people consider, depending on the prior information they have and the display of relevant information by the system.

Table 1. Some types of costs and benefits related to privacy

	Benefits	Dangers and costs
Social	Communicate with others, impression management, maintain relationship	Unintended consequences of information reaching people
Economic	Incentives from sharing information	Possible negative effects (increased insurance rates, etc.)
Functional	Improved services when functions are shared (location based recommendations)	Possible misuse of information (identity theft, etc.)

2 Privacy Engineering

The design of systems that take privacy into account has to deal with numerous aspects of privacy, including the encryption of information, the protection of information from unwanted access, the limitation of information collection, etc. Eventually these boil down to technical decisions made by the people who develop, deploy and maintain systems. These are part of the engineering of systems, and hence the engineering of privacy may be a relevant term. Spiekerman and Cranor (2009) published an analysis of the development of privacy-sensitive systems, with the title "engineering privacy". They describe two approaches in the engineering of privacy. One, which they name "privacy by architecture", is the prevention of privacy violations by designing the system so that the data collection will be minimal or privacy violations will ideally be impossible. The other approach, "privacy by policy", deals with cases in which the possibility of privacy violations still exists. Then system designers need to inform users about possible privacy risks and must leave users the choice whether to expose themselves to such risks or not (the "notice and choice" approach).

Gurses (2014) points out that building systems that cope appropriately with the plethora of legal and societal aspects of privacy is a "bewilderingly complex" task. She describes three major approaches in privacy research in computer science, which can form the basis of the engineering of privacy: (1) Privacy as confidentiality, which means limiting the amount of information collected and the possibility that information can be revealed to others; (2) privacy as control, which means creating mechanisms that allow people to control the collection and use of data about them; and (3) privacy as practice, which considers privacy as part of social interactions in which people exchange information and signals about the use of the information. Gurses doubts that it will be possible to engineer privacy. Rather, this may be a, perhaps unattainable, ideal towards which engineers should strive.

3 Cognitive Engineering

The design of systems that allow people to take adequate control over their privacy requires the understanding of people's decision making process. This includes observing how people obtain information on which they base their decisions, how they use this information to evaluate different alternative actions, and how they choose a particular course of action. The information and the available actions are often displayed by computers, and action implementation is mediated by a computer. Thus, in the context of privacy, a computer may (or may not) tell a person what information is collected if he or she grants a program a specific permission. The computer may also inform the person (correctly or incorrectly) what will be done with this information and how it will be protected. The person's decision should eventually be based on the evaluation of this information, together with some evaluation of the expected benefits from providing the information.

"Cognitive engineering" studies systems in which people and computers interact to perform some task, or as Vicente (1999) defined it, "Cognitive engineering is a multidisciplinary endeavor concerned with the analysis, design, and evaluation of complex systems of people and technology". The field emerged from the attempt to understand and predict human performance in complex systems, such as advanced aircraft cockpits or the control rooms in nuclear power plants. It encompasses a variety of different approaches, ranging from qualitative, descriptive analyses to highly quantitative predictive and analytical models.

3.1 Quantitative Models

Among the different approaches in cognitive engineering the attempt to create an engineering process of the specification and design of human computer systems might be particularly valuable in the context of privacy. In this engineering process (as in engineering in general), the decisions and actions should be based on quantitative models of systems and operator actions in the systems. The American Institute of Aeronautics and Astronautics (1998) defined a model as a "Conceptual / mathematical / numerical description of a specific physical scenario, including geometrical, material, initial, and boundary data."

Such work should aim to generate models of people's decisions, given specific system properties and usage conditions. These models can be used for a number of purposes. For one, they can support design decisions, and they can help develop specifications for the system. For instance, they can be used to decide which functions to automate, so that the computer will perform them and which to leave to the human operator (a process named "function allocation").

In addition, the models can be used for interface design, including the decisions what to display to the users and what actions users should be able to perform (which will affect the choice of displays and input devices for a system). At times exist regulations that specify which information must be provided to the user, such as Article 10 in the EU Data Regulation Directive. It states that people about whom data is collected must be informed about the collection of the data, who collects it, for what purpose is it collected, and other relevant information. The model can be used to predict the conditions that will provide optimal presentation of this information, so that people will become aware of it without too strongly disrupting their interaction with the system.

The analysis can also help in the development of training and simulation facilities by supporting various decisions, such as to understand what skills and knowledge are required for a particular task? What situations should be trained? How frequently should refresher training take place? Etc.

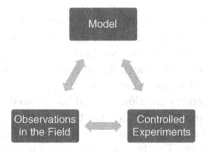

Fig. 1. The relation between models, observations and controlled experiments.

Models are part of the continuous attempt to observe, describe, analyze and predict phenomena. As shown in Fig. 1, models are closely related to observations of the world and to controlled experiments. They are based on intuitions and observations, and they inform interventions, which should be based on conclusions drawn from models. They also generate hypotheses that can be tested in controlled experiments, and they are adjusted, based on the results of the experiments. Finally, the design of the experiment should be informed by observations of the world and ideally resemble the conditions that exist in the world (to ensure the generalizability of the results from the experiment to situations outside the lab, the so-called "external validity"). The process of model development, adjustment and validation is a continuous process, which can never end. There is never a "correct model" that has been reached. Rather, as the statistician George E. Box stated "Essentially, all models are wrong, but some are useful" (Box and Draper, 1987; p. 424).

The engineering model is first a model of the system, incorporating the functions, properties and the behavior of the system that is modeled (see Fig. 2). For instance, the engineering model of a privacy component of a system will describe the way information in the system is stored, who can access it, and how this access is done. The model should not only model the system, but it also needs to model the environment in

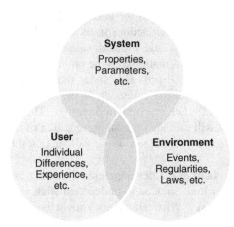

Fig. 2. Aspects to be addressed by a cognitive engineering model.

which the system is deployed. Thus, properties of the environment, such as the likelihood of privacy transgression, the severity of the expected outcomes, the information available to detect privacy problems, etc., need to be incorporated in the model. Finally, in a human-computer model the model also needs to describe and specify the user. It needs to specify relevant stable, general user properties that may affect the user's behavior, such as age, gender, education, cultural background, etc. In addition, it may include situation-specific user variables, such as the individual user's experience with a given situation, the information the user received (perhaps through word of mouth from others) about the situation, etc. The three domains – system, environment and user – are not independent, and properties of the system may alter the user and to some extent also affect the situation in which the system is used (because users may, for example, choose to avoid certain situations).

3.2   The Triad of Privacy-Related Behaviors

The modeling of privacy-related decisions is complicated by the fact that these are not single decisions. Rather, they are decisions that are part of an ongoing sequence of actions, where decisions made at earlier points in time will affect the set of alternatives among which people choose in the future, the available information for making decisions, and the expected outcomes of decisions. Essentially, as in cyber-security decisions (Ben-Asher et al. 2010; Möller et al. 2011), there are three different time perspectives of decision making, which all need to be considered, and which affect the decisions a person makes at some moment in time:

1. *Precautionary actions*. These actions are done in advance, and often only once, when a person begins to use a system. They include the choice of system settings, the installation (or disabling) of functions and services, and the installation and setting of protective mechanisms. These decisions are made, based on the information available to the user at the time at which she or he begins to use the system, and they may often

not be adjusted when the use of the system, the system itself or the environment change. One of the major problems, inherent in these actions, is the fact that people are not very good in deciding how to adjust a system and its settings. These decisions depend on the available information, and they will often deviate greatly from optimal settings, if such can be computed (Botzer et al., 2010).

2. *Exposure to a privacy risk.* These are decisions to engage in activities that make privacy risks possible (e.g., posting information on social networks, providing identifying information when signing up for a service, allowing a mobile app to collect information, etc.). These decisions are made continuously, whenever people encounter situations in which they might reveal information that may be sensitive at some point in time and under certain conditions.

3. *Actions when a negative event occurs.* These decisions are made at the moment when possibly sensitive information is revealed to somebody who is not supposed to have access to this information. Unfortunately, in most cases, this will happen without the person about which the information is revealed having control over the event or even knowing about it (thus he or she will usually not be able to make a decision and take action at this point). In systems in which people are somehow involved (e.g., are alerted when someone tries to access their information or tries to download personal material), the involvement is tied to alerts and warnings. These can be followed, or, quite often, especially if they occur frequently, they will be ignored. Overall, people's responses to alerts differ systematically from the optimal responses to such information, if these can be computed (e.g., Meyer, Wiczorek and Günzler, 2014).

The three behaviors, related to these three times, can be considered a "triad of privacy-related behaviors", in parallel to the "triad of risk-related behaviors" we describe in the context of cyber-security (Ben-Asher and Meyer, 2015).

An additional challenge in the modeling of privacy-related decisions is that the decisions are not necessarily the ones a classic economic decision-making model would prescribe. The expected value maximization can perhaps be a starting point for developing a model, but it needs to be adjusted to properties of the decision process, such as risk aversion and non-linear utility functions, and bounded rationality due to limited time and cognitive abilities. It must also take into account characteristics of behavioral decision making, such as deviations from classical probability theory in the estimation of the likelihood of outcomes and the computation of preferred alternatives.

4   Discussion

The design of information systems and the mechanisms involved in having people manage their personal information should be based on systematic analytical tools, similar to the tools used in other engineering disciplines. Such models should combine an understanding of the technical, as well as the behavioral aspects of a system and a situation.

To develop such models, we should adapt the standards and views of engineering modelers. For one, in contrast to scientific models which often strive to be as accurate as possible, we aim to develop as simple models as possible. Models need not be complete (and actually never can be). Rather, they should provide sufficient information to be used to make the decisions for which they were developed. If the outcomes from choosing either of a number of different design alternatives are very similar, it will not particularly matter which of the alternatives one chooses. Thus the accuracy of model predictions needs not to be very high.

Also, models should be easy to develop. The development should be doable with relatively simple tools, and even people with limited experience in modeling should be able to develop models. To do so, it may be necessary to develop software tools that can support and guide the modeling process. Models should also be easy to communicate. The modeler should be able to present the outcome of the modeling in a simple and convincing way to stakeholders for whom the model predictions are relevant. And finally, models need to verifiable, so that people who want to inspect the model can relatively easily see if model predictions were computed correctly and can recreate the computations leading to these predictions.

Although we strive to develop simple models, modeling of privacy decisions is inherently difficult. There are large individual differences in people's preferences and the factors they consider when evaluating outcomes, in most cases consequences of choices are not known when choices are made, and the values of consequences may change over time (a person who prides himself of an active social life as a student, may be less happy to reveal this information after accepting an executive position). At the moment of the decision, the situational characteristics, the information that is salient, and the recent experiences a person has (or events the person heard about) may all affect the decisions. Thus the timing and context in which people make decisions will all have to be taken into account.

Gurses (2014) expresses some doubt about the possibility to engineer privacy. If by engineering privacy, one means that there will be full control of privacy including all its aspects, this statement is certainly correct. However, design decisions, and in particular decisions regarding the information provided to people regarding the implications of their choices, should be based on scientifically validated models, rather than on the intuitions, gut feelings, and impressions of software developers, designers or project managers. Even if such models currently often cannot provide predictions, their development helps to structure the thinking about the design decisions and can point to a subset of alternatives among which one may find an adequate solution to the problem. This may help us develop systems that are better adapted to protect users' privacy and that provide people with the ability to make the choices that are required to manage the collection and exposure of information about themselves.

References

Acquisti, A., Grossklags, J.: Privacy and rationality in individual decision making. IEEE Secur. Priv. **3**(1), 26–33 (2005)

AIAA (American Institute of Aeronautics and Astronautics): Guide for the verification and validation of computational fluid dynamics simulations, AIAA-G-077-1998. American Institute of Aeronautics and Astronautics Reston, VA (1998)

Ben-Asher, N., Meyer, J.: The triad of risk related behaviors. Unpublished Manuscript (2015)

Ben-Asher, N., Meyer, J., Parmet, Y., Möller, S., Englert, R.: An experimental microworld for evaluating the tradeoffs between usability and security. Usable Security Experiment Reports (USER) Workshop in the Symposium on Usable Privacy and Security (SOUPS), Redmond, WA, USA, 14–16 July 2010

Botzer, A., Meyer, J., Bak, P., Parmet, Y.: Cue threshold settings for binary categorization decision. J. Exp. Psychol. Appl. **16**, 1–15 (2010)

Box, G.E.P., Draper, N.R.: Empirical Model Building and Response Surfaces. Wiley, New York (1987)

Gurses, S.: Privacy and security: Can you engineer privacy? Commun. ACM **57**(8), 20–23 (2014)

Meyer, J., Wiczorek, R., Günzler, T.: Measures of reliance and compliance in aided visual scanning. Hum. Factors **56**(5), 840–849 (2014)

Möller, S., Ben-Asher, N., Engelbrecht, K.-P., Englert, R., Meyer, J.: Modeling the behavior of users who are confronted with security mechanisms. Comput. Secur. **30**(4), 242–256 (2011)

Spiekerman, S., Cranor, L.F.: Engineering privacy. IEEE Trans. Softw. Eng. **35**(1), 67–82 (2009)

Vicente, K.: Cognitive Work Analysis. Lawrence Erlbaum Associates, Mahwah (1999)

Westin, A.: Privacy and Freedom. Atheneum, New York (1967)

The Value of Personal Data

Marc van Lieshout[(✉)]

TNO, Van Mourik Broekmanweg 6, 2618 XE Delft, The Netherlands
Marc.vanlieshout@tno.nl

Abstract. This chapter discusses the value of personal data from two complementary perspectives: the value of personal data for firms and the value of personal data for individuals. The chapter starts with a short introduction into the rise of personal data markets – markets basically driven by the economic exploitation of personal data. Then the chapter discusses how firms asses the value of personal data. This can be done from different angles, such as stock value and revenues. Another inroad is the costs of data breaches. A second perspective which is discussed is the valuation of personal data by individuals. Some empirical studies are presented that show how individuals value their personal data and what choices they tend to make. The chapter concludes with placing these developments in the frame of the upcoming data protection regulation. Data protection by default has relevance when taking the empirical studies seriously.

Keywords: Behavioural economics · Data protection by design · Economic value of privacy · Personal data markets · Privacy

1 Introduction

Personal data are an important asset in today's data-driven society. A report by the Boston Consulting Group in 2012 stated that the value created through digital identities would amount to approximately 8 % of GDP for the EU-27 countries [3]. With regard to personal data, a privacy paradox seems to exist: individuals state that they consider privacy to be important, but they hardly are willing to undertake action to protect their personal data. The sharing of personal information on social networking sites, and the provision of personal data in exchange for apps and other web-based services seem to support this view. However, several arguments can be presented to explain this apparent contradiction. For instance, users do not have a choice but to accept that they hand over their personal data in exchange for the service to be delivered. Or, the distinction which users make between what they consider privacy relevant and what not, is different from the formal distinction between 'ordinary' personal data and sensitive data. Another explanation is that although users seem to reveal quite some personal data when using social media, accepting a new app or buying something on

---

This chapter is largely a reproduction of Chap. 2 of the TNO-report: Roosendaal A. Lieshout, M van, Veenstra AF van (2014). Personal Data Markets. TNO report R11390 [10]. The original chapter has been written by the author. It has been adapted for this publication.

© IFIP International Federation for Information Processing 2015
J. Camenisch et al. (Eds.): Privacy and Identity 2014, IFIP AICT 457, pp. 26–38, 2015.
DOI: 10.1007/978-3-319-18621-4_3

the internet, they use informal strategies to protect their privacy (for instance by supplying incorrect personal information) [1, 9].

Literature in the field of behavioral economics shows that there is a very limited willingness to pay for the protection of privacy [1, 5]. People are willing to accept privacy intrusions when it serves their interests. One should therefore wonder whether privacy plays a role at all when personal data can offer financial benefits to individuals. Still, the fundamental right to privacy is not an issue that can simply be put aside. One needs a more thorough analysis, both of how these personal data markets are organized and of how individuals appreciate the economic or monetary value of their data. In this Chap. 1 will start with an introduction to the rise of personal data markets (Sect. 2). The largest part of this chapter will be dedicated to the presentation and the discussion of the various ways in which the monetary value of personal data can be measured.

2 The Market for Personal Data

Over the years, a number of studies have investigated the rise of personal data markets [3, 4, 14, 15]. The studies differ in their focus; two of them look at the overall impact of changes in the use of personal data [14, 15], one study is dedicated to the size and the features of the European markets on personal data [3] and a fourth study investigates the economic value of Individual-Level Consumer Data (ILCD) [4]. The WEF 2010 study highlighted the relevance of personal data as an economic asset that could be perceived as the new 'oil' [14]. The metaphor of personal data as oil is an interesting one. It covers both the use of personal data as a product in itself and as being a substance that is basic to a large number of economic activities. The WEF study was one of the first in capturing the phenomenon of 'big data' developments, and identified a number of interesting features of these developments. It introduced an - arguably contestable – distinction between types of personal data that enables a kind of classification of the data processing and collecting processes (based on either voluntary, observed or inferred data, see below). Due to the contested nature of the first category (data being provided 'voluntarily') the WEF changed its phrasing in follow-on reports in the more apt phrasing 'personally provided'.[1]

The Boston Consulting Group presented a study in which it estimated the economic value of personal data markets in Europe, introducing a new inventory of relevant economic sectors [3]. The study arrives at an expected value of personal data markets of 8 % of European GDP in 2020. It bases its forecast on a composite average of growth of some prominent economic sectors at present. The three most relevant ones are online communication and entertainment (Compound Average Growth Rate 22 %), e-Commerce (CAGR 15 %) and web-communities (100 %). Given the present market size, a presumed CAGR of 22 % over the next years would yield a market of €330 Billion in 2020 with consumer benefits of €670 Billion because of reduced prices, time savings (because of self-service transactions) and the valuation of free online services.

---

[1] See the change in phrasing between [14, 15] on this subject.

The US-based study on Data Driven Market Economies, published by the Data Driven Marketing Institute, on the role of Individual-Level Consumer Data (ILCD) in providing marketing services, estimated the size of the ILCD market to be about $156 Billion, offering work to approximately 676,000 people in 2012. With a total US marketing and advertising market of $298 Billion the contribution of ILCD-based marketing added up to slightly more than 50 %. The largest contribution to the economic value of DDME is related to the direct (50 %) and indirect (21 %) exchange of ILCDs between firms, with only some 29 % related to the collection of use of ILCD within a single firm [4] (pp. 15−16). The role of personal data in marketing activities is manifold, and ranges from personalized targeting, to measuring benefits of marketing activities and lowering the entry costs for small firms (for which mass-advertising is too costly). The study indicates the relevance of DDME for stimulating technology development and realizing start-up entrepreneurship.

The relevance of personal data has a public element as well. Personal data are a prime asset for public services. Having access to (reliable) personal data may improve the efficiency of public services. The relevance of collecting, aggregating, analyzing and using personal data thus extends beyond monetary terms. An example is provided by Kaiser Permanente, a US-based health insurance firm, which has collected a database with over 3 million patient records. It offers patients fast access to their medical files, allowing them for instance to schedule an appointment and to receive text messages for prescription refills, leading to cost savings for Kaiser Permanente of many hundreds of thousands of dollars [7]. Meanwhile, the same data can be used to investigate correlations between incidences of diseases and use of medicines. By using data analytics, Kaiser Permanente discovered a correlation between use of anti-depressants by pregnant women and the incidence of a form of autism by newborns [14]. These results enable adapting medical practices in anti-depressant prescriptions for pregnant women.

Massive personal data collection can thus serve multiple purposes. The area identified in the US study relating to advertisement networks in online environments can be seen as a growing and interesting part of personal data markets. The market is expanding with the growth of personal data that people leave, knowingly or unknowingly, when using one of the several digital platforms they have at their disposal. An estimation presented in the BGC study mentions a growth figure of 45 % per year through 2015 to a volume of 7 zetabytes, being the equivalent of more than 1,000 gigabytes of data for each person on earth [3]. The advertisement market has already matured to some respect, being based on a large number of 'Freemium' services; the business model of these Freemium services is quite simple: personal data in exchange for a free service. The personal data are, as indicated, the 'raw material' for added value services such as personalized and targeted advertisement..

A market of personal data brokers has emerged. Large service providers such as Google, AOL and Yahoo have taken over personal data brokers to secure their own position in this advertisement market. Google now owns a number of brokers such as AdMob and Double Click. Apple has its own ad-broker with iAd. The role of these ad-brokers is growing. The ad-broker MobClix for instance, matches 25 advertisement networks with 15,000 different apps that are looking for advertisers [14]. An organization as BlueKai offers a data exchange platform that captures more than 30,000 attributes over 300 Million users. It handles over 75 Million auctions a day (an auction being a tool with which advertisement space is offered to potential advertisers; ad networks are the intermediaries between advertisers and those offering advertisement space) [14].

3 The Value of Personal Data

The digitization of communication and information has given rise to an abundance of data-sharing practices. People share details about their whereabouts, their moods and their activities through a multitude of platforms. They leave traces that go unnoticed for themselves, such as their geo-location when carrying a mobile phone, or their click behaviour. The value of this information is well understood by marketers who try to collect as much data about personal conducts and preferences as possible, allowing them to learn about purchasing habits and strategies, and to make the best suited offers to their customers. As indicated above, it is not only the commercial value of personal data that is of interest. The public value of these data analytics can be substantial as well. An example is the provision of medical information by patients with rare diseases.[2] The network of patients with rare diseases started as a social interaction between these patients but resulted in an extremely interesting network with very interesting personal experiences in medical treatments and use of medicines for medical practitioners (and pharmaceutical agencies).

3.1   The Monetary Value of Personal Data – A Firm Perspective

To measure the monetary value of personal data, two main perspectives can be used. The first is by assessing the monetary value of the firm that collects, aggregates, processes, stores and/or disseminates the personal data. Various approaches are possible for this assessment [8]. The second perspective determines which monetary value persons attach to their data. This can be assessed in various manners as well and is covered in the next section.

To start with the monetary value of personal values from a firm's perspective, the OECD study mentioned before [8] distinguishes between three perspectives: one can look at the stock value of a firm, at the revenues of a firm or at the price of data records on the market. Alternatively, one can also look at the costs of a data breach and at the price of personal data on an illegal market. All of these approaches show some features of the value of personal data but all have specific drawbacks as well.

A general feature of data is that it can be sold over and over again without loss of its intrinsic value. The copy is just as good as the original, enabling multiple offers without loss of price or value. A single item of personal data thus will hardly have a commercial value. It is the composite of personal data that makes a commercial difference. Combining specific classes of personal data to profiles is another way to realise commercial value. Profiles can be created bottom up (using the available data to create meaningful

---

[2] See www.patientslikeme.org.

subsets of data) or top down (using pre-configured profiles to check in what group specific people would belong). Both forms of profiles add to the monetary attractiveness of personal data, since the grouping of data add to the original value of the data.

The stock value of a firm is a measure of trust in the firm's capacity to produce valuable revenues. It expresses the expectation of shareholders in the growth potential of the firm. For firms trading in personal data as their primary source of revenues, the stock value can be used as a proxy for the value shareholders attach to the data collected and the processes that turn the data into profitable products. However, stock values will fluctuate because of contextual factors that do not bear a direct relationship with the primary process of the firm. Fluctuations of stock prices can induce further fluctuations, as was shown by the introduction of Facebook to the stock market. Only in relatively stable markets one might expect a relatively stable relation between the value of a firm's shares and the revenues it realizes on the basis of its business activities.

The revenues of a firm may serve as a better proxy since it indicates real cash flows on the market, due to the firm's ability to sell products to customers. It enables cross-comparisons between firms acting on a similar market, since one would expect these firms to encounter similar problems in selling their products. The revenues per record may be an indication of the ability of a firm to overcome the complexity of the market, yielding higher revenues against lower costs. Revenues should be compared to the total number of data records a firm owns in order to yield a comparative indicator (revenues per data record in a specific period of time). A drawback of this method is that external factors may influence the prices third parties are willing to pay for specific data on the market, and that there may be a dependency on the total number of records a firm possesses (synergistic effects due to the fact that a firm is able to offer a larger sample of personal data records) [8].

Costs can vary considerably between firms and between markets. This may influence the value of personal data as well.

An example that shows the variance between the indicators above is provided by Experian [8]. Experian is a data broker. Over 2011, Experian reported total revenues of USD 4.2 Billion realized over 600 Million individual records and 60 Million business data records. Its stock value fluctuated between USD 10 and 12 Billion. Market capitalization thus is about USD 19 per record, and annual revenues were about USD 6 per record. Profits were roughly USD 1 per record. By means of comparison, I compared the situation of Experian with the situation of Facebook (see Table 1). The stock market prices of Facebook have seen huge fluctuations since its introduction (from an initial USD 38 to a low USD 20 low per stock two months later to a value of USD 55 in December 2013).[3] Market capitalization of Facebook developed from USD 90 Billion at the start of its presence at the stock market up to USD 140 Billion in December 2013.[4] Over the past four quarters (Q4-2012 up to Q3-2013), Facebook earned a total of USD 6.9 Billion (with USD 2.0 Billion in 2013 Q3) and had a profit of USD 1.04 Billion

---

[3] http://en.wikipedia.org/wiki/Initial_public_offering_of_Facebook (accessed March 17, 2015).

[4] http://en.wikipedia.org/wiki/Initial_public_offering_of_Facebook (accessed March 6, 2015).

(with USD 0.43 Billion in 2013 Q3).[5] Over this year (Q4 2012 – Q3 2013), Facebook has a market capitalization of USD 116 per subscriber, revenues of USD 5.75 per subscriber and a profit of USD 0.87 per subscriber. Though not all revenues are due to selling ads, a large part is. The market capitalization of Facebook thus is considerably larger than the market capitalization of Experian while other indicators are in the same range (though positive revenues and profits for Facebook only started at Q4 2012).

Table 1. Comparison between Experian and Facebook [8, 15]

	Experian 660 M users		Facebook 1,1 B users	
	Total value	Per record	Total value	Per record
Market Capitalisation	$10-12 billion	$19 (2011)	$90-140 billion	$110 (Q4-2012; Q3-2013)
Revenues	$4 billion	$6	$6.9 billion	$6.25
Profit	$660 million	$1	$1.04 billion	$0.92

The prices of personal data as these are sold at the market place offer another indicator. This price reflects the value purchasers attach to these data, which in turn will depend on the profitability purchasers expect to realize. The Financial Times offers an interactive sheet that enables calculating market prices for specific sorts of data.[6] It distinguishes between demographic data, family and health data, property, sport and leisure activities and consumer data. Demographic data such as age, gender, ethnicity, zip-code and education level are worth USD 0.005 per piece. Job information is worth USD 0.1 if being an entrepreneur up to USD 0.72 if being a health professional, pilot or non-profit worker. Over the five data categories, a total of 24 data entries can be discerned, each worth a specific (usually very modest) price. For information on credit history, criminal records, bankruptcies, convictions etc. of persons one has to pay USD 30–40 per record.[7] Firms specialize in inquiries for this kind of background information. Apparently, one is willing to pay higher prices for specific records of particular persons. Information that is available on black market prices shows that data on credit

---

[5] http://techcrunch.com/2013/10/30/facebooks-q3-13-beats-with-2-02b-revenue-0-25-eps-with-49-of-ad-revenue-now-mobile/ (accessed March 6, 2015).

[6] http://www.ft.com/intl/cms/s/2/927ca86e-d29b-11e2-88ed-00144feab7de.html (accessed March 6, 2015). BTW: in order to access these pages one has to register oneself, thus adding to the value FT derives from its subscribers!.

[7] https://ioptconsulting.com/ft-on-how-much-is-your-personal-data-worth/, referring to http://backgroundreport360.com/ (visited March 6, 2015).

card numbers, personal health records and the like may cost in the range of 1–30 USD per record, depending on the sensitivity of the data but also on the occurrence of data breaches (which provide new data on the market but may also lead to a saturated market) [15].

Data breaches themselves offer another inroad to measuring the value of personal data. A data breach as occurred to the Sony PlayStation Network between April 17 and April 19 2011 led to the theft of personal data of 77 Million subscribers. It led Sony to stop its services for 24 days. Together with the costs of recovering from the hack and the fines to be paid, the data breach cost Sony USD 171 Million, this being the directly attributable costs. Per subscriber this led to a cost figure of USD 2.20. The indirect costs (loss of subscribers, negative brand image which may lead to a decline of purchases of other equipment as well, impact on stock market prices) have been estimated at USD 1.25 Billion, being USD 16 per subscriber.[8] Stock market prices showed a dip of approximately 6 % when Sony entered the stock market again, but it is hard to decide whether this is due to the data breach or to the overall fall of stock market prices that Sony experienced in the period February 2011 – November 2012 (steadily falling down from USD 37 to USD 9 over this period).[9]

Bringing the various perspectives together, we can conclude that calculating prices per data record helps in understanding the value of personal data. A calculation from general revenues or the stock value of a firm to a price per record offers some insight in the value that is represented by the personal records a firms owns. However, stock value is a measure that is very dependent on external influences that bear no relationship with the value of the personal data. Revenues and profit per data record seem to offer a better perspective on the value of these data records. From the illustration I presented it showed that, while Experian and Facebook are active on different markets, the value of the data records they own is more or less similar. Other methods to calculate the commercial value of personal data show that the direct commercial value of personal data is usually relatively low, except for sensitive data and very specific data. Data breaches represent a specific measure of the price of personal data as well. The Sony PlayStation data breach showed that the costs per subscriber of this breach surpassed the net profits that Facebook and Experian made in a year per subscriber.[10]

3.2   The Monetary Value of Personal Data – The Individual Perspective

I will now shift the perspective from the value firms attribute to personal data to the value individuals attribute to their personal data. This valuation could vary considerably between individuals. What one individual would consider to be highly private

---

[8] Juro Osawa, May 9 2011. 'As Sony counts hacking costs, analysts see billion-dollar repair bill.' *Wall Street Journal.* http://online.wsj.com/news/articles/SB100014240527487038593045763076641746 67924 (accessed March 6, 2015).

[9] http://quotes.wsj.com/SNE/interactive-chart (accessed March 6, 2015).

[10] Having only a few illustrations in which the price of personal data was calculated, the findings are only illustrative. More research is needed to turn the findings in more robust conclusions. However, this is outside the scope of this article.

information (such as income or health data), another individual might not bother to share or sell.[11] The case of Shawn Buckles is an interesting illustration of this last position.[12] Shawn Buckles, set up an auction in 2014 to sell his personal data to the highest bidder. The firm that offered the highest price for his personal data would acquire a subscription of a year to data that were collected on Shawn Buckles. These data encompassed his personal profile, his location track records, his train track records, his personal calendar, his email conversations, his online conversations, his consumer preferences, his browsing history, and his thoughts.[13] The highest bidder for this data set was The Next Web. This firm offered €350, - for the full data set. Shawn Buckles used the auction to raise awareness for the commercialization of personal data and the consequences for privacy.[14]

In dealing with how people value personal data I will present two perspectives. Firstly, people could attribute a specific monetary value to these data as exemplified by Shawn Buckles. This is the commercial value of personal data. It forms the counter part of the overview I presented in the preceding section. Secondly, one can investigate what people are willing to pay to keep personal data private. The reasons for keeping these data private could vary. Data could be seen as delicate or sensitive data which people want to keep for themselves. Besides that, people might not want to have data made public because they think the economic benefits do not outweigh the disadvantages (getting loads of advertisements for instance).

The role of personal data in today's society is undisputed. In a Eurobarometer Survey, stemming from 2011, 74 % of respondents indicated that they accept that personal data need to be disclosed when participating in today's society [13]. The same number of people consider financial information, medical information and identity card numbers to be personal information. The survey showed that higher educated people and people living in West and North European countries are more sensitive to what they consider personal data [13].

In understanding what people value in privacy, the traditional economic models have been supplemented with models that look at behavioural features. These models study the impact of attitudes and preferences on choices people make. A number of mechanisms that influence behaviour have been identified [2, 6, 9, 12]. People perceive losses differently than gains, and are more willing to prevent a loss than achieving a similar gain (prospect theory) [2]. People tend to value situations nearby differently

---

[11] The webforum 'Patients like me' offers an example that shows that patients are willing to share sensitive and personal data, hoping it will help in improving treatments for the rare diseases which they suffer. See http://www.patientslikeme.com/ (visited March 7, 2015).

[12] See http://shawnbuckles.nl/dataforsale/ (visited March 7, 2015).

[13] http://shawnbuckles.nl/dataforsale/. While some of these data categories seem to be rather straightforward, some pose problems. Email conversations, for instance, do not only contain information on Shawn Buckles but could reveal information on those with whom he communicates as well. And what precisely Shawn Buckles considered to be his thoughts is not identified at his website.

[14] Shawn Buckles published a Privacy Pamphlet on his website. The Pamphlet intends to raise awareness for the way how personal data are used for marketing purposes, and how the market of personal data 'lures' people in the trap to sacrifice privacy for 'free' services.

from situations further away (hyperbolic discounting [9]. People tend to value what they own higher than what they do not own (endowment effect) [12]. People are risk averse and People tend to overvalue immediate rewards and undervalue long term rewards (instant gratification) [6]. People tend to mimic behaviour shown by predecessors: if many people already entered a specific site or social medium, it seem to be OK (informational cascading) [6]. The absence of real choices may impact upon how people will behave. When one can only chose between accepting specific conditions and getting access to a service or rejecting the conditions and thus having no access to that service, one may be tempted to accept unfavourable or unclear conditions. This practice is well-known in the internet-economy. Many services are offered as a 'take it or leave it' option. For many youngsters it is absolutely prerequisite to have a subscription to Facebook, if one wants to keep in close contact with one's friends, and thus one has to accept the conditions Facebook poses, whether one likes this or not.

Empirical research that tries to identify the relevant parameters of behaviour in order to understand how people assess the value of their personal data, is relatively scarce. An ENISA study mentions four papers dealing with an empirical field- or lab-related study of privacy behaviour [5]. ENISA itself performed a case study in which it investigated whether people are willing to pay for additional data protection [5]. When buying a ticket for the cinema, participants could choose between a number of – varying – offers. The minimum set of data asked was name, e-mail address and date of birth. Variations existed in the usage of the data (indicating that the e-mail address provided would be used for advertisement options) and a request for additional information (phone number). On top of this, in some experiments the price was kept the same for different options while in other options the price was different between the privacy-friendly and the privacy-unfriendly firm. The experiment was conducted as a lab experiment (with 443 participants), in which different options were offered in sequence, and as a hybrid field experiment (with more than 2,300 participants). The study showed that the privacy-unfriendly option was chosen by the majority of the participants when this ticket was 50 cent cheaper than the privacy-friendly offer. A minor part of 13 % chose to pay the additional 50 cents. Without price difference, the majority of participants chose the privacy-friendly option. The experiment also showed that participants, when buying two tickets consecutively, remained to a large extent (142 of 152 participants) loyal to their first choice, even when they could swap from the more expensive to the cheaper ticket [5].[15]

In an experiment performed in 2011 Acquisti checked how people evaluated the willingness of people to pay for protection of their data vis-à-vis the willingness of people to accept the use of these data. The experiment was focused on revealing whether the gap between 'Willingness-to-Pay' and 'Willingness-to-Accept' as identified in several studies, exists as well when dealing with privacy and data protection

---

[15] This could identify those people who really care about their privacy. The study did not conclude on this matter since it could not be asked (being a purely observational study that was constructed such that no direct link to privacy was made in the design of the field study).

issues.[16] The Willingness-to-Pay for the protection of personal data was relabeled as Willingness-to-Protect. This was juxtaposed against the Willingness-to-Accept: users were offered a financial reward in return for release of specific personal data. The experiment was performed with 349 (female) participants in a shopping mall. The participants first filled in a quiz and then answered some sensitive questions, such as the number of sex partners the participants had had. After filling in the questionnaire, participants could either protect information (at a specific cost) or sell it. The bonus they received was a gift card which price was 10 USD if no sensitive information was provided and 12 USD when they were willing to provide the sensitive information. Different scenarios were tested. In one scenario first the cheaper gift card was presented and participants were then asked to provide more sensitive information in exchange for the more expensive gift card (Willingness to Accept). Another scenario started with participants having revealed sensitive information in exchange for the gift card of 12 USD and were then enabled to change to the cheaper gift card in exchange for protection of their sensitive data (Willingness to Protect). Other, more complex scenarios were added. The gift cards were real, and the participants were not informed that this was an experiment directed at testing the difference between WtP and WtA. The experiments validated the different attitudes with respect to WtP and WtA. When first offered the 10 USD card, 52 % of the participants kept the card and decided not to go for the more valuable card at the expense of revealing additional information. The other way around, only 10 % of the participants decided to exchange the 12 USD gift card for the 10 USD gift card in order to protect their data. When the two cards were offered consecutively, 42 % chose the 10 USD card when this was offered first, while 27 % chose the 10 USD card when this was offered second.

A final study worth mentioning is a study performed by Spiekermann in which she investigated the willingness of participants to pay for their own data which they had left on Facebook before [11]. The – hypothetical – situation Spiekermann sketched is the announcement by Mark Zuckerberg that he pulls the plug out of Facebook. Facebook participants could either buy their information back or have it destroyed. In a second scenario a third party took over Facebook. Participants had the choice to leave their data at the platform or to buy their data back. A third scenario offered participants a share in the revenues of the third party that took over Facebook. The experiment was performed with over 1,500 Facebook participants. The results of the experiment showed that the Willingness to Pay/Protect was lowest in the first option (money one was willing to pay in order to have data saved): €16, - (median). In the second option Willingness to Pay/Protect was higher: €54, - (median) for preventing the data were sold to a third party. In the option of sharing in the revenues, people assessed the value of their data considerably higher: €507, - (median). The study supported the existence of the endowment effect: when people feel they own their data (shown by the possibility to share in the revenues) they consider the value of their personal data higher than in the other two

---

[16] This gap is identified in many studies. People tend to value what they own above what they do not own and are thus willing to pay a higher price for keeping what they have than for achieving the same when not having it. See [1, 2].

scenarios. Spiekermann concludes that psychology of ownership is more relevant than privacy concerns in explaining attitudes of people vis-à-vis their personal data.

4 Conclusions

The market for personal data is growing explosively. Expectations are of double digit growths in the coming years. New services will be developed on the basis of the collection, aggregation and dissemination of personal data. The value of new businesses is hidden in the stock of personal data that can be collected. Personalised and targeted advertising enables offering services for free. Personal data are the new 'oil': they fuel new services and they can be used to deliver additional services, based for instance on profiles constructed of the aggregation of personal data. In estimating the value of personal data from a firm's perspective, I used a number of proxies (such as stock market valuation, revenues or profits per data record). This yields some comparative indicators. They highlight different aspects of the valuation of personal data. Revenues and profits per data record are more reliable indicators than stock market value. Comparing the situation of Experian and Facebook, it showed that the revenues and profits per data record were almost similar. The impact of data breaches is high, as the Sony PlayStation data breach shows. Costs per subscriber were twice as high as the annual revenues per subscriber of Experian and Facebook.

Empirical studies on how people value their personal data and what they are willing to pay to protect personal data to be used are scarce The few studies available indicate a sensitivity of individuals for ownership of data, and the relevance of concepts such as instant gratification (evaluating immediate returns higher than returns on the longer term), hyperbolic discounting (difficulty of evaluating costs at the longer term against benefits at the shorter terms), and endowment effects (the relevance of a sense of ownership). The privacy paradox (people indicate they care about privacy but do not act accordingly) is at least partly situated in these behavioural features. The direct valuation of personal data is shown to be modest in the case of Facebook. When some kind of ownership is introduced, people start to bother more about their data and want a fairer share of the revenues that can be realized with the data. The experiments done in this respect showed that people prefer a privacy friendly approach when it is for free but that they are hardly willing to pay for additional privacy protection.

These mechanisms may help to understand how people deal with their privacy and may help to develop systems that meet these expectations. One issue that springs to mind is the interpretation of privacy by default (or, to be more precise: data protection by default) as this is mentioned in the General Data Protection Regulation (article 23). Behavioural economics shows that it is very relevant to have a high level of data protection as starting point (by default). People appreciate what they have. Any privacy feature already built in into a system will likely be appreciated as OK and 'nice to have'. When this feature is offered as a choice it is likely that people will only accept it when it comes for free and does not impose any mental or financial effort. Designing data protection by default such that it makes initial decisions for individuals in protecting their privacy is one approach towards 'nudging' individuals into privacy protection, as Acquisti proclaims [1].

Another issue is whether the fundamental right to privacy can be traded away by making good offers for personal data. The right to privacy is a fundamental right and will always have to be balanced against other fundamental rights. The very moment privacy becomes a tradable good, other fundamental rights, such as non-discrimination, will be put under pressure. The emergence of personal data markets and the increasing importance of profiles encompass opportunities for various forms of discrimination, both on commercial markets (people who are excluded from specific services or people who are offered specific services at a higher price) and in the public domain (health insurers who will use profiles to discriminate in health services and insurance packages offered).

A prominent issue that needs to be tackled in this discussion is the proximity of the right to data protection and the right to privacy. Both rights are safeguarded in the European Charter of Fundamental Rights. This is an interesting observation since the European directive on data protection (which is expected to be replaced by the General Data Protection Regulation within the coming two to three years) is based upon economic and not fundamental principles, namely the free flow of such data (as expressed in the full title of the directive). By uplifting the principle of data protection to the level of a fundamental right the European Parliament seems to lend more moral support to safeguarding this principle against market forces. In that sense, a preliminary conclusion can be – for the European situation – that sheer market forces are not sufficient to determine the price against which privacy and/or data protection can be traded away. This requires further study, especially with the advent of the era of big data and data analytics.

References

1. Acquisti, A.: Nudging privacy: the behavioural economics of personal information. IEEE Secur. Priv. 7, 82–85 (2009)
2. Acquisti, A., Grossklags, J.: What can behavioral economics teach us about privacy? In: Acquisti, A., Gritzalis, S., Di Vimercati, S., Lambrinoudakis, C. (eds.) Digital Privacy: Theory, Technologies, and Practices, pp. 363–379. Auerbach Publications, New York (2007). ISBN 1420052179
3. BCG: The value of our digital identity. Boston Consulting Group (2012)
4. Deighton, J., Johnson, P.A.: The Value of Data: Consequences for Insight, Innovation and Efficiency in the US Economy. Harvard (2013)
5. ENISA: Study on monetizing privacy. In: An economic model for pricing online information. ENISA, Brussels (2012)
6. Hoogveld, N., Straathof, S.M.: De nieuwe privacyverordening en keuzemogelijkheden voor consumenten. Priv. Identity 16(6), 262–266 (2013)
7. Katibloo, F.: Personal identity management: preparing for a world of consumer–managed data. Forrester, 30 September 2011
8. OECD: Exploring the economics of personal data - a survey of methodologies for measuring monetary value. OECD Digital Economy Papers (2013)
9. Rabin, M.: Incorporating limited rationality into economics. J. Econ. Lit. 51, 528–543 (2013)

10. Roosendaal, A., van Lieshout, M., van Veenstra, A.F.: Personal data markets. TNO report R11390, Delft (2014)
11. Spiekermann, S.: Privacy Property and Personal Information Markets. Acatech - Deutsche Academie der Wissenschaften, Berlin (2012)
12. Thaler, R.: Towards a positive theory of consumer choice. J. Econ. Behav. Organ. **1**, 39–60 (1980)
13. TNS-NIPO: Attitudes on data protection and electronic identity in the European union. In: Eurobarometer 359. European Commission, Brussels (2011)
14. World Economic Forum: Personal data: the emergence of a new asset class. World Economic Forum (2010)
15. World Economic Forum 2013: Unlocking the value of personal data: from collection to usage. World Economic Forum (2013)

Privacy and Security Perceptions of European Citizens: A Test of the Trade-Off Model

Michael Friedewald[1]([envelope]), Marc van Lieshout[2], Sven Rung[1],
Merel Ooms[2], and Jelmer Ypma[2]

[1] Fraunhofer Institute for Systems and Innovation Research ISI, Breslauer Straße 48,
76139 Karlsruhe, Germany
{michael.friedewald,sven.rung}@isi.fraunhofer.de
[2] Strategy and Policy Department, The Netherlands Organisation for Applied
Science (TNO), P.O. Box 155, 2600 AD Delft, The Netherlands
{Marc.vanLieshout,merel.ooms}@tno.nl

Abstract. This paper considers the relationship between privacy and
security and, in particular, the traditional "trade-off" paradigm that
argues that citizens might be willing to sacrifice some privacy for more
security. Academics have long argued against the trade-off paradigm, but
these arguments have often fallen on deaf ears. Based on data gathered
in a pan-European survey we show that both privacy and security are
important to European citizens and that there is no significant correlation between people's valuation of privacy and security.

Keywords: Privacy · Public opinion · Security · Trade-off

1 Introduction

The relationship between privacy and security has often been understood as a
zero-sum game, whereby any increase in security would inevitably mean a reduction in the privacy enjoyed by citizens. A typical incarnation of this thinking is
the all-too-common argument: "If you have got nothing to hide you have got
nothing to fear". This trade-off model has, however, been criticised because it
approaches privacy and security in abstract terms and because it reduces public opinion to one specific attitude, which considers surveillance technologies as
useful in terms of security but potentially harmful in terms of privacy [15,17].
Some people consider privacy and security as intrinsically intertwined conditions
where the increase of one means the decrease of the other. There are also other
views: There are those who are very sceptical about surveillance technologies and
question whether their implementation can be considered beneficial in any way.
Then there are people who do not consider surveillance technologies problematic
at all and do not see their privacy threatened in any way by their proliferation.
Finally there are those who doubt that surveillance technologies are effective
enough in the prevention and detection of crime and terrorism to justify the
infringement of privacy they cause [12].

© IFIP International Federation for Information Processing 2015
J. Camenisch et al. (Eds.): Privacy and Identity 2014, IFIP AICT 457, pp. 39–53, 2015.
DOI: 10.1007/978-3-319-18621-4_4

Insight into the public understanding of security measures is important for decision makers in industry and politics who are often surprised about the negative public reactions showing that citizens are not willing to sacrifice their privacy for a bit more potential security. On the back of this the PRISMS project aims to answer two central questions:

– Do people actually evaluate the introduction of new security technologies in terms of a trade-off between privacy and security? Our hypothesis is that people do not "naturally" think this way.
– If there is no simple trade-off between privacy and security perceptions, what then are the important factors that affect public assessment of the security and privacy implications of security technologies?

The PRISMS project has approached these questions by conducting a large-scale survey of European citizens. This is, however, not simply a matter of gathering data from a public opinion survey, as such questions have intricate conceptual, methodological and empirical dimensions. Citizens are influenced by a multitude of factors. For example, privacy and security may be experienced differently in different political and socio-cultural contexts. Therefore PRISMS has not only conducted a survey of public opinion, but has also explored the relationship between privacy and security from different disciplinary perspectives [14]. In this paper, however, we focus on results derived from the survey. The results presented have a European orientation but do not address Member State specifics, dissimilarities or similarities.[1]

2   Measuring Privacy and Security Perceptions

Researchers investigating the relationship between privacy and security have to deal with the so-called privacy paradox: It is well known that while European citizens are concerned about how the government and private sector collect data about citizens and consumers, these same citizens seem happy to freely give up personal and private information when they use the Internet. This "paradox" is not really paradoxical but represents a typical value-action gap which has been observed in other fields as well.[2]

Measuring privacy and security perceptions thus has to deal with problems similar to ecopsychology at the beginning of the environmental movement in the 1970s: What is the relationship between general values and concrete (environmental) concerns and how do they translate into individual behaviour?

In PRISMS we follow the concept of "planned behaviour" that suggests that if people evaluate the suggested behaviour as positive (attitude), and if they think their significant others want them to perform the behaviour (subjective norm), this results in a higher intention and they are more likely to behave in a certain way (Fig. 3). A high correlation of attitudes and subjective norms to behavioural intention, and subsequently to behaviour, has been confirmed in many studies [2].

---

[1] These and other analyses of the survey data can be found in [6].
[2] E.g. in the context of environmentalism consumers often state a high importance of environmental protection that is not reflected in their actual behaviour [11].

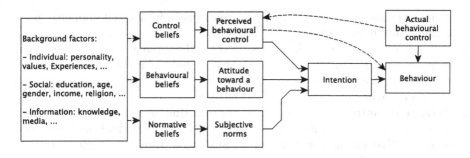

Fig. 1. Model of "planned behaviour" [2, p. 194]

As a consequence the PRISMS survey comprises of questions exploring respondents' perceptions of privacy and security issues as well as values questions including political views, attitudes to rights and perceptions of technology.

2.1 Seven Types of Privacy

Privacy is a concept that is not only hard to measure but also difficult to define, or, as Daniel Solove once deplored: "Privacy is a concept in disarray. Nobody can articulate what it means" [17, p. 3]. It is, however, a key lens through which many new technologies, and most especially new surveillance or security technologies, are critiqued. Changes in technology have continually required a more precise reworking of the definition in order to capture the ethical and legal issues that current and emerging surveillance and security technologies engender. In this endeavour, scholars have primarily utilised two perspectives to define privacy. On the one hand Solove [19] and Kasper [10] have defined privacy negatively by focussing on privacy intrusions and attempted to systemize the potential infringements that privacy is meant to protect against.

For the PRISMS work, on the other hand, we have used a taxonomy developed by Finn et al. [4] who suggest seven different types of privacy which ought to be protected and that receive different attention and valuation in practice. Such a detailed taxonomy facilitates the overcoming of the problem that privacy is too abstract as a concept. It helps to deal with the fact that people can (and do) understand the term in very different ways. It is a known problem that though people know rather little about the facts and rights related to privacy [9] they often voice (even strong) opinions about it. Finally the taxonomy can help to sort out the difference between "privacy" and "data protection" which are related but not identical [7]. The seven types of privacy comprise [4, pp. 7–9]:

1. **Privacy of the person** encompasses the right to keep body functions and body characteristics (such as genetic codes and biometrics) private. This aspect of privacy also includes non-physical intrusions into the body such as occur with airport body scanners.
2. **Privacy of behaviour and action** includes sensitive issues such as sexual preferences and habits, political activities and religious practices. However, the

notion of privacy of personal behaviour concerns activities that happen in public space *and* private space.

3. **Privacy of communication** aims to avoid the interception of communications, including mail interception, the use of bugs, directional microphones, telephone or wireless communication interception or recording and access to e-mail messages.

4. **Privacy of data and image** includes protecting an individual's data from being automatically available or accessible to other individuals and organisations and that people can "exercise a substantial degree of control over that data and its use" [3].

5. **Privacy of thoughts and feelings** is the right not to share one's thoughts or feelings or to have those thoughts or feelings revealed. Privacy of thought and feelings can be distinguished from privacy of the person, in the same way that the mind can be distinguished from the body.

6. **Privacy of location and space** means that individuals have the right to move about in public or semi-public space without being identified, tracked or monitored. This conception of privacy also includes a right to solitude and a right to privacy in spaces such as the home, the car or the office.

7. **Privacy of association** (including group privacy) is concerned with people's right to associate with whomever they wish, without being monitored.

2.2   Seven Types of Security

The concept of security is at least as difficult to approach as privacy. Firstly, for a pan-European study it is a problem that the term "security" can have multiple meanings, depending, for example, on language or use context. First, the German term "Sicherheit" can be understood as "security" (against an external threat), safety (against a threat originating from a system or situation) or, rather more generally, as "certainty". Such linguistic ambiguity exists in other European languages as well. Second, "security" can be defined as "protecting people and the values of freedom and democracy, so that everyone can enjoy their daily lives without fear" [8, p. 13] and is thus negatively defined as the absence of insecurity. Perfect objective security thus implies the absence of any threat. Even if this was achieved today it remains open to societal negotiations of new threats in the future. Finally, security can also refer to a subjective notion. What one considers insecure, the other may perceive as secure. Consequently we must distinguish objective from subjective security [20, p. 14].

Apart from these conceptual considerations it is also difficult to delineate the content of "security". The discourse in the media and among (European Union) policy makers is often narrowed down to issues of terrorism, crime and, increasingly, border security. For the general public, however, security is usually much more, including socio-economic conditions, health or cultural security. Therefore we have used a broad definition, in order not to exclude interesting perspectives. We have identified seven general types of security contexts and the accompanying measures to safeguard and protect these contexts [13]:

1. **Physical security** deals with physical measures designed to safeguard the physical characteristics and properties of systems, spaces, objects and human beings.
2. **Political security** deals with the protection of acquired rights, established institutions/structures and recognised policy choices.
3. **Socio-economic security** deals with economic measures designed to safeguard the economic system, its development and its impact on individuals.
4. **Cultural security** deals with measures designed to safeguard the permanence of traditional schemas of language, culture, associations, identity and religious practices while allowing for changes that are judged to be acceptable.
5. **Environmental security** deals with measures designed to provide safety from environmental dangers caused by natural or human processes due to ignorance, accident, mismanagement or intentional design, and originating within or across national borders.
6. **Radical uncertainty security** deals with measures designed to provide safety from exceptional and rare violence/threats, which are not deliberately inflicted by an external or internal agent, but can still threaten drastically to degrade the quality of life.
7. **Information security** deals with measures designed to protect information and information systems from unauthorized access, use, disclosure, disruption, modification, perusal, inspection, recording or destruction.

2.3   The Questionnaire and the Survey

In the survey, the seven types of privacy and security were translated into items that are part of overarching questions about privacy and security (the exact questions can be found in the annex). In the survey, the construct of "security" has been split up into "general security" and "personal security", both being worked out in terms of items reflecting the seven types of security. This was done as people can respond differently to issues that affect them personally, such as "someone hacking into your computer" as opposed to more abstract items, such as "viruses damaging the national Internet infrastructure". The result is that, in the survey, three batteries of questions measure citizens' attitudes towards privacy, general security and personal security. The questions reflect the considerations that were derived from the hypothesis, namely:

- In the survey, the two terms "security" and "privacy" are not explicitly used due to the lack of a clear and commonly shared definition. Instead, the questions were designed to address the different, more concrete types of privacy and security.
- For privacy we have asked how important the different types of privacy are for the interviewee (see QD1 in the appendix).
- Since we have defined security as the absence of threats, citizens were asked about their security worries.
- Finally people were never asked if they think in terms of a trade-off directly as this would have biased respondents' views (and hence their answers).

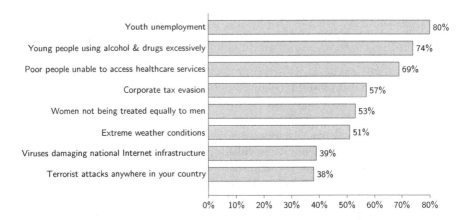

Fig. 2. General security worries. Question C3: "How often, if at all, have you worried about each of the following in your country in the last year?" Base: All valid responses (n=18 080), answers including "most days", "at least once a week", "at least once a month"

Fieldwork took place between February and June 2014. The survey company Ipsos MORI conducted around 1 000 telephone interviews in each European Union member state except Croatia[3] (27 195 in total) comprised of a representative sample (based on age, gender, work status and region) within each country (the sample composition is presented in the appendix).

3   Descriptive Results

All in all, European citizens share a commitment to privacy *and* security. In an introductory question we asked citizens about the importance of protecting their privacy and taking action against important security risks. In both cases 87 % of the respondents said that this is important or very important for them. This is a first indication for a shared commitment to privacy and security, and evidence against a trade-off. The answers to the three batteries of questions representing the concepts privacy, general security and personal security show what this commitment means in detail. First, the answers to the items measuring these concepts are shown, to get an idea of how the respondents score these.

With respect to *security in general* (in their respective countries) citizens made clear that social issues, such as unemployment, healthcare and young people are top concerns with more than 60 % of the respondents saying that they worry about them at least once a month (cf. Fig. 2). A much smaller share of European citizens (under 40 %) are worried about security issues with a potential privacy impact, such as virus attacks against the ICT infrastructure or becoming a victim of terrorist attacks.

---

[3] Croatia had not acceded to the European Union at the time of the project planning.

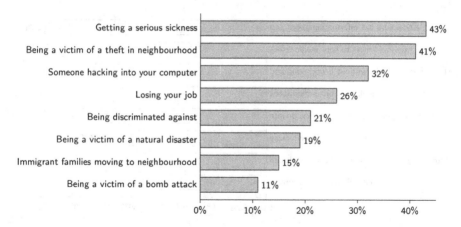

Fig. 3. Personal security worries. Question C4: "How often, if at all, have you worried about each of the following in your country in the last year?" Base: All valid responses (n=18 080), answers including "most days", "at least once a week", "at least once a month"

With respect to *personal security* the level of concern is much lower than that for general security (cf. Fig. 3). There is an indication that feelings of safety and health are more important to people personally than generally. At the same time, issues such as becoming a victim of crime in the neighbourhood, or someone hacking into one's computer are relatively more important than similar general security issues.

Regarding *privacy*, the survey results show that for many citizens personal control over their data is crucial, as is freedom of everyday association (cf. Fig. 4). In this context, personal is understood widely, ranging from the freedom to decide and to know who is collecting personal data, to the ability to move and communicate without being monitored. Compared to general and personal security worries the importance of privacy is rated relatively high. This result can, however, be an effect of the difference between expressions of people concerning their worries and expressions on what they consider important. It might as well be partly explained as socially desirable responding (Fig. 4).

Overall, it can be stated that while general security is a an important issue for citizens there is a higher concern about general socio-economic phenomena such as employment, healthcare and discrimination. Criminality and terrorism is only a secondary concern for most citizens. This also applies for individual security though the concern is on average lower here ("The world is in crisis, but I am doing relatively fine"). On the other hand, however, it is noteworthy that there is high concern about individual monitoring whether e.g., telephonically, electronically, or physically. This highlights the tension that exists between security as a collective and privacy as a (mainly) individual value [18].

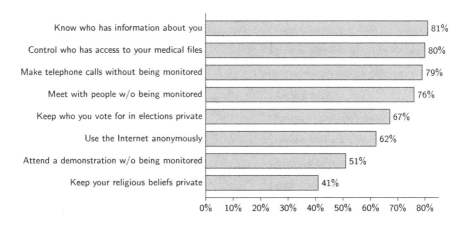

Fig. 4. Importance of privacy. Question D1: "How important, if at all, is it for you to be able to. . ." Base: All valid responses (n=27 195), answers including "essential", "very important", "fairly important"

4   Testing the Privacy-Security Trade-Off Hypothesis

4.1   Methodology

As mentioned before, the survey did not include a question directly addressing whether people think about privacy and security in terms of a trade-off. This does not only prevent biased answers, but also makes it less straightforward to analyse whether a trade-off exists or not. To test the validity of the trade-off model we investigated whether perceptions of general and personal security and privacy are related or independent. If the trade-off exists, we expected that people who worry a lot about security, think privacy is less important and vice versa. Our hypothesis was that the trade-off does not exist, and therefore there would be no correlation between privacy and security attitudes. For this test, the three batteries of questions regarding general security, personal security and privacy that embrace different types of privacy and security are used. First, factor analysis was used to investigate whether the three constructs that are supposed to be there really emerge in the data. When they are found to be present, they can be used for further regression analyses.

4.2   Factor Analysis Results

Previously it was stated that privacy and security have many different aspects. This was taken into account by asking respondents about seven different types of both privacy and security in the questionnaire. The concept of security was split up into both general security and personal security. In total the analysis included 24 items. Instead of analysing them individually, we reduced the number of variables in the analysis without losing valuable information by using factor analysis.

Table 1 shows the factor loadings which indicate which items can be combined into one construct. All items with factor loadings above a threshold in one column

Table 1. Factor loadings of principal axis factoring personal security, general security and privacy

	Privacy	Security personal	Security general
How often, if at all, have you worried about each of the following in your country in the last year?			
Poor people not being able to access healthcare services	0.060	0.187	0.624
Youth unemployment	-0.018	0.177	0.672
Corporate tax evasion	0.077	0.225	0.523
Women not being treated equally to men	0.106	0.253	0.499
Terrorist attacks anywhere in your country	-0.042	0.497	0.386
Young people using alcohol and drugs excessively	-0.055	0.273	0.549
Extreme weather conditions	0.066	0.356	0.359
Viruses damaging the national internet infrastructure	0.138	0.360	0.250
And how often, if at all, have you worried about each of the following in the last year?			
Getting a serious sickness	0.012	0.509	0.218
Losing your job	0.000	0.389	0.172
Being a victim of a theft in your neighbourhood	-0.015	0.553	0.162
Being discriminated against	0.108	0.508	0.231
Being a victim of a bomb attack (in your country/city)	-0.046	0.681	0.147
Immigrant families moving to your neighbourhood	-0.006	0.465	0.048
Being a victim of a natural disaster	-0.012	0.619	0.250
Someone hacking into your computer	0.201	0.445	0.066
How important, if at all, is it for you to be able to...			
Know who has information about you	0.614	0.095	0.070
Control who has access to your medical files?	0.593	0.079	0.035
Use the Internet anonymously?	0.641	0.009	-0.030
Make telephone calls without being monitored?	0.711	-0.002	0.068
Keep who you vote for in elections private?	0.539	0.049	-0.003
Keep your religious beliefs private?	0.492	0.064	-0.063
Attend a demonstration without being monitored?	0.592	-0.039	0.133
Meet with people without being monitored?	0.728	-0.052	0.059

(cells shaded in grey) constitute the three constructs that are expected, namely "privacy", "general security" and "personal security".

For the data on the European level the table shows that all items in battery QD1, the privacy question, are strong predictors for each other (someone answering positive on one of the privacy questions will respond positively as well on the other privacy questions). This indicates that they measure the same underlying construct of "privacy". It seems largely independent of the other two constructs; these items do not explain many of the security items. Based on the factor loadings, the majority of items in QC3, the general security question, can be considered as part of the construct which we labelled for rather obvious reasons "general security". Only "extreme weather conditions" and "viruses damaging the internet infrastructure" do not correlate well with the other items. They do, however, correlate with the "personal security" items, which makes sense since these are easier to relate to an individual's "real life" than, for example, "youth unemployment", which is a rather abstract concern when you are not part of this group. The last construct is "personal security" which is composed mainly of the items in question QC4, the "personal security" question. In addition, the QC3 questions on "extreme weather conditions", "damages to the Internet infrastructure" and "terrorist attacks" are relevant for this construct.

In summary, the factor analysis indicates that on the European level citizens' attitudes towards different aspects of privacy, general security and personal security correlate for each of these concepts. The answers on one item are good predictors for others in the same construct.[4]

4.3   Correlations Between Privacy and Security Attitudes

To examine the correlation between the privacy and security constructs the scales were plotted pairwise against each other.[5] This gives a visual impression as to whether people who score high on "privacy importance" score low on "security worries" – as would be expected in the trade-off model – or not.

Figure 5 displays the values for the two security scales in a scatter graph. A regression line is computed to assess the relationship between the newly constructed variables. As was expected, the explained variance of the scores on

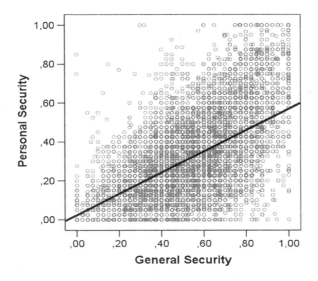

Fig. 5. Correlation between the General and Personal Security constructs. $R^2=0.316$

---

[4] While this holds on the European level, different results are found when investigating on a country level. In most countries, the construct of privacy is separate from security, although the general and personal security items overlap in many cases [6].

[5] Even though we are using a categorical tt scale for the constructs, they can be treated like numerical, continuous variables due to the high number of manifestations ($>$100).

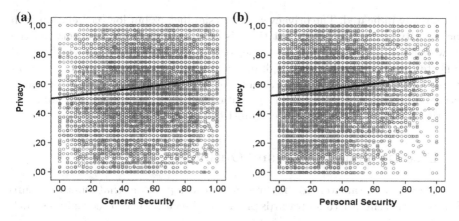

Fig. 6. Correlation between security and privacy constructs (a) $R^2=0.012$; (b) $R^2=0.023$

general security and on personal security shown by the R^2 Linear is quite high at 0.316. This is not surprising since these are comparable concepts.

Next, the general and personal security and privacy scales are plotted to see whether there is a relation between these constructs that can indicate evidence for or against the trade-off hypothesis. See Fig. 6 with general security (a) and personal security (b). In both cases, the explained variance of one variable in relation to the other is very low, at 0.012 for general security and 0.023 for personal security. There is a slight positive relationship indicating that when you think privacy is important, you also worry more about security. This is evidence against the trade-off hypothesis – albeit not convincing evidence. More convincing is that there is no negative relationship visible showing that respondents who worry more about security think their privacy is less important and vice versa. This is evidence against the existence of the trade-off model in the data.

To further assess this relationship between the privacy and security scales, correlation coefficients are calculated, using Pearson correlations ranging from 0 (no correlation) to 1 (complete correlation) (cf. Table 2). There is a relatively strong and significant correlation of 0.562 between both security scales – as the scatter

Table 2. Correlation between privacy, general security, and personal security scales

		Privacy scale	Personal security scale	General security scale
Privacy scale	Pearson correlation	1	0.111**	0.123**
	N	27 292	18 123	18 063
Personal security scale	Pearson correlation	0.111**	1	0.562**
	N	18 123	18 133	8 907
General security scale	Pearson correlation	0.123**	0.562**	1
	N	18 063	8 907	18 074

** Correlation is significant at the 0.01 level (2-tailed)

plot already indicated. The privacy scale has significant, but low, correlation with the security scale, indicating that there is only a small connection between the answers given to these scales. Also, the correlation is not negative, which would indicate that people who score high on the one, score low on the other. A negative correlation would have been evidence for the trade-off hypothesis. The results retrieved here show there is no clear relation between the privacy scale and the security scales, providing evidence against the trade-off hypothesis.

5   Discussion of Results and Outlook

Our analysis of the answers to the three batteries of questions that aim to measure European citizens' attitudes towards privacy and security had three main results:[6]

1. By applying factor analysis to a large number of items reflecting different types of privacy and security, it was possible to distinguish three "constructs" that reflect attitudes towards privacy, general security and personal security in a rich way. Something that needs more investigation is the fact that the results of the factor analysis are less clear on the national level. While in most cases the items in the privacy question contribute exclusively to the privacy construct, the assignment of QC3 and QC4 questions to the two security constructs is more variable.
2. Perception of general security and personal security are highly correlated. This result was to be expected as the individual feeling of security is (among other, often contextual factors) influenced by the general security feeling. We expect to gain greater insight into the mechanism of this translation process with the results from the analysis of the eight vignettes used in the survey.
3. There is no significant statistical correlation between people's valuation of privacy and their worries about security on the level of attitudes. This is first evidence against the trade-off hypothesis. The result only applies to people's attitudes, since these were measured in the variables used for the analyses in this paper. When it comes to actual behaviour people have to make choices that include trade-offs. It should be investigated further whether and how people make these trade-offs in their behaviour (for comparable work with focus on economic decision-making see e.g. [1]).

Finally we need to bear in mind that for citizens privacy and security are not always subject matter number one – most people have other day-to-day concerns. While our research shows that both privacy and security are important to people, the process of weighing the two values in specific situations is a contingent one that needs to take other factors into account as well.

Since we have shown that a simple trade-off between citizens' privacy and security perceptions does not exist, the next step is to define a structural model that describes the relationship of the main constructs. This will be a translation of the theory of planned behaviour into a survey based empirical model. This model

---

[6] Another ongoing research project has come to similar empirical findings, altough using a different methdolology [16].

will, in particular, take into account that attitudes towards a specific surveillance practice and the perceived as well as actual behavioural control may differ significantly. Such an enriched model may then support decision-makers in industry, public authorities and politics to implement security measures that raise fewer concerns in the population and are thus more acceptable along the lines stated in many policy documents.[7]

Acknowledgement. This work was carried out in the project "PRISMS: Privacy and Security Mirrors" co-funded from the European Union's Seventh Framework Programme for research, technological development and demonstration under grant agreement 285399. For more information see: http://prismsproject.eu.

Appendix 1: Composition of the survey sample

		Responses	Per cent
Total		27 195	100 %
Gender	Male	12 566	46 %
	Female	14 629	54 %
Age	16-24	2 793	10 %
	25-34	4 006	15 %
	35-44	4 704	17 %
	45-54	4 960	18 %
	55-59	2 435	9 %
	60-64	2 305	8 %
	65-74	3 643	13 %
	75+	2 294	8 %
Work status	Working	13 775	51 %
	Unemployed or in education	5,788	21 %
	Retired	7 209	27 %
Geographic areas	Big city	6 535	24 %
	Suburban area or small city	12 833	47 %
	Rural area	7 748	28 %

Appendix 2: Extract from the Survey Questionnaire

Privacy – 8 items

QD1. How important, if at all, is it for you to be able to...

1. ...know who has information about you?
2. ...control who has access to your medical files?

---

[7] The most notable is maybe the European Union's "Stockholm programme" that states "[t]he challenge will be to ensure respect for fundamental freedoms and integrity while guaranteeing security in Europe" [5, p. 4].

3. ... use the Internet anonymously?
4. ... make telephone calls without being monitored?
5. ... keep who you vote for in elections private?
6. ... keep your religious beliefs private?
7. ... attend a demonstration without being monitored?
8. ... meet with people without being monitored?

Possible Answers: Essential / Very important / Fairly important / Not very important / Not at all important / (Don't know)

General Security Worries – 8 Items

QC3. How often, if at all, have you worried about each of the following in your country in the last year?

1. Poor people not being able to access healthcare services.
2. Youth unemployment.
3. Corporate tax evasion.
4. Women not being treated equally to men.
5. Terrorist attacks anywhere in your country.
6. Young people using alcohol and drugs excessively.
7. Extreme weather conditions.
8. Viruses damaging the national Internet infrastructure.

Possible Answers: Most days / At least once a week / At least once a month / At least once in the last year / Not in the last year / Never / (Don't know)

Personal security worries – 8 items

QC4. And how often, if at all, have you worried about each of the following in the last year?

1. Getting a serious sickness.
2. Losing your job.
3. Being a victim of a theft in your neighbourhood.
4. Being discriminated against.
5. Being a victim of a bomb attack (in your country/in your city).
6. Immigrant families moving to your neighbourhood.
7. Being a victim of a natural disaster.
8. Someone hacking into your computer.

Possible Answers: Most days / At least once a week / At least once a month / At least once in the last year / Not in the last year / Never / (Don't know)

References

1. Acquisti, A., Grossklags, J.: Privacy attitudes and privacy behavior: losses, gains, and hyperbolic discounting. In: Camp, J.L., Lewis, S. (eds.) The Economics of Information Security, pp. 165–178. Kluwer, Dordrecht (2004)

2. Ajzen, I., Fishbein, M.: The influence of attitudes on behavior. In: Albarracin, D., Johnson, B.T., Zanna, M.P. (eds.) The Handbook of Attitudes, pp. 173–221. Erlbaum, Mahwah (2005)
3. Clarke, R.: Introduction to Dataveillance and Information Privacy, and Definitions of Terms. Xamax Consultancy, Chapman (1997–2006). http://www.rogerclarke.com/DV/Intro.html
4. Finn, R.L., Wright, D., Friedewald, M.: Seven types of privacy. In: Gutwirth, S., Leenes, R., De Hert, P., Poullet, Y. (eds.) European Data Protection: Coming of Age, pp. 3–32. Springer, Dordrecht (2013)
5. European Council: the Stockholm programme - an open and secure Europe serving and protecting the citizens. Official Journal of the European Union C 115, 1–38 (2010)
6. Friedewald, M., van Lieshout, M., Rung, S., Ooms, M., Ypma, J.: Report on statistical analysis of survey results, PRISMS Deliverable 10.1 (2015). http://prismsproject.eu
7. Gellert, R., Gutwirth, S.: The legal construction of privacy and data protection. Comput. Law Secur. Rev. 29, 522–530 (2013)
8. General Secretariat of the Council (ed.): Internal Security Strategy for the European Union: Towards a European Security Model. Publications Office of the European Union, Luxembourg (2010)
9. Hallinan, D., Friedewald, M., McCarthy, P.: Citizens' perceptions of data protection and privacy. Comput. Law Secur. Rev. 28, 263–272 (2012)
10. Kasper, D.V.S.: The evolution (or devolution) of privacy. Sociol. Forum 20, 69–92 (2005)
11. Kollmuss, A., Agyeman, J.: Mind the gap: why do people act environmentally and what are the barriers to pro-environmental behaviour? Env. Edu. Res. 8, 239–260 (2002)
12. Kreissl, R., Norris, C., Krlic, M., Groves, L., Amicelle, A.: Surveillance: preventing and detecting crime and terrorism. In: Wright, D., Kreissl, R. (eds.) Surveillance in Europe, pp. 150–210. Routledge, New York (2015)
13. Lagazio, M.: The evolution of the concept of security. Thinker 43(9), 36–43 (2012)
14. van Lieshout, M., Friedewald, M., Wright, D., Gutwirth, S.: Reconciling privacy and security. In: Friedewald, M., Pohoryles, R.J. (eds.) Privacy and Security in the Digital Age, pp. 119–132. Routledge, London (2014)
15. Pavone, V., Esposti, S.D.: Public assessment of new surveillance-oriented security technologies: beyond the trade-off between privacy and security. Public Undestanding Sci. 21, 556–572 (2012)
16. Pavone, V., Esposti, S. D., Santiago, E.: Key factors affecting public acceptance and acceptability of SOSTs, SurPRISE Deliverable 2.4 (2015). http://surprise-project.eu/
17. Solove, D.J.: "I've got nothing to hide" and other misunderstandings of privacy. St. Diego Law Rev. 44, 745–772 (2008)
18. van Schoonhoven, B., Roosendaal, A., Huijboom, N.: Privacy versus collective security. In: Hansen, M., Hoepman, J.-H., Leenes, R., Whitehouse, D. (eds.) Privacy and Identity 2013. IFIP AICT, vol. 421, pp. 93–101. Springer, Heidelberg (2014)
19. Solove, D.J.: Understanding Privacy. Harvard University Press, Cambridge (2008)
20. Zedner, L.: Security. Routledge, London (2009)

Privacy and Confidentiality in Service Science and Big Data Analytics

Christine M. O'Keefe[✉]

CSIRO Digital Productivity Flagship,
GPO Box 664, Canberra, ACT 2601, Australia
Christine.OKeefe@csiro.au
http://people.csiro.au/O/C/Christine-OKeefe

Abstract. Vast amounts of data are now being collected from census and surveys, scientific research, instruments, observation of consumer and internet activities, and sensors of many kinds. These data hold a wealth of information, however there is a risk that personal privacy will not be protected when they are accessed and used.

This paper provides an overview of current and emerging approaches to balancing use and analysis of data with confidentiality protection in the research use of data, where the need for privacy protection is widely-recognised. These approaches were generally developed in the context of national statistical agencies and other data custodians releasing social and survey data for research, but are increasingly being adapted in the context of the globalisation of our information society. As examples, the paper contributes to a discussion of some of the issues regarding confidentiality in the service science and big data analytics contexts.

Keywords: Privacy · Statistical disclosure control · De-identification

1 Introduction

The future internet in the age of globalisation is turning the so-called *information super-highway* into an *information super-mountain* of data. The Internet of Things continues to grow and touch every aspect of our lives, and every interaction generates a digital record, leading to vast data archives accumulating in repositories everywhere. Put together, these data repositories reveal more and more details about ourselves, our behaviours, and our preferences. On the one hand, these detailed data hold a wealth of information vital to informed decision making, research, services personalisation, and debate within governments and the community. On the other hand, there is a risk that personal privacy will not be protected, where privacy is understood as the interest an individual has in controlling the dissemination of information about themselves.

In this paper, we focus on the use of data archives, irrespective of how they have been established, populated and maintained, and on methods for assuring confidentiality of the people or organisations represented in the data. Such methods are called *statistical disclosure control* methods, since they seek to reduce or

J. Camenisch et al. (Eds.): Privacy and Identity 2014, IFIP AICT 457, pp. 54–70, 2015.
DOI: 10.1007/978-3-319-18621-4_5

control the risk of disclosure from statistical analysis. To provide a full solution, they must be implemented with an appropriate governance framework and with appropriate information security processes. The methods we will present and discuss were developed in the context of a national statistical agency making census and survey data available for research. Confidentiality remains a major concern for national statistical agencies [11,19], as well as for a broader range of agencies and organisations which now find themselves holding significant data archives and receiving access requests from researchers.

Thus, this paper aims to contribute to the investigation of what technologies, frameworks, and tools we might need to gain, regain and maintain informational self-determination and lifelong privacy while still extracting useful information from our growing data archives. This would be in addition to the minimum standard required by applicable privacy, data protection, and related legislation.

2   Preliminaries

In this section we describe preliminary notions regarding confidentiality and privacy, where confidentiality is *a status accorded to information about a person* [11, Section 1.1], and: *A disclosure occurs when a person or organisation recognises or learns something that they did not know already about another person or organisation, via released data* [19].

2.1   Types of Data

Microdata refers to datasets in which each record is contributed by an individual in the population, so that the record typically comprises values of a number of variables for that individual. A variable can be either continuous or categorical, where a continuous variable value is numeric and a categorical variable value is a category label.

Tabular data result when microdata are summarised and presented as a table with axes corresponding to explanatory variables and cells corresponding to a response variable. Table cells can contain counts, where each data record contributes 1 to its tabulation cells and 0 to all other cells, in which case the data is called *tabular count data* and the table is called a *contingency table*. Table cells can also contain aggregates of one response variable, for example the total or average value of that variable for individuals contributing to that cell, in which case the data is called *magnitude data*.

2.2   Types of Disclosure

There are two basic types of disclosure, namely identity and attribute disclosure [10], resulting from a data release. An *Identity Disclosure* occurs if an individual is identifiable from the data release. An *Attribute Disclosure* occurs when the released data make it possible to infer the characteristics of an individual more accurately than would have otherwise been possible.

The main ways that an identity disclosure can occur are:

- Release of identifying information
- Spontaneous recognition - where an individual is sufficiently unusual in a data collection, or the data user knows sufficiently many attributes of an individual, so that individual can be recognised from normally non-identifying attributes. This may occur if the attributes have extreme values such as extreme old age or an unusual combination of attributes. For example, it is generally accepted that households have distinctive patterns of inhabitants and other features that make them vulnerable to spontaneous recognition.
- Matching to another data base - where combinations of so-called key variables in the data occur in other databases sufficiently rarely that data matching reveals identity.

Attribute disclosure is usually achieved through identity disclosure; an individual is first identified through some combination of variables and then disclosure of values of other variables included in the released data follows.

2.3 Balancing Disclosure Risk with Data Utility

The balance between protecting confidentiality and allowing the use of data for research has been represented as a trade off between disclosure risk and data utility [10], where *disclosure risk* attempts to capture the probability of a disclosure of sensitive information, while *data utility* attempts to capture some measure of the usefulness of the released data. Confidentiality methods are technical approaches designed to reduce disclosure risk, and are applied in addition to governance and information security measures. Unfortunately, any confidentiality method will also reduce data utility.

The idea of balancing risk and utility advanced by Duncan et al. [10] is that in a specific situation, the data custodian creates a *Risk-Utility (or R-U) Map* as a two-dimensional plot of disclosure risk versus data utility for various parameter instances of a range of confidentiality methods, and chooses the method and parameter instance with the maximum utility given a maximum tolerable risk.

3   Approaches for Protecting Confidentiality in Data

In this section we provide a structured overview of a broad range of approaches for protecting confidentiality in data archives. Many of these appear in the literature, and are described in [11,19]. The structure of our overview depends at a high level on the system design, the type of method, and the type of data [30].

3.1   Types of Methods

In the remainder of this Section we provide a structured overview of approaches to reducing disclosure risk when making data available for research. Importantly, each approach only addresses the disclosure risk inherent in the data, and so each must be implemented within an appropriate legislative and policy environment and governance structure, and with user community management and IT security, including user authentication, access control, system audit and follow-up. The approaches have different strengths and weaknesses, and so none dominates the others in all data access scenarios. In fact, because there is a range of scenarios, it is desirable to have a range of disclosure risk reduction approaches, so the most appropriate one can be chosen to meet the requirements of a particular situation involving a particular dataset, data custodian, analyst and so on.

Traditionally, there have been two different general approaches with regard to enabling the use of data while protecting confidentiality [12]:

- *restricted or limited access*, wherein the access to the information is restricted; and
- *restricted or limited information*, wherein the amount or format of the information released is restricted.

Often these two approaches are used in combination, such as when access to data is restricted to approved analysts and the data themselves have had identifying information removed and/or dates aggregated to months or years. The relationship between the degree of access restriction and the degree of information restriction required is perhaps best represented in the framework of Marsh et al. [26], who noted that a successful disclosure involves first an attempt at disclosure, then success of that attempt. In probabilistic terms, this is $\Pr(\text{disclosure}) = \Pr(\text{attempt}) \cdot \Pr(\text{disclosure} \mid \text{attempt})$. Restricted access seeks to reduce $\Pr(\text{attempt})$ while restricted data seeks to reduce $\Pr(\text{success} \mid \text{attempt})$.

3.2   Restricted Access Methods

In this Section we discuss various data access strategies used to restrict access to information, noting that they are predominantly implemented as system designs. We present these in generally increasing order of restriction, so that the degree of requirement for information restriction generally decreases correspondingly. At opposite ends of this spectrum are the familiar data access strategies of providing no information to non-authorised users, and full information to fully authorised users.

User Agreements for Offsite Use. Under this approach, sometimes called *Licensing*, users are required to register with a custodian agency, and sign a user agreement, before receiving data to be analysed offsite. Typically such agreements specify restrictions on the user, such as, restrictions on the manner of storage and further dissemination of the data, as well as prohibiting attempts to re-identify data records. Such agreements also typically specify sanctions for breaches, and are legally binding. The user community is managed by the custodian, including, possibly, the use of external audits to verify compliance with the restrictions in the agreement.

Examples of this approach include the many Public Use Files disseminated by organisations and agencies, including national statistical and health agencies, see [3, 8, 27].

Remote Analysis Systems. In remote analysis, the analyst submits statistical queries through an interface, analyses are carried out on the original data in a secure environment, and the user then receives the (confidentialised) results of the analyses [16, 44]. In particular, the analyst does not receive any data at all, but only analysis results. Since analysis results can reveal information about the underlying data, the output needs to be confidentialised.

The Australian Bureau of Statistics Remote Access Data Laboratory (RADL) is a secure online data query service that clients can access via the Australian Bureau of Statistics web site [2]. The Australian Bureau of Statistics has recently developed the TableBuilder and DataAnalyser remote analysis systems with automated confidentiality routines that allow uses to build their own custom tables or undertake regression analyses on secured ABS microdata [46]. The Microdata Analysis System under development by the U.S. Census Bureau will allow users to receive certain statistical analyses of Census Bureau data, including regression analyses, without ever having access to the data themselves [23].

We remark that remote analysis systems need to be protected against attacks including massively repeated queries, subsetting to create very small datasets and never-ending loops. Recently-developed systems do not allow user-submitted code but rather implement a menu-driven interface to prevent these and other types of attack.

Virtual Data Centres. Virtual data centres are similar to remote analysis systems, except that the user has full access to the data [31], and are similar to on-site data centres except that access is over a secure link on the internet from the researcher's institution.

An example of a virtual data centre is the US NORC Data Enclave, that provides a confidential, protected environment within which authorised social science researchers can access sensitive microdata remotely [49]. Another interesting example is the Australian Population Health Research Network Secure Unified Research Environment [41], see [29]. Similar systems include the United Kingdom Office For National Statistics (ONS) Virtual Microdata Laboratory [28], and the UK Secure Data Service, that provides secure remote access to data operated by the Economic and Social Data Service [47].

Secure On-Site Data Centres. Many national statistical agencies allow researchers access to confidential data in secure, on-site research data centres. Usually the data have undergone a confidentialisation process such as de-identification and some light statistical disclosure control, but have more detail than datasets confidentialised for release to researchers. Analysts are generally not restricted in the analyses they can perform and the intermediate results they can generate and view. However, only results which have been checked to ensure low disclosure risk, or which have been confidentialised if necessary to reduce disclosure risk, can be removed from the laboratory. Currently this output checking is done manually, as in the guidelines in [19].

Examples of on-site data centres include the U.S. Census Bureau Research Data Centers (RDC) [48] and the Australian Bureau of Statistics (ABS) On-site Data Laboratory [5].

3.3 Restricted Information Methods - Microdata

Restricted information methods normally comprise the application of some statistical disclosure limitation techniques, see [11,19]. Statistical disclosure control techniques can be perturbative or non-perturbative. Perturbative methods operate by modifying the data values, whereas non-perturbative methods do not modify the data values. Perhaps the most well-known perturbative method is the addition of random "noise" to a dataset, and perhaps the most well-known non-perturbative method is suppression of sensitive values.

In this section we describe the main techniques developed for microdata. The methods are presented in the order of generally increasing restriction on released information, so decreasing disclosure risk, from removal of identifying information to synthetic data. The amount of trust in the analyst therefore generally decreases across the methods, and so access restrictions may also be able to be relaxed across the methods.

3.3.1 Removal of Identifying Information

Probably the most common method of reducing disclosure risk in data sets is to remove identifying information such as name, address, date of birth, and unique identifiers such as social security number or healthcare identifier. This is often called *de-identification*.

As examples, the Population Health Research Network [33] will enable existing Australian health data to be brought together and made available for health and health related research purposes under protocols that use linkage keys to replace personal information in health records. Similarly, the University of British Columbia Centre for Health Services and Policy Research [6] is the central access point for researchers wishing to obtain and use health data in de-identified format for research in the public interest.

3.3.2 Non-perturbative Methods for Microdata

Suppression of Variables or Variable Values. Entire sensitive variables, such as name of surgeon in clinical data, can be suppressed. It is also possible to suppress certain values of categorical individual variables, where such a value is sufficiently unusual that it leads to unacceptable risk of disclosure via matching.

Variable Recoding. A widely-used method for reducing disclosure risk is *variable recoding,* or *coarsening,* that can be either part of the data collection design phase or applied to the resulting dataset. The method can be applied to either tabular data or microdata, and can be applied to any number of the variables.

Variable recoding usually involves reporting the values of the variable with less than full detail. For example, geographic information such as address can be recoded to suburb or postal code area, age can be recoded to 5-year or 10-year intervals, and age over a certain threshold can be recoded to simply being over that threshold.

Sampling. Disclosure risk can depend on the existence of microdata records that are both unique in the sample and in the population on a set of potentially identifying cross-classified key variables, since such records can be matched to external datasets with high confidence [42].

3.3.3   Perturbative Methods for Microdata

Rounding. Original variable values are replaced by rounded values rounded to multiples of a given number such as 3 or 5.

Data Swapping. Data swapping transforms a database by interchanging values of sensitive variables between records in a microdata file.

Additive or Multiplicative Noise Addition. Randomly-distributed noise values can be added to the data, or the data can be multiplied by randomly-distributed values. Additive noise can be uncorrelated or correlated, and can be augmented with a linear or non-linear transformation.

Micro-aggregation. Micro-aggregation is applied by clustering records into small groups of similar records and replacing individual record values by the cluster average values.

Post-randomisation Method (PRAM). The Post-Randomisation Method technique is applied to categorical data and involves a form of intended misclassification using a known and pre-set probabilistic mechanism. Under PRAM, for each record in a microdata file, the value of one or more categorical variables is changed with a certain probability.

Synthetic Data. Rubin [39] suggested the approach of generating and releasing (fully) *synthetic data*, see also [22,35]. In the generalisation to partially synthetic data, the data custodian releases a dataset comprising the original records with some observed values replaced with multiple imputations drawn from distributions designed to preserve important relationships in the confidential data, or from models generated by a machine learning technique.

3.3.4   Examples of Restricted Information Approaches on Microdata

Internationally, IPUMS-International is a project dedicated to collecting and distributing census data from around the world [27]. IPUMS-International works with each country's statistical office to minimise the risk of disclosure of respondent information. The details of the confidentiality protections vary across countries, but in all cases, names and detailed geographic information are suppressed and top-codes are imposed on variables such as income that might identify specific persons. In addition, IPUMS-International uses a variety of technical procedures to enhance confidentiality protection, including:

- Swapping an undisclosed fraction of records from one administrative district to another to make positive identification of individuals impossible.
- Randomizing the placement of households within districts to disguise the order in which individuals were enumerated or the data processed.
- Aggregating codes of sensitive characteristics (e.g., grouping together very small ethnic categories)
- Top- and bottom-coding continuous variables to prevent identification of extreme cases.

There are several examples of partially synthetic datasets already released for research. For example, the US Bureau of the Census has released a partially synthetic, public use file for the Survey of Income and Program Participation including imputed value of Social Security benefits information and dozens of other highly sensitive variables [1]. More recently, a synthetic public use file for the U.S. Longitudinal Business Database, an annual economic census of U.S. establishments, has been approved for release by the U.S. Bureau of the Census and the Internal Revenue Service [21].

3.4 Restricted Information Methods - Tabular Data

Although tabular data are aggregated, there still may be unacceptable disclosure risk. Perhaps the most common disclosure risk is associated with a cell of a table that relates to only one individual, where an identity disclosure may occur by data matching from the characteristics in the table.

Restricted information methods normally comprise the application of some statistical disclosure limitation techniques for tabular data, see [11,19]. As in the case of microdata, tabular statistical disclosure control techniques can be perturbative or non-perturbative. There are two main classes of confidentiality methods for tabular data, namely, pre-tabular and post-tabular. *Pre-tabular* methods modify microdata before aggregation into a table, while *post-tabular* methods modify a table directly.

Pre-tabular Methods. Perhaps the most widely-used pre-tabular method is table redesign, including collapsing of categories along any axis. In fact, any of the methods presented in Sect. 3.3 could be used as a pre-tabular confidentiality method.

Post-tabular Methods. In post-tabular Statistical Disclosure Control for tabular data, the first task is to determine whether any of the cells are sensitive, where a sensitive cell is one for which the release of the data in the cell could lead to a disclosure. The most commonly-used cell sensitivity tests are:

- *Threshold rule* - a cell is sensitive if less than n individuals contribute to its value (frequency and magnitude tables)
- (n, k) *-rule* - a cell is sensitive if less than n individuals contribute at least $k\%$ of its value (magnitude tables) [9]

For a discussion of the shortcomings of these techniques, see [37].

After the sensitive cells in a table have been identified, the second task is to take steps to address the disclosure risk. The most commonly-used techniques are:

- *Deletion of variables* - removing table axes corresponding to sensitive variables and/or variables that lead to sensitive cells.
- *Variable recoding* - adjusting the level of aggregation of variables to reduce the number of sensitive cells. This method aggregates all cells involving the recoded variable, whether sensitive or not.
- *Cell collapsing* - merging pairs of cells until no sensitive cell remains. This method only aggregates the sensitive cells, but can make analysis more difficult.
- *Cell suppression* - suppression of the entry in each sensitive cell, then suppression of entries in non-sensitive cells sufficient to prevent reconstruction of any sensitive value.
- *Rounding* - rounding all cells to a multiple of a chosen positive integer, for example, 3 or 5.
- *Addition of noise* - altering sensitive cell values (and usually also non-sensitive cell values) by the addition of noise sampled from some distribution. Examples of this method include the *Post-Randomization Method* [17] and the key-based method in [25].

The Australian Bureau of Statistics Census TableBuilder [4] is an online tool that allows users to create confidentialised, custom tables of Census data from variables including age, education, housing, income, transport, religion, ethnicity, occupation, family composition and more for all ABS geographic areas [46].

3.5   Analysis Output Confidentialisation Methods

Currently virtual data centres rely on manual checking for confidentiality protection, such as those outlined in [19]. This solution may not be feasible in the long term given the trend of rising user demands for data access. Although it is acknowledged that developing valid output checking processes that are automated is an open research question [11], there have been some recent advances in such methods for remote analysis systems, see [16, 23, 34, 36, 43, 44, 46].

Remote analysis systems now in development in the US Census Bureau and the Australian Bureau of Statistics do not rely on restricted output methods alone, but also make use of a combination of protective measures from the restricted access, restricted data, restricted analysis and restricted output groups of methods.

4   Confidentiality in Service Science and Big Data Analytics

In this paper, our aim is to contribute to the investigation of what technologies, frameworks, and tools we might need to gain, regain and maintain informational self-determination and lifelong privacy while still extracting useful information from our growing data archives. We do this by means of two examples of growing importance due to the rise of the future internet in the age of globalisation, namely, service science and big data.

4.1 Confidentiality in Service Science

The world is dominated by service-based economies. In developed countries, the sector accounts for over 70 % of economic activity, and in a significant number of developing countries it accounts for over 50 % [14]. A *service* can be defined as: the application of competencies for the benefit of another [24], see [45]. Further, "Service is performed in close contact with a client; the more knowledge-intensive and customized the service, the more the service process depends critically on client participation and input, whether by providing labor, property or information" [40] see [45]. According to the Journal *Service Science,* "Leading and competitive services enabled by service systems are all remarkably delineated with information-driven, people-centric, e-oriented, and satisfaction/success focussed characteristics". Market and consumer trends in the service economy include: demand for personalisation, customisation of services, and improvement of the customer service experience.

It is clear that a successful service economy relies fundamentally on customers providing information to service providers. This information is needed in the service provision, for example, a delivery address is needed for goods delivery, and service requests often include choice of options. The service provider may need to share the information internally or externally, for example with a courier service.

It is highly likely that service providers also store client information, for future use in service improvement and innovation, including personalisation, customisation and customer experience improvement. Issues of privacy and commercial sensitivity arise, since client information can be complex, personal and sensitive. For example, the information may include direct data such as health status, employment status, or financial status, or may include indirect information revealing behaviours, movements, and preferences. In some cases, such as government services, the client may not have a choice whether to interact or not, so must accept that the information needs to be provided. In addition, given the trends of the future internet in the age of globalisation, service providers would be increasingly collecting as much transactional and auxiliary information as possible. The service provider may be motivated to address these issues, since assurances of confidentiality protection during service provision may increase the information the client is willing to give, so improving the service and the level of personalisation possible, and hence improving the overall service experience for the client.

Interestingly, we have been unable to locate any articles in the academic press relating primarily to privacy or confidentiality technologies in service science (via a title search on a popular publications database). There has been some discussion of policy aspects, see for example [32], who note that "technology has

	Service Science	Research Use
Data providers	Clients	Census and survey participants
Motivation for providing information	In exchange for a service, but may be compulsory	Voluntary or compulsory
Data custodians	Service provider agencies and companies	National statistical agencies and other service provider agencies
Dataset size	Moderate trending to big data	Moderate trending to big data
Data sharing	Shared amongst a community of service provider agencies and companies	Usually held by custodian agency, some initiatives in data linkage
Authorised data users	Staff in service provider agencies and companies; increasingly outsourced to contractors	Staff in service provider agencies. Researchers, policy analysts, increasingly the general public
Confidentiality protection needed against:	Unauthorised users – most privacy policies include use for service provision, improvement and personalisation	Unauthorised users and some classes of authorised users

Fig. 1. Main similarities and differences between the scenarios of service science and research use of data archives

the potential to regulate behaviour by enabling or disabling it, in contrast with law, which regulates mainly be imposing sanctions. ... Therefore, it is necessary to consider these approaches simultaneously ..."

It is therefore worthwhile to analyse the similarity between the confidentiality protection scenario in service science and that in the research use of data scenario as discussed in this paper. We consider the applicability of the approaches described in Sect. 3, in order to better understand the need for new methods of protecting confidentiality in service science. This is consistent with the approach advocated by service science experts, including: "Services science is an emerging field that seeks to tap into these and other relevant bodies of knowledge, integrate them, and advance three goals - aiming ultimately to understand service systems, how they improve and how they scale", "The study of service systems is an integrative, multidisciplinary undertaking and many disciplines have knowledge and methods to contribute" [45], and "Synthesis of partial knowledge from individual disciplines is vital for future of service science" [14].

The table in Fig. 1 gives a summary of the main similarities and differences between the scenarios of service science and research use of data archives.

We see from Fig. 1 that the data providers and data custodians in the two scenarios are broadly similar. The differences in motivation for providing information are probably not sufficient to impact on the data providers' expectations of confidentiality of their data. For the implications of big data on confidentiality protection, see Sect. 4.2.

One of the main differences between the two scenarios is in the area of data sharing - specifically, whether the dataset is held by the collecting agency or is held in trust for a different collecting agency. In the research use of data, this issue arises in data linkage centres which bring together data from various sources, see the Manitoba Centre for Health Policy and Evaluation, Canada [38], the Oxford Medical Record Linkage System [15], the Scottish Medical Record Linkage System [20], Western Australian Data Linkage Branch [18] and the Welsh Secure Anonymised Information Linkage (SAIL) system [13]. In this situation the issue is best addressed in the governance layer, supported by technological implementations and information security measures.

Finally, two areas of broad similarity between the two scenarios are the range of authorised users and the cohort against which confidentiality protection is needed, if we accept that there is broad analogy between contractors and researchers, policy analysts, and the general public.

Given the similarities between the two scenarios of service science and research use of data, we believe that the approaches for protecting confidentiality outlined in Sect. 3 are broadly applicable in service science. We note that within the broad service science context, there is still likely to be a range of more detailed scenarios involving a particular dataset, data custodian, analyst and so on. We reiterate that it is important to choose the appropriate confidentiality protection method to address the particular scenario in question.

4.2   Confidentiality in Big Data

As mentioned in the introduction, technological advances and the increasing connectivity of a growing number of computers, devices, and sensors are resulting in massive amounts of data being generated and stored. The term "Big Data" was coined in response to the realisation that traditional methods of storing, processing, and analysing data were breaking down in the face of the so-called "3 V's of big data", namely, volume (amount of data), variety (range of data sources and data types), and velocity (speed of collection and dissemination).

In the big data scenario, it is worthwhile to think about whether the 3 V's of big data pose additional privacy or commercial sensitivity risks. Again, we analyse the similarity between the confidentiality protection scenario in big data and that in the research use of data scenario as discussed in this paper. We further consider the applicability of the approaches described in 3, in order to understand the need for new methods of protecting confidentiality in big data.

Big data involves massively increasing volumes of data, often leading to a situation in which values for more and more characteristics of an individual are being stored. This in turn increases disclosure risk, since the more information we have about an individual, the more likely it is to be able to identify an individual in the data and learn something that we did not know already about that individual. Massively increasing volume of data also places stress on storage and computational infrastructure. These challenges are being addressed through new infrastructure and computational approaches. A important additional privacy or commercial sensitivity risks would therefore arise in the context of information security - the question is whether the new infrastructure and computational approaches for big data are still adequately protecting data from unauthorised access and use.

	Big Data	Research Use
Data providers	Any individual interacting with the internet or other electronic device – knowingly or unknowingly	Census and survey participants
Motivation for providing information	Generally trading information for goods and services, but increasingly data collected while individuals go about their daily lives	Voluntary or compulsory
Data custodians	Anyone with a website, electronic equipment, sensors, etc	National statistical agencies and other service provider agencies
Dataset size	Big data	Moderate trending to big data
Data sharing	Anecdotally could be huge and range from controlled to uncontrolled	Usually held by custodian agency, some initiatives in data linkage
Authorised data users	Authorised users for a range of applications	Staff in service provider agencies. Researchers, policy analysts, increasingly the general public
Confidentiality protection needed against:	Unauthorised users and some classes of authorised users	Unauthorised users and some classes of authorised users

Fig. 2. Main similarities and differences between the scenarios of big data and research use of data archives

Massively increasing variety of data has the potential to increase again the likelihood that an individual is identified, with subsequent increased disclosure risk.

Massively increasing velocity of data bring challenges in terms of ensuring that data processing is fast enough to keep up with the rate of data arriving. For example, if it is necessary to remove direct identifiers from data in order to reduce disclosure risk, then how fast does this need to be done in order to ensure that only de-identified data are stored or accessed? Again, these challenges seem to be best addressed through the integration of confidentiality protection routines with the new infrastructure and computational approaches under development to cope with big data velocity.

There have been a number of books and articles published in the academic press relating primarily to privacy or confidentiality technologies in big data. Many of these address the socio-legal or information security perspectives. We believe it is still worthwhile to analyse the similarity between the confidentiality protection scenario in big data and that in the research use of data scenario as discussed in this paper. We consider the applicability of the approaches described in Sect. 3, in order to better understand the need for new methods of protecting confidentiality in big data.

The table in Fig. 2 gives a summary of the main similarities and differences between the scenarios of big data and research use of data archives.

We see from Fig. 2 that there are significant differences between the nature of data providers and the motivation for providing information between the two scenarios of big data and the research use of data. In the situation of big data, data providers may not even know they are providing data, or may have little or no choice in the data provision. Given these observations, there is a higher moral/ethical responsibility on data custodians to protect confidentiality in big data, which would be addressed in the design of information management systems, see [7].

There are also significant differences between the nature of data custodians in the two scenarios. While in research use, the relatively few data custodians are subject to enabling legislation containing specific confidentiality protection requirements, in big data almost any entity can be a data custodian subject to more general privacy or data protection laws. Similarly, while data sharing is quite controlled in research use, in big data it could be trending to uncontrolled. The degree of community awareness of data collection would also impact community expectations of confidentiality protection from data custodians during collection, storage, sharing and use. There would appear to be an imperative to ensure that legislative frameworks are robust and widely applicable enough to cover the activities of all data custodians, not just the traditionally-recognised ones.

There is broad similarity between the two scenarios with respect to the range of authorised users and the cohort against which confidentiality protection is needed, though these populations may be vastly different sizes. The main difference is in the size of the datasets, though this may disappear in time as research data sets also become larger and larger. In the big data scenario, it will be generally infeasible to transfer datasets to users, implying that there will be a preference for remote analysis systems, virtual data centres and secure on-site data centres. These are likely to rely on a combination of microdata confidentialisation methods with techniques to confidential analysis outputs. The growing user numbers are likely to cause a greater reliance on automated methods.

We note that within the broad big data scenario, there is still likely to be a range of more detailed scenarios involving a particular dataset, data custodian, analyst and so on. We reiterate that it is important to choose the appropriate confidentiality protection method to address the particular scenario in question.

5   Conclusion

In this paper our aim was to contribute to a discussion of some of the issues regarding confidentiality in the service science and big data analytics contexts. We believe that these two areas are growing in importance as the future internet in the age of globalisation is transforming our economy into a service economy and is turning the so-called *information super-highway* into an *information super-mountain* of data.

We provided an introduction to a consideration of what technologies, frameworks, and tools we might need to gain, regain and maintain informational self-determination and lifelong privacy while still extracting useful information from our growing data archives. In particular, we gave an overview of methods for protecting confidentiality in the use of data for research, as developed in the context of a national statistical agency making census and survey data available for research and policy analysis. We then discussed the general applicability of these methods to the new scenarios, in order to help pinpoint where existing methods might be applicable and where new methods might be in demand.

In the service science scenario, we found that the approaches for protecting confidentiality in the research use of data are broadly applicable, with adaptations as needed to particular situations. In the case of big data on the other hand, we found that only certain of the approaches were applicable, namely, remote analysis servers, virtual data centres, and secure on-site data centres with automated output confidentialisation routines. We remark that this is a trend underway for enabling the research use of data, and we echo the following: ... *recent events in the development of remote analysis servers herald the dawn of a new era in automated confidentiality protection for analysis and we look forward to invigorated research collaborations among NST's and academic institutions to further this research* ... [46].

Acknowledgments. I warmly thank the organisers of the International Federation for Information Processing (IFIP) 9th Summer School on *Privacy and Identity Management for the Future Internet in the Age of Globalisation,* for their invitation to participate. I acknowledge the financial support of the *Authentication and Authorization for Entrusted Unions (AU2EU)* project funded by the European Commission Seventh Framework Programme for Research and Technological Development.

References

1. Abowd, J.M., Stinson, M., Benedetto, G.: Final report to the social security administration on the sipp/ssa/irs public use file project. Technical report (2006)
2. Australian Bureau of Statistics: Remote Access Data Laboratory (RADL) (2014). http://www.abs.gov.au. Accessed 23 October 2014
3. Australian Bureau of Statistics: About CURF Microdata. Website (nd) (2014). http://www.abs.gov.au/websitedbs/D3310114.nsf/home/About+CURF+Microdata. Accessed 23 October 2014
4. Australian Bureau of Statistics: Census TableBuilder (nd) (2014). http://www.abs.gov.au. Accessed 23 October 2014
5. Australian Bureau of Statistics: (website) (2014). http://www.abs.gov.au. Accessed 23 October 2014
6. British Columbia Linked Health Database (BCHLD) (2014). http://riskfactor.cancer.gov/tools/pharmaco/epi/british_columbia.html. Accessed 23 October 2014
7. Cavoukian, A., Jonas, J.: Privacy by design in the age of big data. Published online (2014). http://privacybydesign.ca/content/uploads/2012/06/pbd-big_data.pdf. Accessed 23 Dec 2014
8. Centers for Disease Control and Prevention: Public-use data files and documentation. Website (2014). http://www.cdc.gov/nchs/data_access/ftp_data.htm. Accessed 23 Oct 2014
9. Cox, L.: Linear sensitivity measures in statistical disclosure control. J. Stat. Plan. Infer. **5**, 153–164 (1981)

10. Duncan, G.T., Keller-McNulty, S.A., Stokes, S.L.: Disclosure risk vs data utility: The R-U confidentiality map. Technical report LA-UR-01-6428, Los Alamos National Laboratory (2001)
11. Duncan, G., Elliot, M., Salazar-Gonzàlez, J.J.: Statistical Confidentiality. Springer, New York (2011)
12. Duncan, G., Pearson, R.: Enhancing access to microdata while protecting confidentiality: prospects for the future. Stat. Sci. **6**, 219–239 (1991)
13. Ford, D.V., Jones, K.H., Verplancke, J.P., Lyons, R.A., John, G., Brown, G., Brooks, C.J., Thompson, S., Bodger, O., Couch, T., Leake, K.: The SAIL databank: building a national architecture for e-health research and evaluation. BioMed central. Health Serv. Res. **9**, 157 (2009)
14. Geczy, P., Izumi, N., Hasida, K.: Service science, quo vadis? Int. J. Serv. Sci. Manage. Eng. Technol. **1**(1), 1–16 (2010)
15. Gill, L.: OX-LINK: The oxford medical record linkage system. Record Linkage Techniques. Technical report, 19, University of Oxford, Oxford (1997)
16. Gomatam, S., Karr, A., Reiter, J., Sanil, A.: Data dissemination and disclosure limitation in a world without microdata: a risk-utility framework for remote access systems. Stat. Sci. **20**, 163–177 (2005)
17. Gouweleeuw, J., Kooiman, P., DeWolf, L.W.P.P.: Post randomisation for statistical disclosure control: theory and implementation. J. Official Stat. **14**, 463–478 (1998)
18. Holman, C.D.J., Bass, A.J., Rouse, I.L., Hobbs, M.S.: Population-based linkage of health records in Western Australia: development of a health services research linked database. Aust. N. Z. J. Public Health **23**, 453–459 (1999)
19. Hundepool, A., Domingo-Ferrer, J., Franconi, L., Giessing, S., Nordholt, E., Spicer, K., de Wolf, P.P.: Statistical Disclosure Control. Wiley Series in Survey Methodology. Wiley, United Kingdom (2012)
20. Kendrick, S., Clarke, J.A.: The scottish medical record linkage system. Health Bull. Edinb. **51**, 72–79 (1979)
21. Kinney, S.K., Reiter, J.P., Reznek, A.P., Miranda, J., Jarmin, R.S., Abowd, J.M.: Towards unrestricted public use business microdata: the synthetic longitudinal business database. Int. Stat. Rev. **79**(3), 362–384 (2011)
22. Little, R.: Statistical analysis of masked data. J. Official Stat. **9**, 407–426 (1993)
23. Lucero, J., Zayatz, L., Singh, L., You, J., DePersio, M., Freiman, M.: The current stage of the microdata analysis system at the U.S. census bureau. In: Proceedings of the 58th Congress of the International Statistical Institute, ISI 2011 (2011)
24. Lusch, R., Vargo, S. (eds.): The Service-Dominant Logic of Marketing: Dialog, Debate, and Directions. ME Sharpe, Armonk (2006)
25. Marley, J., Leaver, V.: A method for confidentialising user-defined tables: statistical properties and a risk-utility analysis. In: Proceedings of the 58th Congress of the International Statistical Institute, ISI 2011, 21–26 Aug 2011
26. Marsh, C., Skinner, C., Arber, S., Penhale, B., Openshaw, S., Hobcraft, J., Lievesley, D., Walford, N.: The case for samples of anonymized records from the 1991 census. J. Roy. Stat. Soc.: Ser. A **154**, 305–340 (1991)
27. Minnesota Population Center, University of Minnesota: Ipums international. Website (2014). https://international.ipums.org/international/. Accessed 23 Oct 2014
28. Office for National Statistics: (website) (2014). http://www.statistics.gov.uk. Accessed 23 Oct 2014
29. O'Keefe, C.M., Gould, P., Churches, T.: Comparison of two remote access systems recently developed and implemented in australia. In: Domingo-Ferrer, J. (ed.) PSD 2014. LNCS, vol. 8744, pp. 299–311. Springer, Heidelberg (2014)

30. O'Keefe, C.M., Rubin, D.B.: Balancing the research use of health and medical data with confidentiality protection, preprint
31. O'Keefe, C.M., Westcott, M., Ickowicz, A., O'Sullivan, M., Churches, T.: Protecting confidentiality in statistical analysis outputs from a virtual data centre. Working Paper (29–30 October 2013), joint UNECE/Eurostat work session on statistical data confidentiality, Ottawa, Canada, p. 10 (2014). http://www.unece.org/stats/documents/2013.10.confidentiality.html. Accessed 23 Oct 2014
32. Pitkänen, O., Virtanen, P., Kemppinen, J.: Legal research topics in user-centric services. IBM Syst. J. **47**(1), 143–152 (2008)
33. Population Health Research Network (2014). http://www.phrn.org.au/. Accessed 23 Oct 2014
34. Reiter, J.: Model diagnostics for remote-access regression systems. Stat. Comput. **13**, 371–380 (2003)
35. Reiter, J.: Using CART to generate partially synthetic public use microdata. J. Official Stat. **21**, 441–462 (2005)
36. Reiter, J., Kohnen, C.: Categorical data regression diagnostics for remote systems. J. Stat. Comput. Simul. **75**, 889–903 (2005)
37. Robertson, D.A., Ethier, R.: Cell suppression: experience and theory. In: Domingo-Ferrer, J. (ed.) Inference Control in Statistical Databases. LNCS, vol. 2316, p. 8. Springer, Heidelberg (2002)
38. Roos, L.L., Wajda, A.: Record linkage strategies: Part 1: Estimating information and evaluating approaches. Technical report 28, University of Manitoba, Winnipeg (1990)
39. Rubin, D.: Discussion: statistical disclosure limitation. J. Official Stat. **9**, 462–468 (1993)
40. Sampson, S., Froehle, C.: Foundations and implications of a proposed unified services theory. Prod. Oper. Manag. **15**(2), 329–343 (2006)
41. Sax Institute: Secure Unified Research Environment (SURE). Website (2014). http://www.sure.org.au. Accessed 23 Oct 2014
42. Skinner, C., Shlomo, N.: Assessing identification risk in survey microdata using log-linear models. J. Am. Stat. Assoc. **103**, 989–1001 (2008)
43. Sparks, R., Carter, C., Donnelly, J., Duncan, J., O'Keefe, C.M., Ryan, L.: A framework for performing statistical analyses of unit record health data without violating either privacy or confidentiality of individuals. In: Proceedings of the 55th Session of the International Statistical Institute, Sydney, p. 4 (2005)
44. Sparks, R., Carter, C., Donnelly, J., O'Keefe, C.M., Duncan, J., Keighley, T., McAullay, D.: Remote access methods for exploratory data analysis and statistical modelling: privacy-preserving analytics^{TM}. Comput. Methods Programs Biomed. **91**, 208–222 (2008)
45. Spohrer, J., Maglio, P., Bailey, J., Gruhl, D.: Steps toward a science of service systems. Computer **40**, 71–77 (2007)
46. Thompson, G., Broadfoot, S., Elazar, D.: Methodology for automatic confidentialisation of statistical outputs from remote servers at the Australian Bureau of Statistics. In: Joint UNECE/Eurostat Work Session on Statistical Data Confidentiality, Ottawa, Canada, 28–30 October 2013, p. 37 (2013)
47. UK Data Archive: Secure data service (website) (2014). http://ukdataservice.ac.uk/get-data/how-to-access/accesssecurelab.aspx. Accessed 23 Oct 2014
48. United States Census Bureau: (website) (2014). http://www.census.gov. Accessed 23 Oct 2014
49. University of Chicago: NORC (website) (2014). http://www.norc.org. Accessed 23 Oct 2014

Legal Privacy Aspects
and Technical Concepts

The Court of Justice of the European Union, Data Retention and the Rights to Data Protection and Privacy – Where Are We Now?

Felix Bieker[(⊠)]

Walther Schücking Institute for International Law at the University of Kiel
and ULD (Independent Centre for Privacy and Data Protection),
Kiel, Schleswig-Holstein, Germany
fbieker@wsi.uni-kiel.de

Abstract. In a recent judgment the CJEU found the Data Retention Directive to be incompatible with the rights to privacy and data protection under the EU Charter of Fundamental Rights. However, the Court's interpretation of these fundamental rights needs further development, especially with regard to their respective scopes. While the Court declared the EU Directive to be invalid, there remain questions with regard to the Member States' national implementation measures, which remain in force. Nevertheless, they do no longer comply with EU law and therefore need to be repealed or altered substantively. While it should be for the national legislator to achieve this, it might be necessary for service providers and citizens to challenge these provisions before the competent national courts.

Keywords: Data Retention · Privacy · Data Protection · European Union · Fundamental Rights · Court of Justice · Data Retention Directive · Data Protection Directive · e-Privacy Directive

1 Introduction

In Europe, the retention of traffic data for criminal investigations has been and continues to be a subject for much debate as well as litigation. With the long-awaited and substantive judgment of the Court of Justice of the European Union (in the following: CJEU or the Court) in the cases of *Digital Rights Ireland and Seitlinger*[1], this article argues that the blanket retention of traffic data for the fight against crime and terrorism has been ruled out. However, there remain questions to be answered, most prominently the scope of the right to data protection under Article 8 of the EU Charter on Fundamental Rights (in the following: CFR or the Charter) and the consequences of the Data Retention Directive's (in the following: DRD or the Directive)[2] invalidity for Member States' law.

---

[1] Joined Cases C-293/12 and 594/12 *Digital Rights Ireland and Seitlinger*, Judgment of 8 April 2014, not yet reported.

[2] Directive 2006/24/EC of the European Parliament and of the Council of 15 March 2006 on the retention of data generated or processed in connection with the provision of publicly available electronic communications services or of public communications networks and amending Directive 2002/58/EC, OJ 2006 L 105/54.

© IFIP International Federation for Information Processing 2015
J. Camenisch et al. (Eds.): Privacy and Identity 2014, IFIP AICT 457, pp. 73–86, 2015.
DOI: 10.1007/978-3-319-18621-4_6

This article explains the genesis and scope of the Data Retention Directive (2), before briefly summarizing the Court's judgment (3). The Court's reasoning is then assessed with a focus on the interpretation of Article 8 CFR and the Court's role in the European system of fundamental rights protection (4). Section 5 analyzes the consequences of the DRD's invalidity for the Member States' own regulations on data retention. The conclusions (6) provide a brief outlook on future developments.

2   The Genesis and Scope of the Data Retention Directive

The regulation of data retention on a European level gained momentum after the terrorist attacks of Madrid and London in 2004 and 2005 respectively. In the aftermath of these tragic events, there was an endeavor to pass a Framework Decision in the then third pillar of the European Union, the Police and Judicial Cooperation in Criminal Matters.[3] The cooperation of police was governed by ex-Articles 30, 31 and 34 TEU. Under these provisions however, a unanimous vote in the Council was required. When, in the early stages of the negotiations, Ireland threatened to use its veto on the proposal, the legislation was in jeopardy.

Nevertheless, while some Member States did not have any form of data retention, there also were many variations of data retention in other Member States. This provided the impetus to further pursue the subject as a harmonization measure under ex-Article 95 TEC (now Article 114 TFEU). The subsequent Data Retention Directive, due to the change in legal basis, could then be adopted by a majority vote in the Council.

The DRD obliged Member States to order providers of publicly available electronic communication services or of public communications networks (in the following: service providers) to retain data to identify the source and destination of fixed network and mobile telephony – including text messages – as well as internet telephony, E-Mail communications and internet access according to its Article 5 para. 1. These data include numbers or user names, date, time and duration, and for mobile telephony the subscriber's IMSI (international mobile subscriber identity), the cell phone's IMEI (international mobile station equipment identity) and the location by Cell ID. These sets of data, at a first glance, might appear rather innocuous, as they do not contain any contents of the communication. In fact, the DRD expressly prohibits the storing of any data which may reveal the contents of a communication in its Article 5 para. 2. However, for two different projects a German and a Swiss politician made their data publicly available and had them visualized in an interactive map showing their location. This was correlated with a list of calls, text messages and internet communications to and from other (identifiable) persons.[4] From this combined information, it is possible to draw comprehensive conclusions about the everyday life of these politicians.

---

[3] Terhechte, Rechtsangleichung zwischen Gemeinschafts- und Unionsrecht – die Richtlinie über die Vorratsdatenspeicherung vor dem EuGH, Europäische Zeitschrift für Wirtschaftsrecht 2009, 199.

[4] Biermann, Betrayed by our own data, Zeit Online of 26 March 2011, available at: http://www.zeit.de/digital/datenschutz/2011-03/data-protection-malte-spitz/komplettansicht; Digitale Gesellschaft, The life of National Councillor Balthasar Glättli under surveillance, available at: https://www.digitale-gesellschaft.ch/dr.html.

Soon after the Directive's adoption, Ireland filed an annulment action according to Article 263 TFEU before the CJEU, solely attacking the choice of legal basis, which was rejected by the Court in 2009.[5] Simultaneously, the Member States' implementation measures for the DRD were challenged before numerous national constitutional courts and declared invalid in Romania, Germany and the Czech Republic.[6] None of these courts made a preliminary reference to the CJEU under Article 267 TFEU, arguing that the national legislator had not exercised the margin granted by the Directive in a way compatible with the national constitution.[7] While a German Administrative Court in 2009 asked the Court about the Data Retention Directive's validity, the CJEU found the question inadmissible, as it did not bear any relation to the case referred.[8] In 2012 however, the Austrian Constitutional Court as well as the Irish High Court referred questions concerning the compatibility of the DRD with fundamental rights to the CJEU, which resulted in the present judgment.

3 The Court's Judgment

In its judgment, the Court stressed that the Directive's wide scope allowed detailed insights into the daily life of all citizens. Even though no contents of the communications were stored, the retention of the data might change the use of these services, which affected the users' and subscribers' right to freedom of expression under Article 11 CFR. The question whether the data of users and subscribers could be retained had to be assessed with regard the right to privacy according to Article 7 CFR. Further, Article 8 of the Charter, the right to protection of personal data, imposed requirements on the protection of personal data.[9]

3.1 Interference with Fundamental Rights

However, when assessing the interference, the Court no longer referred to Article 11 of the Charter. Instead, it affirmed that for the right to privacy, there was no requirement of sensitivity of the data or any inconvenience for the users or subscribers. In accordance with its own and the jurisprudence of the European Court for Human Rights (in the following: ECtHR), it held that the obligation to retain the data as well as the granting of access for national authorities to this data constituted two independent interferences

---

[5] Case C-301/06 *Ireland v Parliament and Council* [2009] ECR I-593.

[6] Constitutional Court of Romania, Decision no. 1258 of 9 October 2009, available at: http://www.legi-internet.ro/fileadmin/editor_folder/pdf/decision-constitutional-court-romania-data-retention.pdf; Federal Constitutional Court of Germany, Judgment of 2 March 2010, 1 BvR 256/08, English press release available at: http://www.bundesverfassungsgericht.de/pressemitteilungen/bvg10-011en.html; Constitutional Court of the Czech Republic, Judgment of 22 March 2011, Pl. ÚS 24/10, available at: http://www.slidilove.cz/sites/default/files/dataretention_judgment_constitutionalcourt_czechrepublic.pdf.

[7] Cf. for example Federal Constitutional Court of Germany (note 6), paras. 183 and 185–187.

[8] Joined Cases C-92 and 93/09 *Schecke and Eifert* [2010] ECR I-11063, paras. 35 and 42.

[9] Joined Cases C-293/12 and 594/12 *Digital Rights Ireland and Seitlinger* (note 1), paras. 28–30.

with Article 7 CFR. Additionally, the processing of personal data in itself interfered with Article 8 CFR. The Court emphasized that due to the mass scale of the data retention, this measure was likely to create a feeling of constant surveillance.[10]

3.2 Justification of the Interference

Under the horizontal justification clause of Article 52 para. 1 of the Charter, interferences with all rights granted may be justified when they are provided for by law, respect the essence of the rights and are proportionate. The Court started with an assessment whether the DRD respected the essence of the rights concerned. Before the Charter entered into force, the CJEU stated that interferences may not impair the very substance of fundamental rights, but has since adopted the Charter's wording.[11] In an earlier decision the Court defined the essence of a right as its 'core content'[12] and thus interpreted it as a principle separate from proportionality.[13] In the case at hand, the Court found that while the retention was a particularly serious interference, it respected the essence of Article 7 CFR as it did not include the retention of any contents of communication. With regard to Article 8 CFR the Court argued that the essence of this right was not concerned, as the Directive itself contained rules on the integrity and protection of the data retained.[14]

In the review of the Directive's proportionality the Court found the fight against terrorism and serious crime to be its 'material objective'[15]. Yet, due to the sensitivity of personal communications and the large scale of the retention, the Court held that this measure called for strict judicial review.

Assessing the appropriateness, the CJEU argued that the retained data was a valuable tool for criminal investigation, which was unchanged by the fact, that the measures could be circumvented by taking recourse to anonymous forms of communication. However, the fight against serious crime, did not in itself justify the retention of all communication data with regard to necessity. Rather, the restriction had to be limited in so far as it was strictly necessary, due to the right to data protection's particular importance for the right to private life. As the DRD encompassed traffic data from all means of electronic communication and all subscribers and users, it affected, without any exception, all European citizens using electronic communication. This called for legislation with a precisely defined scope as well as safeguards against abuse and unlawful processing of the data.[16] In particular, the CJEU criticized four aspects:

Firstly, the collection of data neither required a nexus with a threat to public security, nor did it demand any temporal, geographical or personal limitations.

---

[10] *Ibid.*, paras. 34–37.

[11] Cf. Case C-5/88 *Wachauf* [1989] 2609, para. 18.

[12] Case C-283/11 *Sky Österreich*, Judgment of 22 January 2013, not yet published, para. 49.

[13] This line of assessment was also conducted in a judgment after *Seitlinger* in Case C-129/14 PPU *Spasic*, Judgment of 27 May 2014, not yet published, para. 58.

[14] Joined Cases C-293/12 and 594/12 *Digital Rights Ireland and Seitlinger* (note 1), para. 40.

[15] *Ibid.*, para. 41.

[16] *Ibid.*, paras. 49-58.

Secondly, access to and use of the data retained was not limited: the definition of serious crime as well as the substantive and procedural conditions were left to the Member States. Further, the Directive required no limitation on the persons who were granted access and there was no prior review by a court or other independent body. Thirdly, the range of data retention from a period of six to 24 months was not justified by any reasons and thus arbitrary. These three points constituted grave interferences with Articles 7 and 8 of the Charter.[17]

Lastly, the Court criticized the lack of safeguards against abuse and rules for protection of the data retained. The organizational measures to protect the data against loss and misuse were to be weighed against economical interests of the service providers and there was no obligation to store the data within the territory of the EU and thus no supervision by an independent body. This did not conform to the requirements of Article 8 CFR.[18] Therefore, the CJEU found that the data retention was disproportionate and the interference not justified. Consequently, the Court ruled that the DRD was invalid.

4 Assessment of the Judgment

Keeping in mind the controversy surrounding data retention for years now, which included the CJEU in two instances, it seems as though the Court needed a push to finally assess the validity of the DRD. However, with a view to previous judgments concerning EU legislation and the strict proportionality review conducted by the Court,[19] the judgment does not come as a surprise.

The CJEU assesses the rights of the Charter extensively and for the first time scrutinizes Article 8 CFR as a right independent from Article 7 of the Charter. In previous cases, the Court assessed the rights jointly, under the premise that Article 8 para. 1 and Article 7 CFR were closely connected and their scope of protection was a right to respect for private life with regard to the processing of personal data.[20] When stating in *Digital Rights Ireland and Seilinger*, that the question of the retention of the data affects the scope of Article 7 CFR, while Article 8 of the Charter sets out data protection requirements,[21] the Court allows for a nuanced shift in the assessment of the scopes of these rights.

As far as the interference is concerned though, the Court relies on its own jurisprudence to hold the storing of the data to interfere with Article 7 CFR and refers to the

---

[17] *Ibid.*, paras. 59–65.

[18] *Ibid.*, paras. 66–68.

[19] Case C-291/12 *Schwarz v Stadt Bochum*, Judgment of 17 October 2013, not yet published; Joined Cases C-92 and 93/09 *Schecke and Eifert* (note 8).

[20] Joined Cases C-92 and 93/09 *Schecke and Eifert* (note 8), paras. 47 and 52; Case C-468/10 *ASNEF* [2011] I-12181, paras. 41 *et seq*; Case C-291/12 *Schwarz v Stadt Bochum* (note 19), paras. 24 *et seq*; However, in one case between private parties, where according to Article 51 para. 1 CFR the Charter does not apply, the Court mentioned – without any assessment of its scope or an interference – the right to data protection safeguarded by Article 8 CFR without reference to Article 7 of the Charter, cf. Case C-70/10 *Scarlet Extended* [2011] I-11959, para. 50.

[21] Joined Cases C-293/12 and 594/12 *Digital Rights Ireland and Seitlinger* (note 1), paras. 29 *et seq*.

ECtHR's case law when finding the access to this data as a separate interference with this very provision.[22] While it is to be welcomed that the Court refers to the jurisprudence of the ECtHR, which has developed extensive and long-standing case-law on the right to privacy under the European Convention on Human Rights (in the following: ECHR), the CJEU's adoption of this strand of case law leads to problems with regard to Article 8 CFR. This is due to the fact that the ECHR contains no separate right to data protection. Interpreting the obligation of service providers to store the data and the subsequent access of national authorities to this data as interferences with Article 7 CFR is in line with the ECtHR's jurisprudence on interferences with Article 8 ECHR.[23] As Article 7 CFR guarantees a right corresponding to Article 8 ECHR in the sense of Article 52 para. 3 CFR according to the Explanations to the Charter[24] such an interpretation is sensible. Even though the Explanations are not a legally binding document, they are awarded interpretative force for the Charter by Article 52 para. 7 CFR and Article 6 para. 1 TEU.

When, however, the Court goes on to consider the processing of the data as interference with Article 8 CFR, this leads to overlaps between the scopes of these rights. In order to interpret the notion of processing as laid down by Article 8 para. 2 CFR, recourse can be taken to the Explanations to the Charter. For Article 8 CFR, they refer to the Data Protection Directive (in the following: DPD)[25] for conditions and limitations of the right to data protection. According to the definition of Article 2 lit. b Data Protection Directive, the processing of personal data consists inter alia of their collection, storage and use. Thus, when analyzing the judgment with due regard to the secondary law, the term 'processing' which is used to describe an interference with Article 8 of the Charter has to be interpreted as the collection, storage and subsequent use of the personal data. Then however, the interference with Article 8 CFR is exactly the same as the interferences by retention of the communication data with Article 7 CFR, i.e. the obligation of service providers to store the data and the subsequent access to the data by national authorities.

Although the Court apparently tried to differentiate between the right to privacy and the right to data protection in this case, it ended up with identical definitions for both rights. Consequently, whenever data is stored or accessed, this constitutes simultaneous interferences with the right to privacy and the right to data protection. If this had been an intended outcome, the Court would not have bothered to differentiate between the rights. Therefore, the CJEU's interpretation of the scope of the rights of Article 7 and 8 CFR is not yet convincing and requires further elaboration by the Court.

However, if the current approach of the CJEU is followed and the rights to privacy and data protection are interpreted in the same manner, Article 8 CFR could be regarded as a lex specialis to the more general provision of Article 7 CFR.[26] As the

[22] *Ibid.*, paras. 33–35.

[23] *Leander v. Sweden,* Judgment of 26 March 1987, no. 9248/81, para. 48; *Rotaru v. Romania,* Judgment of 4 May 2000, no. 28341/95, para. 46.

[24] Explanations Relating to the Charter of Fundamental Rights, OJ 2007 C 303/17.

[25] Directive 95/46/EC of the European Parliament and of the Council on the protection of individuals with regard to the processing of personal data and on the free movement of such data, OJ 1995 L 281/31.

[26] Kingreen, Article 8, in: Calliess/Ruffert, EUV/AEUV, 4th ed., Munich 2011, MN. 1.

ECHR does not include a separate right to data protection, the ECtHR employed the right to private life in order to develop the right to privacy as one of its facets. With time, the case law evolved and the ECtHR also covered aspects of data protection, as detailed above. While the CJEU could just adopt this case law for its own jurisprudence before the Charter, there is now an express right to data protection, which has to be taken into account. In this regard, the specific right to data protection of Article 8 CFR could be awarded precedent over the more general right to private life in Article 7 of the Charter, which – in its verbatim – does not contain any reference to either privacy or data protection. This lex specialis interpretation would ensure consistency with the ECHR, while allowing a broader scope for Article 8 of the Charter with regard to the extensive individual rights granted by the DPD. Nevertheless, the existence or non-existence of a distinction between privacy and data protection is a contentious issue in doctrine.[27] The ultimate resolution of this problem is not within the scope of this article, which is instead focused on the discussion of the CJEU's judgment in the *Digital Rights Ireland and Seitlinger* case.

Yet, the judgment at hand does include a new aspect concerning the right to data protection: that is the Court's interpretation of Article 8 para. 3 CFR – which states that an independent authority supervises adherence to the provision – as requiring storage of the data within the European Union. This is a very welcome statement. The CJEU thereby demonstrates that it takes the revelations about mass-surveillance by US and UK intelligence services seriously and is not willing to let European law turn a blind eye to these substantial threats to privacy and data protection. In the way the Court assesses this provision as a part of the right to data protection, it adds an element of an individual right to Paragraph 3 of Article 8 CFR, which could have been seen as a merely formal requirement.

Although the interpretation of the rights to privacy and data protection may not be followed in its reasoning, the Court is to be commended for its extensive assessment of the privacy implications of data retention. However, the issue that it took eight years to arrive at the conclusion that the DRD gravely violated fundamental rights remains. Yet, it should be borne in mind that it is a legal obligation of the legislator to draft regu-lations in a way consistent with fundamental rights. The DRD in its Article 14 para. 1 contained a clause requiring an evaluation of its impact and effectiveness. In the subsequent report the Commission, evaluating its own work, suggested several chan-ges, inter alia to the storage of the data and the reimbursement of service providers, but found the Directive in general to conform to fundamental rights.[28] However, with

---

[27] Cf. inter alia Tzanou, Data protection as a fundamental right next to privacy? 'Reconstructing' a not so new right, International Data Privacy Law 3 (2013), 88; Kranenborg, in: Peers et al. (eds.), The EU Charter of Fundamental Rights – A commentary, Oxford/Portland 2013, MN. 08.21-08.27; Kokott/Sobotta, The distinction between privacy and data protection in the jurisprudence of the CJEU and the ECtHR, International Data Privacy Law 3 (2013), 222; and even AG Villalón, Joined Cases C-293/12 and 594/12 *Digital Rights Ireland and Seitlinger*, Opinion of 12 December 2013, paras. 62–67.

[28] European Commission, Report from the Commission to the Council and the European Parliament, Evaluation report on the Data Retention Directive (Directive 2006/24/EC) of 18 April 2011, COM (2011) 225 final.

regard to the measure's fundamental rights implications the report merely summarized the case law of the CJEU and the ECtHR without applying it to the Directive itself.[29] In this regard, improvement is necessary: the Commission needs to take the assessment of fundamental rights implications of regulations more seriously. A two page description of the fundamental rights concerned cannot be sufficient for measures interfering with the rights of the entire European population.

In safeguarding fundamental rights the CJEU comes into play only on a secondary level, when it interprets Union law and rules on the validity of the acts adopted by the legislator according to Article 19 para. 3 TEU. As any other court, the CJEU cannot render decisions by its own motion, but is limited to the cases brought before it. In the aftermath of its first decision on the proceedings instigated by Ireland, the CJEU attracted wide-spread criticism.[30] However, it could have been anticipated that the Court would only assess the choice of Article 114 TFEU (ex-Article 95 TEC) as legal basis as this was the only claim made by Ireland.[31] As the infringement proceedings under Article 263 TFEU are based on the French legal system, there is a long-standing practice of the Court to limit its review to the claims of the applicants, rather than conduct an extensive ex-officio scrutiny.[32]

The issue of fundamental rights was, however, raised by the Slovak Republic, which supported Ireland's action before the CJEU and questioned the retention's compatibility with Article 8 ECHR.[33] Under Article 130 of the Rules of Procedure of the Court, Member States may be granted leave to join proceedings, but this is limited to supporting the claims of the party according to Article 129 para. 1 cl. 2 of the Rules of Procedure. Even though the CJEU's case law on claims and defences is not always consistent,[34] the Court does not allow interveners the right to seek forms of order unconnected to those of the party.[35]

While the Court's judicial self-restraint in this context as a whole has been[36] and continues to be subject to criticism, especially when it comes to the compatibility of a measure with fundamental rights,[37] the CJEU's limited review cannot be ascribed to an attempt to circumvent an assessment of fundamental rights. Rather, the suggestion that

---

[29] *Ibid.*, 28 *et seq.*

[30] Cf. inter alia, Simitis, Der EuGH und die Vorratsdatenspeicherung oder die verfehlte Kehrtwende bei der Kompetenzregelung, Neue Juristische Wochenschrift 2009, 1782; Petri, Rechtsgrundlage der EG-Richtlinie zur Vorratsdatenspeicherung, Europäische Zeitschrift für Wirtschaftsrecht 2009, 212, 214 *et seq*; Braum, „Parallelwertung in der Laiensphäre": Der EuGH und die Vorratsdatenspeicherung, Zeitschrift für Rechtspolitik 2009, 174; Terhechte (note 3).

[31] Case C-301/06 *Ireland v Parliament and Council* (note 5), para. 24.

[32] Case C-367/95 P *Commission v Sytraval and Brink's France* [1998] ECR I-1719, para. 67.

[33] Case C-301/06 *Ireland v Parliament and Council* (note 5), para. 34.

[34] Cf. Pechstein, EU-Prozessrecht, 4th ed., Tübingen 2011, MN. 212.

[35] Case C-155/91 *Commission v Council* [1993] I-939, paras. 23 *et seq.*

[36] Everting, Überlegungen zum Verfahren vor den Gerichten der Europäischen Gemeinschaft, in: Colneric et. al, Une communauté de droit, Berlin 2003, 537.

[37] Giegerich, Spät kommt Ihr, doch Ihr kommt: Warum wird die Grundrechtskonformität der Vorratsdatenspeicherung erst nach acht Jahren geklärt?, Zeitschrift für Europarechtliche Studien 2014, 3, 9 *et seq.*

Ireland's annulment action was motivated by the aspect concerning EU competence and the circumvention of a unanimous vote in the third pillar can be considered an explanation for the absence of any claim concerning the compatibility of the DRD with fundamental rights.[38] After this judgment, as noted above, there were several instances where national courts were concerned with the compatibility of the DRD with fundamental rights. Yet, until the reference by the Austrian Constitutional Court and the Irish High Court none of the courts submitted a reference to the CJEU. This is a further point for improvement: in a multi-level system for the protection of fundamental rights, such as the EU, all depends on the cooperation of the various actors.[39]

5 Consequences of the Judgment

As an immediate consequence of the judgment, the infringement proceedings instigated by the Commission against Germany under Article 258 TFEU for failure to implement the Data Retention Directive were dropped, as this obligation no longer exists.[40] Additionally, the Commission will reimburse Sweden, which had already been ordered to pay the costs for the infringement proceedings instigated against it.[41]

More importantly however, should the EU legislator opt for a new approach to data retention, it will not be able to employ Article 114 TFEU as a legal basis. As the Court has required it to lay down the details of storage and access to the data, a definition for serious crime as well as procedural safeguards, this is evidently not a measure to harmonize national legislation for the benefit of the internal market. Rather, the measure will have to be based on the police cooperation rules, which with the entry into force of the Lisbon Treaty have been integrated into the former first pillar. Most likely, data retention could be based on Article 87 TFEU, which allows joint measures for police cooperation.[42]

Aside from this question of competence, it needs to be assessed, whether Member States, which do not have rules on data retention such as Germany, are now free to pass national legislation. Further, as the CJEU's jurisdiction only covers EU law the national rules implementing the DRD remain in force in many Member States. For these Member States, it is important to know whether they can uphold their national laws. With the DRD declared invalid, the national transposition measures can no longer transpose European law. As the competence of the EU in the Area of Freedom, Justice and Security is a shared competence according to Article 4 para. 2 lit. j TFEU and there no longer is EU legislation with regard to data retention, the Member States are in principle free to exercise their own competences and legislate on the matter. However, as the Court pointed out, the DRD was a derogation from the general EU data

---

[38] Terhechte (note 3), 201.

[39] Cf. Giegerich (note 37), 14–17.

[40] Case C-329/12 *Commission v Germany*, case closed.

[41] Case C-185/09 *Commission v Sweden*, [2010] ECR-14.

[42] Cf. in greater detail Wendel, Wider die Mär von Grundrechtsblinden: Der EuGH und die Vorratsdatenspeicherung, Verfassungsblog, available at: http://www.verfassungsblog.de/wider-maer-vom-grundrechtsblinden-eugh-und-vorratsdatenspeicherung/.

protection regime, i.e. the DPD and the e-Privacy Directive (in the following: ePD)[43], which according to its Article 1 para. 2 complements the DPD for the electronic communications sector.[44] The Court further held that data retention concerns the detection and prosecution of serious crime. For measures concerning cooperation in the area of police and judicial cooperation in criminal matters, there is an exemption clause in Article 1 para. 3 ePD. An almost identically phrased clause is contained in Article 3 para. 2 DPD. In a previous judgment, the CJEU interpreted the latter provision to apply to the transfer of data collected by private operators to a third country.[45] The transfer fell within a framework established by public authorities that related to public security. Applied to the case of data retention this implies that the access of public authorities serves the aim of fighting serious crime and improving public safety. Thus, the exemption clauses apply. However, the 'mere' collection, which served the harmonization of the internal market, is not covered by Article 1 para. 3 ePD and Article 3 para. 2 DPD. While this differentiation might seem artificial, it is the only interpretation consistent with Article 15 para. 1 cl. 2 ePD, which exceptionally allows Member States to impose an obligation on service providers to retain communication data for a limited period. If the storage of data by service providers was covered by the exemption clauses, there would be no scope of application for Article 15 para. 1 cl. 2 eDP.[46] Furthermore, the Court already stated in its judgment on the action brought by Ireland that national measures on data retention before the DRD fell under Article 15 para. 1 ePD.[47] Therefore, the storage of communication data falls under the scope of the ePD and the Member States may derogate from the confidentiality of communications guaranteed by Article 5 ePD and the obligation to have traffic data deleted or anonymized by the service providers once they are no longer required under Article 6 ePD. However, the derogation clause of Article 15 para. 1 ePD allows such exceptions only where these restrictions serve public security, the prevention, investigation, detection and prosecution of criminal offences. While this is certainly the case for any national legislation on data retention, the provision further calls for the restriction to be limited to necessary, appropriate and proportionate measures needed in a democratic society. Further, the third clause of Article 15 para. 1 ePD calls for the measures to be in concordance with the general principles of EU law, including those of Article 6 para. 1 TEU. This refers to the fundamental rights of EU law, which are enshrined in the Charter, which has gained binding legal force with the coming into force of the Lisbon Treaty according to Article 6 para. 1 cl. 2 TEU.

---

[43] Directive 2002/58/EC of the European Parliament and of the Council of 12 July 2002 concerning the processing of personal data and the protection of privacy in the electronic communications sector (Directive on privacy and electronic communications), OJ 2002 L 201/37.

[44] Joined Cases C-293/12 and 594/12 *Digital Rights Ireland and Seitlinger* (note 1), para. 32.

[45] Joined Cases C-317/04 and 318/04 *Parliament v Council and Commission* [2006] ECR I-4721, paras. 56-59.

[46] Cf. Wagner, Die Vorratsdatenspeicherung in der Grundrechtsunion, Ju-Wiss Blog, available at: https://www.juwiss.de/54-2014/; Lehofer, Nochmals zum VDS-Urteil: auch "autonome" nationale VDS (auf Basis des Art 15 Abs 1 RL 2002/58) muss den Anforderungen des Urteils genügen, available at: http://blog.lehofer.at/2014/04/noch-zwei-kurze-anmerkungen-zum.html; dissenting Wendel (note 42).

[47] Case C-301/06 *Ireland v Parliament and Council* (note 5), para. 67.

With the present judgment of the Court, it has been ruled that the DRD did not conform to the fundamental rights of EU law. From this judgment, it follows immediately, that national measures, which – as it has been demonstrated still fall under the ePD and therefore come within the scope of EU law – have been adopted in order to implement the DRD, do not meet the standards of the ePD and therefore violate Union law. Even where the national legislator has restricted access to and use of the data, the retention period will still be set arbitrarily and there will be no restriction as to the personal scope of the retention. If that would be the case, the national measure would have violated the very provisions it was supposed to implement. Therefore, Member States with rules on data retention are under a legal obligation to repeal them.

In case Member States do not repeal the national laws themselves, affected service providers and citizens can challenge these provisions before national courts claiming a violation of EU law in order to have these provisions set aside in accordance with the primacy of EU law.[48] With the judgment at hand, there should not be any issues as to the interpretation of the DPD's and eDP's provisions. However, if a national court had any doubts or wished to derogate from the CJEU's judgment, at least a court of last resort would be under an obligation to submit a reference for a preliminary ruling under Article 267 para. 3 TFEU. When a national court refuses to make a reference or deliberately deviates from the case law of the CJEU it violates EU law. Thus, the Commission may instigate proceedings under Article 258 TFEU against the Member State. Additionally, the refusal to refer to the CJEU may be a violation of national constitutional law. If in Germany, for instance, a court arbitrarily fails to refer a case to the CJEU, it violates the individual's right to the jurisdiction of his or her lawful judge under Article 101 para. 1 cl. 2 of the Basic Law.[49] Such an interpretation of the national law conforms to the Member States' obligation to provide effective remedies in areas concerning Union law under Art. 19 para. 1 cl. 2 TEU.

However, even where Member States repeal their implementing measures, critical review of new data retention legislation is needed. The United Kingdom, in the wake of the CJEU's judgment, has already passed new legislation to continue the retention of users' and subscribers' data with the Data Retention and Investigatory Powers Act 2014 (in the following: DRIP).[50] Under Sect. 1 paras. 1 and 2 DRIP, retention may be ordered by the Secretary of State relating to one or multiple service providers. According to Sect. 1 para. 5 DRIP the maximum period of retention must not exceed twelve months. With regard to details of the retention the Secretary of State is authorized by Sect. 1 paras. 3 and 4 DRIP to further specify these by means of regulations. Despite its recent enactment, this legislation has already been subject to

---

[48] Cf. Genna, Messy Consequences for National Legislation following Annulment of EU Data Retention Directive, LSE Media Policy Project, available at: http://blogs.lse.ac.uk/mediapolicyproject/2014/04/08/messy-consequences-for-national-legislations-following-annulment-of-eu-data-retention-directive/.

[49] Federal Constitutional Court of Germany, Reports of Decisions (BVerfGE) 75, 223.

[50] Data Retention and Investigatory Powers Act 2014 of 17th July 2014, available at: http://www.legislation.gov.uk/ukpga/2014/27/pdfs/ukpga_20140027_en.pdf, the Act also broadens investigatory powers of UK agencies and contains a clause on extra-territoriality, which are, however, outside the scope of this article.

severe criticism by Members of the UK Parliament, who announced that they would challenge the act before national courts[51] as well as several legal scholars, who argued in an open letter to the Home Office that the law was incompatible with the CJEU's criteria for data retention.[52] Indeed, while it does not require default storage of all communications data, the DRIP allows storage of the entire data of one or more service providers, which still entails a very wide range of persons affected without any suspicion or link to criminal activities. Nevertheless, the scope of the retention depends on the subsequent regulations, which shape the requirements for the retention notice and its contents under Sect. 1 paras. 3 and 4 DRIP. Until these rules are set up, a final assessment of the measure's compatibility is hardly possible, although the wide scope of the DRIP does not seem to be reconcilable with the CJEU's requirements.

Concerning Member States which still wish to implement data retention it is hard to see how this could be accomplished. Although it is unclear to what extent the requirements of the Court are cumulative,[53] i.e. whether all of them have to be fulfilled or whether the CJEU would be willing to allow measures, which comply with a minimum core, it seems hardly possible to reconcile the idea of data retention with the requirements set up by the Court. While it stated that the fight against serious crime is of great importance and for this purpose communication data may be retained under certain conditions, it has been made clear, that the blanket retention of data of all citizens without any occasion or relation to serious crime is not in conformity with EU fundamental rights.[54] Therefore, Member States will have to settle for alternatives such as the 'quick freeze' process, where law enforcement authorities need to obtain a court order, which obliges a service provider to retain specified data of an individual or a group of individuals linked to criminal or terrorist activities. In a second step, the relevant authorities have to provide evidence within a limited time-frame, to obtain another court order, which obliges service providers to transfer the traffic data to them.[55] This concept addresses the Court's main point of criticism: the blanket retention of data of all European citizens. If implemented with the appropriate procedural and technical safeguards, this process has the potential to conform to the CJEU's requirements.

---

[51] Travis, Drip surveillance law faces legal challenge by MPs, The Guardian of 22 July 2014, available at: http://www.theguardian.com/world/2014/jul/22/drip-surveillance-law-legal-challenge-civil-liberties-campaigners.

[52] Basu et al., An open letter from UK internet law academic of 15th July 2014, available at: http://www.law.ed.ac.uk/__data/assets/pdf_file/0003/158070/Open_letter_UK_internet_law_academics.pdf.

[53] For reading the requirements as cumulative cf. Kühling, Der Fall der Vorratsdatenspeicherungs-richtlinie und der Aufstieg des EuGH zum Grundrechtsgericht, Neue Zeitschrift für Verwaltungsrecht 2014, 681, 683; Reading the requirements as 'essential elements': Priebe, Reform der Vorratsdatenspeicherung – strenge Maßstäbe des EuGH, Europäische Zeitschrift für Wirtschaftsrecht 2014, 456, 458.

[54] Roßnagel, Neue Maßstäbe für den Datenschutz in Europa – Folgerungen aus dem EuGH-Urteil zur Vorratsdatenspeicherung, Multimedia und Recht 2014, 372, 375.

[55] Cf. The Federal Commissioner for Data Protection and Freedom of Information, Peter Schaar: "Quick Freeze" instead of data retention, Press Release of 15 June 2010, available at: http://www.bfdi.bund.de/EN/PublicRelations/PressReleases/2010/22_%22QuickFreeze%22.html?nn=410156.

6   Conclusions

It follows from the foregoing considerations that the present judgment of the Court has effectively ended the blanket retention of traffic data in the European Union. Although it may take additional time and litigation before national courts to implement this judgment, a system like that envisaged by the DRD has been clearly identified as the grave violation of fundamental rights that it is.

This case is also a step forward in the exploration of the innovative and, from the perspective of EU jurisprudence, yet uncharted right to the protection of personal data as laid down by Article 8 CFR. However, the Court's reasoning in this regard needs further development. So far, the relationship of Article 8 CFR with the right to privacy according to Article 7 of the Charter remains opaque.

Additionally, the relationship of the fundamental right to data protection with the general data protection regime of the Union remains to be explored with regard to the individual rights such as the right to access to data granted by Article 12 DPD. Yet, as this very data protection regime of the EU is currently in a process of reform, the future cannot be ascertained with certainty. While attention has largely focused on the envisaged General Data Protection Regulation[56], which is currently under discussion in the Council,[57] there is also a proposal for a directive concerning data protection with regard to criminal investigations,[58] which has been partially agreed on after a first reading by the European Parliament and is now under deliberation in the Council.[59]

While the last Commissioner for Home Affairs, Cecilia Malmström, announced that she had no plans to introduce any new legislation concerning data retention,[60] her successor in office, Dimitris Avramopoulos, after the tragic attacks of Paris in January 2015 stated that the Commission is monitoring the situation in the Member States and assesses the need for data retention.[61] Similarly, German chancellor Angela Merkel

---

[56] European Commission, Proposal for a regulation of the European Parliament and of the Council on the protection of individuals with regard to the processing of personal data and on the free movement of such data (General Data Protection Regulation) of 25 January 2012, COM(2012) 11 final.

[57] On the state of the legislative process cf. http://ec.europa.eu/prelex/detail_dossier_real.cfm?CL=en&DosId=201286.

[58] European Commission, Proposal for a directive of the European Parliament and of the Council on the protection of individuals with regard to the processing of personal data by competent authorities for the purposes of prevention, investigation, detection or prosecution of criminal offences or the execution of criminal penalties and free movement of such data of 25 January 2012, COM(2012) 10 final.

[59] Cf. http://ec.europa.eu/prelex/detail_dossier_real.cfm?CL=en&DosId=201285.

[60] Eder/Schiltz, EU will keine neuen Regeln für Vorratsdaten, Die Welt of 4 June 2014, available at: http://www.welt.de/politik/ausland/article128698101/EU-will-keine-neuen-Regeln-fuer-Vorratsdaten.html.

[61] European Commission, Speech by Commissioner Avramopoulos on Counter-Terrorism, SPEECH/15/3860 of 28 January 2015, available at: http://europa.eu/rapid/press-release_SPEECH-15-3860_en.htm.

endorsed traffic data retention in conformity with the CJEU's requirements.[62] Thus, the possibility of a recurrence of some form of data retention on the EU level cannot be excluded with certainty. However, the Member States, at least for the time being, are under a legal obligation to implement the Court's ruling immediately.

The enforcement of the present judgment against Member States who are unwilling to abolish or revise their national laws will presumably require more litigation and is thus unlikely to be achieved in the near future. Moreover, as the example of the United Kingdom illustrates, even where a Member State adopts new legislation, the changes may not reflect the spirit of the judgment and also require further scrutiny by the judiciary. Despite these limitations with regard to the short term implementation of the judgment, the ruling at hand, in the long term, further advances the Court's role as a supreme court of the European Union which ensures the protection of individuals' fundamental rights.

---

[62] Statement by Chancellor Merkel of 15 January 2015, available at: http://www.bundeskanzlerin.de/Content/DE/Regierungserklaerung/2015/2015-01-15-regierungserklaerung.html.

EUROSUR – A Sci-fi Border Zone Patrolled by Drones?

Daniel Deibler[✉]

Unabhängiges Landeszentrum Für Datenschutz, Kiel, Germany
daniel@funkpark.de

Abstract. In the context of the smart border initiative, the European Union also established a mass surveillance and data exchange programme, called European External Border Surveillance System (EUROSUR). This paper will look at the compliance of the respective European regulation and the implementation of the system with Article 8 ECHR (European Convention on Human Rights, hereinafter: ECHR.) as well as Articles 7 & 8 EUFRCh (Charter of Fundamental Rights of the European Union (2000/C 364/01), hereinafter: EUFRCh.). This paper will argue that due to the concrete circumstances of the data processing and the large scale of the surveillance, the EUROSUR system constitutes a serious interference with the right to data protection and privacy. While the necessity of such an additional and intrusive border management tool is already highly questionable, in the end, the interference is not justified. In particular, the vagueness in most parts of the regulation and the lack of specific privacy protecting safeguards preclude the fulfilment of the 'quality of law' requirements. Furthermore, it will be shown that a more privacy preserving version is conceivable. As a result, EUROSUR is neither in accordance with law, nor necessary, nor proportionate, and therefore violates Article 8 ECHR as well as Articles 7 & 8 EUFRCh.

Keywords: Privacy · Data protection · EUROSUR · Surveillance · Border control · European convention on human rights · Charter of fundamental rights of the European Union · European Union · Frontex

> *The EU is going down a very dangerous route of tracking, storing and accessing data on individuals' movements without an adequate grip on the consequences for privacy, notably through 'profiling', misuse and carelessness.* (Goldirova, R.: *EU unveils plans for biometric border controls*; EUobserver, 13th February 2008; http://euobserver.com/justice/25650.).

> Baroness Sarah Ludford
> Member of the European Parliament

Lucht, H.: *The Watery Tomb Europe Tolerates*, The New York Times, 7th October 2013; http://www.nytimes.com/2013/10/08/opinion/the-graveyard-at-europes-doorstep.html.

© IFIP International Federation for Information Processing 2015
J. Camenisch et al. (Eds.): Privacy and Identity 2014, IFIP AICT 457, pp. 87–109, 2015.
DOI: 10.1007/978-3-319-18621-4_7

1 Introduction

In the above quote baroness Ludford was criticising the 'smart border' initiative of the European Commission which was announced in February 2008. This initiative consisted of two proposed instruments to manage the external borders of the European Union (Entry/Exit System, Registered Traveller Programme) and was complemented by a proposal for the creation of a European External Border Surveillance System (EUROSUR). The subsequent criticism from data protection authorities and privacy promoting organisations concentrated mostly on the smart border initiative while the EUROSUR proposal was implemented without any mayor outcry or public discussion. The little expressed criticism for the – in the meantime established – surveillance system came mostly from NGOs in the field of migrant and refugee protection. Organisations such as Pro Asyl[1] or the Jesuit Refugee Service[2] have scrutinised the compliance of EUROSUR with the obligations deriving from the 1951 Geneva Convention relating to the status of refugees as well as other migrant protecting agreements. Consequently this paper sets out to close the existing void and will therefore examine the possible interferences of EUROSUR with the right to privacy and data protection. On the basis of the EUROSUR Regulation[3] the first part of the paper (Sect. 2) will outline the structure and functioning of EUROSUR and describe which information from which sources are imported into the so called 'system of systems'. In addition, the compliance with the rights to privacy and data protection will be examined (Sect. 3). It will be argued that due to the concrete circumstances of the data processing and the large scale of the surveillance, EUROSUR constitutes a serious interference with the right to data protection and privacy (Sects. 3.1.2 and 3.1.3). In the end this interference is ultimately not justified (Sect. 3.2). In particular, the vagueness in most parts of the regulation and the lack of specific privacy protecting safeguards preclude the fulfilment of the 'quality of law' requirements (Sect. 3.2.1). Furthermore, the necessity of such an additional and intrusive border management tool is highly questionable and raises concerns in regards to its usefulness (Sect. 3.2.3). Last but not least it will be shown that the interference by the current system and the legislation is greater than necessary, since a more privacy preserving version is conceivable (Sect. 4). As a result, EUROSUR is neither in accordance with law, nor necessary, nor proportionate and therefore violates Article 8 ECHR[4] as well as Articles 7 & 8 EUFRCh.[5]

---

[1] Pro Asyl: *EU-Asylpolitik nach Lampedus: Abschottung geht weiter*, 09.10.2013, http://www.proasyl.de/de/news/detail/news/eu_asylpolitik_nach_lampedusa_abschottung_geht_weiter-1/.

[2] Jesuit Refugee Service Europe: *Proposals for amendments to EUROSUR Regulation.*

[3] Regulation (EU) No 1052/2013 of the European Parliament and of the Council of 22 October 2013 establishing the European Border Surveillance System (Eurosur), hereinafter: EUROSUR Regulation.

[4] European Convention on Human Rights, hereinafter: ECHR.

[5] Charter of Fundamental Rights of the European Union (2000/C 364/01), hereinafter: EUFRCh.

2 EUROSUR – A System of Systems

By establishing a European Border Surveillance System the European Union is attempting to move away from the traditional patrolling of borders to a more risk-based approach to border control. This approach is described in the EUROSUR Regulation as improving the situational awareness and increasing the reaction capability at the external borders.[6] This fairly vague description of EUROSUR and the extent of the surveillance becomes clearer by looking at the definition of 'situational awareness' included in the regulation:

> 'situational awareness' means the ability to monitor, detect, identify, track and understand illegal cross-border activities in order to find reasoned grounds for reaction measures on the basis of combining new information with existing knowledge, (...)[7]

To achieve this improved situational awareness the regulation establishes a common framework for the exchange of information and for the cooperation between the national authorities responsible for border surveillance as well as Frontex.[8] EUROSUR has been described as a 'system of systems' because it does not establish one centralised database but connects the different so-called National Coordination Centres (NCC) of the participating Member States with each other and Frontex via a communication network which allows:

- information exchange in near-real-time;
- audio and video conferencing;
- handling, storing, transmission and processing of information.

Furthermore, to streamline the information exchange via the National Situational Pictures, the regulation obliges the NCCs to collect the relevant information from a vast array of sources (including national border surveillance systems, liaison officers, border authorities from third countries and ship reporting systems)[9] and to establish and

---

[6] Article 1 EUROSUR Regulation.

[7] Article 3 (b) EUROSUR Regulation.

[8] European Agency for the Management of Operational Cooperation at the External Borders of the Member States of the European Union; established by Regulation (EC) No 2007/2004; hereinafter: Frontex.
The name of EU's external border agency derives from the French term *frontiers extérieures* (external borders). Its main responsibilities are the following:

- Planning, coordination and implementation of joint border control operations;
- Training of national border guards;
- Risk analysis, research and intelligence gathering;
- Provision of rapid response capabilities;
- Assisting in deportations;
- Information exchange.

For more information see: http://frontex.europa.eu/.

[9] The list of sources entailed in Article 9(2) EUROSUR Regulation includes ten different sources for relevant information; nevertheless by further including 'others' the list is not exclusive and gives the Member States an extensive margin of appreciation to collect information from every source possible.

maintain their picture. The Situational Pictures from the different NCCs will be shared which each other and Frontex. Frontex itself, however, will moreover supplement the national information with information from European Union bodies, offices and agencies as well as other undefined sources to create a European Situational Picture, which will subsequently be shared over the network too. Similar sources will be used by Frontex to maintain an additional Common Pre-frontier Intelligence Picture, increasing the knowledge about activities beyond the external borders of the Schengen Area.

The above mentioned range of different sources of information hinders every examination of the information which will be processed in the NCCs. Nevertheless, since the collection of data on a national level as well as the exchange of information between national authorities is regulated by the national law of the Member States, it falls outside the scope of the EUROSUR Regulation and consequently of this paper. However, the data processed in the NCCs is the foundation of the information exchanged in the EUROSUR system and therefore relevant for the Situational Pictures. The regulation itself provides only limited instructions on which information should be included in the Situational Pictures. According to Article 8 EUROSUR Regulation it consists of an event, an operational and an analysis layer. The event layer shall contain information about incidents regarding unauthorised border crossings, cross border crime and crisis situations. Furthermore the event layer will provide.

> information on unidentified and suspect vehicles, vessels and other craft and persons present at, along or in the proximity of, the external borders of the Member State concerned, as well as any other event which may have a significant impact on the control of the external borders.[10]

The operational layer will provide information on the position, status and type of border control assets. Last but not least, the analysis layer consists of analysis and risk assessments for the relevant border sections. However, it also includes reference imagery and analysed information relevant for the purpose of the regulation. Beyond these general descriptions of the exchanged data no concrete information is publicly available. The relevant documents explaining the specifications of the information exchange are not yet available,[11] are EU-restricted and government-use-only, or have been presented and discussed in confidential project advisory boards and the EUROSUR Member States' expert group.[12] Nevertheless, presentations by Frontex and the European Commission, such as the infographic EUROSUR,[13] allow us to catch a glimpse of the event layer of the European Situational Picture. The included exemplary incident reports of the European Picture show that each event is filed under the location, time, date and type of the incident and illustrated on a map of Europe. Furthermore, each event is described in a free text field (e.g. persons involved, arrests or

---

[10] Article 9 (3)(d) EUROSUR Regulation.

[11] E.g. EUROSUR Handbook.

[12] An overview can be found in the European Commission Staff Working Paper SEC(2011) 1538 final, Annex 1.

[13] European Union: *Infographic European Border Surveillance System (EUROSUR)*, http://ec.europa.eu/dgs/home-affairs/e-library/multimedia/infographics/index_en.htm#080126248ad359ff/c_.

seizures, additional comments) and the user interface allows attaching images, videos, or other documents as well as to create linkages, or add historical backgrounds. It seems that the National and the Pre-Frontier Situational Picture will also include the above mentioned information since, according to the regulation, they are all structured the same way.

This information exchange will be further complemented by the common application of surveillance tools. According to the regulation ship reporting systems, satellite imagery and any sensors mounted on a vehicle, vessel or craft shall be used to monitor third country ports and coasts, pre-frontier areas and areas in the maritime domain, as well as to track vessels or other crafts in the high seas. Frontex is free to use these surveillance tools on its own initiative and the collected information can also be requested by the NCC of a Member State. For this purpose Frontex shall combine the information from the different sources and analyse the data to create so-called surveillance information on the external borders and on the pre-frontier area.[14]

3   EUROSUR and the Right to Privacy and Data Protection

EUROSUR is in its core a mass-surveillance tool combined with a large-scale exchange of data. Consequently, the activities under the EUROSUR regulation raise questions in regards to its compliance with the fundamental rights of respect for private life and protection of personal data (Articles 7, 8 EUFRCh and Article 8 ECHR). While the EUFRCh differentiates between the right to privacy – as part of the right to respect for private life – and the right to data protection, both fundamental rights are embraced in the broad term of 'private life' in the ECHR.[15] However, since both rights inter-relate strongly the ECJ[16] favours a joint reading of Articles 7 and 8 EUFRCh and relies heavily on the jurisprudence of the ECtHR[17,18]. Therefore, based on the jurisdiction of the ECJ and the ECtHR, this section will examine if EUROSUR interferes with these fundamental rights.

3.1   Interference with the Right to Privacy

Regarding the legality of surveillance the ECtHR stated in the *Peck case*[19] that

---

[14] Article 12 EUROSUR Regulation.

[15] ECtHR, App. 6825/74, *X v Iceland*, Decision of 18 May 1976, (1976) 5 DR 86; ECtHR, App. 23841/95, *Rotaru v Romania*, 4 May 2000 [GC], ECHR 2000-V, § 46; ECtHR, App. 27798/95, *Amann v Switzerland*, 16 February 2000 [GC], ECHR 2000-II, § 65.

[16] European Court of Justice, hereinafter: ECJ.

[17] European Court of Human Rights, hereinafter: ECtHR.

[18] Article 29 Data Protection Working Party: *Opinion 01/2014 on the application of necessity and proportionality concepts and data protection within the law enforcement sector*, adopted on 27 February 2014, p. 4.

[19] ECtHR, App. 44647/98, *Peck v United Kingdom*, 28 January 2003, ECHR 2003-I.

the monitoring of the actions of an individual in a public place by the use of photographic equipment which does not record the visual data does not, as such, give rise to an interference with the individual's private life.[20]

Nonetheless, while the mere act of monitoring will not interfere with one's right, the recording of such data can constitute an interference.[21] Furthermore, the Court decided in the *Amann case*[22] as well as in the *Rotaru case*[23] that the compilation of data by security services on particular individuals can affect the private lives of the victims,[24] even if only public information is systematically collected and stored in files.[25] Consequently, the interference is independent from the way of surveilling[26] – covert or overt – but dependent from the storing and further processing of the data. Besides the fact that data has to be collected, an interference further presupposes that personal data is processed. Therefore, the right to private life in form of the right to privacy and the right to protection of personal data do not just inter-relate in this context but overlap mostly.

3.1.1 Personal Data

In European law personal data is commonly understood as *'any information relating to an identified or identifiable natural person.'*[27]

The element of 'any information' shows the broad concept of personal data and evidently includes images or other data from CCTV, surveillance sensors or other surveillance tools.[28] However, more problematic is, in the context of surveillance information, the question of whether a person is recognisable or identifiable.[29] This problem will be ascertained in detail below.

The second element requires that the information is relating to someone. However, the concept of 'relating to' is broader than the common understanding of the notion and therefore, data is not only relating to a person if the content of the data is explicitly about this person. According to the Article 29 Working Party, a relationship between data and a specific person can also result from the purpose or the result of the data

---

[20] Ibid. § 59.

[21] Ibid. § 59.

[22] ECtHR, App. 23841/95, *Rotaru v Romania*, 4 May 2000 [GC], ECHR 2000-V.

[23] ECtHR, App. 27798/95, *Amann v Switzerland*, 16 February 2000 [GC], ECHR 2000-II.

[24] ECtHR, App. 23841/95, *Rotaru v Romania*, 4 May 2000 [GC], ECHR 2000-V, § 43–44; ECtHR, App. 27798/95, *Amann v Switzerland*, 16 February 2000 [GC], ECHR 2000-II, § 65–67.

[25] ECtHR, App. 23841/95, *Rotaru v Romania*, 4 May 2000 [GC], ECHR 2000-V, § 43.

[26] ECtHR, App. 9248/81, *Leander v Sweden*, 26 March 1987, Series A No 116.

[27] Article 2 (a) Directive 95/46/EC of the Directive 95/46/EC of the European Parliament and of the Council of 24 October 1995 on the protection of individuals with regard to the processing of personal data and on the free movement of such data; Article 2(a) Convention for the Protection of Individuals with regard to Automatic Processing of Personal Data; Article 2(a) Regulation (EC) No 45/2001 of the European Parliament and of the Council on the protection of individuals with regard to the processing of personal data by the Community institutions and bodies and on the free movement of such data.

[28] Article 29 Data Protection Working Party: *Working Document on the Processing of Personal Data by means of Video Surveillance*, adopted on 25 November 2002, p. 5.

[29] Article 29 Data Protection Working Party, *Opinion 4/2007 on the concept of personal data*, adopted on 20 June 2007, p. 8.

processing. When data is used *"with the purpose to evaluate, treat in a certain way or influence the status or behaviour of an individual"*[30] the processed information relates to a specific person. Similarly, data is relating to a person if the use of the information is likely to have an impact on a certain person's rights and interests, however small the impact is.[31] *"It is sufficient if the individual may be treated differently from other persons as a result of the processing of such data."*[32]

According to the next element of the definition data has to be relating to an identified or identifiable person. While the term 'identified' is self-evident, particular explanations are necessary for the notion of 'identifiability'. In general a person is identifiable if he or she is *"described in the information in a way which makes it possible to find out who the data subject is by conducting further research."*[33] Consequently, it is not necessary to identify a person by finding out his or her name, but it suffices to combine different criteria of personal attributes so that the group, the person belongs to, can be narrowed down and the person can be distinguished from other individuals.[34] Furthermore it is not necessary that the data processor has all the relevant information and significant criteria to identify the individual, since the decision regarding the question if data is personal data is made objectively. Even if only friends or family members can recognise a person on a video due to e.g. his or her figure, haircut and cloth, the data in form of a surveillance tape has to be categorised as personal data.[35] Moreover, the period of data storage becomes relevant in this context. Even if identification is not possible today, data will be personal data if identification becomes possible during the 'lifetime' of the data, due to new information or new technical possibilities. Last but not least, the purpose of the processing also affects the concept of 'identifiability'. In cases where the purpose of the data processing is the identification of specific individuals, the purpose implies that the processor will be able to identify persons and therefore the processed data has to be categorised as personal data again. The Article 29 Working Party explains this concept by the example of video surveillance:

> As the purpose of video surveillance is, however, to identify the persons to be seen in the video images in all cases where such identification is deemed necessary by the controller, the whole application as such has to be considered as processing data about identifiable persons, even if some persons recorded are not identifiable in practice.[36]

Consequently, identification is highly dependent on the particular situation and circumstances of the processing, the additional information that is or will be available, and the purpose of the processing. In particular the issue of contextualisation has to be

---

[30] Article 29 Data Protection Working Party, *Opinion 4/2007 on the concept of personal data*, adopted on 20 June 2007, p. 10.

[31] Ibid. p. 11.

[32] Ibid. p. 11.

[33] European Union Agency for Fundamental Rights: *Handbook on European Data Protection Law*, Luxembourg, Publications Office of the European Union, 2014, p. 39.

[34] Article 29 Data Protection Working Party: *Opinion 4/2007 on the concept of personal data*, adopted on 20 June 2007, p. 13.

[35] Ibid. p. 13, 21.

[36] Ibid. p. 16.

considered regarding depersonalised or statistical data since even if only aggregated data is processed, it might enable the identification of persons if the original sample is too small or additional information is available.

Lastly, the information has to relate to a natural person. Even though the term is self-explanatory, it has to be mentioned that information which seems to relate to objects might also contain personal data. Data about objects such as boats or cars can also contain personal data about the captain or owner of the vessel in question.[37]

3.1.2 EUROSUR and Personal Data

In a next step these general considerations about the concept of personal data have to be applied to the EUROSUR surveillance and data exchange.

Concerning the common application of surveillance tools the European Commission regards the use of modern surveillance technology as a key element of EUROSUR and stated that in particular the fusion of data received from ship reporting systems and satellite imagery plays an essential role.[38] As previously discussed, the data from vessel monitoring systems may already on its own contain personal data relating to the captain or owner of a vessel.[39] Nevertheless, this personal data is furthermore complemented by satellite imagery or data from any sensor mounted on any vehicle, vessel or other craft.[40] While those sensors might not be designed to identify or track natural persons, the images the system takes when monitoring vessels, beaches or ports will also depict individuals.[41] Depending on weather conditions, light, distance, range, and resolution of photographs the data from the surveillance tools can allow identification of individuals and therefore may constitute personal data. Furthermore, the necessary soft- and hardware already exist to post edit imagery and increase its resolution.[42] While this possibility is less likely when using satellites for monitoring, since they only allow detection of objects larger than 50 cm,[43] the EUROSUR Regulation also permits the use of Remotely Piloted Aircraft Systems (RPASs). Currently the use of Unmanned Aerial Vehicles (UAVs) is prohibited in European civil airspace, however, using Optional Piloted Aircrafts (OPAs) is allowed when someone is on board as an

---

[37] Article 29 Data Protection Working Party: *Letter to the Commissioner for Home Affairs Ms. Cecilia Malmström regarding the Proposal for a Regulation establishing the European Border Surveillance System*, p. 2.

[38] European Commission: *Communication from the Commission to the European Parliament and the Council on the work of the Task Force Mediterranean*, COM (2013) 869 final, Brussels, 4.12.2013, p. 17.

[39] Article 29 Data Protection Working Party, *Letter to the Commissioner for Home Affairs Ms. Cecilia Malmström regarding the Proposal for a Regulation establishing the European Border Surveillance System*, p. 2.

[40] Article 12(3) EUROSUR Regulation.

[41] European Union Agency for Fundamental Rights: *Fundamental rights at Europe's southern sea borders*, Luxembourg, Publications Office of the European Union, 2013, p. 60.

[42] Zöller, M. A., Ihwas, S. R.: *Rechtliche Rahmenbedingungen des polizeilichen Flugdrohneneinsatzes*, Neue Zeitschrift für Verwaltungsrecht, 2014, p. 408–414, 410.

[43] Ludwig, A.: *Frontex und Eurosur – Umweltsatelliten der Esa helfen bei Jagd auf Flüchtlinge*, Zeit Online, 20th December 2013; http://www.zeit.de/digital/datenschutz/2013-12/frontex-eurosur-satelliten-fluechtlinge.

additional safety feature, even if the real pilot is operating the craft from a ground station and Frontex is already interested in acquiring an OPA for the surveillance of external borders.[44] As RPASs can be equipped with different sensors (e.g. high-resolution cameras and microphones or thermal imaging equipment)[45] including some that can zoom into 50 cm they would certainly allow the identification of persons from the high resolution images.[46] The EUROSUR regulation permits the use of such sensors and therefore the processing of such personal data. Furthermore, the regulation obliges Frontex not only to gather this surveillance information but also to supply the NCCs with the information. Consequently, the application of common surveillance tools in the EUROSUR Regulation foresees and permits the processing of personal data and thus, interferes with the right to privacy and protection of personal data.

The second element of EUROSUR, relevant regarding the processing of personal data, is the data exchange via the Situational Pictures (National, European and Pre-Frontier). According to the Commission, EUROSUR does not intend to regulate the storage or cross border exchange of personal data[47] and therefore the *"possibility for exchanging personal data in EUROSUR is very limited: At European level, Member States and Frontex are entitled only to exchange ship identification numbers."*[48] Nevertheless, the limitation to the exchange of ship IDs has only found its way into the regulation regarding the European and the Pre-Frontier Situational Picture.[49] Furthermore, the processing of personal data is envisaged in the regulation in specific circumstances, even if they are described as exceptional.[50] Nonetheless, closer scrutiny reveals that the exchange of personal data was broadly enabled by EUROSUR and might even become the norm. A questionnaire regarding the use of personal data in the NCCs showed that nine NCCs were already processing personal data and one NCC was planning to do so in the future. Furthermore, while only two Member States responded that they were not planning on handling personal data for border surveillance purposes, the rest of the states did not reply to the question.[51] In the context of

---

[44] Nielsen, N.: *EU looks to 'hybrid drones' for legal shortcut on migration*, EUobserver, 14th October 2013; http://euobserver.com/priv-immigration/121735.

[45] Article 29 Data Protection Working Party: *Letter to the European Commission regarding Remotely Piloted Aircraft Systems (RPAS) – Response to the Questionnaire*, p. 1.

[46] Hayes, B., Vermeulen, M.: *Borderline – EU Border Surveillance Initiatives – An Assessment of the Costs and Its Impact on Fundamental Rights*, Berlin, Heinrich Böll Stiftung, 2012, p. 38.

[47] European Commission: *Proposal for a Regulation of the European Parliament and of the Council Establishing the European Border Surveillance System (EUROSUR)*, COM (2011) 873 final, Brussels, 12.12.2011, p. 3.

[48] European Commission: *EUROSUR: new tools to save migrants' lives at sea and fight cross-border crime*, Memo/13/578, Brussels, 19th June 2013.

[49] Art. 13 EUROSUR Regulation.

[50] European Union Agency for Fundamental Rights: *Fundamental rights at Europe's southern sea borders*, Luxembourg, Publications Office of the European Union, 2013, p. 62; Recital 13 EUROSUR Regulation.

[51] European Commission: *Commission Staff Working Paper - Impact Assessment accompanying the Proposal for a Regulation of the European Parliament and of the Council establishing the European Border Surveillance System (EUROSUR)*, SEC(2011) 1538 final, Brussels, 12.12.2011, pp. 31, 32.

data exchange and provision of supposedly anonymised data, another statement of the Article 29 Working Party has to be observed:

Thus, it is critical to understand that when a data controller does not delete the original (identifiable) data at event-level, and the data controller hands over part of this dataset (for example after removal or masking of identifiable data), the resulting dataset is still personal data. Only if the data controller would aggregate the data to a level where the individual events are no longer identifiable, the resulting dataset can be qualified as anonymous. For example: if an organisation collects data on individual travel movements, the individual travel patterns at event level would still qualify as personal data for any party, as long as the data controller (or any other party) still has access to the original raw data, even if direct identifiers have been removed from the set provided to third parties.[52]

Additionally, it has to be noted that the perception of personal data differs between European Member States and that for example the relevant authorities of Spain or Romania do not categorise surveillance images as personal data.[53] Furthermore, the EUROSUR Regulation does neither entail any restrictions on the data exchanged between the NCCs nor does the user interface limit the possibilities of the NCCs.

Events uploaded in the system are essentially text boxes where information on persons could be shared. There are no alert pop-ups or other safeguards to ensure that personal data are not inadvertently included or that text boxes are anonymised. Furthermore, EU Member States are also encouraged to report "information on unidentified and suspect platforms and persons present at or nearby the external borders". The system also allows for video and picture attachments to an event.[54]

While these considerations concern only the National Situational Picture, it also affects the European and Pre-Frontier ones, since the latter two are based on the information provided from the different NCCs.

Secondly, data might have to be categorised as personal data because different NCCs have additional information and can, by linking different information and data, identify an individual. In this context the storage period also has to be considered. In most cases the shared information should lead to an interception of vessels or another legal or administrative measure. Consequently, at least the acting state will gather further information about the individuals and therefore be able to identify the persons and relate the previous information (such as the port of departure) to them.

Finally, the purpose and the result of EUROSUR, make it necessary to categorise parts of the exchanged data as personal data. If the purpose of the data processing is the identification of the surveilled individuals or the use of the information will impact the rights and interests of these individuals,[55] the whole application as such has to be

---

[52] Article 29 Data Protection Working Party: *Opinion 05/2014 on Anonymisation Techniques*, adopted on 10 April 2014, p. 9.

[53] European Union Agency for Fundamental Rights: *Fundamental rights at Europe's southern sea borders*, Luxembourg, Publications Office of the European Union, 2013, p. 60.

[54] Ibid. p. 62.

[55] Article 29 Data Protection Working Party: *Opinion 4/2007 on the concept of personal data*, adopted on 20 June 2007, p. 11.

considered as processing data relating to identifiable persons, even if some persons are not identifiable in practice.[56] When examining the creation of EUROSUR the European Commission stated as one of the objectives for the new system the reduction of irregular – 'illegal' according to the Commission – migration. Further explanatory remarks show that the purpose of EUROSUR is to provide the authorities responsible for border control in the Member States with more timely and reliable information, so they are able to detect, identify and intercept those attempting to enter the EU.[57] Therefore, the identification of irregular migrants is one of the objectives of EUROSUR and thus, one of the purposes of the data exchange. Moreover, the data exchange will impact the interests of specific persons, since EUROSUR shall improve

> the ability to monitor, detect, identify, track and understand cross-border activities in order to find reasoned grounds for reaction measures on the basis of combining new information with existing knowledge.[58]

Reaction measures will include interceptions, controls, arrests, etc. and consequently affect person's rights and interests.

In conclusion, while there is no hard evidence available that personal data is exchanged in the EUROSUR Network, since the relevant documents are not publicly available, the examples from the user interface, the data processed in the NCCs as well as the objectives of EUROSUR support the presumption that personal data is exchanged between the NCCs themselves as well as Frontex and the NCCs. Consequently, it will be assumed that the data exchange element of EUROSUR also interferes with the right to privacy and protection of personal data.

3.1.3 Seriousness of the Interference

Since both core elements of EUROSUR interfere with the right to privacy and data protection, it has to be established how serious the interference is. While there are several problematic points concerning EUROSUR, the most concerning one is the sheer amount of different data and data sources that are compiled in EUROSUR. The regulation only entails a non-exhaustive list of sources and therefore provides Frontex and the responsible national authorities with a margin of appreciation to include all data and data sources which they deem necessary for achieving the objectives of the regulation. Furthermore, Frontex is obliged to intensify their cooperation with international organisations and European Union bodies to make use of existing information and available capabilities and systems. While some of the examples stated in the regulation are obvious, such as EUROPOL or the Maritime Analysis and Operations Centre – Narcotics, others are not, such as the European

---

[56] Ibid. p. 16.

[57] European Commission: *Communication from the Commission to the European Parliament, the Council, the European Economic and Social Committee and the Committee of the Regions – Examining the creation of a European Border Surveillance System (EUROSUR)*, COM(2008) 68 final, Brussels, 13.02.2008, p. 3.

[58] Article 3(b) EUROSUR Regulation.

Fisheries Control Agency. Furthermore, the European Space Agency (ESA) is now cooperating with Frontex and ESA's programme Copernicus,[59] which was founded to provide information regarding the environment and climate change, is now providing Frontex with satellite imagery.[60] Similar cooperation is encouraged on a national level, and Member States shall increase their cooperation and data exchange with third countries and regional networks.[61]

Correlating to the amount of sources is the amount of affected persons. The satellite used in the Copernicus programme is able to capture an area as wide as 290 km[62] and the OPA Frontex is interested in has the capability to surveil an area for 12.5 h without refuelling.[63] Furthermore, it has to be considered that in particular the southern European Coasts and the Mediterranean Sea, were most of the surveillance is taking place, is frequently used for leisure purposes during the summer months by many tourists.[64] Additionally, the regulation does not only oblige Frontex to monitor the sea itself but also third country ports and coasts. Since satellites do not enable a specific and targeted surveillance, but create a general image of an area it can be assumed that the common application of surveillance tools will constitute a general surveillance of the area around the European external borders.[65] Consequently, it will include the collection of excessive information concerning everyone present at or around the external borders.

A similar open approach is taken in the regulation regarding the recipients of information.[66] Besides Frontex and all participating states the information shall be shared with European Union bodies, offices and agencies, and international organisations[67] as well as with regional networks and, under certain circumstances, with neighbouring third countries.[68] On a national level the NCC shall distribute the

[59] http://www.esa.int/Our_Activities/Observing_the_Earth/Copernicus.

[60] Ludwig, A.: *Frontex und Eurosur – Umweltsatelliten der Esa helfen bei Jagd auf Flüchtlinge*, Zeit Online, 20th December 2013; http://www.zeit.de/digital/datenschutz/2013-12/frontex-eurosur-satelliten-fluechtlinge.

[61] European Commission: *Communication from the Commission to the European Parliament and the Council on the work of the Task Force Mediterranean*, COM (2013) 869 final, Brussels, 4.12.2013, pp. 5–11.

[62] Ludwig, A.: *Frontex und Eurosur – Umweltsatelliten der Esa helfen bei Jagd auf Flüchtlinge*, Zeit Online, 20th December 2013; http://www.zeit.de/digital/datenschutz/2013-12/frontex-eurosur-satelliten-fluechtlinge.

[63] Nielsen, N.: *EU looks to 'hybrid drones' for legal shortcut on migration*, EUobserver, 14th October 2013; http://euobserver.com/priv-immigration/121735.

[64] European Union Agency for Fundamental Rights: *Fundamental rights at Europe's southern sea borders*, Luxembourg, Publications Office of the European Union, 2013, p. 60.

[65] International Working Group on Data Protection in Telecommunications: *Arbeitspapier zum Datenschutz bei Überwachung aus der Luft*, Berlin, 54th Session, 2–3 September 2013, p. 6.

[66] European Data Protection Supervisor: *Preliminary Comments of the European Data Protection Supervisor on: COM(2008) 69 final; COM(2008) 68 final; COM(2008) 67 final*, Brussels, 3rd March 2008, p. 7.

[67] Article 18 EUROSUR Regulation.

[68] Article 20 EUROSUR Regulation.

information to all authorities with a responsibility for external border surveillance as well as with law enforcement, asylum, and immigration authorities.

Furthermore, EUROSUR entails the possibility to process special categories of data, which are normally stronger protected in European Data Protection Laws.[69] These categories include information regarding racial or ethnic origin, political opinions or religious or other beliefs, as well as personal data concerning health and sexual life or criminal convictions.[70] Surveilling ports or towns, or tracking vessels – including photographic surveillance – for an extended period of time might reveal information regarding person's habits to visit religious institutions or to pray and thereby disclose one's religious beliefs. Furthermore, the incident reports of the situational picture may reveal criminal convictions, and descriptions of the involved persons can entail their ethnic origin.

The next point of concern relates to transparency – or rather the lack of it – as well as the supervision of EUROSUR. Most of the documents revealing the exact scope of data exchange are not publicly available and therefore an exact scrutiny is not possible. Furthermore, since the system is running 24 h a day, 7 days a week and includes inter alia the possibility of audio and video conferencing this unrecorded exchange of information complicates the general difficulty of supervising large-scale international, interconnected databases even more.[71] From the point of view of the data subject, transparency would be of upmost importance to ascertain which authority has which information about oneself. Nonetheless, this seems rather illusory in the context of EUROSUR. Once a NCC inserts information into its National Situational Picture it will be automatically shared with Frontex and the other NCCs, including all the national or international authorities they are further connected with. Only the transfer of information to third countries requires the consent of the NCC which provided the original information. Consequently, not even the NCCs know to which authorities in Europe the information is disclosed. Further concerns are raised by the planned as well as deployed surveillance tools, such as RPAS and satellites. While the use of these tools is openly communicated,

> data subjects would hardly be aware of this kind of processing as it is difficult to notice RPAS, because of their small size and the altitude of operation. Furthermore, it is difficult, if not impossible, even for individuals noticing such devices, to know who is observing them, for what purposes and how to exercise their rights.[72]

---

[69] For example: Article 8 Directive 95/46/EC of the European Parliament and of the Council of 24 October 1995 on the protection of individuals with regard to the processing of personal data and on the free movement of such data, Article 6 Convention for the Protection of Individuals with regard to Automatic Processing of Personal Data.

[70] Only the Convention for the Protection of Individuals with regard to Automatic Processing of Personal Data includes information regarding criminal convictions.

[71] European Data Protection Supervisor: *Preliminary Comments of the European Data Protection Supervisor on: COM(2008) 69 final; COM(2008) 68 final; COM(2008) 67 final*, Brussels, 3rd March 2008, p. 7.

[72] Article 29 Data Protection Working Party, *Letter to the European Commission regarding Remotely Piloted Aircraft Systems (RPAS) – Response to the Questionnaire*, p. 1, 2.

This combination of abstract knowledge regarding surveillance in a certain area but further uncertainty can, according to the ECJ, "*generate in the minds of the persons concerned the feeling that their private lives are the subject of constant surveillance.*"[73] A further problem of secret surveillance was pointed out by the ECtHR in the *Klass case*[74]:

> The Court points out that where a State institutes secret surveillance the existence of which remains unknown to the persons being controlled, with the effect that the surveillance remains unchallengeable, Article 8 (art. 8) could to a large extent be reduced to a nullity. It is possible in such a situation for an individual to be treated in a manner contrary to Article 8 (art. 8), or even to be deprived of the right granted by that Article (art. 8), without his being aware of it and therefore without being able to obtain a remedy either at the national level or before the Convention institutions.[75]

A further factor that elevates the intensity of the interference is the potential abuse of stored data.[76] Notwithstanding the data protection obligations entailed in the EUROSUR Regulation, the system itself and the large-scale collection of data increase the risk of misuse of personal information. As explained before, the user interface allows data exchange via text boxes and does not include any privacy enhancing or depersonalising safeguards. Furthermore, neither the system itself nor the EUROSUR Regulation hinder or permit that the description of an event is illustrated with attached images or videos. As asylum and immigration authorities shall also be provided with relevant information, these might run an asylum seeker's photo against all the uploaded EUROSUR pictures of arrivals by sea to ascertain where he/she first landed or authorities in charge of tracing unaccompanied minors' family members may wish to consult EUROSUR pictures to see if the child arrived accompanied by adults. While both examples are unintended by the regulation they are not only technical possible but also not prohibited by it.[77]

Last but not least, the general application of surveillance or the lack of reasoned grounds for surveillance aggravates the intensity of the interference. EUROSUR aims at finding reasoned grounds for reaction measures on the basis of combining new information with existing knowledge.[78] However, while the objective might be justified, the definition shows that there does not have to exist any initial suspicion or indication. Consequently, all persons who stay, roam or sail in a certain area will be put under a general suspicion until they are categorised as unsuspicious. This can also be seen in the regulation itself, since according to Articles 9(3)(d) the event layer shall contain *information on unidentified and suspect vehicles, vessels and other crafts and persons at, along or in the proximity of the external border*. The ECJ categorised the

---

[73] ECJ, *Digital Rights Irleand Ltd.*, C-293/12 and C-594/12, Judgement of 8th April 2014, § 37.

[74] ECtHR, App. 5029/71, *Klass and others v Germany*, 6 September 1978, Series A No. 28.

[75] Ibid. § 36.

[76] Advocate General Cruz Villalon (ECJ), *Digital Rights Irleand Ltd.*, C-293/12 and C-594/12, Opinion, 12th December 2013, § 75.

[77] European Union Agency for Fundamental Rights: *Fundamental rights at Europe's southern sea borders*, Luxembourg, Publications Office of the European Union, 2013, p. 62.

[78] Articles 1, 3(b) EUROSUR Regulation.

Data Retention Directive[79] as a particular serious interference with the right to private life partly because it applied even to persons for whom there is no evidence capable of suggesting that their conduct might have a link, even an indirect or remote one, with serious crime.[80]

In summary, it can be argued that EUROSUR constitutes a rather serious interference with the right to privacy, even though no personal data in the traditional sense of the term – meaning information about an already identified person – is processed.[81] It has to be reiterated that "*to establish the existence of an interference with the fundamental right to privacy, it does not matter whether the information on the private lives concerned is sensitive or whether the persons concerned have been inconvenienced in any way.*"[82] In particular the general application of surveillance without any reasoned grounds combined with the vast range of data sources and data recipients aggravate the interferences. However, this already grave interference is further intensified by the lack of transparency and the correlating exclusion of data subjects' rights.

3.2 Justification of EUROSUR

After establishing that EUROSUR interferes with fundamental rights it further has to be ascertained if the interference is justified. According to Article 8(2) ECHR an interference is justified if it is in accordance with law, if the restriction targets one of the listed legitimate aims, and if the interference is necessary in a democratic society. A set of similar requirements apply to interferences with rights of the EUFRCh.

> *Article 52(1) of the Charter provides that any limitation on the exercise of the rights and freedoms laid down by the Charter must be provided for by law, respect their essence and, subject to the principle of proportionality, limitations may be made to those rights and freedoms only if they are necessary and genuinely meet objectives of general interest recognised by the Union or the need to protect the rights and freedoms of others.*[83]

3.2.1 Accordance with Law

To be in accordance with law, the interference has to not only be based on a national or European law,[84] which is accessible to the citizens, but the law also has to be formulated with sufficient precision, allowing citizens to foresee the consequences which a given action may entail.[85] While this so-called test of foreseeability does not require

---

[79] Directive 2006/24/EC of the European Parliament and of the Council of 15 March 2006 on the retention of data generated or processed in connection with the provision of publicly available electronic communications services or of public communications networks and amending Directive 2002/58/EC.

[80] ECJ, *Digital Rights Ireland Ltd.*, C-293/12 and C-594/12, Judgement of 8th April 2014, § 58.

[81] Advocate General Cruz Villalon (ECJ), *Digital Rights Irleand Ltd.*, C-293/12 and C-594/12, Opinion, 12th December 2013, § 74.

[82] ECJ, *Digital Rights Ireland Ltd.*, C-293/12 and C-594/12, Judgement of 8th April 2014, § 33.

[83] Ibid. § 38.

[84] ECtHR, App. 45036/98, '*Bosphorus Airways' v Ireland*, 30 June 2005, 2005-VI.

[85] ECtHR, App. 6538/74, *Sunday Times v United Kingdom*, 26 April 1979, Series A No. 30, § 49.

that the law stipulates every detail of surveillance, the legal foundation should not give the executive authorities an excessively broad discretion. *"The law must indicate the scope of any discretion conferred on the competent authorities and the manner of its exercise with sufficient clarity to give the individual adequate protection against arbitrary interference."*[86]

> The Court must be satisfied that, whatever system of surveillance is adopted, there exist adequate and effective guarantees against abuse. This assessment has only a relative character: it depends on all the circumstances of the case, such as the nature, scope and duration of the possible measures, the grounds required for ordering such measures, the authorities competent to permit, carry out and supervise such measures, and the kind of remedy provided by the national law.[87]

When applying these guidelines towards the EUROSUR Regulation the following conclusion can be drawn. Firstly, every inclusion of personal data in the European Situational Picture or the Common Pre-Frontier Intelligence Picture that is not concerning ship identification numbers is illegal, since there is no legal foundation.[88] However, there are sufficient safeguards in place for personal data concerning ship IDs. Secondly, personal data in the National Situational Picture is hardly safeguarded in the regulation, since the only provision concerning the protection of personal data is a general cross reference to European and national provisions on data protection. Consequently, there are no EUROSUR specific safeguards in place. This, however, appears as a surprise, since the Commission stated in 2008 that:

> The processing of personal data within the context of EUROSUR must therefore be based on appropriate legislative measures, which define the nature of the processing and lay down appropriate safeguards.[89]

Furthermore, the Commission was encouraged in this endeavour by the Article 29 Working Party, which states that even the exchange of personal data to a limited extent would require specific boundaries concerning the scope and categories of personal data, and its limited use and retention.[90] Moreover, the possibility that personal data is processed in the common application of surveillance tools is not mentioned once in the regulation. As a result, it has to be concluded that the limitations to the right of privacy based on the EUROSUR Regulation cannot be justified due to the vagueness of the provisions and the lack of safeguards. As it has been explained above, the data sources

---

[86] White, R. C.A., Ovey, C.: *The European Convention on Human Rights*, New York, Oxford University Press, 2010, 5th Edition, p. 367.

[87] ECtHR, App. 5029/71, *Klass and others v Germany*, 6 September 1978, Series A No. 28, § 50.

[88] Article 13(2) EUROSUR Regulation.

[89] European Commission: *Communication from the Commission to the European Parliament, the Council, the European Economic and Social Committee and the Committee of the Regions – Examining the creation of a European Border Surveillance System (EUROSUR)*, COM(2008) 68 final, Brussels, 13.02.2008, p. 11.

[90] Article 29 Data Protection Working Party: *Letter to the Commissioner for Home Affairs Ms. Cecilia Malmström regarding the Proposal for a Regulation establishing the European Border Surveillance System*, p. 1, 2.

and recipients are specified in non-exhaustive lists, the information exchanged is only described vaguely, there are no specific safeguards or remedies, and all relevant decisions are made by the executive authorities in the Member States or Frontex without any direction provided by the regulation. Consequently, the EUROSUR Regulation is not formulated precise enough to qualify as justifying law. In this context it also has to be noted that the legal basis for EUROSUR was negotiated after or at least parallel to the creation of the system. After running pilot projects between 2008 and 2011 by year-end of 2012 Frontex signed a Memorandum of Understanding with 18 Member States and connected them to EUROSUR, one year prior to the adoption of the regulation.

3.2.2 The Essence of Fundamental Rights and Legitimate Aims

Furthermore, it is questionable if the regulation respects the essence of the right to privacy and data protection as required by Article 52(1) EUFRCh. European data protection organisations have declared that:

> The monitoring of travellers has to be well founded and can only be allowed in exceptional cases and for justified and specific purposes. Any general surveillance poses unacceptable risks to the freedom of individuals.[91]
> From its analysis, the Working Party concludes that secret, massive and indiscriminate surveillance programs are incompatible with our fundamental laws and cannot be justified by the fight against terrorism or other important threats to national security.[92]

Nonetheless, EUROSUR does not include a targeted surveillance of people entering Europe, but rather a surveillance of specific areas. Furthermore, the surveillance does not interfere with the core personal sphere but rather with individuals in public or in transit. "*Such an individual in transit may well expect a lesser degree of privacy, but not expect to be deprived in full of his rights and freedoms as also related to his own private sphere and image.*"[93] As EUROSUR does not deprive individuals fully of their privacy, it does respect the essence of their data protection right.

Furthermore, the purposes of EUROSUR of "*detecting, preventing and combating illegal immigration and cross-border crime and contributing to ensuring the protection and saving the lives of migrants*"[94] are legitimate aims (national security, public safety, prevention of crime, amongst others).

3.2.3 Necessary in a Democratic Society

Last but not least, the interference has to be necessary in a democratic society. According to the jurisdiction of the ECtHR this necessity test consists of two elements:[95]

---

[91] Conference of the European Data Protection Authorities: *Border Management Declaration*, Rome, April 2008.

[92] Article 29 Data Protection Working Party: *Opinion 04/2014 on surveillance of electronic communications for intelligence and national security purposes*, adopted on 10 April 2014, p. 2.

[93] Article 29 Data Protection Working Party: *Working Document on the Processing of Personal Data by means of Video Surveillance*, adopted on 25 November 2002, p. 5.

[94] Article 1 EUROSUR Regulation.

[95] See for example: ECtHR, Apps 5947/72, 6205/73, 7052/75, 7061/75, 7107/75, 7113/75, and 7136/75, *Silver v United Kingdom*, 25 March 1983, Series A No. 61, § 97.

- Does the interference correspond to a pressing social need?
- Is the interference proportionate to the legitimate aim? /Is the interference no greater than necessary to address the pressing social need?

Therefore, each of the purposes has to constitute a current pressing social need. While the European Union has a certain margin of appreciation in determining pressing social needs, there has to be at least factual evidence that an issue exists that needs to be addressed with a view to protecting public security. Furthermore, EUROSUR actually has to contribute to tackling the issue.

In general, it cannot be questioned that an effective management and control of the external borders of the European Union is necessary and a social need. Nonetheless, justification of interferences with fundamental rights requires that the tool in question corresponds to a specific issue which requires an urgent response. According to the EUROSUR Regulation and the correlating documents the main goal of EUROSUR is to combat irregular migration into the EU, while the prevention of loss of life at sea as well as fighting cross border crime are only added advantages.[96] However, already in 2008 – when the EUROSUR Regulation was firstly initiated – the European Data Protection Supervisor criticised the proposal for the lack of evidence of the necessity and the lack of evaluation of existing systems.[97] In the following years, the relevant authorities have neither responded to the existing criticism nor have they considered the changes in migration flows. Consequently, several arguments can be produced that question the necessity of EUROSUR.

Firstly it seems that the European Union has a disproportionate focus on irregular arrivals by land and sea.[98] Statistics show, that only a very small percentage of migrants enter Europe irregularly by sea or land, while the majority of migrants without the required documents overstay their visas.[99] Furthermore, it has to be considered, that a vast majority of the migrants arriving by sea are in the need of protection and apply for asylum or another form of protection.[100] In this context it also has to be stressed,

---

[96] European Commission: *Commission Staff Working Paper - Impact Assessment accompanying the Proposal for a Regulation of the European Parliament and of the Council establishing the European Border Surveillance System (EUROSUR)*, SEC(2011) 1538 final, Brussels, 12.12.2011, pp. 8, 9.

[97] European Data Protection Supervisor: *Preliminary Comments of the European Data Protection Supervisor on: COM(2008) 69 final; COM(2008) 68 final; COM(2008) 67 final*, Brussels, 3rd March 2008, pp. 3, 4.

[98] UN Human Rights Council: *Report of the Special Rapporteur on the human rights of migrants, Regional study: management of the external borders of the European Union and its impact on the human rights of migrants*, 24 April 2013, A/HRC/23/46, p. 6.

[99] Ibid; European Union Agency for Fundamental Rights: *Fundamental rights at Europe's southern sea borders*, Luxembourg, Publications Office of the European Union, 2013, pp. 19–23.

[100] According to statistics (from 2009) roughly 70 % of the migrants that arrived in Malta by sea applied for asylum; (UNHCR: *Irregular Migration by Sea: Frequently Asked Questions*, http://www.unhcr.org/4a1e48f66.html).

that within the European Union irregular migration is still considered a security problem and linked to terrorism and cross border crime.[101] Similarly does the term 'illegal migration' – as used in the EUROSUR Regulation – suggest that irregular migration is a criminal offence in line with human trafficking. Nonetheless, the UN-HCR[102] has emphasised repeatedly that irregular migration does not constitute a criminal offence and that the 1951 Geneva Convention[103] explicitly prohibits penalties relating to the illegal entry of refugees. Moreover, the terminology is not only regrettable,[104] but *"defining persons as illegal can also be regarded as denying their humanity"*[105] and challenging their fundamental rights as human beings. Consequently, the issue of irregular migration should not be approached with the same means as the smuggling of humans or contraband. Furthermore, there is no reliable data linking irregular migration to terrorism or proving that the majority of those entering irregularly are serious criminals[106] and the perception of 'migrant criminality' is wrong in most cases.[107]

Secondly, the statistics of the last decade have shown, that the number of migrants entering into Europe is declining – except a short incline resulting from the Arab spring and ongoing civil unrest and war.[108] Nonetheless, the proposal for the EUROSUR Regulation from 2008 has not been abandoned or changed. Furthermore, it is unlikely that migration will be stopped by reinforcing border control or other border management measures. So far statistics have proven that increased surveillance or control measures in one area of the border do not result in a cease of migration but in a shift of

---

[101] See for example: European Commission, *Commission Staff Working Paper - Impact Assessment accompanying the Proposal for a Regulation of the European Parliament and of the Council establishing the European Border Surveillance System (EUROSUR)*, SEC(2011) 1538 final, Brussels, 12.12.2011, pp. 8, 9.

[102] United Nations High Commissioner for Refugees, hereinafter: UNHCR.

[103] Article 31 1951 Convention Relating to the Status of Refugees, hereinafter: 1951 Geneva Convention.

[104] UN Human Rights Council: *Report of the Special Rapporteur on the human rights of migrants, Regional study: management of the external borders of the European Union and its impact on the human rights of migrants*, 24 April 2013, A/HRC/23/46, p. 10.

[105] Koser K.: *Irregular migration, state security and human security*, Global Commission on International Migration, September 2005, p. 5.

[106] European Data Protection Supervisor: *Preliminary Comments of the European Data Protection Supervisor on: COM(2008) 69 final; COM(2008) 68 final; COM(2008) 67 final*, Brussels, 3rd March 2008, p. 3.

[107] Pugh, M.: *Mediterranean Boat People: A Case for Cooperation?*, Mediterranean Politics, 2001, 6, pp. 1–20, 2, 3.

[108] European Union Agency for Fundamental Rights: *Fundamental rights at Europe's southern sea borders*, Luxembourg, Publications Office of the European Union, 2013, pp. 19–23; Grant, H., Provost, C., Allen, P.: *Fortress Europe: have border controls worked? An interactive guide*, The Guardian, 13th January 2014, http://www.theguardian.com/global-development/interactive/2014/jan/13/europes-border-control-interactive-guide.

migration routes, and consequently longer and more dangerous trips for migrants.[109] Furthermore, experiences have already been made with a large-scale high-tech surveillance network (SBI-net) at the border between Mexico and the US since 2006. As a result, the funding of the project was frozen in 2010 and the initiative consequently stopped and seriously altered since the project in its original form did neither meet its capacities nor provide the authorities with the necessary assistance.[110]

According to the Commission EUROSUR will also affect the fight against serious crime in Europe, since *"criminal networks involved in the smuggling of migrants are often using the same routes and methods for cross-border crime activities, such as trafficking in human beings, illicit drug trafficking, illicit arms trafficking, trafficking in radioactive and nuclear substances, and terrorism."*[111] While the linkage between migrants and terrorism has already been discussed above, the described 'use of the same routes' can also be questioned. Since 2003 testimonies of arriving migrants show that normally one of the migrants themselves operates the vessel.[112] Due to increased surveillance and interceptions and a heightened risk of being arrested on sea or upon arrival smugglers are hardly ever on board of the boats.[113] Moreover, it has to be stressed that so far the UN Smuggling Protocol, which is part of the Organised Crime Convention, has never been invoked as legal basis for interceptions during Frontex missions. Therefore, it seems not only questionable that these routes are also used for the trafficking of other goods but also that any arrests would be foreseeable. In the context of serious cross border crimes it further has to be mentioned that abetting or facilitating 'illegal' immigration, which carries a penalty of up to 15 years imprisonment in Italy, is also applied to fishermen or other sailors who render assistance to migrant boats.[114] The *Cap Anamur* case[115] and other cases proved that even though the law contains an exemption if assistance is given to those in need, the exemption is

---

[109] Council of Europe – Parliamentary assembly: *Migration and asylum: mounting tensions in the Eastern Mediterranean,* 23 January 2013, Doc. 13106, p. 10, 15; Lutterbeck, D.: *Policing Migration in the Mediterranean,* Mediterranean Politics, 2006, 11 (1), pp. 59–82,74–77; Parliamentary Assembly of the Council of Europe: *Europe's "boat-people": mixed migration flows by sea into southern Europe – Report of the Committee on Migration, Refugees and Population,* Doc. 11688, 11 July 2008, para 17.

[110] Hayes, B., Vermeulen, M.: *Borderline – EU Border Surveillance Initiatives – An Assessment of the Costs and Its Impact on Fundamental Rights,* Berlin, Heinrich Böll Stiftung, 2012, p. 67.

[111] European Commission: *Commission Staff Working Paper - Impact Assessment accompanying the Proposal for a Regulation of the European Parliament and of the Council establishing the European Border Surveillance System (EUROSUR),* SEC(2011) 1538 final, Brussels, 12.12.2011, p. 9.

[112] European Union Agency for Fundamental Rights, *Fundamental rights at Europe's southern sea borders,* Luxembourg, Publications Office of the European Union, 2013, pp. 25–27.

[113] Hamood S.: *EU-Libya cooperation on migration: a raw deal for refugees and migrants?,* Journal of Refugee Studies, 2008, 21 (1), pp. 19–42, 29–31.

[114] Parliamentary Assembly of the Council of Europe, *Europe's "boat-people": mixed migration flows by sea into southern Europe – Report of the Committee on Migration,* Refugees and Population, Doc. 11688, 11 July 2008, para 36; ITF seafarers: *Damned if they do ...,* http://www.itfseafarers.org/damned.cfm.

[115] Information on the Cap Anamur case can be found at: Statewatch, *Italy: Criminalising Solidarity – Cap Anamur trial underway,* http://www.statewatch.org/news/2007/apr/03italy-cape-anamur.htm.

applied restrictively and that it is not clear if it is also valid in cases where the assistance is given outside of the Italian territorial waters.[116]

Finally, it is questionable how much EUROSUR can actually contribute towards *protection and saving the lives of migrants*.[117] While the high number of migrants' deaths on the way to the Europe is caused in various ways – including suffocation in trucks, car accidents, frostbite, police violence, hunger strikes, landmines, or suicide in detention[118] – the majority loses their lives at sea. Even though the Mediterranean Sea is already one of the closest surveilled maritime spaces in the world, it is estimated that since the mid-1990s at least 20,000 migrants have died there.[119] Consequently, organisations such as the International Federation for Human Rights consider not the lack of information responsible for the death toll at European borders but rather the lack of legal possibilities to reach Europe, the shifting towards more hazardous routes, the reluctance of patrol and fishing vessels to render assistance, the conflicts over search and rescue responsibilities, and the unwillingness of the EU to tackle the root causes of migration.[120] Yet, besides a general statement to contribute towards search and rescue of migrants in distress, the EUROSUR Regulation does not entail any provisions on how exactly this contribution will look like. Currently there are no official procedures detailing how to proceed after a distress-call nor is there an obligation to include national authorities responsible for search and rescue into EUROSUR or the NCC.[121] Additionally, it has to be stressed that surveillance measures on their own are not capable of saving lives. This can be illustrated by a report from a Major of the Maltese Armed Forces in front of the UK House of Lords: After a distress call of a vessel a Maltese aircraft was send to the scene but after some time *"the aircraft was withdrawn for refuelling and sent again to the position. On arriving it did not find a boat either in the position where it had been initially sighted nor within a substantial radius around it."*[122] In conclusion, the UN Special Rapporteur on the human rights of migrants *"fears that EUROSUR is destined to become just another tool that will be at the disposal of member States in order to secure borders and prevent arrivals, rather than a genuine life-saving tool."*[123]

---

[116] Ryan B., Mitsilegas, V.: *Extraterritorial immigration control: legal challenges*, Koninklijke Brill NV, Leiden, The Netherlands, 2010, p. 301.

[117] Art. 1 EUROSUR Regulation.

[118] UN Human Rights Council: *Report of the Special Rapporteur on the human rights of migrants, Regional study: management of the external borders of the European Union and its impact on the human rights of migrants*, 24 April 2013, A/HRC/23/46, p. 6.

[119] International Federation for Human Rights: *Lampedusa: Murderous Europe*, 10 October 2013.

[120] Ibid.

[121] European Union Agency for Fundamental Rights: *Fundamental rights at Europe's southern sea borders*, Luxembourg, Publications Office of the European Union, 2013, p. 62.

[122] House of Lords European Union Committee, *9th Report of Session 2007–08, Frontex: The EU external borders agency*, Report with Evidence, London, United Kingdom, 5 March 2008, p. 19 (Box 1 – The disappearance of 53 Eritrean nationals).

[123] UN Human Rights Council: *Report of the Special Rapporteur on the human rights of migrants, Regional study: management of the external borders of the European Union and its impact on the human rights of migrants*, 24 April 2013, A/HRC/23/46, pp. 10, 11.

In sum, the introduction of the EUROSUR does not seem necessary in a democratic society. While the aims of the regulation are comprehensible, the accompanying documents do not show how EUROSUR will be able to contribute towards achieving these goals. Furthermore, there is no hard evidence that an additional surveillance tool is necessary at the European borders. Neither the proposal of the EUROSUR Regulation nor the following documents have evaluated the already increased surveillance and interception operations of Frontex, the intensified cooperation of Member States in regional networks and with third countries, or the decrease of migrants. However, this would have been necessary to prove that additional measures were necessary in 2008 and still are.

Finally, each interference has to be proportionate, meaning that an interference should not be greater than necessary. From the regulation itself as well as from the accompanying documents and press releases it can be concluded that the EU deems the collection, storage and exchange of personal data generally as not necessary for achieving the goals of EUROSUR. Consequently, the current version of EUROSUR is not proportionate since it gives the actors the possibility and the legal grounds to process personal data. Several properties of the current user interface as well as the common application of surveillance tools could have been implemented less intrusive by following a privacy-by-design approach. Furthermore, this would have limited the possibilities of misuse. The current regulation obliges Member States and Frontex to process data in accordance with the European and national provisions on data protection. However, it does not foresee any specific legal, organisational or technical safeguards. Nonetheless, in particular the latter one would have been desirable, since it can already be observed in the context of border control management *"that where strong human rights standards are incorporated into European Union policy and legislation, there is often a wide discrepancy between the texts and member-State implementation."*[124] In conclusion, the interference by the current EUROSUR system is greater than necessary since a more privacy protecting version seems possible.

4 Conclusion

A more privacy protecting system and regulation would have to observe the following recommendations. Firstly, the regulation should include provisions outlining the exceptional reasons and circumstances in which the processing of personal data is permitted as well as which data will be collected and shared. Furthermore, it should exhaustively list all data sources. This list should result from a thorough evaluation of each source under necessity considerations which should be included into the accompanying documents of a new regulation. A similar procedure is advisable for the recipients of data. Moreover, after the actual exchange of data, the recipients – European and national authorities – should be recorded in the system itself. Additionally, the inclusion of obligatory deletion deadlines as well as organisational and technical measures to protect the personal data is necessary. Concerning the system

---

[124] Ibid. p. 11.

itself, the EU should abstain from using free text boxes to prevent misuse. Furthermore, the possibility to add historical or photographic information to an incident should be abandoned, since it increases the likelihood of persons being identified via the system. Moreover, when applying common surveillance tools, the possibility to identify individuals should be precluded. Therefore, no sensors or cameras should be used that provide a high resolution or zoom capabilities enabling the identification of persons from the recorded images. These improvements could contribute towards a regulation that is more compliant with the right to privacy not only in consideration of the proportionality requirement but also under the aspect of the precision of the legal foundation. Nonetheless, even these improvements will not resolve the issues regarding the necessity of a new surveillance system at the European borders. Furthermore, this paper analysed EUROSUR only from a privacy protection point of view and all the existing issues concerning other fundamental rights of migrants have been left aside.

While there are currently no drones securing European borders, Baroness Ludford was, nevertheless, right, when she warned about the route the European Union is taking in the context of border management. The EUROSUR Regulation is just one of the examples that prove that due to security concerns – justified or not – the Member States are willing to neglect fundamental rights when balancing these competing interests. Furthermore, it shows that the tragedies of irregular migrants at sea are often used as an excuse for interfering with fundamental rights of refugees, asylum seekers, migrants as well as 'normal' travellers. While the deaths at sea of countless migrants are disgraceful for Europe it is very questionable that EUROSUR will improve this situation. Therefore, the criticism of the International Federation for Human Rights seems justified in the context of privacy protection, when they were stating:

> The deaths in Lampedusa, like those from yesterday and from tomorrow, are the victims of a Europe that is locked to the point of obliviousness into a securitarian logic, which has renounced the values that it claims to defend.[125]

---

[125] International Federation for Human Rights: *Lampedusa: Murderous Europe*, 10 October 2013.

Anonymous ePetitions – Another
Step Towards eDemocracy

Hannah Obersteller[(✉)]

Unabhängiges Landeszentrum Für Datenschutz Schleswig-Holstein,
Kiel, Germany
hobersteller@datenschutzzentrum.de

Abstract. This paper addresses the possibility to implement an online petition
platform which allows citizens to petition the public authorities anonymously.
The advantages and possible obstacles of anonymity are discussed. We focus on
the legal admissibility of anonymous petitions in Europe and Germany and
conclude that all related legal requirements could be met by implementing
Privacy-enhancing Attribute-based Credentials.

Keywords: Privacy · Privacy-ABCs · eDemocracy · ePetitions · Anonymity

1 Introduction

A petition is a democratic instrument that allows – in general – the members of a
country, a state or other kinds of community to introduce their concerns to the political
decision-makers and thereby influence the political dialogue. The petition offers the
possibility to raise an issue and obliges the democratically elected representatives to
address this issue. E.g., the German constitution (Grundgesetz; abbr.: GG) guarantees
everyone to petition the public authorities (Art. 17 GG). Art. 45c GG determines that a
committee of petitions shall be established. This text, however, will focus on petitions
to parliaments.

In the last few years, citizens have been provided an increasing number of ways
to get into contact with public administrations. In the context of the so-called
"e-government movement" many administrative issues now can be performed by
sending e-mails or using online services. The current German and European legislation
allows for the possibility to file petitions online. Advantages of information and
communication technologies, as e.g. being independent from time and location (cf. [1],
pp. 357, 358), support these methods of e-participation. This paper focuses on the
advancement and improvement of the existing systems with regard to the protection of
the citizens' right to privacy.

For instance, in 2005 the German federal Parliament (Bundestag) introduced the
possibility to file petitions online. At the same time, a new form of petitions was

The research leading to these results has received funding from the European Community's Seventh
Framework Programme (FP7/2007-2013) under Grant Agreement no. 257782 for the project
Attribute-based Credentials for Trust (ABC4Trust).

J. Camenisch et al. (Eds.): Privacy and Identity 2014, IFIP AICT 457, pp. 110–124, 2015.
DOI: 10.1007/978-3-319-18621-4_8

introduced: public petitions. A public petition is published on the Internet, i.e. on the website of the Bundestag, and can be signed by other people during four weeks. The Directive on public petitions which concretizes the Rules of Procedure of the Bundestag (RoP BT) determines that the petitioner has to indicate his name, permanent address and e-mail address. If the petition is meant to be a public petition, the name and contact address of the petitioner will be published with the petition text. (According to the "Help" section of the Bundestag's website, only the name of the petitioner is published [2].)

While already the fact that a petitioner has to identify herself by revealing her name and full address to the petition committee, as petition recipient, is to be considered as critical, the publication online is an even stronger intrusion in the petitioner's privacy. The employment of Privacy-enhancing Attribute-based Credentials could be a solution. This technology allows petitioners (and signees) to stay completely anonymous while at the same time it is guaranteed that they are legitimized and do not sign a petition several times when only one signature per person is allowed. Note that current systems do not prevent multiple signing if someone has more than one e-mail address.

The objective of this paper is to discuss how far it is possible to introduce a system which allows submitting a petition not only online but at the same time anonymously, i.e. without disclosing one's name and address to the respective petition committees. The reasoning is based on European legislation. In addition, German legislation is analyzed for input on the Member State level. Furthermore, it is debated how far staying anonymous is possible when submitting a simple petition or a petition that is to be signed by other citizens and, finally, if signees can stay anonymous in the latter case, too.

The text is organized as follows: First, key terms are defined in Sect. 2. Section 3 provides an overview of the current legal framework concerning anonymous use of online services and petitions on European and German level. Obstacles to overcome are discussed in Sect. 4. Finally, it is concluded that anonymous ePetitions would support eDemocracy.

2 Definitions

2.1 Petitions and "ePetitions"

Traditionally, a petition is submitted as a document, written on paper, signed in manuscript by the petitioner(s). Nowadays, public authorities increasingly allow the submission via online form. The general process of a petition stays the same and is as follows:

1. A citizen (the petitioner) formulates her concern in writing. Often a (online) form is provided. Inter alia she has to provide her full name and address, in order to allow the public authority to identify the petitioner and contact her by post.
2. The public authority that receives the petition is obliged to examine the admissibility of the petition (compliance with the respective procedural requirements, e.g. competence of the public authority on the petition subject). Mostly, parliaments have established petition committees that process the incoming petitions.

3. If the petition is admissible, the petition committee is obliged to decide on the petition. The exact procedure (oral proceedings/summons of the petitioner or just a written decision with or without grounds) depends on the individual case. But the petition committee is obliged to reply to the petition and to send the petitioner a final reply.

There are different possible understandings of the term "electronic petition" (or: "ePetition"): It can be defined as the submission of a petition to the addressee electronically. In this case the only aspect different for ePetitions compared to "traditional" petitions (in writing) is the modernized way of filing. The actual petitions process would not have to change ([3], p. 11). Another definition of "ePetition" could be "a petition that is published on the Internet". It does not necessarily have to be submitted electronically, but the further petitions process would happen online ([3], p. 11). Within this latter case one can make another distinction between a passive and an active way of use. A passive way of use would be that the petition (and eventually the petition notice) is simply made visible online. An active way of use would mean that an electronic petition system is set up, which especially enables people to file, and others to sign the petition online ([3], p. 12).

In the following "ePetition" will be understood as a petition filed (and possibly published) online and "public ePetition" will be understood as a petition filed online and published on the Internet that can be signed by other people (signees) online. This understanding of "public ePetition" corresponds to the definition of "public petition" laid down in the Rules of Procedure of the Bundestag concerning petitions (see 2 (4) RoP BT). On the European level, only (simple) ePetitions exist. Both kinds of ePetitions can be filed by several petitioners together.

2.2 Privacy-Enhancing Attribute-Based Credentials

Privacy-enhancing Attribute-based Credentials (Privacy-ABCs) give the user control over which, and how much personal information she reveals. They allow authentication towards an online service provider without identification. In a Privacy-ABC system the following entities are mandatory: issuer, user and verifier.

The issuer knows and can vouch for attribute values of the user. The issuer issues a Privacy-ABC credential containing those attributes to the user. The user receives the credential. Whenever the user wishes to authenticate, the credential on her device is combined with her individual secret key that only she possesses. The result is called a token. The user now can use this token to provide proof of certain attributes towards a third party – normally a service provider – which is called the verifier. The verifier offers a certain online service and usually has a presentation policy that determines which information is demanded to access the service. If e.g. the verifier is an information portal of town X that offers the possibility to ask questions on community issues to the inhabitants of town X, the user will only have to prove that she is an inhabitant of town X. Further information that may be contained in the user's credential, like e.g. her name and exact address, she can strip off. If the information stored in the token that the user provides meets the requirements of the verifier's presentation policy, the user is allowed to access the desired service. As a result, the user does not have to reveal more information than absolutely needed to make use of a certain online service. This supports the data minimization principle (see also Sect. 4.2).

Besides the above mentioned mandatory entities, a Privacy-ABC system can additionally comprise further entities: If full anonymity is not desired, ways for conditional identification can be allowed. This would be done by adding the "inspection feature". This means, in order to allow the revealing of the user's identity if necessary, an independent "inspection entity" can be employed. The "inspector" is allowed and enabled to identify the user only if predefined conditions are fulfilled. Those "inspection grounds" could, for instance, allow the revealing the identity of a user in case of misuse or infringement of third parties' rights. They have to be made known to the user in advance. Furthermore, it may become necessary to revoke a credential, e.g. if the user's attributes, stored in this credential, have changed. For this purpose, a "revocation authority" can be established. The inspection and revocation processes have been discussed in detail in [4].

In principle, the user can be enabled to act completely anonymously. However, while Privacy-ABCs allow anonymous authentication, the implementation has to be considered in detail as certain circumstances, such as the specific value of revealed attributes, tracking measures (cookies etc.) and IP addresses, may hinder this capability. An illustrative example of how a Privacy-ABC-based petition system which allows complete anonymity could be implemented was already given and discussed in the past in [5].

2.3 Anonymity

According to the European Data Protection Directive (Directive 95/46/EC of the European Parliament and of the Council of 24 October 1995 on the protection of individuals with regard to the processing of personal data and on the free movement of such data; respectively its national implementing laws), a data subject is considered as anonymous if she is not or no longer identified or identifiable. "(...) To determine whether a person is identifiable, account should be taken of all the means likely reasonably to be used either by the controller or by any other person to identify the said person (...)." (European Data Protection Directive; Recital 26; omissions by the author; cf. the draft General Data Protection Regulation, Recital 23) "Identification" does not only mean that it is possible to retrieve a data subject's name and/or address, but also identifiability by singling out, linkability and interference ([6], p. 10).

The document referenced in [6] also explains in detail different ways of anonymization. In general, identifiability of a single individual depends to a large extent on the distinguishability of this person within a set of individuals. The larger the set of people sharing the same attributes values is, the more unlikely is the identification of an individual. So ideally, an anonymous ePetition system has to avoid storing information that might allow the data controller – or an external attacker – to directly identify the users or link the information with other databases and use the retrieved information in connection, in order to identify the users ([7], p. 42).

Privacy-ABCs systems provide a possible solution, since the service provider – in this case the provider of the ePetition platform – does not receive more data than absolutely necessary and, consequently, cannot store them. In most cases, e.g., it is sufficient to prove that one is citizen of a certain state (or maybe region) to participate in a certain ePetition. Still, Privacy-ABCs allow to make sure that a citizen signs a petition not more often than once. (See also Sect. 4.3. For more details on the technical solution please refer to [8], pp. 128 et sqq.)

However, in case of complete anonymity the European Data Protection Directive is not applicable, since it only regulates the handling of identifying data (Recital 26 Dir. EC/95/46; [6], p. 5). From a legal point of view, anonymity is not given if the user is not identified from the outset but still identifiable ([6], p. 6), i.e. her identity can be revealed. In a Privacy-ABC system which enables the inspection feature, the credentials issued to the user are "inspectable". If the inspection grounds are fulfilled, the inspector is (technically) enabled to reveal the user's identity.

Assuming that an ePetition system will not be accepted by the responsible public authorities if identification is absolutely excluded, it would probably be more accurate to speak of "anonymous or pseudonymous" ePetitions when discussing the possibility of employing Privacy-ABCs with or without the inspection feature for this purpose. But since anonymity (in the legal sense) is technically possible, it seems acceptable to focus on this goal. Pseudonymity, however, means that the linkability of a dataset with the original identity of an individual is reduced ([6], p. 20).

3   Legislation

Since 1992, the right to petition the European Parliament is laid down in the European legal framework. Prior to that, it was recognized by customary law and mentioned in the Rules of Procedure of the European Parliament ([9], p. 344).

Today, it is guaranteed by the Charter of Fundamental Rights of the European Union (CFREU), the Treaty in the Functioning of the European Union (TFEU) and in many constitutions of the EU Member States ([9], p. 344, fn. 1385). As mentioned initially, in Germany it is constitutionally guaranteed in Art. 17 GG. The competence of the respective public authorities depends on the subject of the petition. For instance, the Bundestag is not responsible for the educational policy of the German federal State Schleswig-Holstein. If a petitioner files a petition concerning the inadequate curricula of public schools in Schleswig-Holstein, the Bundestag's petition committee will inform the petitioner that her petition was rejected as inadmissible.

3.1   Anonymity

If the operator wishes to store identifying data of the user (e.g. the IP address), he needs a legal permission. As the IP address commonly is regarded as personal data ([10], p. 16), the European Data Protection Directive is applicable. This means, data may only be collected for specified, explicit and legitimate purposes. Under the current German legislation there is no general legal permission (or even obligation) for website operators to know or to store identifying personal data of their users. While telecommunication providers in Germany are obliged to collect identifying personal data such as name, permanent address, date of birth etc. from their customers (cf. § 111 Telecommunications Act; abbr.: TKG), this does not apply to website operators. The latter (usually) are not telecommunication providers.

A "telecommunication provider" is a natural or legal person offering telecommunication services. "Telecommunication services" are offers of telecommunications, including transmission line offers to broadcasting networks, usually for a consideration (§ 3 Nr. 18 TKG). "Telecommunications" means the technical process of sending, transmitting and receiving any kind of message in the form of signs, voice, images or sounds by means of telecommunication systems (§ 3 Nr. 16 TKG).

Provided that the operator of an online petition platform does not run an own telecommunication network, he does not meet this definition as he does not offer access to a telecommunication network. To website operators the German Telemediengesetz (Telemedia Act; abbr.: TMG) applies. Both the TKG and the TMG serve to implement European legislation on national German level; i.e. the Directive 2002/58/EC of the European Parliament and of the Council of 12 July 2002 concerning the processing of personal data and the protection of privacy in the electronic communications sector (e-Privacy Directive) amended by the Directive 2009/136/EC of the European Parliament and the Council of 25 November 2009. The TMG itself does not oblige (or allow) the website operator to store user data. The responsibility and liability of website operators depend on his role. A website operator who is just running and maintaining the website, but does not provide own editorial contributions is regarded as host provider (Art. 14 Directive 2000/31/EC of the European Parliament and of the Council of 8 June 2000 on certain legal aspects of information society services, in particular electronic commerce, in the Internal Market; "Directive on electronic commerce"). Concerning the content a petitioner publishes at the petition platform, the Bundestag (as website operator) does not provide own contributions online. A moderator will just delete user content which is not compliant to the terms of use [11]. Hence, the Bundestag is to be treated as a host provider in this regard. In consequence, a right to store the user's personal data for own business purposes because this is necessary to safeguard its legitimate interests (according to § 28 (1) Nr. 2 Federal German Data Protection Act; abbr.: BDSG) cannot be derived, as a host provider is not responsible for user content. Otherwise the legitimate interest could be e.g. evidence purposes or own legal actions in case of legal proceedings against the website operator due to content published by a user [12]. The host provider is just required to make sure that such content is deleted, respectively not accessible anymore (§ 10 TMG).

The website operator of an Internet forum is not required to provide an individual with personal data of one of the users, even if this user has published content which violates the rights of personality of this individual [13]. In turn, the operator has to provide the prosecution authorities with stored personal data in cases of suspicion of serious criminal offences committed by the user. But if no identifying data is stored, the website operator cannot provide the authorities with such data. Currently, there is no German data retention law: In 2010 the German Constitutional Court (Bundesverfassungsgericht) ruled that the German transposition law to the European Directive on retention of personal data (Directive 2006/24/EC of the European Parliament and of the Council of 15 March 2006 on the retention of data generated or processed in connection with the provision of publicly available electronic communications services or of public communications networks and amending Directive 2002/58/EC) was void.

This may be regarded as an unintended gap, since the technical possibility of complete anonymity just was not considered. But de facto there is not even a rule of law which regulates a comparable issue and therefore could be applied by analogy.

3.2 Legal Requirements on Petitions

The right to petition grants that the petition recipient examines the petition content. If the petition recipient comes to the conclusion that the petition is not admissible, the right to petition further grants that the petitioner shall be informed about this fact and the reason for the inadmissibility. Reason for this is to allow the petitioner to make a decision on whether she wants to appeal the decision and to allow a judge to review the grounds for lawfulness. Insofar, the right to petition is identical on European and national German level ([14–16]. However, as for the national German level, the German constitutional court ruled that the petition committee is not obliged to provide the petitioner (of an admissible petition) with a statement of grounds for its decision. Once a petitioner got a reply for the purpose of notifying the decision on her petition, she has no right to get another reply if she petitions to the same authority for the same reasons again [14].

Under the current legislation – leaving aside the subordinate Rules of Procedure, which could be attached autonomously by the respective parliaments or petition committees themselves – it is possible to implement an anonymous ePetition system.

The current Rules of Procedure of both the European Parliament and the Bundestag determine that the petitioner has to identify herself towards the petition committees. Staying anonymous or using a pseudonym towards the petition committee is not allowed.

However, the Rules of Procedure stem from the fact that the treatment of petitions is left to the discretion of the public authorities, as long as the minimum conditions are fulfilled ([17], marginal 10). The parliaments could change their respective Rules of Procedure and allow anonymous ePetitions as long as compliance with the "minimum conditions" is assured.

European Union. The European legislation allows every citizen of the European Union and any natural or legal person residing or having its registered office in a Member State to petition the European Parliament alone or jointly with others (Art. 44 CFREU, Art. 227 TFEU). Art. 227 TFEU limits the scope to matters which come within the Union's field of activity and affect the petitioner directly. Petitions will be addressed by the Petition Committee of the European Parliament. According to the Rules of Procedure of the European Parliament (8th parliamentary term, July 2014; abbr.: RoP EP), the Petition Committee is one of the standing committees which are to be set up by the European Parliament (196 RoP EP; Annex VI (XX)).

It is possible to file petitions via an online form (or by post). It is not possible to file a petition as public ePetition, but – as Art. 227 TFEU provides – to file petitions together with as many other petitioners as desired. The petitioner has to indicate her name, permanent address and nationality. If the petition is published online, the name of the petitioner may be published with the petition's content (215 (9) RoP EP). Basically, all registered petitions will be made public documents and may be published by the European Parliament (215 (9) RoP EP). Nevertheless, the European Parliament has itself undertaken to respect the privacy interests of petitioners to such degree as Rule 215 also stipulates the mandatory non-disclosure of the petitioner's name (Rule 215 (10) RoP EP) or the possible treatment of the petition (the content) as confidential (Rule 215 (11) RoP EP) if the petitioner clearly requests this when filing the petition.

In contrast to the German constitution, neither the CFREU, nor the TFEU states clearly that a petition has to be filed in writing. Still, the RoP EP anticipate that petitions are "written" (c.f. 215 (5) RoP EP: "Petitions must be written in an official language of the European Union."), which of course does not necessarily mean in a traditional – meant as "on paper" – way. However, in accordance with the Bundestag, the European Parliament decided to give potential petitioners the ability to file petitions online. But all subsequent communication will happen by post. As this communication could be done electronically as well, there is no absolute hindrance for anonymous ePetitions.

Germany. As stated in the introduction, on the German federal level the right to petition the Bundestag (and other public authorities) is guaranteed in Art. 17 GG. Art. 45c GG determines that a petition committee is to be appointed by the Bundestag. All powers conferred to the petition committee of the Bundestag are regulated by federal law (Gesetz über die Befugnisse des Petitionsausschusses). All details concerning action taken on petitions are laid down in the petition committee's Rules of Procedure (introduced on the basis of § 110 of the Bundestag's Rules of Procedure; abbr.: GOBT).

Art. 17 GG determines that a petition has to be filed in writing. Traditionally, "in writing" requires a piece of paper with the petition text on it, signed by the petitioner. Accordingly, 4 (1) of the Rules of Procedure of the Bundestag's petition committee (RoP BT) states the written form requirement and adds that it is also observed if the petitioner uses the online form and provides her name and postal address. However, this data is not published on the petition platform; everyone who wants to contribute to the platform has to register.

The name and permanent address data of a public ePetition's so-called main petitioner ("initiator of a public petition") is published online together with the petition text (Nr. 6 of the additional Directive on public ePetitions, [18]). Signees have to register, but can choose to sign the petition under a pseudonym (created by the system). However, this only provides pseudonymity towards other users of the platform.

At the same time, the Bundestag introduced a discussion forum to allow interested parties to discuss a public petition's content. Participation in the forum discussions is only possible under a self- or system-chosen pseudonym [2]. Petitions including signee lists and contributions to the discussion forum are accessible online throughout three election periods before they are deleted.

It is questionable whether petitions may be filed online in Germany at all. The electronic form could be regarded as constitutionally excluded: According to the jurisdiction of the German constitutional court, it is constitutionally not permissible to conduct parliamentary elections in Germany solely electronically. In a parliamentary democracy the elections of the representatives are the initial and the key element of the chain of democratic legitimacy. Based in this appraisal, the German constitutional court in its grounds mainly refers to the principle of publicity of elections which is derived from Art. 38, in conjunction with Art. 20 (1) and (2) GG. The court considered the principle as affected, since the usage of electronic voting machines did not allow monitoring the actual voting process (all relevant steps from the voter's individual action to the result) without having expert knowledge [19]. However, the electoral principles only concern parliamentary or general elections and are not transferable to other democratic instruments [20]. Therefore, the petitions process is not affected by the judgement of the German constitutional court initially mentioned and can be conducted electronically (including online). But at the same time, since the electoral principles are not applicable, no rights can be derived from e.g. the principle of secrecy (Art. 38 (1) GG). In other words: The German constitution does not grant the right to be anonymous to petitioners.

Since the Bundestag – resp. its petition committee –accepts petitions that are filed via the online form provided at the Bundestag's website, the definition of "in writing" obviously has been adjusted to the modern world. This is not an exception. § 3a of the federal German Administrative Procedure Act stipulates that – if written form is mandatory by law – it may be replaced by electronic form if this is not excluded by (another) legal norm. In context with the eGovernment movement, it is often said that, in general, there are too many written form requirements (e.g. by ISPRAT, [21], p. 4).

A decrease of written form requirements to simplify or facilitate the proceedings should not have a negative impact on the reliability or sincerity of the respective declaration of intent in sensitive areas. Therefore, it needs to be considered carefully which written form requirements may be abdicable. For this, it has to be analyzed individually why written form is required first.

According to the traditional understanding, the written form requirement in Art. 17 GG is necessary because it (a) allows to identify the petitioner, (b) allows to answer the petition (send a notice), and (c) assures the seriousness of the petitioner's request ([22], marginal 61). Sometimes it is also stated that the (d) anonymous exercise of funda-mental rights is "a contradiction in terms" ([22], marginal 62).

Here, the written form requirement in Art. 17 GG itself is not to be questioned. But it will be discussed that an online petition platform that employs Privacy-ABCs could fulfill all the requirements set up by the traditional understanding of "in writing" and at the same time protect the petitioner's privacy. A system that applies Privacy-ABCs allows to "identify" the petitioner (criteria (a) from the list above), since the system guarantees that the one who participates is duly accredited. It is not necessary to know the name of the petitioner if it is assured that she exists and has the right to petition. Insofar, as the nationality or permanent residence of the petitioner is of relevance (e.g. any citizen of the European Union and any natural or legal person residing or having its registered office in a Member State can petition the European Parliament, cf. 215 (1) RoP EP), the petitioner will only have to prove the country to the system and will be allowed to file her petition. There is no need for the recipient to learn about the exact address of the petitioner.

A Privacy-ABC system allows contacting the petitioner (criteria (b)). It is possible to implement some sort of chat functionality. The petition committee could commu-nicate its decision online. Another, and probably the preferable, option could be to implement a system which offers a "sharing documents" functionality. In a Privacy-ABC-based communication system it is possible to implement a personal "Restricted Area" for every user ([23], pp. 19, 33). This allows the petition committee to upload the petition notice (as a document) to the respective petitioner's Restricted Area. Only the petitioner will have access to this area and, consequently, to the document. The system guarantees that only the petitioner can retrieve this document.

Finally, it is not reasonable that an online form can guarantee the seriousness of a petitioner's request less than, say, a post card – which, by the way, would fulfill the "in writing" requirements if signed with name (criteria (c) and (d)). Still this online form exists today and therefore apparently is regarded as compliant with the constitution. Occasionally it is even doubted that a petition to the Bundestag filed online enjoys the protection by the constitution because it does not fulfill the constitutionally prescribed form requirements ([24], p. 59). But if the public authorities open this door, a discrimination of ePetitions is not acceptable.

Due to the fact that the fundamental right to petition is meant to be exercisable as easily as possible and therefore no other procedural requirements need to be fulfilled ([25], marginal 38), it is worth to make it accessible as easy as technically and legally possible. Especially due to the fact that petitions often are regarded as the "ultimate backup" or an "emergency telephone" for the citizens ([3], p. 36), it would be inappropriate to create artificial obstacles. In contrary, all discretion should be used and bureaucratic requirements – such as a necessarily postal communication with the petitioner, once the petition is filed – rethought.

Schleswig-Holstein. In the German federal State of Schleswig-Holstein the idea of anonymous ePetitions was proposed by a Member of Parliament, but has not met with broad support by the responsible committees, yet.

The right to petition the Parliament of Schleswig-Holstein (Landtag) is not explicitly laid down in the constitution of Schleswig-Holstein, but arises from the federal constitution, which – of course – also is applicable at federal state level. The constitution of Schleswig-Holstein (abbr.: LVerf S-H) just states that the State Parliament shall establish a petition committee (Art. 19 (1) LVerf S-H). So the right to petition is not stated, but preconditioned. The procedural rules are similar to those of the Bundestag, in particular they also foresee public ePetitions. Since the minimal conditions arise from the constitution (i.e. the GG), the same approach as on German federal level (see above) should be applied here. An online platform that allows anonymous (public) ePetitions would be legally permissible.

4   Obstacles to Overcome

Since a democratic system provides instruments of participation, these instruments should be accessible and attractive to as many citizens as possible. Therefore, potential obstacles have to be removed. Based on the assumption that participating online – via an own device, from wherever the user is – is convenient, the next step is to discuss if citizens feel comfortable with raising issues and expressing their opinion towards the public authorities, and if they do not, how the offer can be improved. In the following section, major concerns regarding online petition platforms are addressed in order to show that a Privacy-ABC-based system might foster the democratic participation.

4.1   Fear of Discrimination by Other People or Public Authorities

In principle, a petition can address any subject. However, most petitions will at least indicate the political opinion of the petitioner (and the signees). The sensitivity of personal data can also result indirectly from the context ([26], rec. 56a). This may keep people from participating, since they fear negative consequences, or to be attacked for their opinion. The data protection legislation provides stricter requirements concerning the processing of data about political opinions. It is defined as sensitive data (cf. Art. 8 Dir. 95/46/EC). Against this background, the fact that a petitioner has to identify herself with her full name and permanent address towards the public authorities is unsatisfactory not only from a privacy perspective. Especially, it is incomprehensible why the name and permanent address of the initiator of a public ePetition has to become known even to the Internet public. In fact, it would be sufficient to publish the petition text and use a pseudonym here as well – as for the discussion forum, in the case of the Bundestag. On the European level public ePetitions do not exist. But in general, the European Parliament seems to be aware of the problem and thus allows exceptions from its rule to publish petition texts including the petitioners' names.

Anonymity could prevent a (theoretical) possible "there you go again" -reflex of the petition committees in cases of people who petition repeatedly. In general, anonymous petitions allow the most objective and fair decision by the petition committees, as nothing but the content (and maybe the number of signees) is known to them. In fact, very few petitioners are "heavy users". Most of the users of the Bundestag's online platform do not sign more than two petitions ([3], p. 79]. This may also mean: The fewer "troublemakers", the more likely it becomes that they are known by name.

4.2   Data Security/System Data Protection

There is a difference between "being on a list that, if any, can be consulted at a town hall" – as in case of a traditional referendum, for instance – and "being on a list that is published online". The latter is potentially considerable by the whole online world and – since the information is stored on the public authorities' servers – of course, potential target of cyber criminals (data theft). So, even if one does not fear discrimination by the public entities or other users, such security threats have to be considered. As for parliamentary elections, 57 % of the German citizens would prefer not to vote online for doubts about security in general. 37 % explicitly fear misuse of their data [27]. At the same time, nearly three out of four Germans (74 %) expect the government and business community to actively ensure online security ([28], pp. 9–10). And at least nearly 60 % of Germany's population assumes that responsibility for security and data protection on the Internet primarily rests with companies and/or the government, which they expect to create the necessary conditions ([28], p. 12).

Having said this, it is obvious that such data security problems cannot simply be solved by not publishing the names of petitioners (and signees) online. The less data is stored centrally, the better. Already if information is stored that allows re-identification or linkage to other databases, an attacker could use this information in connection with information stored in service or log files of other data controllers to identify a participant. Since with Privacy-ABCs only the information absolutely necessary is revealed to the service provider, the petition committees', resp. the parliaments', servers would have to deal only with a small amount of data (cf. Sect. 2.3). The data minimization and data avoidance principle addresses this risk. It demands that personal data must be adequate, relevant and not excessive in relation to the purposes for which they are collected and/or further processed (Art. 6 (1) (c) Dir. 95/46/EC). If an anonymous or pseudonymous mode of use is possible, the user shall have this opportunity ([26], marginal 1, 4). A Privacy-ABC-based system could fulfill the requirements arising from the data minimization and data avoidance principle.

4.3   Multiple Participation

Another issue – not from a privacy, but general eGovernment perspective – is to prevent users from participating several times. For instance, the RoP BT determine that if a public ePetition is signed by at least 50,000 people, the petitioner (or several petitioners) will be invited to a personal interview by the petition committee, while normally there is no right to be heard. Even if this may not be considered as a big issue concerning ePetitions, it can be of interest for further use cases such as citizens' initiatives and referendums. In these cases even more rights arise from the achievement of a certain quota.

The current ePetition system of the Bundestag, for instance, checks the e-mail address and the IP address of a signee ([3], p. 74). In times of dynamic IP addresses this is clearly not the most reliable method to exclude multiple participations. A Privacy-ABC system, for instance, could be implemented in a way that in case of repeated participation in the petition, only the last signature would be counted (cf. [29], p. 85; [5], p. 213).

4.4   Contact the Petitioner

As indicated above, the petition committees are legally obliged to send a note to the petitioner in order to communicate its decision. This issue has already been addressed in Sect. 3.2 when discussing reasons for the written form requirement on German federal level.

4.5   Misuse

Cases of misuse are rare under the current Bundestag system ([3], p. 15). Considering the fact that at present people could "invent" identities (e.g. by using an assumed name and creating a fake e-mail account), this is in a way remarkable. However, public authorities might fear that anonymity would open up for every conceivable kind of abuse. A public ePetition to the Bundestag is inadmissible, inter alia, if it contains obviously wrong, distorting or offensive expressions. The same holds if the content is obviously impertinent or is based on fundamentally wrong premises. In principle, deletion seems to be sufficient in such cases. But at present, the petition committee could demand criminal prosecution and provide the respective authorities with potentially identifying data, such as the IP address.

However, if a Privacy-ABC-based system including the inspection feature (as described in Sect. 2.2) was employed, the identification of the user would be regulated. Although it is explicitly not intended at this point to vote for an "all identifiable system through the back door", it might be considerable that it is fairer to let the user know the exact conditions under which her identity will be revealed. This would be the case in a Privacy-ABC system with an implemented inspection feature. At the same time, a Privacy-ABC system would provide a strong authentication. Misuse in terms of illegitimate petitions by illegitimate users could be prevented.

5 Conclusions

It was shown that all guarantees arising from the actual fundamental right to petition can be granted when introducing an anonymous ePetition system which employs Privacy-ABCs. The right to petition is designed as "low barrier" (in terms of "bureaucratic hurdles") democratic instrument and therefore the ideal environment for a completely new and innovative approach. If someone is legitimated to make use of the right to petition, the proof of this legitimization (i.e. being a citizen, living in a specific region etc.) is sufficient. Whether the concern brought up in the petition is legitimate as well is a different matter and does not depend on the person's identity.

The benefit of respecting the citizens' fundamental right to privacy is not just a goal in itself. Even if at the moment most people in Europe live in countries that respect their citizens' rights, unfortunately it cannot be granted that it will stay this way. In the recent past, the European Community has seen political developments in some Member States which indicate that the guarantees of freedom and expression are not as perfectly natural as one may wish for. They need to be watched and defended. Democracy does not work if no one participates due to fear of consequences. Instruments like the petition are a comparatively easy way to report wrongdoing. They deserve reasonable assistance and support from the democratic forces that can be offered.

References

1. Märker, O., Wehner, J.: E-Participation. In: Zechner, A. (ed.) E-Government Guide Germany, pp. 355–369. Fraunhofer IRB Verlag, Stuttgart (2007)
2. Deutscher Bundestag: Petition zur Veröffentlichung einreichen (2015). https://epetitionen.bundestag.de/epet/peteinreichen/oeffentlich.schritt1.html. Accessed 9 March 2015
3. Riehm, U., Böhle, K., Lindner, R.: Elektronische Petitionssysteme: Analysen zur Modernisierung des parlamentarischen Petitionswesens in Deutschland und Europa. Edition sigma, Berlin (2013). http://www.itas.kit.edu/pub/v/2013/riua13a.pdf. Accessed 9 March 2015
4. Bieker, F., Hansen, M., Zwingelberg, H.: Towards a privacy-preserving inspection process for authentication solutions with conditional identification. In: Hühnlein, D., Roßnagel, H. (eds.) Proceeings of Open Identity Summit 2014. Lecture Notes in Informatics, vol. P-237, pp. 85–96. Gesellschaft für Informatik, Bonn (2014). http://subs.emis.de/LNI/Proceedings/Proceedings237/article2.html. Accessed 9 March 2015

5. Diaz, C., Kosta, E., Dekeyser, H., Kohlweiss, M., Nigusse, G.: Privacy preserving electronic petitions. Identity Inf. Soc. 1(1), 203–219 (2008). Springer, Netherlands

6. Article 29 Data Protection Working Party: Opinion 05/2014 on Anonymisation Techniques. WP 216. Adopted on 10 April 2014. http://ec.europa.eu/justice/data-protection/article-29/documentation/opinion-recommendation/files/2014/wp216_en.pdf. Accessed 9 March 2015

7. Abendroth, J., Bcheri, S., Krontiris, I., Liagkou, V., Sabouri, A., Schlehahn, E., Veseli, F., Zwingelberg, H.: ABC4Trust D5.2a Amendment Building Blocks of ABC Technology. Deliverable of the ABC4Trust Project (2013). https://abc4trust.eu/download/ABC4Trust-D5.2a_Amendment_Building_Blocks_of_ABC_Technology.pdf. Accessed 9 March 2015

8. Bcheri, S., Damgård, K.L., Deibler, D., Goetze, N., Knudsen, H.G., Moneta, M., Pyrgelis, A., Schlehahn, E., Stausholm, M.B., Zwingelberg, H.: ABC4Trust D5.3 Experiences and Feedback of the Pilots. Deliverable of the ABC4Trust Project (2014). https://abc4trust.eu/download/D5.3_ExperiencesAndFeedback_Final.pdf. Accessed 9 March 2015

9. EU Network of Independent Experts on Fundamental Rights: Commentary of the Charter of Fundamental Rights of the European Union (2006). http://ec.europa.eu/justice/fundamental-rights/files/networkcommentaryfinal_en.pdf. Accessed 9 March 2015

10. Article 29 Data Protection Working Party: Opinion 4/2007 on the Concept of Personal Data. WP 136. Adopted on 20 June 2007. http://ec.europa.eu/justice/policies/privacy/docs/wpdocs/2007/wp136_en.pdf. Accessed 9 March 2015

11. Deutscher Bundestag: Nutzungsbedingungen (2015). https://epetitionen.bundestag.de/epet/service.$$$.rubrik.nutzungsbedingungen.html. Accessed 9 March 2015

12. VG Berlin, 1. Kammer: Datenschutzrechtliche Anordnung im Fall der Speicherung von Beschäftigtendaten. Urteil vom 13. Januar 2014, 1 K 220.12 (2014). http://www.gerichtsentscheidungen.berlin-brandenburg.de/jportal/portal/t/279b/bs/10/page/sammlung.psml?pid=Dokumentanzeige&showdoccase=1&js_peid=Trefferliste&documentnumber=1&numberofresults=1&fromdoctodoc=yes&doc.id=JURE140003569&doc.part=L&doc.price=0.0#focuspoint. Accessed 9 March 2015

13. Bundesgerichtshof: Urteil vom 1. Juli 2014 – VI ZR 345/13 (2014)

14. Bundesverfassungsgericht: BVerfGE 2, 225 – Beschluß des Ersten Senats vom 22. April 1953 – 1 BvR 162/51 (1953)

15. European Court of Justice: Judgment of the General Court (Sixth Chamber) of 14 September 2011. Ingo-Jens Tegebauer v European Parliament. Right to petition – Petition addressed to the Parliament – Decision to take no action – Action for annulment – Actionable measure – Admissibility – Obligation to state reasons. Case T-308/07 (2011). http://curia.europa.eu/juris/liste.jsf?language=en&num=T-308/07. Accessed 9 March 2015

16. European Court of Justice: Judgment of the General Court (Sixth Chamber) of 27 September 2012. J v European Parliament. Right of petition – Petition addressed to the European Parliament – Decision to take no further action – Action for annulment – Duty to state reasons – Petition not falling within an area of activity of the European Union. Case T-160/10 (2012). http://curia.europa.eu/juris/liste.jsf?language=en&num=T-160/10. Accessed 9 March 2015

17. Uerpmann-Witzack, R.: Artikel 17 GG. In: Münch, I., Kunig, P. (eds.) Grundgesetz-Kommentar, vol. 1, 6th edn. Verlag C.H. Beck, Munich (2012)

18. Deutscher Bundestag: Richtlinie für die Behandlung von öffentlichen Petitionen (öP) gem. Ziff 7.1 (4) der Verfahrensgrundsätze (Engl.: Directive on the Treatment of Public Petitions according to Nr. 7.1 (4) of the Rules of Procedure). https://www.bundestag.de/blob/190940/c0cbbd627e20fcc1519b03dc61db40f3/richtlinie_oeffentliche_petitionen-data.pdf. Accessed 9 March 2015

19. Bundesverfassungsgericht: Urteil des Zweiten Senats vom 3. März 2009 – 2 BvC 3/07, 2 BvC 4/07 (2009). https://www.bundesverfassungsgericht.de/entscheidungen/cs20090303_2bvc000307.html. Accessed 9 March 2015

20. Bundesverfassungsgericht: Beschluss vom 16. Juli 1998 – 2 BvR 1953/95 (1998). http://www.bundesverfassungsgericht.de/SharedDocs/Entscheidungen/DE/1998/07/rs19980716_2bvr195395.html. Accessed 9 March 2015

21. ISPRAT(Interdisziplinäre Studien zu Politik, Recht, Administration und Technologie e.V.): Stellungnahme zum Referentenentwurf der Bundesregierung eines Gesetzes zur Förderung der elektronischen Verwaltung sowie zur Änderung weiterer Vorschriften (E-Government-Gesetz) (2012). http://isprat.net/fileadmin/downloads/pdfs/20120618__ISPRAT_Stellungnahme_E-Government-Gesetz.pdf. Accessed 9 March 2015

22. Klein, H.H.: Artikel 17 GG. In: Maunz, T., Dürig, G. (eds.) Kommentar zum Grundgesetz. Loose-leaf booklet. Verlag C.H. Beck, Münch (2011)

23. Bcheri, S., Björk, E., Deibler, D., Hånell, G., Lerch, J., Moneta, M., Orski, M., Schlehahn, E., Tesfay, W.: ABC4Trust D6.3 Evaluation of the School Pilot. Deliverable of the ABC4Trust Project (2014). https://abc4trust.eu/download/Deliverable%20D6.3.pdf. Accessed 9 March 2015

24. Kellner, M.: Die E-Petition zum Bundestag: Ein Danaergeschenk. Neue Justiz **61**(2), 56–59 (2007). Nomos, Baden-Baden

25. Krings, G.: Artikel 17 GG. In: Friauf, K.H., Höfling, W. (eds.) Berliner Kommentar Zum Grundgesetz. Loose-leaf booklet. Erich Schmidt Verlag, Cologne (2014)

26. Gola, P., Schomerus, R.: § 3 BDSG. In: Gola, P., Schomerus, R. (eds.) BDSG Bundesdatenschutzgesetz, 11th edn. Verlag C.H. Beck, Munich (2012)

27. DIVSI Deutsches Institut für Vertrauen und Sicherheit im Internet: DIVSI Milieu Study on Trust and Security on the Internet – Condensed Version. Hamburg (2012). https://www.divsi.de/publikationen/studien/divsi-decision-maker-study-on-trust-and-security-on-the-internet-condensed-version/. Accessed 9 March 2015

28. DIVSI Deutsches Institut für Vertrauen und Sicherheit im Internet: Jeder Zweite möchte online wählen. Press release, 13 August 2013. https://www.divsi.de/jeder-zweite-moechte-online-waehlen/. Accessed 9 March 2015

29. Deibler, D., Engeler, M., Krontiris, I., Liagkou, V., Pyrgelis, A., Schlehahn, E., Stamatiou, Y., Tesfay, W., Zwingelberg, H.: ABC4Trust D7.3 Evaluation of the Student Pilot. Deliverable of the ABC4Trust Project (2014). https://abc4trust.eu/download/Deliverable%20D7.3.pdf. Accessed 9 March 2015

A Brief Evaluation of Icons in the First Reading of the European Parliament on COM (2012) 0011

John Sören Pettersson[(✉)]

Information Systems, Karlstad University, Karlstad, Sweden
john_soren.pettersson@kau.se

Abstract. We present the result of a small-scale test in which the participants failed to understand the graphic scheme as well as the pictographic parts of the icons appearing in the Annex to Article 13a of the European Parliament legislative resolution of 12 March 2014 on the Proposal for a regulation of the European Parliament and of the Council on the protection of individuals with regard to the processing of personal data and on the free movement of such data (General Data Protection Regulation), COM (2012) 0011.

Keywords: Usable privacy · EU regulations · Computer icons

1 Informed Consent and UI Objects that Make a User Understand Privacy Policies

The principle of "informed consent" as prescribed by national laws and EU directives [3] makes it necessary to inform users about all the intended data processing when they submit data. Conveying the sometimes highly complex clauses of privacy policies to the subjects concerned is generally hard. The solution of providing situated or "just-in-time" information to internet service users has been discussed and investigated in several projects and reports. At the same time, it is known that for psychological reasons it might be hard to divert a user's attention from the primary goals of a transaction to the details of privacy policies.

In order to solve the problem of these competing requirements, expandable short texts as well as icons have been proposed by different authors and project teams (see for instance the overview and discussions in [2], esp. Chap. 2 and Sect. 5.5.2). This report takes a look at the icons appearing in Annex 1 to Article 13a of [5], which is a European Parliament document on a proposal [4] for new EU regulations.[1]

The set of icons presented in the Annex raises some questions. Are these icons as suggestive of the content as intended? The proposal states that icons, texts (= verbal

---

[1] "Compromise amendments on Articles 1–29". COMP0 Article 1. 07.10.2013 [5]. Later adopted as the "European Parliament legislative resolution of 12 March 2014 on the Proposal for a regulation of the European Parliament and of the Council on the protection of individuals with regard to the processing of personal data and on the free movement of such data (General Data Protection Regulation)." COM (2012) 11. Brussels, 25.1.2012 [6].

© IFIP International Federation for Information Processing 2015
J. Camenisch et al. (Eds.): Privacy and Identity 2014, IFIP AICT 457, pp. 125–135, 2015.
DOI: 10.1007/978-3-319-18621-4_9

statements of "essential information"), and a kind of evaluation of whether or not the statements are met shall all be presented in a table. However, as experienced in several experiments, indications of deviations from desired conditions should be marked close to the corresponding fields for entering data or close to any OK or ACCEPT button rather than in a separate window or as a text that the user is likely to scroll away from in order to find the OK button. It is therefore of interest to see how a user would understand the icons in themselves, especially if understood as implied by Annex 1 so that they can be used in notifications and not only in the table (otherwise a user interface designer might end up having two sets of icons with similar meanings).

Furthermore, as the table presents evaluations which are made according to a desired policy, the composition of statements and evaluation symbols is of interest to investigate. (The statements stating the desired policy are called "essential information" in Annex 1.)

In order to assess the suitability of this graphic scheme as well as the pictographic parts of the icons, a minor survey was made with Media and Communication undergraduates to see how they comprehend the icons. Here we report on the thoughts behind the design of the survey and on the results that came out of it. The paper is structured as follows:

Section 2 presents the bulk of Annex 1.

Section 3 explains the rationale of the questionnaire used in the survey.

Section 4 summarizes the results of the survey.

Section 5, finally, presents some further thoughts on the composition of icons for information and alerts.

2   Article 13a and Annex 1 of the Proposed Amendments from 2013

The first page of Annex 1 is here reproduced in Fig. 1 together with Fig. 2 showing two symbols (a) and (b) which are to be inserted in the right-hand column of the table. It is important to note that the table in Fig. 1 is not included in the official amendment text of 2014 [6]. This is probably just a mistake and accordingly we have to refer to the 2013 document [5].

The Annex thus presents a table which matches icons to "essential information" and then continues by explaining that the symbols (a) and (b) will be used in the third column if the conditions in the second column are met or not met, respectively. It is also stated specifically that the words in bold are supposed to be in bold.

As a side note, the information in the first three rows can be questioned. For instance, row 1: the demand of the regulation should rather be that *all* purposes are given than that certain data collections are marked as superfluous for the purposes given. Nevertheless, it can be argued that the sentences and the corresponding icons might be used in slightly modified versions for summaries before data disclosures or later in incident reports.

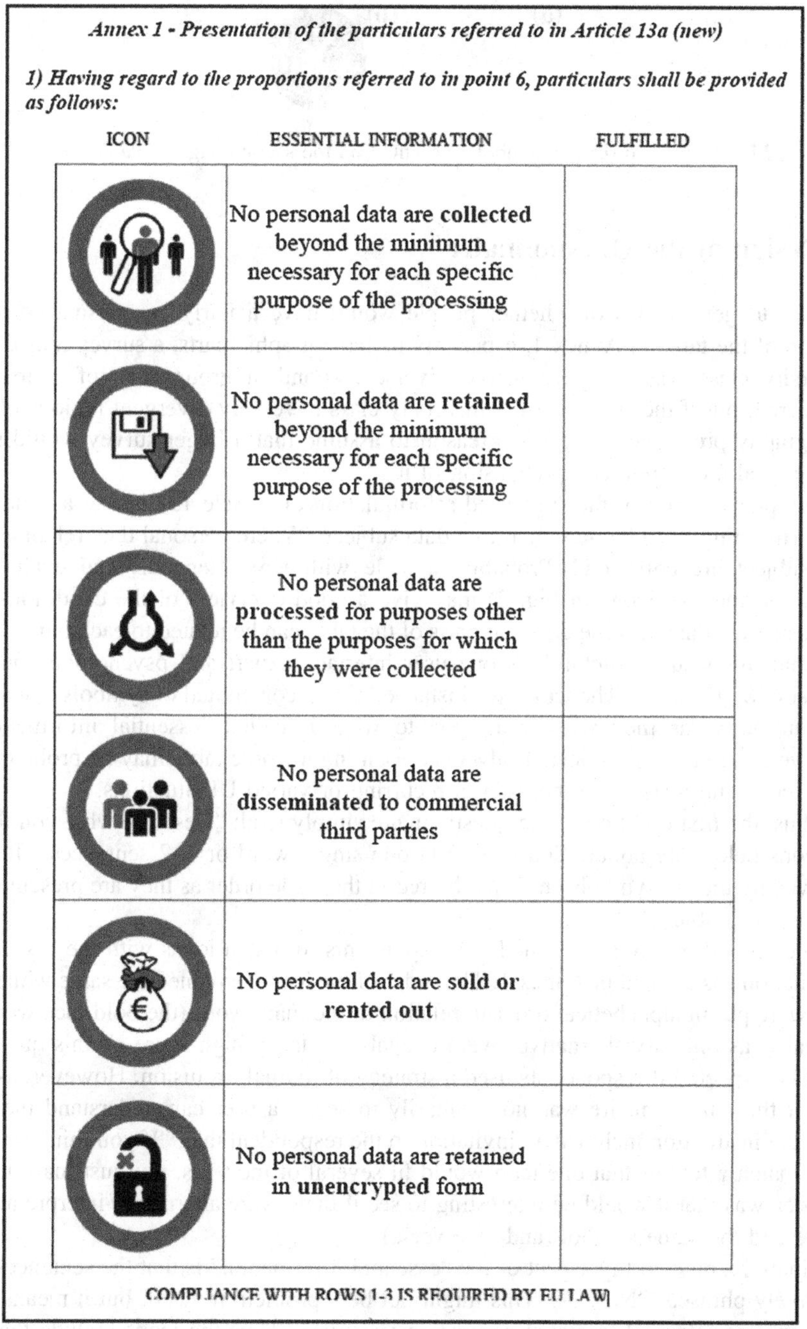

ICON	ESSENTIAL INFORMATION	FULFILLED
Annex 1 - Presentation of the particulars referred to in Article 13a (new)		
1) Having regard to the proportions referred to in point 6, particulars shall be provided as follows:		
	No personal data are **collected** beyond the minimum necessary for each specific purpose of the processing	
	No personal data are **retained** beyond the minimum necessary for each specific purpose of the processing	
	No personal data are processed for purposes other than the purposes for which they were collected	
	No personal data are **disseminated** to commercial third parties	
	No personal data are **sold or rented out**	
	No personal data are retained in **unencrypted** form	

COMPLIANCE WITH ROWS 1-3 IS REQUIRED BY EU LAW

Fig. 1. First page of Annex 1 in [5]

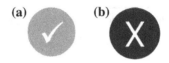

Fig. 2. (a) and (b) are symbols presented on the second page of Annex 1.

3 Design of the Questionnaire

In order to get an idea of whether people would have a fairly consensual comprehension of the table in Annex 1, especially its iconographic parts, a survey aimed at a university class was designed. More diverse respondent groups can of course be considered, but if the students of a university class have very divergent notions of the iconography presented, there is no reason to assume that a larger survey would suddenly reveal a coherent comprehension of it.

The presumption of the suggested reformulation of Article 13a is that a table can easily (meaningfully) be presented to a data subject "Where personal data relating to a data subject are collected". Probably, a table with icons, legends, and evaluation indicators (the two icons in Fig. 2) may give a good overview of the conditions for processing the data because different parts of the table can be related to each other. "We seek and use visual structure" as one user interface expert and psychologist puts it (Johnson [8], Chap. 3). The icons, for instance, can be constituted of symbols that seem quite arbitrary, as they will occur next to what is called "essential information". However, as remarked in Sect. 1, always presenting a whole table may be problematic if the icons and texts are to be used in recurring or varied UI situations.

Thus, the first question in the questionnaire simply read: "Describe what you think the icons below are about. You can write one single word or 1–2 sentences." It was followed by the six symbols encircled by red in the same order as they are presented in the Annex 1 table.

The second question requested the respondents to match icons with the "essential information" as defined in Annex 1. The order of the icons remained the same while the texts were put in alphabetical order in relation to the main word (the bold face words). Naturally, as only six alternatives were available, a fairly high score on this question could be expected if respondents used a strategy of mutual exclusion. However, as the goal of this questionnaire was not primarily to see if a user can understand the full table, the instruction included an invitation to the respondent that, "If you think several icons match a text or that one icon would fit several of the texts, you just mark that." The idea was that it would be interesting to see if there were alternative interpretations of one and the same symbol (and vice versa).

Finally, a noteworthy aspect of the "essential information" is that the sentences are negatively phrased ("No ..."). This might not be a problem in itself, but it means that the icons are intended to signal a negative statement. Thus the icons include the red circle found in traffic signs. However, a red circle with a diagonal bar is presumably more obvious in terms of indicating a negative statement. This is the first problem one can envisage: the proposed icons try to make a compositional statement with an unwanted condition in the middle and a red circle around it to signal, "It is not the case that…".

The situation is further complicated by the third column of the table, where an indicator is supposed to be inserted to signal whether or not the assertion of the composite statement will be fulfilled. The symbol (a) in Fig. 2 is presumably understood as affirmative, but the symbol (b) in fact means that "It is not the case that the statement in the left and middle column will be fulfilled." Thus, for each row with a red cross, the message should be interpreted as: "It's not the case that it's not the case that…".

To see if people were prone to generate such interpretations, the third question was placed above a depicted sample row, and ran as follows: "When you are about to enter some personal data at a site, you notice the row below. What do you think the site is trying to say?"

The questionnaire can be found in a working paper with English translations [11]. Admittedly, there are points where the design of the study can be questioned. For instance, situating the icons (or the whole table) on actual web pages would have been fairer to the proposal. On the other hand, research projects such as PRIME, PrimeLife, and A4Cloud have made clear that there are functions which would provide similar information to data subjects but without the purpose of giving consent (cf. in particular the *Data Track* [1, 2, 12], Sect. 5.3.1). A user interface designer should not end up having two sets of icons with similar meanings; thus, there are reasons to explore how generally understandable the icons in Fig. 1 are. Likewise, there are reasons to investigate how understandable the doubling of negations is.

Pilot Questionnaire: Before the questionnaire was handed out to the class, four people were asked to read the introduction and answer the questions. The pilot group of respondents comprised one administrator, two academic psychologists, and finally one student union representative. The introduction was slightly rephrased after the first pilot run of the test. Moreover it was obvious that the "necessary information" texts had to be given in Swedish (for instance, a word like *dissemination* was not understood by all pilot testers). The order of the texts was not rearranged when Swedish translations were inserted.

4 Summary of the Answers and Some Implications for UI Design

The questionnaire was handed out to an undergraduate class in "Visual communication and design". Everyone was willing to participate, which provided 21 responses. The answers (translated into English) are given in [11].[2]

---

[2] Credits to Julio Angulo for distributing and collecting the questionnaire, to Malin Wik for discussing the translations of the received responses, and to Sofie Liljeborg for the initial draft translations of icon texts.

In question 1, only one respondent, #21, understood the red circle as some kind of negation. The question (translated into English) was: **Describe what you think the icons below are about. You can write one single word or 1–2 sentences.**

We present one example here. It is the 21 comments to the first icon in Fig. 1. Notably, only respondent #21 starts his/her answer with a negative phrase, "not search…". In the list, alternative translations are given in parentheses. Multiple answers are given on separate lines.

Description(s) given

1. search for people (people search)
   more info about the person
2. Detailed information
3. Examination (check, inspection)
4. Search information about a person
5. Examination of an individual
6. Alert (warning) about surveillance
7. Find a person
8. Personal data
9. Identification of person
10. Inspection area
11. This icon means that the page looks up personal data about you, the user
12. Save data [personal data]
13. In order to search person …?
14. Background information
    personal data
15. ?
16. Person check
17. Investigate
18. Investigate deeper (closer)
19. Check (examination) of personal data
20. Searching for people (People search)
21. not search on persons (not searching for people/individuals).

All in all, the interpretation deviated quite often from the concepts intended in Annex 1 of the proposal. Considering how many times the phrase "personal data" is used in the introduction, it is disappointing to see how few references to privacy policy issues are found in the answers. The Swedish term for personal data, *personuppgifter*, seems however to have influenced the wording in some answers as some respondents have used the Swedish non-technical term *uppgifter* rather than *data* or *information*, which in this case would be completely synonymous with *uppgifter*.

Question 2 "Try to match": Only one respondent made multiple matchings so a simple evaluation of the result is reached by counting the total number of correct matches for each respondent. On average, it was not very high:

Matches	6	5	4	3	2	1	0	
Number	4	1	3	6	5	1	1	= 21

A more thorough inspection of the answers, however, reveals that the translation of "are retained" to *bevaras* may have confused respondents, since the standard Swedish term for saving files in computer programs is *Spara* and this word is often associated with the floppy disk symbol. Choosing *Sparas* instead of *bevaras* in the questionnaire might have raised the number of all-corrects with some 25–50 %.[3]

The lesson to be drawn from this is that if icons are used that distinctly resemble well-known icons from other user interfaces, the wording in each language must match the standard "textual" translation of the icon. Thus, the intended message must be conveyed in the same words and also be close in meaning to the standard use of the icon + word.

In question 3, icon number three gets a definitive interpretation because the icon and the "essential information" are put together just as in the table in the Annex of the amendments. This of course influenced the respondents and it explains why the answers actually deviate from the explanations provided by the respondents in relation to the same icon in question 1. What is interesting is instead that in spite of the "essential information" provided in the table row, many respondents extended the meaning to cover also the forwarding of data. Four examples are included here:

Description(s) given

1. Personal info is not shared with third party
2. Info will not be furthered to other parties, will not be used
3. The information is not shared with others.
4. One will not share the [personal] data.

Moreover, as the icon and the textual statement were combined with the red cross-out icon (Fig. 2b), the meaning should be interpreted as "It is not the case that the statement is valid." However, from the four samples just quoted, and all other answers, it is obvious that the system of negation of negation presupposed by the table semantics does not work. Perhaps equally telling is the fact that respondent #21 (like two others) left no comments to this question. One can of course not draw any definitive conclusion

---

[3] It is to be noted that the Swedish Personal Data Act from 1998 [10] hardly uses any word for passively storing data: *lagring* and *lagra* ('store') occur 1 + 3 = 4 times, but otherwise *behandla* ('to process') is used while the person is called 'the registered person'. The words for collecting, registering, organizing, and storing are used in the same sentence in the initial definition of *behandling*, 'processing', which seems to differentiate between registering and storing, but the differentiation is not drawn upon as all concepts are collected under 'to process'.

from only one case, but it is highly suggestive that the only respondent that seemed to have grasped the negation indicated by the red circle gave up when it came to the double negation of red circle plus red cross-out.

5 Some Further Thoughts on Future UI Design

For the future, the different needs of different user interface designs should be considered. For instance, icons do not have to make statements but rather only indicate area; this is appropriate when an icon is only used to open a table or dialog box which outlines the conditions of the particular data request made by that particular service provider. The icon then has a classifying function (a headline function). In order to call the data subject's attention to a specific and potentially problematic fact, a classifying icon can get a warning triangle superscript. The composition can still function as a place to click or hover over when one wants to read more.

There might be other alerts a user wants to receive than the ones prescribed by an EU directive. Therefore, customer-tailored integration of alerts must be considered.

Additionally, the information texts do not cover all the information that could be conceived as pertinent for cloud processing. The "essential information" may need to be extended and then icons or parts of icons may need to be reused.

Now let us turn to the ecology of the icons. It has already been mentioned above that situating the icons from the amendments in a web-based scenario might have increased their correct interpretation. Even if the reported survey was argued to provide meaningful data in spite of this, it is worthwhile to bring up the issue of situational interpretation for a final discussion to illuminate pitfalls and promises.

We will refer to two experiments conducted within the A4Cloud project ([7], chap. 3). In one of them, a paper-based mockup was used to see how test subjects would respond to a set of icons. The mockup was used to demonstrate a hotel booking scenario.[4] In a post-questionnaire, there were two icons to express the portability and non-portability of personal data to the data subject when he/she terminates a service contract. Graphical designers had provided us with icons that suggested a portfolio in the shape of a case. A few participants in the experiment interpreted this icon as signaling something to do with travelling, e.g. "OK to bring luggage" and "No help with the luggage". Hardly the kind of interpretations we had anticipated in a set of privacy policy icons, but of course, in a specific scenario centered on hotel booking this was not too far-fetched. To create effective privacy tools for the future, one must consider the possibility that, initially, people who are presented with a set of icons may believe that the icons are event-specific rather than general and that such a belief may lead to misunderstandings. (These responses also illuminate why general functional categories for icons, such as for instance the ones recently presented by Jakob Nielsen [9], do not offer any a priori help in design work: the correct applications of a category are not obvious until after user testing.)

---

[4] Credits to Henrik Andersson for producing the mockup and collecting the data.

The other experiment was a survey of the same kind as the one reported here. To illuminate the effect that the situation can have on the apprehension of the same set of icons, it is interesting to contrast responses in this survey to responses to a similar questionnaire in the mockup-based scenario mentioned in the last paragraph: one question displayed alternative symbols for the area where EU regulations are applicable. A simple EU symbol (blue with the letters "EU" encircled by yellow stars) might be questioned as there are some non-EU countries that also follow EU regulations. As the questionnaire explained: "Some states outside the EU also follow EU regulations. Together with EU they form EEA – The European Economic Area (EU + Iceland, Lichtenstein and Norway)." The respondents in both questionnaires were asked "What symbol would you prefer is used to show that data processing takes place inside EEA?" The icons they could choose among were the three depicted in Fig. 3. In all three cases, the icon legends read "DATA PROCESSED INSIDE THE EUROPEAN ECONOMIC AREA".[5]

The survey respondents, who had no other priming to this set of icons than the explanation that EAA is not identical with EU, all voted for one of the EEA icons except for three persons as Fig. 3 shows ($N = 49$). On the other hand, in the small mockup-based evaluation of icons ($N = 10$), the respondents had in the mockup seen the ordinary EU logo indicating data processing within the countries regimented by EU regulations. The scenario would have been less casual if there had been prior discussions of the political extension of supranational regulations why we had avoided to use any of the two EEA icons. This conditioning seems to have had a strong influence on the answers as nearly all respondents in this test preferred the common EU logo despite the icon legend matching the EEA explanation in the question.

	Questionnaire the only priming	EU symbol priming in mockup
EEA (DATA PROCESSED INSIDE EUROPEAN ECONOMIC AREA)	13 "avoid confusion with EU"	1
★EEA★ (DATA PROCESSED INSIDE EUROPEAN ECONOMIC AREA)	33 "an inspired combination of a well-known symbol and a new content"	1
★EU★ (DATA PROCESSED INSIDE EUROPEAN ECONOMIC AREA)	3	8 "easier to understand"

Fig. 3. Acceptance of new symbols with typical arguments from respondents.

---

[5] Credits to Jessica Edlom and Mia Toresson for the icons. Credits to Elisabeth Wennö and Anna Linzie for a professional language check of the entire document.

These results show how volatile results can be, how much they depend on the design of the investigation (and this problem cannot be remedied by means of a larger number of respondents; the proportions might be the same more or less for the same priming factor). At the same time, there is also the promise that if standardized information policies are designed with due consideration of the "total" user interfaces of web sites and specific privacy tools, and vice versa, then correct understanding may be facilitated far beyond what an individual icon or icon legend can manage. Another implication should also be stressed; in relation to user testing, namely, that such contextual features should be reported so that workable UI solutions are presented with information on the contextual background – we are tempted to say *enabling* background.

Acknowledgements. Credits to Elisabeth Wennö and Anna Linzie for a professional language check of the entire document.

References

1. Angulo, J., Fischer-Hübner, S., Wästlund, E., Pulls, T.: Towards usable privacy policy display and management. Inf. Manag. Comput. Secur. **20**(1), 4–17 (2012)
2. Angulo, J., Fischer-Hübner, S., Pettersson, J.S.: General HCI principle and guidelines for accountability and transparency in the cloud. Deliverable D:C-7.1 within the A4Cloud project (2013). http://www.a4cloud.eu/deliverables
3. European Commission: Directive 95/46/EC of the European Parliament and of the Council of 24 October 1995 on the protection of individuals with regard to the processing of personal data and on the free movement of such data. Office Journal L. 281, 23 November 1995
4. European Commission: Proposal for a Regulation of the European Parliament and of the Council on the protection of individuals with regard to the processing of personal data and on the free movement of such data (General Data Protection Regulation). COM (2012) 11 Final. Brussels, 25 January 2012
5. European Parliament: Compromise amendements on Articles 1–29. COMP Article 1. 7 October 2013. www.europarl.europa.eu/meetdocs/2009_2014/documents/libe/dv/comp_am_art_01-29/comp_am_art_01-29en.pdf
6. European Parliament: European Parliament legislative resolution of 12 March 2014 on the proposal for a regulation of the European Parliament and of the Council on the protection of individuals with regard to the processing of personal data and on the free movement of such data (General Data Protection Regulation) (COM(2012)0011 – C7-0025/2012 – 2012/0011 (COD)) (Ordinary legislative procedure: first reading) (2014). http://www.europarl.europa.eu/sides/getDoc.do?type=TA&reference=P7-TA-2014-0212&language=EN
7. Fischer-Hübner, S., Pettersson, J.S. (eds.): Report on end-user perceptions of privacy-enhancing transparency and accountability. Deliverable D:C-7.3 within the A4Cloud project (2014). http://www.a4cloud.eu/deliverables
8. Johnson, J.: Designing with the Mind in Mind, 2nd edn. Morgan Kaufmann, San Francisco (2014)
9. Nielsen, J. Icon classification: Resemblance, reference, and arbitrary icons (2014), http://www.nngroup.com/articles/classifying-icons/

10. Personal Data Act (Swedish "Personuppgiftslagen") (1998). http://www.government.se/content/1/c6/01/55/42/b451922d.pdf
11. Pettersson, J.S.: A brief evaluation of icons suggested for use in standardised information policies. Referring to the Annex in the first reading of the European Parliament on COM (2012) 0011. Working paper, Karlstad University. urn:nbn:se:kau:diva-32217 (2014)
12. Pettersson, J.S., Fischer-Hübner, S., Bergmann, M.: Outlining "Data Track": Privacy-friendly Data Maintenance for End-users. In: Nilsson, A.G., et al. (eds.) Advances in Information Systems Development, vol. 1, pp. 215–226. Springer, Heidelberg (2007)

Privacy by Design and Privacy Patterns

Privacy by Design – The Case of Automated Border Control

Pagona Tsormpatzoudi$^{(\boxtimes)}$, Diana Dimitrova,
Jessica Schroers, and Els Kindt

Interdisciplinary Centre for Law and ICT/Center for Intellectual Property,
KU Leuven, Leuven, Belgium
{pagona.tsormpatzoudi,diana.dimitrova,
jessica.schroers,els.kindt}@law.kuleuven.be

Abstract. Function creep, i.e. when the purpose specification principle is breached, is a major challenge for personal data processing operations. This is especially a clear risk in the field of Identity Management when biometric data are deployed. The concept of privacy by design, set forth in the data protection reform, could, in principle, contribute to mitigating function creep. An implementation is discussed hereunder in relation to Automated Border Control ('ABC').

Keywords: Function creep · Automated border control · ABC · Identity management · Biometric data · Privacy by design · Automated erasure · Attribute based credentials · Pseudo-identities

1 Introduction

In the era of globalization, mobility becomes fast and easy. People on touristic or professional travels flood airports, which becomes a challenge for border authorities. Automated Border Control is proposed by some as a solution. While there is no formal definition yet, ABC is understood as an automated system which performs several border control functions: travel document authentication, verification that the traveller is the rightful holder of this document, database checks, and automated verification that the entry conditions are fulfilled (FRONTEX 2012; European Commission 2013).

ABC represents a new concept and trend in the technologies for external border control in the EU. External border control refers to the entry and exit checks carried out at the external borders of the Schengen Member States[1] (e.g. when one travels between Poland and Costa Rica), as the internal checks between the Schengen States have been abolished (e.g. between France and Germany). ABC in the EU is designed for people traveling internationally, which means crossing the external borders of the EU. External borders can be Schengen borders but also some EU non-Schengen bor-ders, e.g. UK. While national ABCs are different from one another and are currently primarily used by EU/EEA/CH citizens, proposals are being made to allow certain Third-Country

---

[1] All EU Member States, except the UK, Ireland, Bulgaria, Romania, Cyprus, Croatia, but including 4 non-EU Member States: Iceland, Norway, Liechtenstein and Switzerland.

© IFIP International Federation for Information Processing 2015
J. Camenisch et al. (Eds.): Privacy and Identity 2014, IFIP AICT 457, pp. 139–152, 2015.
DOI: 10.1007/978-3-319-18621-4_10

Nationals to use it as well (see Smart Borders Package). Thus, the future might bring an increasing number of travellers from all over the world using ABC.

At the same time, the amount of existing and available data has globally exploded. This amount of data is often too big to be traditionally managed and from this factor the notion of Big Data emerged. Viktor Mayer-Schöneberger and Kenneth Cukier describe Big Data as "things one can do at a large scale that cannot be done at a smaller scale" which could change the relationship between citizens and governments (Mayer-Schöneberger & Cukier 2013). What is special about this, is that Big Data is the "technique to mine relevant patterns from stored or even streaming data" (Hildebrandt 2013). A common criticism with regard to big data is that much information is collected to the largest possible amount whereas the patterns emerging from it will determine how data will be used later (Andrejevic 2014). The use of big data analytics can bring a lot of advantages, since their claimed main potential is "the ability to uncover new purposes in the data which may create a win-win situation" (Hildebrandt 2013). However, Big Data might also give rise to function creep, as it might enable data processing activities for purposes not foreseen when the data was initially collected.

In such a context and taking into account the opportunities that emerging technologies, such as ABC, are able to offer, traveller data is often of interest for law enforcement. Even though crossing the border is related to the protection of public and national security, the act of crossing a border is not registered and is not a criminal act per se. Thus, in general, the processing of personal data in a border control context and subsequently by ABC falls within the Directive 95/46/EC soon to be replaced by the proposed General Data Protection Regulation.[2] Therefore, the purpose specification principle of article 6(1) b of the Directive applies and has to be considered in the case of ABC. Hence, the purpose should be clearly defined and personal data, especially biometric data, when used, for example for border control purposes, should not be further processed in ways incompatible with those purposes.

The same Directive 95/46/EC provides in article 13 for derogations on different grounds that provide the possibility to deviate from the principle of purpose specification, for example, in case of the prevention of criminal offences, national and public security on a case-by-case basis and when safeguards are put in place.

In this paper, we first examine ABC as an identity management application and its risks. We present the specificities of ABC as a new trend in border control, and we dive into the concept and factors that trigger function creep (Sect. 2). Later on, we explore the potential of the concept of Privacy by Design to present some measures for privacy preserving ABC, by proposing certain privacy enhancing technologies as viable technical applications (Sect. 3). Finally, we conclude that Privacy by Design is an approach which certainly offers many advantages but that the peculiarities of certain applications, such as ABC, require particular attention and further specifications (Sect. 4).

---

[2] The data processed by the Schengen Information System II (Council Decision 2007/533/JHA) on wanted persons and objects, consulted occasionally when EU/EEA/CH cross external borders of the EU, is not subject to Directive 95/46/EC.

2 From Manual to Automated Border Control: New Trend, New Challenges

2.1 ABC as a New Trend in Border Control

The number of e-Gates[3] and national ABC programmes throughout the EU has been growing (e.g. No-Q and PRIVIUM in the Netherlands; PARAFE in France).[4] Depending on the national implementation, some systems rely on prior registration into a programme. Other systems do not require a prior registration and they are based on verification of the facial or fingerprint image against the chip of the EU biometric passport.

Currently, border checks are regulated by the Schengen Borders Code (SBC). The SBC, however, does not constitute a sufficient legal basis for ABC, as it regulates the process as carried out by border guards, not by self-service e-Gates (article 7 and 15 SBC). To solve the problem of the missing legal basis, national authorities either amended their national laws or used article 7 of Directive 95/46/EC. Those national ABC programmes that rely on consent (article 7 a), must ensure that consent is informed and freely given (article 2 h). Travellers must be informed about how, why and by whom their data are going to be processed and how they can exercise their rights as data subjects. In addition, consent implies a voluntary act, which requires the existence of a viable alternative (Art. 29 WP 2012), i.e. a real opportunity to choose between ABC and manual border control.

We will examine the case of automation of the manual border checks for EU/EEA/CH citizens; in case of Third-Country Nationals the process is more complex.

2.2 ABC as Identity Management Application

Identity management at the Schengen borders raises the issue of trust. The Schengen Member States must ensure that the used token(s) and identifier(s) to claim/verify traveller identity are reliable, and not fake, forged, or stolen. Passports are in general considered to provide reliable identification although they can still be counterfeit or forged. In order to maintain this high level of trust between Schengen Member States, ABC proponents propose biometric processing for verification and/or identification purposes, as biometrics are considered to be a reliable link between travellers and their travel documents or the biometric data stored on a database for registered travellers.

---

[3] Although the e-Gates in the EU differ in their design and functionality, in general terms they refer to an electronic gate where the border control check is carried out in a self-service manner by the travellers themselves. Normally it is equipped with a travel document reading device and a device for biometric scanning and verification or identification and is connected to the relevant background systems (e.g. for wanted individuals, such as the Schengen Information System II).

[4] The enumerated programmes are national ABC programmes introduced by the individual Member States and exemplify different implementations of ABC. While both PRIVIUM and PARAFE require a prior registration, in the case of PRIVIUM the biometric data (iris) is stored on a smart card, while in PARAFE the biometrics (fingerprints) are stored on a central database (French citizens do not need to register). No-Q, on the other hand, does not require pre-registration.

Biometric-based ABC hence changes the nature of identity management at borders, e.g. the method of registration and authentication. This raises privacy and data protection concerns as will be examined below.

The border control process can be split in the several steps of an Identity Management process. While there are numerous approaches to Identity Management, the two basic steps are always registration and authentication.[5]

Registration. The first step is the enrolment/registration. In case of border crossing the identity provider is the national issuing governmental authority of the traveller's home country. This authority verifies that the traveller is registered as citizen and issues a token (usually a passport). In addition to personal information like nationality and name, the passport contains a facial image of the person and his/her fingerprints as identifiers on the chip of the passport. These tokens can be used for both manual and automated border control, but in the case of a Registered Traveller Programme ("RTP"), a separate pre-registration is necessary to use the system.[6] Currently, there are different national implementations of RTPs across the EU and the processes are not harmonized (e.g. PARAFE in France and PRIVIUM in the Netherlands). Generally, for registration in RTPs, first the identity of the traveller needs to be verified with the passport. Then it is examined that the traveller fulfils the entry requirements. Afterwards the identity is registered in the database and linked to the biometric identifiers of the traveller. These biometric identifiers could be stored either on a central database (e.g. PARAFE) or on a separate token, like a card (e.g. PRIVIUM).

Authentication. Authentication is the process of verifying the claimed identity of a user (OECD 2007). Border control in general seeks to address three issues: whether the passport (1) is valid and authentic, (2) has not been stolen, lost or misappropriated (and therefore has been revoked), and (3) that it belongs to the person presenting it (Article 7 (2) SBC). In order to establish the link between the person presenting the identifier and the identifier itself, sometimes an additional verifier is used. A verifier is an attribute which is somehow hard to produce or a secret between the system and the user (Wayman 2008). In ABC biometrics are used as verifier or identifier as it is claimed to be more secure and trusted.

The ABC systems which do not make use of pre-registration can only make use of biometric data already included in the travel document. Usually this is done with a 1:1 comparison, comparing, for example the face of the traveller automatically against the

---

[5] For example: OECD, Digital Identity Management: Enabling Innovation and Trust in the Internet Economy, 2011, describes registration, authorization, authentication, access control and revocation as IdM processes. A. Jøsang divides IdM in the Registration -, Operation - and Termination phase: Identity management and trusted interaction in Internet and mobile computing, IET Information Security, 2014, 8/2, p. 71.

[6] For example, the European Commission has tabled a proposal for a Registered Traveller Programme that would apply to some Third Country Nationals, who fulfill certain requirements. It is part of the Smart Borders Package, which is currently subject to a feasibility test (study and pilot). As it concerns Third Country Nationals and not EU/EEA/CH citizens, the proposal is outside the scope of this paper. See Proposal for a Regulation of the European Parliament and of the Council establishing a Registered Traveller Programme, COM (2013) 97 final, Brussels, 28.2.2013.

data in the passport. Since the verification is done by comparing the information on the chip of the passport, in principle no registration or data base of the biometric data is needed. But the possibility that the information presented is retained after automated verification to build a database or the information is to be checked with other databases cannot be ruled out, unless appropriate measures are taken to prevent this.

RTPs are not restricted to the information on the passport and can make use of additional biometric and alphanumeric data. The authentication can take place in three ways: i. the biometric identifier is registered in a database and then becomes the only identifier of the traveller in a 1:n comparison against all biometrics in the database, ii. the biometric information in the database is linked to a key which the traveller gets in order to open the database and perform a 1:1 verification, or iii. the registered traveller gets a token (e.g. a smartcard) with the biometric identifier for a 1:1 verification against the token.

2.3 Function Creep as a Risk of ABC

Automated Border Control changes the nature of identity verification at external borders through the automated processing of biometrics during the check. During the manual check, the border guard visually compares the facial image on the passport with the persona standing in front of him. However, in the ABC process, the verification is automated, i.e. the biometrics on the chip of the passport are verified against the live image. Article 29 WP recognized that the deployment of biometrics poses specific data protection and privacy challenges, due to its sensitive nature and thus their processing should be examined, inter alia, in light of the purpose for which they are processed (Art. 29 WP 2012).

Nevertheless the processing of biometric data in ABCs raises, amongst other legal concerns,[7] privacy and data protection risks. One of these risks is the problem of function creep. Function creep refers to the "gradual widening of the use of a system or database beyond the purpose for which it was originally intended" (EDPS 2012, p. 7). This entails the risk that the new usage of the data might have a more severe effect on the rights of data subjects than the initially planned usage (EDPS 2012; Lodge 2010). In addition, since the incompatible usage of data would violate the purpose limitation principle (EDPS 2012; EDPS 2006), this could result in an "erosion" of all other related data protection principles by using already available data beyond the purposes for which they were originally collected (Art. 29 WP 2012).

In the context of ABC, function creep could emerge as a result of several factors. These factors could be central storage of (biometric) data in databases if registered traveller databases are created or data from the e-Gates is not deleted and technical

---

[7] Another relevant legal concern is, for instance, the question of legality – on what occasions is the comparison of live fingerprints against the chip of the passport allowed (cfr. Opinion of Advocate General in the case of Schwarz (Court of Justice of theEuropean Union: Schwarz, C – 291/12 2013). According to the Advocate General, the fingerprints of EU citizens are to be verified when there is a suspicion as to the whether the passport belongs to the one presenting it but this is at present not officially decided.

interoperability between different databases. This in turn enables the re-use of the already stored data for incompatible purposes, e.g. law enforcement.

Central Storage. Creation of central databases which store biometric identifiers of travellers is one important factor enabling function creep, as it facilitates the later use of them for further purposes, such as law-enforcement purposes. The core issue is that the biometric data, when stored centrally, are not under the control of the traveller, and thus he or she cannot effectively determine their use and re-use. This is especially problematic in the case of biometric data, which are unique and irreplaceable, in contrast to PINs and passwords. Thus, their misuse could have severe consequences for individuals. Central databases can be established in the framework of an RTP or when live biometric data are presented at the border only for verification purposes, but they are stored for later, instead of being deleted as soon as the traveller crosses the border. In addition, the storing of any personal data of EU/EEA/CH citizens using ABC technology challenges the Union right to freedom of movement, as it provides the opportunity to track their movements in and out of the Schengen area and there is currently no legal basis to track the entry and exit of EU/EEA/CH citizens.

Interoperability. Once databases are created, technological interoperability enables interlinkages between them. This blurs the functional separation between databases created for different purposes. Data from different databases, e.g. national and European databases[8] used for border control, are cross-matched with each other or even with other databases, not used for border control purposes such as law enforcement databases.[9] From the combined information further knowledge about travellers can be derived, which is enabled with big data analytics (Rubinstein 2013).[10] This is further facilitated by the usage of biometric identifiers, which can serve as the primary key to these databases (Kindt 2013a, 2013b). In this way biometrics can become universal identifiers, instead of every database producing its own unique identifier. For example, the live biometric may be presented for verification at e-Gates and at the same time may be used to search national and European databases in real time with little effort.

Re-use of Data for Law-Enforcement Purposes. The breach of the purpose limitation principle could lead to a function creep and potentially have a negative impact on individuals, in a sense that storage and cross-matching of data might enable re-use of data in a way that it can be used against travellers.

ABC processes automatically (biometric) data of the travellers who use it. The majority of these travellers are presumably innocent individuals. Saving and cross-checking their data on a systematic basis with law-enforcement databases would be

---

[8] The databases meant here, in the context of EU citizens, are the Schengen Information System ("SIS II"), which can store facial images and fingerprints, relevant national databases which can contain biometric data, as well as national RTP programmes, such as PARAFE in France.

[9] E.g. a database of registered travellers is cross-matched against a police database on wanted criminals.

[10] Rubinstein refers to Big Data as the "... more powerful version of knowledge discovery in databases or data mining, which has been defined as 'the non-trivial extraction of implicit', previously unknown, and potentially useful info from data".

disproportionate, as EU/EEA/CH citizens should be checked in criminal databases such as SIS II only on a non-systematic basis (article 7 (2) Schengen Borders Code). Thus there is no legal basis for checking whether all EU/EEA/CH travellers that use ABCs are in some way suspects, under investigation, etc. That is why it is important to keep the functional separation between databases.

Such further usage of biometric data, e.g. for law-enforcement purposes, when not regulated by a law which enshrines sufficient safeguards for data subjects, could create a legal vacuum and place in effect all travellers under general suspicion without a sufficient level of protection for their rights. An illustrative example is a potentially false hit of the fingerprints of a registered traveller against a law-enforcement database and subsequent proceedings against the individual. Access to law-enforcement authorities has already been granted in the case of EURODAC, which was not initially envisaged in the original Regulation. Thus, the purpose of EURODAC was extended from regulating the asylum application process to law-enforcement, without sufficient corresponding safeguards to individuals, as the EDPS criticized the Commission Proposals of 2008, 2009 and 2012 to extend access to the data for law- enforcement purposes (EDPS 2012). EURODAC was officially amended anyway to grant access to law-enforcement authorities (Official Journal of the European Union 2013). The Visa Information System (VIS) was also amended to allow access to law-enforcement authorities (Council, 13.8.2008). When the access by law-enforcement authorities is not clearly regulated, including the consequences on individuals of such access, as well as measures to prevent arbitrariness and to allow individuals to exercise their rights, a legal vacuum emerges. Thus, the issue of legal vacuum, which can be observed also in ABC, is another factor which has to be taken into account when considering function creep. (Kindt 2013a, 2013b; CBP 30.03 2007).

The issue of access by law-enforcement authorities to data processed via ABC, if such access is deemed to be necessary to be granted in the first place, has to be clearly regulated in law as the authorities cannot evoke randomly article 13 Directive 95/46/EC. It is important to bear in mind that article 13 requires a legislative measure before a derogation is applied and this measure should be justified under article 8 ECHR (Court of Justice of the European Union 2003).

For the reasons above, a law regulating the access of law enforcement authorities to ABC data should be adopted. This law should contain sufficient safeguards for individuals. In practice, any restriction of the rights of travellers or any re-use of their data for purposes such as security must be carefully assessed and only applied on a case by case basis.

3   Is Privacy by Design a Solution?

To address function creep triggered by applications employing biometrics in the field of ABC, one should consider relevant legal, technical and organisational measures. A concept that promises tremendous benefits to the way relevant measures should be implemented is Privacy by Design.

Privacy by Design is an approach to privacy that helps enforce the privacy rules and ensures that new technologies, products or services do not create new privacy concerns but protect individuals' privacy. Its quintessence is to identify and mitigate privacy risks from the very beginning, when the means for the processing of data are determined and throughout the lifecycle of the processing (Alvaro 2012). It is often argued that Privacy by Design is about using technology as a regulatory instrument and thus has been referred to as "code as code" or "techno-regulation" (Lessig 2000; Koops et al. 2009).

However, in this paper, Privacy by Design is not perceived just as a general requirement for system developers to embed as many data protection requirements as possible in the design of the system, in a sense of strictly automating compliance with the legal framework (Leenes & Koops 2013). Rather, privacy by design is understood as a whole mind-set which embodies the idea to respect privacy at technical and organisational level (Leenes & Koops 2013). This means that privacy should be reflected in the culture of an organisation and drive choices regarding technical design and data processing as well as strategy development and top-level decisions.

In order to unveil Privacy by Design and understand its implications in the context of ABC we first consider its development. Further, we discuss certain Privacy by Design technical applications in light of their potential to address the challenges attached to the use of biometrics without undermining the need for security of the ABC process. Special attention is given to the ISO/IEC 24745, from which we finally derive prerequisites to specify Privacy by Design.

3.1   Development of the Concept

The concept of Privacy by Design is not explicitly included in the Directive 95/46/EC. However, the intention of the legislator to enforce privacy and data protection principles through technology is clear, since it provided that the data controller has to take technical and organizational measures both at the stage of the design of the system as well as at the time of the processing of personal data[11]. While legal and administrative instruments have been exhausted on policy development and monitoring, the introduction and elaboration on Privacy Enhancing Technologies have been an alternative approach to implement Privacy by Design (Koorn et al. 2004). Privacy Enhancing Technologies have extensively been developed in relation to two data protection principles: data quality (article 6 Directive 95/46/EC) that includes both the principles of fairness and of data minimization and data security (article 17 Directive 95/46/EC). Departing from Privacy Enhancing Technologies, it was illustrated that privacy-aware design cannot be seen independently from other processes that are related to organisational aspects (Cavoukian 2011; Koorn et al. 2004). Besides technologies, privacy should, therefore, have an impact on the border control processes as well as on border authorities' attitude towards privacy concerns raised by data processing activities.

Within the preparatory work for the data protection reform, both the Article 29 WP and the EDPS expressed the opinion that Privacy by Design should be recognised as a

---

[11] Recital 46 and article 17 of Directive of the European Parliament and of the Council of 24 October 1995 on the protection of individuals with regard to the processing of personal data and on the free movement of such data (OJ L 281 31).

general principle and has to be articulated in provisions of specific legal instruments (Cavoukian 2010; Art. 29 WP 2009; EDPS 2010), as an extension of the current rules on organizational and technical security measures and the general principle of accountability (EDPS 2010). The recent Proposal for a Draft General Data Protection Regulation (European Commission 2012), refers to data protection by design (article 23). Following the Parliament discussions, data protection by design requires that privacy should be embedded within the entire life cycle of the technology, from very early design stage, right through to its ultimate deployment, use and final disposal[12]. The Council in its report of 3rd October 2014 deleted this definition. The new Recital 61, as proposed by the Council, reads: "In order to be able to demonstrate compliance with this Regulation, the controller should adopt internal policies and implement appropriate measures, which meet in particular the principles of data protection by design and data protection by default. Such measures could consist inter alia of minimising the processing of personal data, (…) pseudonymising personal data as soon as possible, transparency with regard to the functions and processing of personal data, enabling the data subject to monitor the data processing, enabling the controller to create and improve security features" (Council of the EU 3rd October 2014).

3.2 Applications

Automated Erasure. Automated erasure is a Privacy by Design routine that can potentially fulfil the procedural safeguards mentioned in article 23 of the Draft General Data Protection Regulation, regarding the accuracy, confidentiality, integrity, physical security and deletion of personal data. It can be perceived as an expression of data minimization, as deriving from article 6.1(b) and (c) of Directive 95/46/EC. It requires from the data controller not to collect more personal data than what is absolutely adequate, appropriate and necessary in order to accomplish a specified purpose. In that sense automated erasure can take several forms, including installing in the system data self-destructing mechanisms (Mayer-Schönberger 2009; Art. 29 WP 2012). In light of the opportunities often arising from big data analytics (Polonetsky 2012), which for example could be useful to enhance the functionalities of the system, automated erasure should be applied on the basis of proportionality. Storing and analysing huge data sets of travellers might enhance the security functionalities of the system but would not be necessary provided that security measures already exist at the airports. In the case of ABC, data processing involves not only alphanumeric but also biometric data, which have recently been included in the special categories of data under article 9 of the Draft General Data Protection Regulation. The fact that this sensitive data could be useful for general security purposes does not overweight the privacy risks that might emerge from such operations. It should be noted that security mechanisms are already in place, such as general surveillance measures in the airports as well as criminal law enforcement

---

[12] Recital 61 of the European Parliament legislative resolution of 12 March 2014 on the proposal for a regulation of the European Parliament and of the Council on the protection of individuals with regard to the processing of personal data and on the free movement of such data (General Data Protection Regulation).

data bases. Thus a reuse of sensitive data under the excuse that they are intended to overcome security concerns would be unnecessary.

In an ABC context, automated erasure could be embedded at the stages of registration and authentication. As to the stage of registration, it is a privacy enhancement that can be achieved by not storing, i.e. erasing automatically, the original image of the biometric characteristic or any other intermediate data between the extraction steps and the (protected) template (Kindt 2010). In this way any unprotected captured data are deleted automatically in order to prevent their misuse and mismanagement (Art. 29 WP 2012). At the stage of authentication, any stored biometric data shall be used only for the purposes of border control and therefore should be automatically erased after the transaction with the ABC technology. They further should not be retained for longer than necessary to accomplish their intended purpose (EDPS 2010). Other data, such as time and place of crossing, data from the biometric passport, etc., should be deleted as well, unless storage is required by law.

Use of Attribute-Based Credentials for ABC? The use of Attribute-based Credentials is a Privacy by Design technique which decouples the process of identification from the process of authentication in an Identity Management system. Attribute-based Credentials are cryptographically secured carriers of properties for a particular individual and allow authentication on the basis of certain required attributes that are necessary for ABC (Jacobs & Alpár 2013).

As described in Sect. 2, the Schengen Borders Code provides the requirement of article 7 (2) of the Schengen Border Code to conduct minimum checks to establish identities on the basis of a travel document. Additionally the article provides that on a non-systematic basis, border guards may consult national and European databases in order to ensure that EU/EEA/CH travellers do not represent a threat to the Member State.

Applying attribute-based credentials to ABC would mean in practice that the traveller would be issued in advance with a token on which certain hashed personal data are stored. The hashed attributes could represent names, passport number and country code, expiration date of the passport and age of the traveller. This could be useful to establish whether the traveller is eligible to use the ABC by confirming he has an EU/EEA/CH nationality, is above 18 and his passport has not expired yet.

Nevertheless, to establish the identity and carry out the accompanying checks as required by the SBC, the actual personal data of the traveller would be needed. For the establishment of identities, the names, sex, passport number and issuing authority, date of birth and expiration date of the passport are required. Further, to search the SIS II and relevant national databases on alerts for lost, stolen, misappropriated and invalidated documents, border guards need at least the passport number and country code, but could also use names, date of birth, sex, etc. The above-mentioned personal data are also needed to search these databases for alerts on persons (non-systematically).

For these reasons, the attribute-based credentials may not be a workable solution for ABC. However, if in principle a specific law regarding ABC would be introduced, information minimizing techniques such as attribute-based credentials could possibly be taken into account in the wording of the legislation. In such a case, the inherent loss of usable/searchable information due to the use of such a technique would be expected to face opposition from the side of the border guards.

Pseudonymous Biometric Identities. Function creep stemming from the factors attached to biometric authentication in the context of ABC could possibly be further addressed with pseudonymous biometric identities. Pseudonymous biometric identities, sometimes also referred to as 'pseudo-identities', as a generic framework for existing biometric template protection techniques, propose an architecture, which does not reveal any information permitting retrieval of the original biometric data of its owner by any person besides the enrolled data subject. In this sense, they are diversifiable, protected identity verification strings within a predefined context (i.e. the protected biometric ecosystem) (Breebaart et al. 2008).

Pseudonymous biometric identities are able to materialize biometric authentication for ABC in a privacy-respecting way. They allow storage of information which is able to perform biometric verification. As pseudonymous biometric identities represent a solution which focuses on biometric and not on alphanumeric data, it is still possible to establish the identity of the traveller on the basis of biometrics and to search the relevant databases with alphanumeric data. They can ensure data minimization and secure processing of biometric data according to Directive 96/45/EC. Further, they are able to address the requirements for the protection of biometric information posed by ISO/IEC 24745, as described below, since they are irreversible, unlinkable and revocable.

These requirements for the protection of biometric identifiers are:

Irreversibility of the biometric identities: It calls for transformation of the biometric data in such a form that the stored biometric information cannot be reversed to the initially captured biometric data. The fact that a system is not able to trace back the data subject significantly eliminates the possibilities for misuse and mismanagement of biometric data. Subsequently function creep, which could take place in case of law enforcement access to biometric data of travellers that were collected for the purposes of border control, is avoided. Irreversibility seems however hard to achieve.

Unlinkability of the biometric identities: It prevents comparison of the biometric information with other databases or applications and calls for random generation of cancellable identifiers (Kindt 2013a, 2013b). Implementing this requirement would not allow further reuse of biometric data for cross-linkages between interoperable databases, such as data stored for border control purposes and for example national (law enforcement) databases. Pseudonymous biometric identities can be renewed and diversified; multiple independent protected templates can derive from the same biometric data in order to allow travellers' authentication that cannot be linked with previous ones (Breebaart et al. 2008). Even though interoperability of databases is generally associated with function creep, use of pseudonymous biometric identities do not allow linking data subjects across databases, for surveillance purposes or across applications of the law enforcement systems.

Revocability of the biometric identities: This requirement allows that the data subject or the data controller request revocation. This would be useful in case of data breach or of function creep occurring as a result of excessive failures of the ABC or because a traveller does not wish to participate to the ABC system anymore.

Finally, pseudonymous biometric identities are universal and flexible, as they can support combinations of biometric modalities in any architecture for ABC and can be integrated in existing verification methods (Breebaart et al. 2008); i.e. two-factor verification with passport and biometric.

4 Conclusions

With the examples of automated erasure and pseudonymous biometric identities we illustrated that Privacy by Design offers promising solutions for ABC to handle identity verification based on biometric information in a privacy friendly way. In the event that the proposed reform data protection package comes into force, it will certainly foster privacy risk management through provisions such as the one on Privacy by Design. The obligation to implement a principle which proposes proactive embedding of privacy into systems design is expected to reduce the leeway for misuse and mismanagement of biometric data in the context of ABC.

As it has been particularly illustrated in the case of pseudonymous biometric identifiers, Privacy by Design could be inspired by technical standards in applications employing biometrics, as for instance the ISO/IEC 24745:2011, on biometric information protection (ISO/IEC 2011). We support the idea that implementation of the requirements for biometric template protection would satisfy the requirement for building privacy into the design of the system, as Privacy by Design stipulates.

As it has been shown, to mitigate the risks of function creep in ABC, Privacy by Design should be approached in a holistic way and namely with technical, organisational and legal measures. Guidelines or specific legal measures should be developed in order to respond to the particularities of crucial Identity Management applications, as ABC. In addition, further legislative measures such as a proper legal basis for ABC, defining clearly the purpose, scope and functionalities of ABC, including safeguards for travellers, should be taken. Finally, as in the case of all legal principles, while Privacy by Design calls for safeguards that can enhance data protection at the e-Gates and kiosks, the question for actual implementation through enforcement remains.

Acknowledgements. This paper has been partially funded by the European Commission FP7 projects PRIPARE (PReparing Industry to Privacy-by-design by supporting its Application in Research) under Grant Agreement n° No: 610613, FastPass (A harmonized, modular reference system for all European automated border crossing points) under Grant Agreement No: 312583 and FutureID (Shaping the Future of Electronic Identity) under Grant Agreement No: 318424.

References

Alvaro, A.: Lifecycle data protection management: a contribution on how to adjust the European data protection to the needs of the 21st century. Privacy & Compliance 02-06/2013 (2012)

Andrejevic, M.: Surveillance in the big data era. In: Pimple, K. (ed.) Emerging Pervasive Information and Communication Technologies (PICT) - Ethical Challenges, opportunities and safeguards, pp. 55–69. Springer, Heidelberg (2014)

Art. 29 WP: Art. 29 Working Party - The Future of Privacy - Joint Contribution to the Consultation to the European Commission on the legal framework for the fundamental right to protection of personal data (WP168) (2009)

Art. 29 WP: Art. 29 Working Party - Opinion 3/2012 on Development in Biometric Technologies 00720/12/EN (WP193) (2012)

Breebaart, J., Busch, C., Grave, J., Kindt, E.: A reference architecture for biometric; template protection based on pseudo identities. In: Gesellschaft für Informatik (GI): BIOSIG 2008, Proceedings of the Special Interest Group on Biometrics and Electronic Signatures, pp. 25–37. Gesellschaft für Informatik, Bonn (2008)

Cavoukian, A.: Resolution of Privacy by Design. In: 32nd International Conference of Data Protection and Privacy Commissioners, Jerusalem (2010)

Cavoukian, A.: Privacy by design: the 7 foundational principles. Information and Privacy Commissioner of Ontario (2011)

CBP.: College Bescherming van Persoonsgegevens Wijziging Paspoortwet advies z 2007-00010 (invoering biometrie), 30 March 2007. http://www.cbpweb.nl/downloads_adv/z2007-00010. pdf

Council of the European Union: Council Decision 2008/633/JHA of 23 June 2008 concerning access for consultation of the Visa Information System (VIS) by designated authorities of Member States and by Europol for the purposes of the prevention, detection and investigation of terrorist offences and of other serious criminal offences, O.J. L 218

Council of the EU: Proposal for a Regulation of the European Parliament and of the Council on the protection of individuals with regard to the processing of personal data and on the free movement of such data (General Data Protection Regulation) [First reading] – Chap. IV, 3rd October 2014

Court of Justice of the European Union: Österreichischer Rundfunk, C-465/00, 138/01, 139/0 (2003)

Court of Justice of the European Union: Schwarz, C – 291/12 (2013)

EDPS: Opinion of the European Data Protection Supervisor on the Proposal for a Council Decision concerning access for consultation of the VIS by the authorities of Member States responsible for internal security and by Europol for the purposes of the prevention, OJ 2006/C97/03 (2006)

EDPS: Opinion of the European Data Protection Supervisor on Promoting Trust in the Information Society by Fostering Data Protection and Privacy, OJ C280/01 (2010)

EDPS: Opinion of the European Data Protection Supervisor on the amended proposal for a Regulation of the European Parliament and of the Council on the establishment of 'EURODAC' for the comparison of fingerprints for the effective application of Regulation (EU) No [.../...] [.....] (Recast version) (2012). https://secure.edps.europa.eu/EDPSWEB/ webdav/shared/Documents/Consultation/Opinions/2012/12-09-05_EURODAC_EN.pdf

EDPS: *Data minimisation*. Retrieved May 5, 2014, (n.d.) from Glossary: https://secure.edps. europa.eu/EDPSWEB/edps/site/mySite/pid/74

European Commission: Regulation of the European Parliament and of the Council on the protection of individuals with regard to the processing of personal data and on the free movement of such data (General Data Protection Regulation) 25.1.2012 COM(2012) 11 final (2012)

European Commission: Proposal for a Regulation of the European Parliament and of the Council amending Regulation (EC) No 562/2006 as regards the use of the Entry/Exit System (EES) and the Registered Traveller Programme (RTP), COM (2013) 96 final, 28 February 2013

European Commission: Regulation (EU) No 603/2013 of the European Parliament and of the Council of 26 June 2013 Regulation (EU) No 603/2013 of the European Parliament and of the Council of 26 June 2013 on the establishment of Eurodac for the comparison of fingerprints for the effective application of Regulation (EU) No 604/2013 establishing the criteria and mechanisms for determining the Member State responsible for examining an application for international protection lodged in one of the Member States by a third-country national or a stateless person and on requests for the comparison with Eurodac data by Member States' law enforcement authorities and Europol for law enforcement purposes, and amending Regulation (EU) No 1077/2011 establishing a European Agency for the operational management of large-scale IT systems in the area of freedom, security and justice, O.J. L 180/1-30

FRONTEX: Best Practice Operational Guidelines for Automated Border Control (ABC) Systems, 31 August 2012

Hildebrandt, M.: Slaves to big data. Or Are We? IDP Rev. Internet Derecho y Política **17**, 7–26 (2013)

ISO/IEC: ISO/IEC 24745/2011, Information Technology - Security Techniques - Biometric Information Protection (2011)

Jacobs, B., Alpár, G.: Credential design in attribute-based identity management. In: 3rd TILTing Perspectives Conference, Tilburg, pp. 189–204 (2013)

Kindt, E.: The use of privacy enhancing technologies. In: Bezzi, M. (ed.) Privacy and Identity Management for Life: 5th IFIP W P9.2 (2010)

Kindt, E.: Best practices for privacy and data protection for the processing of biometric data. In: Campisi, P. (ed.) Security and Privacy in Biometrics. Springer, London (2013a)

Kindt, E.: Privacy and Data Protection Issues of Biometric Applications: A Comparative Legal Analysis. Springer, Heidelberg (2013b)

Koops, B.-J., Bodea, G., Hoepman, J.-H., Leenes, R., Vedder, A.: D3.4 Code as Code Assessment. VIRTUOSO FP7 project (2009)

Koorn, R., van Gilsm, H., ter Hart, J., Overbook, P., Borking, J.: Privacy Enhancing Technologies: White Paper for Decision-Makers. Ministry of Interior and Kingdom Relation, Directorate of Public Secotr Innovation and Information Policy (2004)

Leenes, R., Koops, B.-J.: Privacy Regulation cannot be hardcoded. A Critical Comment on the 'Privacy by Design' Provision in Data Protection Law. International Review of Law, Computers and Technology (2013)

Lessig, L.: Code and Other Laws of Cyberspace. Basic Books (2000)

Lodge, J.: Biometrics in Europe: inventory on politico-legal priorities in EU27. Best Network Deliverable D 7.1 (2010)

Mayer-Schönberger, V.: Delete: The Virtue of Forgetting in the Digital Age. Princeton University Press, Princeton (2009)

Mayer-Schöneberger, V., Cukier, K.: Big Data - A Revolution that will transform how we live, work, and think, New York (2013)

OECD: Recommendation on Electronic Authentication and OECD Guidance for Electronic Authentication. OECD (2007)

Polonetsky, O.T.: Privacy in the age of big data: time for big decisions. Stan. Law Rev. **64**, 215 (2012)

Ronald Koorn, H.V: Privacy Enhancing Technologies: White Paper for Decision-Makers. Ministry of Interior and Kingdom Relations, Directorate of Public Sector (2004)

Rubinstein, I.: Big data: the end of privacy or a new beginning. Int. Data Priv. Law **3**(2), 74 (2013)

Wayman, J.: Biometrics in identity management systems. IEEE Secur. Priv. **6**(2), 30–37 (2008)

Patterns in Privacy - A Pattern-Based Approach for Assessments

Jörn Kahrmann and Ina Schiering[✉]

Ostfalia Hochschule für angewandte Wissenschaften, Wolfenbüttel, Germany
{joern.kahrmann,i.schiering}@ostfalia.de

Abstract. The concept of patterns was first developed in the context of architecture and is now widely used in different fields such as software design or workflow design. In the last years the idea of patterns is also used to incorporate privacy in the life-cycle of Information Technology (IT) services. Concerning privacy and security, patterns are mainly used in the design phase of IT services in the form of design patterns. In this paper we propose a pattern-based approach to assess the compliance with privacy regulations continuously during the operation phase of an IT service. The central idea of patterns in this area is to provide an abstract representation of typical automated processing procedures for the processing of personal data. Since these patterns represent abstracted versions of workflows, we use as an illustration diagrams with a notation derived from Business Process Management Notation (BPMN). The aim of the approach presented here is to increase the transparency of assessments for all participants and to allow an easy adjustment of existing assessment results when changes occur.

Keywords: Assessment · BPMN · Compliance · IT service · Pattern · Privacy

1 Introduction

Patterns are an important concept in computer science which is widely used especially in the design phase of the software development life-cycle. Beside the very generic design patterns of e.g. Gamma et al. [1], there are also approaches for design patterns in the area of security, privacy, and patterns for workflows. These approaches are described in Sect. 3.

In the approach presented here, a concept of patterns is proposed that facilitate assessments concerning the compliance with privacy regulations during the operations phase of IT services. In this context patterns represent abstract versions of workflows with hints concerning typical weaknesses encountered in practice. The potential weaknesses can be used as hints during the interviews of an assessment. Hence processes in organisations that are supported by IT services can be assessed continuously for potential weaknesses. The concept of patterns for assessment is presented in Sect. 4. Since the concept of patterns presented here is more related to the concept of workflow patterns, the definition of

© IFIP International Federation for Information Processing 2015
J. Camenisch et al. (Eds.): Privacy and Identity 2014, IFIP AICT 457, pp. 153–166, 2015.
DOI: 10.1007/978-3-319-18621-4_11

patterns used as a basis in this paper is the definition used also by van der Aalst et al. [2] in the context of workflow patterns. They based their considerations on the definition proposed by Riehle et. al. [3] "A pattern is the abstraction from a concrete form which keeps recurring in specific non-arbitrary contexts."

The approach of pattern-based assessments was developed in the project "Datenschutz-Cloud". The concept of patterns as described above is used as a basis for tool-based assessments with a focus on small and medium sized companies (SMEs). The general architecture is presented in Sect. 5 followed by a description of assessments that are based on the tools developed during the project in Sect. 6. The technical solution is described in more detail in [4]. Here the focus is on the underlying concept of patterns for assessment.

Since the project has to adhere to German Data Protection Law [5], we have derived our patterns mainly from the German Federal Data Protection Act (BDSG) and other national laws. Still the patterns are not limited to a German scope since data protection law in European Member States is harmonized via the European Data Protection Directive 95/46/EC [6]. In the near future a General Data Protection Regulation (GDPR) [7], currently under discussion, will have direct effect on data protection in the Member States. This may lead to some refinements of our patterns, but the changes in the European data protection framework won't require major changes in our approach.

The aim of the use of pattern as a basis for assessment is to provide transparency in interviews and to support experienced data protection officials in the sense of the BDSG [5] by an effective representation of the central elements of data privacy assessments. The motivation is to provide a compromise between a common thread for the interviews of the assessments and sufficient depth for experienced professionals. The structure, which is based on visualisations of workflows accompanied by a description and hints concerning potential weaknesses, instead of a large amount of questions, also allows adapting the results of the assessment in the case of changes efficiently. This approach is supported by a lightweight tool-set. An overview of existing assessment methodologies and tool support in this area is presented in Sect. 2.

2 Background for Assessments Concerning Privacy

The focus of the approach described here is checking for legal compliance concerning privacy in SMEs by assessments. The basis of the investigation is compliance with the German Data Protection Law. In the following we provide an overview of assessments and tools which are present in this context.

According to the German Data Protection Law [5] "personal data shall mean any information about the personal or material circumstances of an identified or identifiable natural person (data subject)." Typical examples are name, address, telephone number, and information about bank accounts. Concerning SMEs typical personal data is data concerning customers that are natural persons or data about employees.

General principles of German Data Protection Law according to Bizer [8] are

- Lawfulness of data collection, processing and use of personal data.
- Consent of the data subject.
- Limitation of the purpose.
- Necessity concerning the defined purpose and the retention period.
- Transparency of data processing for the data subject.
- Data Security.
- Control of compliance by data protection officials and supervisory authorities.

Concerning data security in the Annex to Section 9 of the BDSG, requirements are stated for access control, disclosure control, input control, job control, availability control and separate processing of data collected for different purposes.

According to §4d, §4e BDSG automated processing procedures for personal data must be documented. This is typically realised in the form of a directory of automated processing procedures. Examples of automated processing procedures are payroll accounting, customer relationship management, application procedure, and time reporting of employees.

In §4f BDSG it is stated that private bodies are obliged to appoint a data protection official if at least 10 employees are carrying out the automatic processing of personal data. The data protection official of the company provides access to the directory of automated processing procedures. To create and update this directory, typically assessments are used to assess the compliance of automated processing procedures with privacy regulations, document weaknesses and give advice concerning measurements which should be applied.

Assessments employed for this aim are focussed on checking for the compliance of processes and supporting IT services in the operation phase, i.e. after the initial roll-out or after changes. Examples are the privacy module of IT Grundschutz of the Federal Office for Information Security (BSI) [9] or a variant targeted for SMEs called ISIS12 [10]. For these assessments *verinice*[1] can be used as a tool to manage questionnaires. Beside this there exist other tools like *2B Secure*[2] or *privacyGUARD*[3] which are mainly based on questionnaires. With a focus on cloud services there exists also the tool *CARiSMA* [11] that is based on the risk model of the IT Grundschutz catalogues and uses ontologies to derive questionnaires from legal regulations.

All these assessments and tools intend to give a complete and detailed guideline how to check for weaknesses concerning data privacy and security. That is very important for skill training and to build up experience. But experts in the field tend to derive from their experience a very personal style to conduct interviews. That is a normal development, but it makes it difficult to work in teams with a comparable approach for assessments. Here the intention is to provide an assessment methodology based on patterns that supports experienced data

---

[1] http://www.verinice.org/.
[2] http://www.2b-advice.com/.
[3] http://www.privacyguard.de/.

protection officials in the assessment process and proposes a general structure for interviews.

Another important aspect for data protection officials is to keep track of changes concerning workflows and technologies efficiently. When the initial analysis was based on a large questionnaire it is a complex task to update these initial answers continuously, since a change might have various implications. The model proposed here addresses the adaptation to changes by modelling the status in the form of a graph. In a connected model it is easier to identify implications of changes.

The concept of Privacy Impact Assessments (PIAs), mentioned as Data Protection Impact Assessment in §33 GDPR, has a different focus. A PIA is integrated in the risk management process of projects or the development process of a product. But beside a PIA there are other means needed to check for compliance during the operation phase as referred to in §33 GDPR. The CORAS approach [12,13] also addresses risk management. It is based on Unified Modelling Language (UML) models, where risks are modelled individually based on the concrete service and its environment. This approach allows also for easy adjustment of models. Whereas the focus of CORAS is modelling of individual risks, the focus of the approach presented in this paper is on checking for compliance. Instead of modelling individual situations, abstract standard models for workflows with typical weaknesses are used in the form of patterns as a basis for all assessments.

3   Existing Pattern Concepts

The idea of patterns was first proposed by Alexander et al. [14] who investigated the use of design patterns in architecture. Gamma et al. transferred these ideas to software engineering [1]. According to Buschmann et al. [15] a design pattern "provides a scheme for refining the subsystems or components of a software system, or the relationships between them. It describes a commonly recurring structure of communicating components that solves a general design problem within a particular context". In software design, patterns are formulated in the form of Unified Modelling Language (UML) diagrams as an illustration augmented with a documentation consisting of the name, the addressed problem, the solution and consequences. UML diagrams are well understood and lead therefore to transparency and ease of use of patterns. These design patterns are widely used and accepted as guidelines for good software architecture. The patterns are organised typically in the form of a hierarchical structure.

A similar approach is followed by van der Aalst et al. [2] for workflow patterns which are design patterns in the area of workflow design[4]. There petri nets are used as a visualisation accompanied by a documentation with a similar structure as for software design patterns. In a recent approach for design patterns for social applications by Bramilla et al. [16] BPMN is used as a visualisation of social

---

[4] http://www.workflowpatterns.com/.

interactions. All these approaches for design patterns organise the patterns in the form of a catalogue which constitutes a hierarchical structure for patterns.

There are several approaches to transfer the idea of patterns to the field of security and privacy. There are approaches proposed by Hafiz [17] to formulate Privacy Enhancing Technologies (PETs) in the form of patterns as part of a pattern language for security [18]. Since patterns as "oblivious transfer" and "random wait" are difficult to visualise, patterns in this field consist of a thorough description. The patterns are organised in the form of a hierarchical pattern language, which is an acyclic graph where abstract patterns lead to more concrete patterns. For an overview how privacy design patterns are integrated in the software development life-cycle and incorporated in a system of design strategies see Hoepman [19].

Another approach by Doty and Gupta describes good practices for concrete aspects in the form of privacy patterns[5]. In [20] in addition risks caused by the wrong application of patterns are investigated.

4 Patterns for Assessments

The definition for patterns, used also in van der Aalst et al. [2], by Riehle et al. [3] "a pattern is the abstraction from a concrete form which keeps recurring in specific non-arbitrary contexts", is used for the approach of assessment

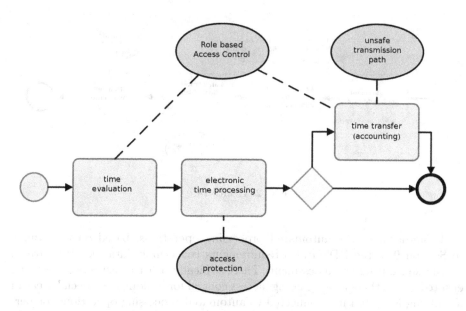

Fig. 1. Time reporting

---

[5] http://privacypatterns.org/.

patterns presented here. As a visualisation for abstracted workflows for auto-mated processing operation, a notation based on Business Process Management Notation (BPMN) [21] is adapted.

The patterns for assessment represent abstracted versions of typical work-flows, used for automated processing procedures concerning the processing of personal data in the sense of the German Data Protection Law [5]. Instead of modelling individual workflows in organisations, these abstract patterns should be usable in a broad range of situations.

BPMN diagrams of abstract workflows are augmented by information about weaknesses with respect to the activities. Possible weaknesses are denoted in the form of an ellipse that is connected via a dotted line to an activity. Weaknesses can occur at several activities, and several possible weaknesses can be connected to one activity. A description is added to workflows and specific weaknesses. For a proof of concept of the tool-set, automated processing operations of SMEs are used. A typical example is e.g. time reporting of employees performed by an IT service or by a paper based approach (Fig. 1).

Another example for an automated processing operation in the sense of BDSG is that companies are obliged to report about the health of employees in the form of a so called health rate (Fig. 2). In both examples of patterns there are typical weaknesses proposed, as role based access control is not sufficient, and the transmission path is not sufficiently secured. Concerning the health rate it is important to ensure the anonymity of employees.

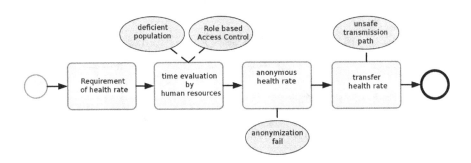

Fig. 2. Health rate

In addition to the automated processing operations, based on the Annex to Section 9 of the BDSG also requirements concerning data security have to be checked during the assessment. There typically a list of aspects have to be ensured. Since these aspects as e.g. access control for buildings or special areas in a building are often not connected to automated processing operations for per-sonal data, a visualisation derived from BPMN diagrams is used with a central activity denoting the area surrounded by several possible weaknesses (Fig. 3).

These patterns constitute a knowledge pool that can be used for assessment. Patterns are organised in the form of a patterns pool. This is a collection of

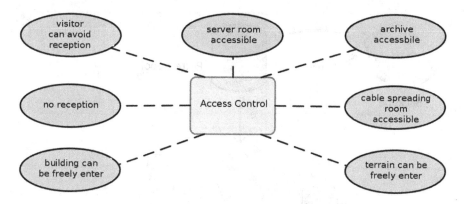

Fig. 3. Access control

patterns with a hierarchical structure based on the idea that patterns should facilitate the interviews in assessments. Hence they are ordered by the roles of interview partners and the automated processing procedures they illustrate. Since this collection is not intended to be complete, but to be augmented whenever there are important new variants of processes and IT services, it is called a pool and there is a backend service that allows to add patterns, weaknesses and measurements to this pattern pool.

This pattern pool is integrated in a mobile client as a basis for assessments where weaknesses of specific organisations can be marked and annotated in the representation of the patterns which are used.

After the assessment the result is transferred to a backend service that facilitates the investigation of the assessment result based on the analysis of former assessments and allows the assignment of measurements to the specific weaknesses encountered during the assessment.

5   Architecture

The tool-set that supports the use of the patterns presented above consists of a mobile client for assessments, a web client for the management of the pattern pool and a web client for associating measurements to weaknesses in the graph resulting from the interviews of the assessment. The web clients together with the pattern pool are called the backend of the tool-set in contrast to the frontend which is the mobile client that supports the interviews of the assessment.

The communication between backend and frontend is realised in the form of JavaScript Object Notation (JSON) data structures. The visualisations of patterns are stored and transferred as Scalable Vector Graphics (SVG). The mobile client is an HTML5 client that creates the representation of the assessment dynamically from the JSON data structures representing the pattern pool and if applicable combined with the results of the last assessment.

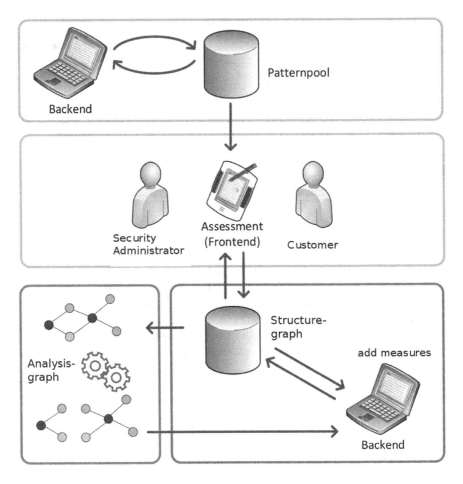

Fig. 4. System overview

The result of the interviews is a data structure consisting of the applicable patterns and the identified weaknesses as nodes. If a weakness is present in a patterns, there is an edge connecting the pattern and the weakness. Hence in the case of common weaknesses like inadequate role based access control it is transparent if the weakness occurs only in special cases or if a general concept is lacking.

6   Tool-Based Assessments

In the following the components of the architecture described above are detailed based on the use cases concerning the pattern pool, the mobile client and the investigation after the interview (Fig. 4).

6.1   Modelling Patterns in the Pattern Pool

Weaknesses, measurements and workflows based on automated processing operations can be documented in the pattern pool using a web client in the backend of the IT service. Additional documentation for every element can be added. First, all needed weaknesses and measurements are added to the pattern pool and connections to possible measurements are connected to weaknesses. Via the pattern editor (see Fig. 5) patterns can be created. Beside the BPMN elements only weaknesses which are already documented in the pattern pool can be used in patterns.

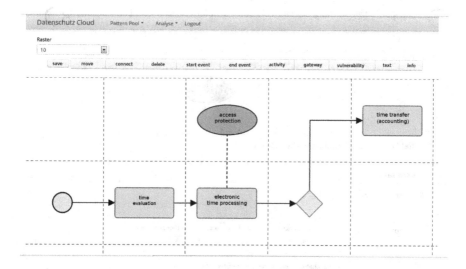

Fig. 5. Editor for pattern pool

For each workflow it is documented further which automated processing procedure, e.g. time reporting, payroll accounting, is represented and what is the role of the intended interview partner concerning this procedure, e.g. management, IT, human resources. These two categories induce a hierarchical structure on the pattern pool. Categories can be added as needed.

6.2   Interviews in Assessment Based on Patterns

To perform an assessment, the actual pattern pool and (if already existent) in addition the result of the last assessment are transferred to a mobile device. The representation of the pattern pool on the mobile device is used as the common thread for all interviews.

After selecting the role of the interview partner, a list of automated processing procedures which are in the responsibility of the role, is presented. If applicable

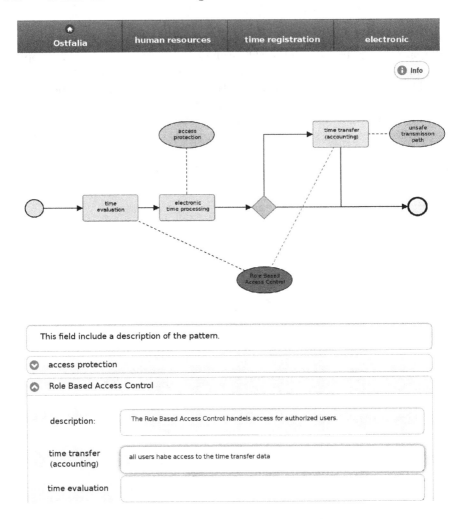

Fig. 6. Client

also aspects of data security are included. After choosing an automated processing procedure, a specific pattern can be selected from a list of variants based on
the process in the organisation. Since SMEs typically use standard applications
and employ relatively simple processes, the list of abstract variants of automated
processing procedure according to the experience of the data protection officials
in the project stays relatively short and an appropriate abstraction for reuse is
possible.

Then the pattern as shown in Fig. 6 can be used as a transparent basis for
the discussion about possible weaknesses. Occurring weaknesses can be selected
in connection with the corresponding activity and are highlighted. Additional
notes can be introduced for the pattern in general and each identified weakness.

The mobile client allows an overview which areas are already covered and where weaknesses occurred by marking areas red resp. green.

6.3 Associating Measurements to Weaknesses in the Backend

The result of the assessment consists of the patterns, which describe the processes in the company or considered aspects of data security. In addition occurring weaknesses connected to patterns and activities in the pattern with supplementary notes are integrated. Because a weakness that occurs in several patterns is represented by the same element of the pattern pool, the result is a graph where patterns are connected by common weaknesses.

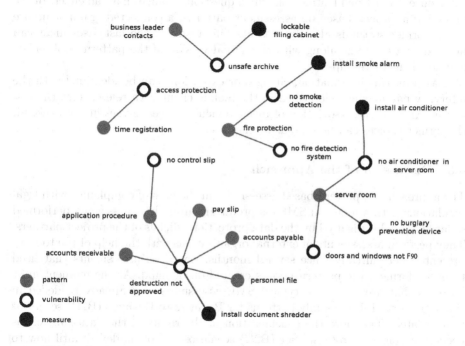

Fig. 7. Overview of results of an assessment with added measurements

This enables the data protection official to get an overview concerning the compliance with privacy regulations. Using a web client in the backend of the tool-set, measurements can be associated to weaknesses from a list of suggestions. The result of the assessment, including the associated measurements, the so-called *structure graph*, is presented in Fig. 7.

After the assessment is finished the intention is to generate experience based knowledge from this result without revealing the organisation and specific information about the situation. For this purpose small sub-graphs, so-called analysis graphs, consisting of a weakness with connected patterns and measurements are extracted and stored in a pool of analysis graphs. This knowledge can be used in the analysis phase of assessments. Suggestions for measurements addressing weaknesses in a specific situation are ranked based on a similarity measurement for analysis graphs. This concept has to be evaluated further, when there is an appropriate number of assessments finalised, such that the pool of analysis graphs is sufficiently large.

6.4   Performing Updates of Assessments

Assessments concerning compliance with legal regulations for privacy need to be updated continuously because of changes in processes, IT infrastructure or other changes. For assessments that are based on questionnaires this is an intricate task, since it must be identified on which questions changes have an effect. In the presented approach based on assessment patterns, a connected graph structure of the former status is already present. This result of the last assessment can be used as a base line along with the actual version of the pattern pool on the mobile client for the update.

Based on this information, changes or extensions can be identified with the interview partners and described in the mobile client with reference to the last status. Also for the association of measurements to weaknesses in the backend, the former choices can be used as a reference.

6.5   Discussion of the Approach

The approach of a pattern based assessment in the area of compliance with legal regulations with a focus on SMEs is promising after the assessments performed so far. The tool-set is used by the data protection officials of the project partners. They perform assessments of external organisations with the help of the tool-set presented here already since several months. Based on assessments that need to be performed, the pattern pool is created on demand. At the moment most patterns that are needed in typical SME assessments are already modelled in the pattern pool. But mainly patterns for Business to Business (B2B) scenarios were created. Therefore the consideration of the rights of the data subject, as needed in Business to Customer (B2C) scenarios, is not modelled until now to the full extent.

To keep the concept of patterns simple, the case that potentially a measurement can lead to additional weaknesses is not modelled in the tool-set. Hints concerning these situations documented in the description of patterns. When such a situation occurs, the weakness has to be added to the assessment result.

7   Conclusion

The proposed concept of patterns for assessment is already used in a prototype of the described tool-set for assessments at SMEs, by a project partner. There also the current pattern pool was developed based on the experience of data protection officials. In the future, the pattern concept, which seems very promising, has to be evaluated further. Beside that, the concept of analysis graphs has to be investigated after an appropriate amount of assessments is performed.

It is an interesting question to what extent the concept of patterns for assessment can be generalised to other fields or larger organisations. There a corporate pattern pool might be needed to model the specifics of the organisation. The question there is to what extent the benefits that are present in the case of SMEs as transparency and a common thread in interviews can be kept while the effort for the modelling of patterns is still reasonable.

Acknowledgement. This work was supported by the Federal Ministry for Economic Affairs and Energy through the Central Innovation Programme for SMEs (ZIM) (grants KF3081801KM2, KF2842903KM2).

References

1. Gamma, E., Helm, R., Johnson, R., Vlissides, J.: Design Patterns: Elements of Reusable Object-Oriented Software. Pearson Education, Upper Saddle River (1994)
2. van der Aalst, W.M.P., ter Hofstede, A.H.M., Kiepuszewski, B., Barros, A.P.: Workflow patterns. Distrib. Parallel Databases **14**(1), 5–51 (2003)
3. Riehle, D., Züllighoven, H.: Understanding and using patterns in software development. TAPOS **2**(1), 3–13 (1996)
4. Rodeck, M., Voigt, C., Schnütgen, A., Schiering, I., Decker, R.: Toolgestützte assessments zu datenschutz und datensicherheit in kleinen und mittelständischen unternehmen. In: GI-Jahrestagung, pp. 575–586 (2014)
5. Federal data protection act in the version promulgated on 14 January 2003 (Federal Law Gazette I, p. 66), as most recently amended by Article 1 of the act of 14 August 2009 (Federal Law Gazette I, p. 2814). http://www.gesetze-im-internet. de/englisch_bdsg/englisch_bdsg.html
6. Directive 95/46/EC of the European parliament and of the council of 24 October 1995 on the protection of individuals with regard to the processing of personal data and on the free movement of such data. http://eur-lex.europa.eu/LexUriServ/ LexUriServ.do?uri=CELEX:31995L0046:EN:HTML
7. Proposal for a regulation of the European parliament and of the council on the protection of individuals with regard to the processing of personal data and on the free movement of such data (General data protection regulation). http://eur-lex.europa.eu/legal-content/EN/TXT/HTML/?uri=CELEX: 52012PC0011&from=EN
8. Bizer, J.: Sieben goldene regeln des datenschutzes. Datenschutz und Datensicherheit-DuD **31**(5), 350–356 (2007)
9. Federal office for information security (BSI): BSI-Standards 100–1 100–2 100–3 100–4 (2008). http://www.bsi.bund.de/EN/Publications/BSIStandards/ BSIStandards_node.html
10. Gruber, M.: Isis12 - informationssicherheit für mittelständische unternehmen. In: D-A-C-H Security 2013, Nürnberg, pp. 275–282. syssec (2013)

11. Humberg, T., Wessel, C., Poggenpohl, D., Wenzel, S., Ruhroth, T., Jürjens, J.: Ontology-based analysis of compliance and regulatory requirements of business processes. In: Proceedings of the 3rd International Conference on Cloud Computing and Services Science (Closer 2013), pp. 553–561. SciTePress (2013)

12. Houmb, S.H, Braber, F.D, Lund, M.S, Stølen, K.: Towards a UML profile for model-based risk assessment. In: Critical Systems Development with UML-Proceedings of the UML 2002 Workshop, pp. 79–91 (2002)

13. Lund, M.S., Solhaug, B., Stølen, K.: Model-driven Risk Analysis: the CORAS Approach. Springer, Heidelberg (2010)

14. Alexander, C., Ishikawa, S., Silverstein, M.: A pattern language: towns, buildings, construction (center for environmental structure series) (1977)

15. Buschmann, F., Meunier, R., Rohnert, H., Sommerlad, P., Stal, M., Sommerlad, P., Stal, M.: Pattern-oriented software architecture, volume 1: a system of patterns (1996)

16. Brambilla, M., Fraternali, P., Vaca, C.: BPMN and design patterns for engineering social BPM solutions. In: Daniel, F., Barkaoui, K., Dustdar, S. (eds.) BPM Workshops 2011, Part I. LNBIP, vol. 99, pp. 219–230. Springer, Heidelberg (2012)

17. Hafiz, M.: A pattern language for developing privacy enhancing technologies. Softw.: Pract. Exp. **43**(7), 769–787 (2013)

18. Hafiz, M., Adamczyk, P., Johnson, R.E.: Growing a pattern language (for security). In: Proceedings of the ACM International Symposium on New Ideas, New Paradigms, and Reflections on Programming and Software, pp. 139–158. ACM (2012)

19. Hoepman, J.-H.: Privacy design strategies. In: Cuppens-Boulahia, N., Cuppens, F., Jajodia, S., Abou El Kalam, A., Sans, T. (eds.) SEC 2014. IFIP AICT, vol. 428, pp. 446–459. Springer, Heidelberg (2014)

20. Doty, N., Gupta, M.: Privacy design patterns and anti-patterns patterns misapplied and unintended consequences. http://citeseerx.ist.psu.edu/viewdoc/summary?doi=10.1.1.385.6907

21. Business process model and notation (BPMN). Version 2.0. Object Management Group specification (2011)

Privacy Technologies and Protocols

A Survey on Multimodal Biometrics and the Protection of Their Templates

Christina-Angeliki Toli[(✉)] and Bart Preneel

Department of Electrical Engineering, ESAT/COSIC - KU Leuven, Kasteelpark
Arenberg 10, bus 2452, 3001 Leuven-Heverlee, Belgium
{christina-angeliki.toli,bart.preneel}@esat.kuleuven.be
http://www.esat.kuleuven.be/cosic/

Abstract. In order to guarantee better user-friendliness and higher
accuracy, beyond the existing traditional single-factor biometric systems,
the multimodal ones appear to be more promising. Two or more biometric measurements for the same identity are extracted, stored and compared during the enrollment, authentication and identification processes.
Deployed multimodal biometric systems also referred to as multibiometrics or even as multimodalities are commonly found and used in electronic chips, embedded in travel documents. The widespread use of such
systems, the nature of the shared data and the importance of applications introduce privacy risks. A significant number of approaches and
very recent advances to the relevant protection technologies have been
published. This paper illustrates a comprehensive overview of research in
multibiometrics, the protection of their templates and the privacy issues
that arise. Up-to-date review of the existing literature revealing the current state-of-art suggestions is provided, based on the different levels
of fusion and the employed protection algorithms, while an outlook to
future prospects is also discussed.

Keywords: Multimodal biometric systems · Multibiometrics · Multimodalities · Levels of fusion · Biometric template protection scheme ·
Biometric cryptosystem · Privacy · Security · Cryptography

1 Introduction

Biometric authentication is the science of establishing the identity of a user,
towards a system, based on his/her physical or behavioral attributes [1]. During
the last decade, the field of biometric authentication has gained growing popularity as biometric traits are becoming the next generation method that will
widely replace the user name and password as the primary way of authentication, in the next 2–3 years. In addition to the idea that biometric characteristics
are only useful in forensics, the pronounced necessity for reliable day-to-day
transactions, has led to a range of applications that verify the identity of a person using human properties. Systems are increasingly being deployed and used
throughout the world [53], from limited simple home or business applications

© IFIP International Federation for Information Processing 2015
J. Camenisch et al. (Eds.): Privacy and Identity 2014, IFIP AICT 457, pp. 169–184, 2015.
DOI: 10.1007/978-3-319-18621-4_12

(the controlled access to a room), to large-scale projects, which are involved in societal functions, such as user verification for on-line transactions (e.g. banking ePayments, mobile devices). Finally, it is a common secret that biometrics have been used in the scope of surveillance themes. Remarkably, not only the industry, but also the military, law enforcement, and security agencies invest in the development and manufacture of facial, iris and voice recognition technologies, capable of detecting and identifying anyone.

Traditional deployments are mainly uni-modal biometric systems and may have limited usage. The fact is that no single sample from the modality biometric is sufficiently accurate in real-world applications [28], where it is demanded from designers to produce robust systems with low error rates and sufficient tamper proof protection [43]. Nevertheless, they constitute the starting point of each research into the direction of multibiometric systems which seeks to reduce some of their drawbacks [20], by consolidating recognition process using multiple templates extracted from the same person (e.g., fingerprint, iris, face, hand geometry, gait, keystroke dynamics) [36,37].

A biometric system is essentially a pattern recognition scheme that compares the tested features of a user with the stored ones, from the process of a previous enrollment. Each system can operate in identification or verification mode, where the system processes a measurement from which a biometrics template is extracted [19]. The concept of fusion in biometrics, helps to expand the feature space used to claim an identity, and thus, affects the matching accuracy of the system [24]. Multibiometric recognition in different levels of fusion can improve the performance, deter spoofing, and increase the overall accuracy of these systems. Considering these enrichments, the system will be more reliable and thus, more acceptable to be used in a number of related applications [4,28,42].

Studies in these areas [5,32,37,38,45], aim to answer a crucial question: *How can the leakage of stored biometric characteristics, to unauthorized individuals, be prevented?* A variety of risks exist that call for protection of the stored elements, after the fusion of the templates. From a privacy viewpoint, most concerns against the common use of biometrics arise from the multiple modalities used to describe a single user, the sensitive nature of these data and the potential leakage of this information from devices that store it. Taking this into consideration, the security of the user's identity should be addressed, with a privacy perspective [21] and should be examined by different points of view. The elements that can reveal the identity of the user should be protected, while simultaneously, preventing him/her from opening multiple accounts using false data and covering the requirements for unique identifiers. Solutions such as the helper data system, fuzzy vault algorithms, cancelable biometrics and others come to promise improvements in this filed, while experimental studies have shown that these technologies can bring improved verification performance.

Multibiometric template protection is the source that has motivated numerous works in the field of the combination of pattern recognition methodologies with the world of cryptography. From research perspective, results about the significant advantages in accuracy, reliability and security of biometric systems can promise protection of their storage. State-of-the-art proposals offer different scenarios to these concerns, while very recent experiments shift the target to the deployment of a unique generic category of systems [6,52]. The idea behind this statement is that the systems development will be able to support many applications based on multiple pieces of evidence under one human identity, capable of performing well on large-scale datasets. They should be designed in such a smart way that can offer overall security, beyond well-known risks or the nature of the transactions.

This work is motivated by very recent advances in the areas of multibiometric recognition and biometric template protection, and its aim is to contribute to the studies of the interaction between biometrics and cryptography, presenting concrete, published results of the last four years. The time period of the works is carefully selected to serve the research in the entrance of biometrics in cryptography world, reflecting the increasing number of projects that aim to suggest solutions for the protection of user's identity, in case of risks during on-line transactions. These complementary security technologies can bring improvements in security and reliability of the systems, while strengthening public acceptance of the involved applications [7]. The remainder of this survey is organised as follows: In the next section, the importance of multimodalities against single modals is underlined, the different levels of fusion for multibiometric data are analysed, and template protection techniques are reviewed. Using this as the background of a new promising idea, the section of related work contains a comparative summary of multimodal biometrics and template protection in combination. The fourth section introduces the major privacy and security issues that arise. Finally, in the last section, a comprehensive conclusion, including the current approaches, is given and some remarks for discussion are presented.

2   Background

This section presents briefly the basic knowledge around the technology of biometric systems, starting from the way that these can be gathered, and suggesting the cryptographic methods that can be used for the protection of a biometric element in a database, in terms of security. The process, according to the application, the type of scenarios, the nature of the stored templates and their representation play an important role to the characterization of each system as a reliable and secure enough or not. The literature review in this area is extensive and it could not be fully addressed in this part. The target of the next subsections is to present the fusion of biometrics and the use of cryptographic techniques, introducing readers to enlightenment.

2.1   Multibiometric System Recognition

Data fusion in biometric systems is commonly an active area with numerous applications being not only a solution to the problems of uni-modalities, but also an active research field [3,28]. Vendors are already deploying systems that use two or three patterns for the same user, providing recognition even on large-scale datasets. Information fusion constitutes a way to enhance the matching accuracy of the system without resorting to other measurements or techniques, but just, being based only on the template.

Information Fusion. The three different factors of recognition performance of the gathered data are given in the following list.

Feature Level Fusion. The specific method comprises the strategies which pertain to the sensor, the set, rank and decision level. For the first one, in a concrete way, it is worth to be mentioned that this fusion level involves augmenting the vectors arising from the extractors and subjecting the vector to a transformation algorithm [35,48]. The elements can enhance the performance.

Furthermore, information from multiple feature sets can be used to refine the template. Using the third category, a rank level fusion is suitable for biometric systems operating in the identification mode.

Finally, the last level fusion consists of artifacts coming from the final outputs of an individual sub-system, and wisely is mentioned as the simplest form of fusion. The correlation between the main inputs has to be examined, in order to evaluate the improvements in matching performance.

Score Level Fusion. On this level of fusion, matching scores are returned by each individual sub-system and the obtained output scores are combined. The suggested ways underline the necessity for a normalised score, aiming to improve the reliability of the system. There are three basic groups: density based, transformation based and classifier based schemes. The performance of each scheme depends on the quantity and the quality of the involved informative data. Major issues, like the limited number of the available training samples, or, the lack of homogeneity, can be further investigated, using the previously mentioned approaches [10].

To conclude, always considering that a multibiometric system is affected by the correlation [50], the combination of the weak uncorrelated biometric matchers can lead to better performance, than combining the strong ones, positively correlated. Using this starting point, score level becomes the most popular level among the others, and uncorrelated traits are applied in recognition systems, increasing, successfully, the desirable accuracy [40].

Decision Level Fusion. This level fusion is termed so because it depends on the final, acceptance or rejection, decisions. Auxiliary information is available to systems with high dependence from the application. Gathering the information by independent sub-systems, and fusing the results, constitutes a way to increase the overall precision, supporting the idea for universality of the entire system [13]. Mainly, the conducted research in this area is still immature. Fusion schemes that incorporate parts into a whole final scheme have not been yet explored [9]. Suggestions for combining soft biometric characteristics [48], like the gender, age or the ethnicity of the user, with the inputs of biometric samples, can be used to verify the person's identity.

The presented themes provide an overview of the first tendency to the direction of covering the problematic areas of conventional biometric systems. The combination of popular traits, such as the iris and the fingerprints, is embedded in many applications. The conducted tests demonstrate advantages, while introducing new tasks. The evaluation of a complete biometric system is a complex issue and requires stronger user involvement for feature level schemes [31]. Compact multibiometric templates need to be generated, offering, in this way, an improved concrete content of information. Nevertheless, the most important drawback of fusion is the central storage of the data, coming from the same or different sources. This is a complex characteristic that should be addressed in order to prevent further privacy threats. Last, but not least, the precision of the model feature distributions, and the estimation of the possibilities to practice the theory in large databases, are still intricate issues [33].

2.2 Biometric Template Protection

Template Protection can be simply described as a straightforward and novel cryptographic construction. Biometrics can be found where personal information is employed to authenticate users, and here the readings are inherently noisy, not only because of their nature, but also, because of the pattern recognition techniques [14,31]. However, such architectures have been used in a number of real-world, error-prone environments. Due to security concerns that arise from the storage of these data, several techniques [26] provide mechanisms, that can face the technical weaknesses of parameterization, representing a primitive with a special property of error-tolerance. The final aim is to improve the reliability of the systems and enlarge the chances for public acceptance and user confidence [17].

Categories. Biometric characteristics are largely immutable and any kind of compromise is undesirable [1,27]. The standard encryption algorithms do not support a comparison of biometric templates in an encrypted domain, leaving important personal information totally exposed, during the authentication. While user authentication is based on possession of secret keys, key management is performed introducing another layer of authentication. In this way, encryption of data inherits the security of according biometrics applied to release correct decrypting keys. Biometric template protection schemes are usually categorised in two main groups and are designed to meet the requirements of biometric data protection [48]. Schematic illustration is shown in Fig. 1.

Cancelable Biometrics also referred to as feature transformations are designed in a way, that it should be computationally difficult to recover the original information [37,56]. The idea is to apply transformations that do not affect the elements, while are tolerant to variations. The basic fact, in this category, is that cancelable biometrics consist of intentional distortions of signals that are repeatedly transformed, similarly to those between templates in the transformed domain.

Techniques of transformation modify the template in a user specific way. During authentication, the same transformation is applied to the biometric query,

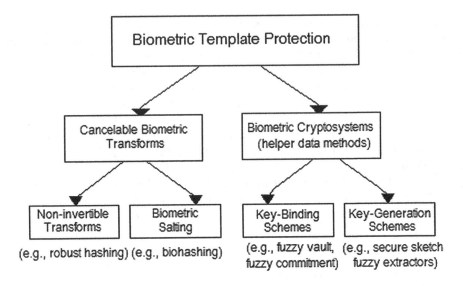

Fig. 1. Categorisation of template protection schemes.

and the matching is performed in the already transformed area, so as to avoid the exposition of the original stored template [47].

A weak point of the system is that the transformation key is stored along with the biometric template. One solution for this can be the non-invertibility of the used transformation function, even in those cases, where the attacker knows the key. Furthermore, assuming beforehand that the transformed biometric data may be compromised, the parameters should be changed, in order to secure the template. Finally, to prevent the tracking subjects by cross-matching databases processes, recent studies have tested methods for applying different transformations for different applications [9, 33].

Cancelable biometrics are distinguished in two categories: non-invertible transforms and biometric salting. Academic research in this area consists of numerous works that can be further classified. It is worth mentioning that published works, in this area, apply the techniques of robust hashing systems and bio-hashing in specific modalities, studying the error rates, with remarkable results. These examinations also include analysis of the design from a constructional and security aspect, and evaluating the behavior of those schemes against potential attacks [35].

Biometric Cryptosystems are designed to securely bind a digital key to a biometric feature or generate a key from it. The idea, for a design of robust keys, started as a solution to threats like copying, sharing and distributing biometrics from the initial genuine storage. This is the reason for their second name, as helper data methods. Based on schemes which perform fuzzy comparisons, using decision thresholds, original templates are replaced through biometric-dependent public information. Specifically, secure sketches are derived from the biometric template after the enrollment process. This sketch is stored in the system, instead of the original template, in a form of a function. This mixture is obtained by binding the template with an error-correcting code, which itself is defined by a key. The strength, in terms of security, is the absence of the user's data, which however is a drawback for this design. Security relies on the difficulty to recover the template, using as attacks an authentication query or an error-correcting code. Some examples of biometric cryptosystems are fuzzy vault schemes, fuzzy extractors, and secret sharing approaches, secure sketches and others. Typically, these are separated into two main categories according to the schemes, as key-binding or key-generation [17].

Both technologies aimed to meet some requirements like non-invertibility where, given a protected template, it should be difficult for the attacker to find a biometric feature set that will match with the initial one. Second, we need revocability where versions of protected templates can be generated from the same biometric data and, concurrently, the protected templates should not allow cross-matching process, obeying to the necessity for diversity of data representations [40]. The use of these techniques can offer advantages, taking into account the uses cases, a fact that is also underlined in some published works [13,16,21,54], where different approaches and combinations can be presented. In general, comparing the two methods of protection, cryptosystems tending to have stronger non-invertibility transformation schemes also offer unlinkability. Separately, or using hybrid products of their connection, several traditional attacks against systems have been prevented and the generated template is usually strong enough to be reconstructed, which is a feature that increases privacy and, consequently, the social acceptance [38].

3   Related Work

As it was mentioned above, the limited security of multimodal recognition systems, the drawbacks of biometric template protection technologies and the major absence of practicality to the recognition algorithms, involved in these creations, have motivated researchers to examine the possibilities for a fortunate combination of the two areas [2,37]. From an academic perspective, multibiometric template protection has several different facets [20]. At the same time, industrial actions attempt to establish a framework that can be effectively used to understand the issues and progress in the area while evaluating the needs of the applications [29,50]. At any rate, the relation between biometrics and protection techniques brings new challenges and illustrates efforts for further scenarios which can promise better overall accuracy of the system [19,32]. Literature survey has revealed a number of experimental works or approaches that are focused on the most frequently used biometrics (iris, fingerprint, face pattern) and aim at reducing the errors and providing higher security [15,50]. This section, briefly, refers to the most notable architectures, according to current methods that aim to equip sensors used in environments, where the personal data constitute a sensitive element [2,14,39,40].

3.1   Multibiometric Template Protection

Current literature in biometric template protection, key approaches to cryptosystems or cancelable biometrics and multiple biometric templates from the same source have been examined. Early studies, which required an alignment of biometric templates, have demonstrated efficiency with specific combinations of personal data. Different techniques have been proposed to overcome the shortcomings of pre-alignment methods [9,45]. Some of the schemes have been applied to physiological or behavioral biometrics [46]. Respecting the necessity for use the most easily captured biometric features, from a pattern recognition aspect, biometrics have been selected to map biohashing, block permutation, fuzzy vaults and commitments schemes [41,44].

As a second approach, the collaboration of template protection with multibiometrics can be achieved with several notable approaches that have been proposed and evaluated according to the ability to correct the error ratio. For example, multi-algorithm fusion at feature level, multibiometric cryptosystem fuzzy vault based on fingerprint and iris [51], fuzzy commitments for face [49] and other ideas for score fusion level were successfully applied to fingerprints with security advances and many other combinations under various scenarios have been proposed during the last three years [23,51]. The target is to provide a uniform distribution of errors [30], combining successfully the data and covering research gaps of previous works, and thus, contributing to secure, stable systems [25,54], while offering, a fast comparison of protected templates suitable for biometric recognition in identification mode.

3.2   Ideas for Incorporation

Industrial projects are focused on the creation of a generic framework, similar to the one schematically presented below. The system should be capable of incorporating n templates, without the necessity to follow specific fusion levels for their representation, (k representations could be involved). The process is continued with a common representation and then the generic system is applied for the protection of the template (Fig. 2).

Analysing the idea from the levels aspect, focusing on the first part of this representation, it seems that biometrics fusion on feature level is the most suitable approach for the protection of the templates. Of course, score level fusion is not enough, besides the approaches of a solutions that offers to many systems. Nevertheless, cancelable biometric systems based on score level fusion can be reconstructed, in an analogous way to conventional, but their use to cryptosystems applications is not really popular [55]. Decisions based on final decisions can be successfully implemented to both system protection areas. Following the design of this framework, some issues arise, such as the template alignments, the way of the combination for modalities, the implementation in applications for the representation of the features [16], the level of the obtained recognition performance, the correction of the errors and the overall security of the system, and the way the latter comes to solve any privacy related themes [11].

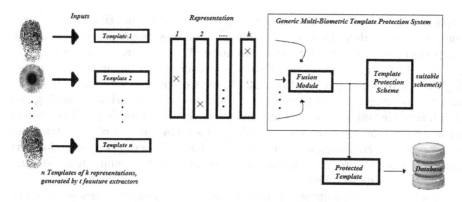

Fig. 2. A framework of a generic multibiometric template protection at feature level.

More precisely, a construction of an align-invariant biometric cryptosystem or cancelable biometrics is not yet fully investigated. Feature level fusion of templates hinders a proper alignment of protected templates, while auxiliary data for the use of alignment may leak information on stored templates. Helper data techniques can probably provide some solution, but this is still unsure. The desired code length also remains evasive, and this comes to affect the necessity for error-correction codes. The fact that false rejection rates are lower bounded by error-correction capacities emerges as a great challenge since each change can make the system more vulnerable. The representation of the feature can bring better results but it may necessitate extended efforts in the direction of combination of many different templates using the fuzzy vault schemes methodology. Finally, from a biometric template protection perspective, the length of the keys remains a major topic for discussion.

In conclusion, experiments that have been carried out in different studies with use of multiple combinations of biometric samples from the same identity and implemented in several template protection technologies, illustrate significant improvements with regards to reliability of the relevant applications. Different proposals of frameworks for the design of cryptosystems or cancelable biometrics that contain many modalities, have been presented enriching this research field. In spite of the encouraging results, several other issues might occur and demand further investigation [23]. Current literature studies are focused on the possibility to establish a generic model, which will cover the necessity for irreversibility and unlinkability, and secure enough to be used in many applications. The next section is dedicated to the emerging issues, from biometrics recognition to the protection categories, as those were presented above.

4 Security and Privacy Issues

A great number of biometric characteristics are being used in various applications. The nature of each biometric trait makes it eligible for a variety of applications. Beyond, the well-known, common seven factors that underline the suitability of the data, that is universality, uniqueness, permanence, measurability, performance, acceptability, circumvention [37], there are, also, other factors that should be taken into consideration, especially when biometric systems are deployed in real-world applications [22,39,40]. Computing environments present security challenges related to aspects of multimodality [28] while extending and facilitating the ways of accessing may cause security threats [7]. The system must, at the same time, behave according to a certain policy of biometrics and be properly instrumented against attacks and actions performed by non-expert users, in order to protect information, thus meeting the requirements of irreversibility and unlinkability.

After overcoming engineering and technical performance issues [6], the primary research question to be addressed with regards to a multibiometric system is: *How does the system address privacy concerns regarding its level of provided security to the relevant application?* A starting point is the idea that with improvements of security, privacy as well as systems reliability of two or more biometrics could be combined in a method that enhances the efficiency. Following this assumption, multibiometric systems not only can reduce some threats, but also can be compromised in many ways [18]. In that sense, the leakage of template information to unauthorized individuals becomes a serious theme. One should bear in mind, however, that the storage of multiple biometric records of a fused template of elements, extracted from different traits, under the same identity, may offer a solution to many risks, but still, this storage has to be protected [9].

4.1 Multibiometric Systems

A multibiometric system increases the degree of confidence while the accuracy, throughput and scalability could be well estimated. Approximately, using the proposed fusion levels for different biometric traits in unconstrained environments and after the experimental performance analysis, there is an ability to reduce the levels of noise [6,48]. On the other hand, multimodalities overcome limitations such as error-correcting capability and non-universality and this is a field which requires improvements [12,42].

4.2 Biometric Template Protection Technologies

Biometric template protection technologies present several advantages over generic biometric systems. In particular, attention is paid to immutability, because it is the basic characteristic of biometrics. The schemes, as these are previously categorised using this point, enhance privacy providing reliable authentication at a significant level. Specifically, the original template is concealed, the reconstruction becomes extremely efficient [9,42] and the methods ensure, in some sort, the revocability and renewability of the template. Published studies provide tests using traditional attacks against the systems and introduce not only the strong fundamental spots, but also, the obscured ones [21,42,49]. For biometric cryptosystems, the key entropy, the tolerance levels, during the processes, and the metrics are the quantities that lack further investigation [9,19]. Then, the amount of the applicable parameters should be examined closely, considering their important role in the definition of a restricted key space, something that puts at risk the security of the methods which use cancelable biometrics. In conclusion, in order to avoid fraud, privacy leakage should be decreased and the major requirement of unlinkability must be met. Furthermore, the alignment affects the recognition performance, the absence of a unified architecture brings confusion across the applications [25] and the desired properties for error-correction codes remain unattained.

4.3   Combination of Cryptography and Multimodalities

It is an undeniable fact that the combination of cryptography and multibiometrics introduces a number of successful mechanisms that ensure information privacy. Some of the approaches presented in the previous paragraphs of this section may be adopted as solutions, but, still other situations will occur. Precisely, the alignment of the protected templates is an essential task [9], and the representation of feature vectors remains an important line of research. Experiments on protected biometric data [42] lead to the assumption that the low boundaries between the false rejection rates and the error-correction capacities compound a more vulnerable system and at the same time, the requirements for stable biometric features are, definitely, non-trivial. Some of the approaches show that the protocols in the literature do not secure the encoding procedures [25] while others provide multiple suggestions for the distribution of reliability, or concentrate the efforts to the improvement of recognition rates [34]. With respect to the different multimodal biometrics template protection schemes, the interesting side contains the concentrated trials for a generic framework, focused on unified representation of biometric features, under the combination of the suggested protection designs. Relevant to the mechanisms and for the improvement of security and privacy, the requirements, according to Biometric Template Protection Standardization ISO/IEC 24745 [58] need to be covered and clearly addressed, while the accuracy of each concept should be tested.

The last element in this list is some of the most popular introduced privacy methods and the security issues currently on debate. Beyond all the technical cases that arise from the use of multimodalities, when those are applied to template protection schemes, their fusion leads to a number of issues. While, researchers suggest the use of multimodalities, other approaches [57] induce different findings and set the dilemma about the choice of the use of multimodal biometrics instead of uni-modal ones, in order to contribute to a protection of the user against undesired biometric checking. Some other open research questions from privacy aspect, which need to be further examined are: *Does the system exclude the threats that can arise, considering the possibility to perform the biometric procedure without notice and/or against the will of the user? How can the user protect himself/herself against undesired biometric checking?* One step further, the biometric databases, created to support a range of applications, the possibility of data correlation with health information [7,8,40,49], and the security requirements for data, stored in ePassports or ID cards, cause a risky uncertainty. Also, the very nature of template protection schemes, introduce questions about their efficiency for on-line fast identifications, or situations that involve government applications, and these are some of the areas that need to be covered extensively.

5   Conclusions and Discussion

In this work, we have presented a concrete approach on the protection of multimodal biometric templates, underlying critical privacy issues, while focusing on the suggestions for future research. Multimodal biometric systems are mostly discussed for the impact of their use on publicly accepted, reliable identification systems [31,53], overcoming the obstacles of uni-modal ones.

Researchers propose different methods for combination of biometric traits, testing the possibilities that can induce to an effective fusion scheme for highly accurate recognition systems. During this study, there is an analysis of the three main fusion levels, in terms of theoretical [37] and recently published experimental knowledge [6,43]. The limitations of the single characteristic as a verification tool are revealed, while the vitality of multimodalities against fraudulent technologies is under examination.

While biometric vendors are deploying multibiometric systems, at the same time concerns arise from the storage and misuse of the data [9]. The security of the templates is especially crucial for the confidentiality and integrity of this sensitive information. In the direction of facing a number of threats, works on the two main categories of biometric template protection schemes offer important advantages [19]. However, the significant number of studies on single biometric data [51] and the lack of security for multimodalities beyond their advantages, shift the organised and dedicated efforts to the connection of these areas. The incorporation of multiple biometrics in template protection schemes seems that can offer suggestions for solution against many drawbacks, while new security interrogations arise. During the last years, studies attempt to generate a compact generic framework and evaluate each proposed multimodal cryptosystem on large-scale datasets. In this line, there are still many open research questions, and the merit of biometric cryptosystems should ideally be expanded. The nature and privacy properties of a system, that can be used in a generalised multimodal way, are highly counter-intuitive and deserve a deeper exposition and evaluation of the ways that could significant to the problematic areas.

Summarising, the selection of the optimal fusion level and the choice for the appropriate modals as well as their combination present special interest, because they are the basic challenges in the requirements of each system according to the application design. After all, biometrics is the new digital enabler in a fast-advancing technological world and their greatest strength is their uniqueness, which is also one of their greatest weakness. And if biometric elements are compromised during the verification process, the identity of the user is the primary concern. And it is at this point where cryptographic issues for multibiometrics need to be further investigated.

Acknowledgments. This research will contribute to FIDELITY (Fast and trustworthy Identity Delivery and check with ePassports leveraging Traveler privacy), project funded by the European Commission, under the Security theme of the Seventh Framework Programme (Grant agreement no: 284862).

The authors would like to thank the reviewers for their ideas and support, regarding improvements for this survey.

References

1. Abaza, A., Ross, A., Hebert, C., Harrison, M.A.F., Nixon, M.S.: A survey on ear biometrics. ACM Comput. Surv. **45**(2), 22 (2013)
2. Maiorana, E., Campisi, P., Fierrez, J., Ortega-Garcia, J., Neri, A.: Cancelable templates for sequence-based biometrics with application to on-line signature recognition. IEEE Trans. Syst. Man Cybern. Part A: Syst. Humans **40**(3), 525–538 (2010)
3. Adams, C.: Achieving non-transferability in credential systems using hidden biometrics. Secur. Commun. Netw. **4**(2), 195–206 (2011)
4. Dodis, Y., Ostrovsky, R., Reyzin, L., Smith, A.: Fuzzy extractors: how to generate strong keys from biometrics and other noisy data. SIAM J. Comput. **38**(1), 97–139 (2008)
5. Nagar, A., Nandakumar, K., Jain, A.K.: Multibiometric cryptosystems based on feature-level fusion. IEEE Trans. Inf. Forensics Secur. **7**(1), 255–268 (2012)
6. Sim, H.M., Asmuni, H., Hassan, R., Othman, R.M.: Multimodal biometrics: weighted score level fusion based on non-ideal iris and face images. Expert Syst. Appl. **41**(11), 5390–5404 (2014)
7. Hao, F., Anderson, R., Daugman, J.: Combining crypto with biometrics effectively. IEEE Trans. Comput. **55**(9), 1081–1088 (2006)
8. Jain, A.K., Nandakumar, K., Nagar, A.: Biometric template security. EURASIP J. Adv. Signal Process. **2008**, 113 (2008)
9. Rathgeb, C., Busch, C.: Multi-biometric template protection: Issues and challenges. In: New Trends and Developments in Biometrics, pp. 173–190 (2012)
10. Argones Rua, E., Maiorana, E., Alba Castro, J.L., Campisi, P.: Biometric template protection using universal background models: an application to online signature. IEEE Trans. Inf. Forensics Secur. **7**(1), 269–282 (2012)
11. Isobe, Y., Ohki, T., Komatsu, N.: Security performance evaluation for biometric template protection techniques. Int. J. Biometrics **5**(1), 53–72 (2013)
12. Simoens, K.: Security and privacy challenges with biometric solutions. LSEC Biometrics (2011)
13. Lu, L., Peng, J.: Finger multi-biometric cryptosystem using feature-level fusion (2014)
14. Hoang, T., Choi, D.: Secure and privacy enhanced gait authentication on smart phone. Sci. World J. Article ID 438254, 8 p. (2014). doi:10.1155/2014/438254
15. Peng, J., Li, Q., El-Latif, A.A.A., Niu, X.: Finger multibiometric cryptosystems: fusion strategy and template security. J. Electron. Imaging **23**(2), 023001–023001 (2014)
16. Chin, Y., Ong, T., Teoh, A., Goh, K.: Integrated biometrics template protection technique based on fingerprint and palmprint feature-level fusion. Inf. Fusion **18**, 161–174 (2014)

17. Maiorana, E.: Biometric cryptosystem using function based on-line signature recognition. Expert Syst. Appl. **37**(4), 3454–3461 (2010)
18. Bringer, J., Chabanne, H., Patey, A.: Privacy-preserving biometric identification using secure multiparty computation: an overview and recent trends. IEEE Sig. Process. Mag. **30**(2), 42–52 (2013)
19. Rathgeb, C., Uhl, A.: A survey on biometric cryptosystems and cancelable biometrics. EURASIP J. Inf. Secur. **2011**(1), 1–25 (2011)
20. Kumar Ramachandran Nair, S., Bhanu, B., Ghosh, S., Thakoor, N.S.: Predictive models for multibiometric systems. Pattern Recogn. **47**(12), 3779–3792 (2014)
21. Simoens, K., Bringer, J., Chabanne, H., Seys, S.: A framework for analyzing template security and privacy in biometric authentication systems. IEEE Trans. Inf. Forensics Secur. **7**(2), 833–841 (2012)
22. Cavoukian, A., Stoianov, A.: Privacy by design solutions for biometric one-to-many identification systems (2014)
23. Rathgeb, C., Busch, C.: Cancelable multi-biometrics: mixing iris-codes based on adaptive bloom filters. Comput. Secur. **42**, 1–12 (2014)
24. Cavoukian, A., Stoianov, A.: Biometric encryption. In: van Tilborg, H.C.A., Jajodia, S. (eds.) Encyclopedia of Cryptography and Security, pp. 90–98. Springer, US (2011)
25. Sutcu, Y., Li, Q., Memon, N.: Secure sketches for protecting biometric templates. In: Campisi, P. (ed.) Security and Privacy in Biometrics, pp. 69–104. Springer, London (2013)
26. Breebaart, J., Yang, B., Buhan-Dulman, I., Busch, C.: Biometric template protection. Datenschutz und Datensicherheit-DuD **33**(5), 299–304 (2009)
27. Tuyls, P., Akkermans, A.H.M., Kevenaar, T.A.M., Schrijen, G.-J., Bazen, A.M., Veldhuis, R.N.J.: Practical biometric authentication with template protection. In: Kanade, T., Jain, A., Ratha, N.K. (eds.) AVBPA 2005. LNCS, vol. 3546, pp. 436–446. Springer, Heidelberg (2005)
28. Lee, D.G., Hussain, S., Roussos, G., Zhang, Y.: Editorial: special issue on security and multimodality in pervasive environments. Wireless Pers. Commun. **55**(1), 1–4 (2010)
29. Butt, M., Henniger, O., Nouak, A., Kuijper, A.: Privacy protection of biometric templates. In: Stephanidis, C. (ed.) HCI 2014, Part I. CCIS, vol. 434, pp. 153–158. Springer, Heidelberg (2014)
30. Wang, N., Li, Q., Ahmed, A., El-Latif, Abd., Peng, J., Yan, X., Niu, X.: A novel template protection scheme for multibiometrics based on fuzzy commitment and chaotic system. Sig. Image Video Process., 1–11 (2014). doi:10.1007/s11760-014-0663-2
31. Buchmann, N., Rathgeb, C., Baier, H., Busch, C.: Towards electronic identification and trusted services for biometric authenticated transactions in the single euro payments area. In: Preneel, B., Ikonomou, D. (eds.) APF 2014. LNCS, vol. 8450, pp. 172–190. Springer, Heidelberg (2014)
32. Connaughton, R., Bowyer, K.W., Flynn, P.J.: Fusion of face and iris biometrics. In: Burge, M.J., Bowyer, K.W. (eds.) Handbook of Iris Recognition, pp. 219–237. Springer, London (2013)
33. Awad, A.I., Hassanien, A.E.: Impact of some biometric modalities on forensic science. In: Muda, A.K., Choo, Y.-H., Abraham, A., Srihari, S.N. (eds.) Computational Intelligence in Digital Forensics: Forensic Investigationand Applications, pp. 47–62. Springer, Switzerland (2014)
34. Campisi, P.: Security and Privacy in Biometrics. Springer, London (2013)

35. Jillela, R.R., Ross, A.A., Boddeti, V.N., Kumar, B.V.K.V., Hu, X., Plemmons, R.J., Pauca, P.: Iris segmentation for challenging periocular images. In: Burge and Bowyer [11], pp. 281–308
36. Burge, M.J., Bowyer, K.W. (eds.): Handbook of Iris Recognition. Advances in Computer Vision and Pattern Recognition. Springer, London (2013)
37. Ross, A.A., Nandakumar, K., Jain, A.K.: Handbook of Multibiometrics, vol. 6. Springer, New York (2006)
38. Kong, A., Zhang, D., Kamel, M.: Palmprint identification using feature-level fusion. Pattern Recogn. 39(3), 478–487 (2006)
39. Wouters, K., Simoens, K., Lathouwers, D., Preneel, B.: Secure and privacy-friendly logging for egovernment services. In: Third International Conference on Availability, Reliability and Security, ARES 2008, pp. 1091–1096. IEEE (2008)
40. Juels, A., Molnar, D., Wagner, D.: Security and privacy issues in e-passports. In: First International Conference on Security and Privacy for Emerging Areas in Communications Networks, SecureComm 2005, pp. 74–88. IEEE (2005)
41. Kelkboom, E.J., Breebaart, J., Buhan, I., Veldhuis, R.N.: Analytical template protection performance and maximum key size given a gaussian-modeled biometric source. In: SPIE Defense, Security, and Sensing, pp. 76670D–76670D. International Society for Optics and Photonics (2010)
42. Rathgeb, C., Uhl, A., Wild, P.: Reliability-balanced feature level fusion for fuzzy commitment scheme. In: 2011 International Joint Conference on Biometrics (IJCB), pp. 1–7. IEEE (2011)
43. Siddiqui, A.M., Telgad, R., Deshmukh, P.D.: Multimodal biometric systems. Study Improv. Accuracy Perform. 4(1), 165–171 (2014)
44. Nandakumar, K., Jain, A.K.: Multibiometric template security using fuzzy vault. In: 2nd IEEE International Conference on Biometrics: Theory, Applications and Systems, BTAS 2008, pp. 1–6. IEEE (2008)
45. Kelkboom, E., Zhou, X., Breebaart, J., Veldhuis, R., Busch, C.: Multi-algorithm fusion with template protection. In: IEEE 3rd International Conference on Biometrics: Theory, Applications, and Systems, BTAS 2009, pp. 1–8. IEEE (2009)
46. Sutcu, Y., Li, Q., Memon, N.: Secure biometric templates from fingerprint-face features. In: IEEE Conference on Computer Vision and Pattern Recognition, CVPR 2007, pp. 1–6. IEEE (2007)
47. Radhika, K., Sekhar, G., Venkatesha, M.: Pattern recognition techniques in online hand written signature verification-a survey. In: International Conference on Multimedia Computing and Systems, ICMCS 2009, pp. 216–221. IEEE (2009)
48. Rajibul Islam, M., Shohel Sayeed, M., Samraj, A.: Multimodality to improve security and privacy in fingerprint authentication system. In: International Conference on Intelligent and Advanced Systems, ICIAS 2007, pp. 753–757. IEEE (2007)
49. Yang, B., Hartung, D., Simoens, K., Busch, C.: Dynamic random projection for biometric template protection. In: 2010 Fourth IEEE International Conference on Biometrics: Theory Applications and Systems (BTAS), pp. 1–7. IEEE (2010)
50. Simoens, K., Yang, B., Zhou, X., Beato, F., Busch, C., Newton, E.M., Preneel, B.: Criteria towards metrics for benchmarking template protection algorithms. In: 2012 5th IAPR International Conference on Biometrics (ICB), pp. 498–505. IEEE (2012)
51. Nandakumar, K.: A fingerprint cryptosystem based on minutiae phase spectrum. In: 2010 IEEE International Workshop on Information Forensics and Security (WIFS), pp. 1–6. IEEE (2010)
52. Bringer, J., Chabanne, H., Pointcheval, D., Zimmer, S.: Generation and use of a biometric key, US Patent 8,670,562, Mar 11 2014

53. Yang, B., Busch, C., Bringer, J., Kindt, E., Belser, W.R., Seidel, U., Springmann, E., Rabeler, U., Wolf, A., Aukrust, M.: Towards standardizing trusted evidence of identity. In: Proceedings of the 2013 ACM Workshop on Digital Identity Management, pp. 63–72. ACM (2013)
54. Bolle, R.M., Chikkerur, S.S., Connell, J.H., Ratha, N.K.: Methods and apparatus for generation of cancelable fingerprint template, US Patent 8,538,096, 17 September 2013
55. Cheng, W., An, G.: Face template protection using chaotic encryption (2013)
56. Abt, S.: Assessing Semantic Conformance of Minutiae-based Feature Extractors. Ph.D. thesis, M.Sc. thesis (2011)
57. http://www.cl.cam.ac.uk/jgd1000/combine/combine.html
58. ISO/IEC 24745/2011, Information Technology - Security Techniques - Biometric Information Protection (2011)

Event Invitations in Privacy-Preserving DOSNs
Formalization and Protocol Design

Guillermo Rodríguez-Cano[(✉)], Benjamin Greschbach, and Sonja Buchegger

School of Computer Science and Communication, KTH Royal Institute
of Technology, Stockholm, Sweden
{gurc,bgre,buc}@csc.kth.se

Abstract. Online Social Networks (OSNs) have an infamous history of privacy and security issues. One approach to avoid the massive collection of sensitive data of all users at a central point is a decentralized architecture.

An event invitation feature – allowing a user to create an event and invite other users who then can confirm their attendance – is part of the standard functionality of OSNs. We formalize security and privacy properties of such a feature like allowing different types of information related to the event (e.g., how many people are invited/attending, who is invited/attending) to be shared with different groups of users (e.g., only invited/attending users).

Implementing this feature in a Privacy-Preserving Decentralized Online Decentralized Online is non-trivial because there is no fully trusted broker to guarantee fairness to all parties involved. We propose a secure decentralized protocol for implementing this feature, using tools such as storage location indirection, ciphertext inferences and a disclose-secret-if-committed mechanism, derived from standard cryptographic primitives.

The results can be applied in the context of Privacy-Preserving DOSNs, but might also be useful in other domains that need mechanisms for cooperation and coordination, e.g., Collaborative Working Environment and the corresponding collaborative-specific tools, i.e., groupware, or Computer-Supported Collaborative Learning.

Keywords: Event invitation · Privacy · Decentralized Online Social Networks

1 Introduction

The most common form of Online Social Networks (OSNs) are run in a logically centralized manner (although often physically distributed), where the provider operating the service acts as a communication channel between the individuals. Due to the popularity of these services, the extent of information the providers oversee is vast and covers a large portion of the population. Moreover, the collection of new types of sensitive information from each individual simply keeps increasing [19]. Users of these centralized services not only risk their own privacy

© IFIP International Federation for Information Processing 2015
J. Camenisch et al. (Eds.): Privacy and Identity 2014, IFIP AICT 457, pp. 185–200, 2015.
DOI: 10.1007/978-3-319-18621-4_13

but also the privacy of those they engage with. Whether intentional, or unintentional, data leakages [18], misuse [13] or censorship are some of the issues affecting the users.

Decentralization has been proposed to reduce the effect of these privacy threats by removing the central provider and its ability to collect and mine the data uploaded by the users as well as behavioral data. A Decentralized Online Social Network (DOSN) should provide the same features as those offered in centralized OSNs and at the same time it must preserve the privacy of the user in this different scenario. The latter is not straightforward, as in addition to the decentralization challenge itself, new privacy threats arise when the gatekeeper functionality of the provider that protects users from each other disappears [8].

One of the standard features of OSNs is the handling of event invitations and participation, i.e., a call for an assembly of individuals in the social graph for a particular purpose, e.g., a birthday celebration, demonstration, or meeting. There is usually metadata related to each event, such as date, location and a description. An implementation of this feature must provide security properties to the participants, e.g., that a user can verify that an invitation she received was actually sent by the organizer. Furthermore, it must support certain privacy settings. For example, an organizer could choose that only invited users learn how many other users were invited and that only after a user has committed to attend the event, she learns the identities of these other invited users.

Realizing this in a decentralized scenario is non-trivial because there is no Trusted Third Party (TTP) which all involved users can rely on. This is a problem, especially for privacy properties where information shall only be disclosed to users with a certain status, because any user should be able to verify the results to detect any possible cheating. In the example above, a neutral, trusted broker could keep the secret information (the identities of invited users) and disclose it only to users who committed to attend the event. This would guarantee fairness to both the organizer and the invited users. It becomes more challenging to implement this without a central TTP and still allowing different types of information about the event to be shared with different groups of users in a secure way.

1.1 Our Contribution

We describe and formally define two basic and five more complex security and privacy properties for the event invitations feature.

We propose and discuss a distributed and privacy-preserving implementation of the event invitations feature without using a TTP. The suggested protocols cover all of our defined properties, considering 20 different parameter combinations for the tunable privacy properties.

We also describe three privacy-enhancing tools that we use in our implementation: storage location indirection, controlled ciphertext inference and a commit-disclose protocol. They are based on standard cryptographic techniques such as public key encryption, digital signatures and cryptographic hashes, and can be useful for other applications as well.

1.2   Paper Outline

We discuss related work in Sect. 2, describe the problem of implementing the event invitation feature in a decentralized way and formalize security and privacy properties in Sect. 3. Our proposed implementation together with privacy-enhancing tools follow in Sect. 4, and we discuss this solution in Sect. 5. We conclude with a summary and future work in Sect. 6.

2   Related Work

Groupware tools have been widely researched since they were first defined in 1978 by Peter and Trudy Johnson-Lenz [10]. Choosing between centralized and distributed implementations has been a major concern for these applications as pointed out in [15]. While the traditional model uses the client-server architecture [12,20], there have been some projects on decentralized collaborative environments: Peer-to-pEer COLlaborative Environment [4], a P2P multicast overlay for multimedia collaboration in real-time, although synchronous; YCab [2], a mobile collaborative system designed for wireless ad-hoc networks; or a hybrid P2P architecture with centralized personal and group media tools in [21].

Security features in collaborative applications were already introduced in the popular client-server platform for businesses, IBM Notes/Domino (formerly Lotus Notes/Domino), to allow for usable authentication, and digital signature and encryption by means of a Public Key Infrastructure (PKI) to end-users [22]. Control policies in Computer-Supported Collaborative Work (CSCW) are considered in [16], including distributed architectures.

Protocol design guidelines in collaboration scenarios, where the privacy of a group member does not lessen by participating in the environment, have been studied and proposed in [11]. These guidelines aim at minimizing the amount of information a member has to provide to the group for the common activities, and making the protocols and the tasks transparent to everyone in the group.

Another type of related work lies within the domain of DOSNs [1,3,5]. To the best of our knowledge the event invitations feature has not been investigated in a privacy-preserving manner in this decentralized scenario.

3   Decentralizing the Event Invitation Feature

We already described the intuition of an event, where a group of people gathers with the intention of carrying out some activity. Now we more formally model the event invitation feature and desirable security and privacy properties. We denote the set of users as $U = u_1, \ldots, u_n$. The event invitation happens in three main stages:

- **Creation:** When a user $u_i \in U$ decides to create a new event e_k, she becomes the organizer o_{e_k} and creates the event object $event_k$ including different information, e.g., a description, date, time and location.

- **Invitation:** The organizer o_{e_k} selects the set of users to be invited to the event e_k, denoted by I_{e_k}, crafts the invitation objects $i_{e_k}^{u_j}$ for each of these invitees, and sends them to the respective users.
- **Commitment:** The invitees I_{e_k} have the chance of confirming the invitation, i.e., "commit" to attend the event e_k, by issuing commitment objects $c_{e_k}^{u_j}$. We denote the set of all attendees, i.e., the users who committed to the event e_k, as C_{e_k}.

Figure 1 shows an example with eight users, $u_1 \ldots u_8$, where one of them, u_1, is the responsible organizer o_{e_k} of the event e_k. The organizer issues invitations to $u_2 \ldots u_6$, depicted with a dashed line. These users form the group of invitees, denoted with I_{e_k}. Invited users who confirm their attendance, (u_2, u_4 and u_6 in this example), provide a commitment to the organizer, depicted with a continuous line. They form the group of attendees, denoted with C_{e_k}.

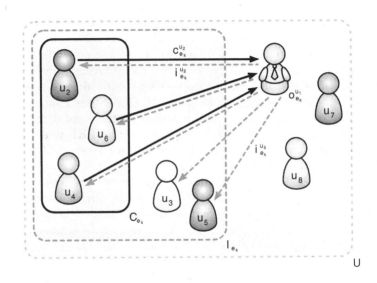

Fig. 1. Example of one event invitation.

A possible privacy setting could specify that invited users learn how many other users are invited but only attending users learn their identities. That is, u_3 and u_5 would learn that five users are invited (while this is kept secret from u_7 and u_8). u_2, u_4 and u_6 would additionally learn the identities of $I_{e_k} = u_2 \ldots u_6$.

3.1 System Model and Assumptions

In the following, we assume basic functionalities of popular OSNs to be available in a decentralized manner, such as user search [9] and user messaging [17]. We also assume that users are identified by a public key and the ability to verify the identity of other users via some sort of PKI, which can be realized in a decentralized manner, e.g., a "Web of Trust" model or a Bitcoin block-chain binding friendly usernames to public keys [6]. Moreover, we rely on a distributed storage featuring access right management, e.g., that a certain storage object is only writeable by a specific user, and "append-only" storage objects, where new data can be appended, but existing data cannot be modified or removed without notice. The latter can be realized in a decentralized fashion, e.g., in a similar manner as the Bitcoin block-chain is secured against modifications [14].

3.2 Threat Model

We assume that users in all roles, e.g., invited users or the organizer of an event, might act maliciously, i.e., become adversaries. The capabilities of an adversary range from passively learning information accessible in that role (e.g., an invited user might have access to a list of all other invited users, depending on the privacy settings for the event), to actively interacting with other parties, e.g., writing arbitrary data to accessible storage objects or sending arbitrary messages to other users. We also assume that powerful adversaries might have the possibility to pervasively monitor a large fraction of the network traffic. While we try to mitigate threats like traffic analysis and correlation attacks arising from this, we cannot completely protect against them and come back to this in the discussion section. We do not assume that adversaries can subvert the storage layer. So we assume the availability of a secure distributed storage including features like append-only lists and authorization mechanisms, as mentioned above.

We want to keep malicious users from undermining the reliability of the event invitation feature for legitimate users. This means that an adversary should not be able to violate the security and privacy properties that we define in the next section. This comprises guaranteeing the authenticity and non-repudiation of statements made by the involved parties, such as issued invitations or commitments. Furthermore it includes keeping information such as the identities of invited/attending users, the number of invited/attending users or a private event description secret from unauthorized users while guaranteeing its availability and authenticity for legitimate users. An example for the latter would be to keep an organizer from withholding or lying about the number of attending users. We do not focus on denial-of-service attacks and leave them for future work.

3.3 Security and Privacy Properties

A protocol for event invitations can comply with different security and privacy properties. We first list the following basic security properties:

- A user u_j can prove that she was invited to the event e_k if and only if the organizer o_{e_k} invited u_j, i.e., issued an invitation $i_{e_k}^{u_j}$.

  This property is two-sided and guarantees that a user cannot forge an invitation she did not get, while an organizer cannot deny that she invited a user. This implies that an invitation $i_{e_k}^{u_j}$ is tied to a user u_j that was chosen by the organizer o_{e_k} and cannot be transferred to another user.

– *An organizer o_{e_k} can prove that the invited user u_j committed to attend the event e_k if and only if u_j actually committed, i.e., issued a commitment $c_{e_k}^{u_j}$.*

This property also has two sides. The organizer cannot forge a commitment of a user that did not commit to the event. And a user cannot deny that she committed to an event once she did so.

More challenging properties are those defining which groups of users are allowed to see what information, namely,

Invitee Identity Privacy (IIP)

For an event e_k, only a chosen set of users (e. g., U, I_{e_k}, C_{e_k} or only o_{e_k}) learns who else is invited (i. e., sees all members of I_{e_k}).

This property defines who can see information about who is invited to an event. This can be all users (U) or be restricted so that only other invited users see who else is invited (I_{e_k}). Another possibility is that even an invited user first learns who else is invited when she committed to attend (C_{e_k}). Finally, this information could be kept completely secret, so only the organizer o_{e_k} knows the complete list of invited users.

Invitee Count Privacy (ICP)

For an event e_k, only a chosen set of users (e. g., U, I_{e_k}, C_{e_k} or only o_{e_k}) learns how many users are invited (i. e., learns $|I_{e_k}|$).

This property is a variant of property IIP where the number of the invited people I_{e_k} is disclosed to a set of users (while the identities of the invited people might remain hidden).

Property IIP and ICP are closely related in the sense that if IIP holds for a certain set of users, then ICP trivially holds for the same set (and all its subsets – note the subset relation of the possible sets to choose from, $U \supseteq I_{e_k} \supseteq C_{e_k}$).

This constrains the possible combinations of these two properties' parameters. If, for example, for a certain event all invited users I_{e_k} should see who else was invited, i.e., property IIP with parameter choice I_{e_k}, then it does not make sense to choose that only the attendees C_{e_k} should learn the number of invited people, i.e., property ICP with parameter choice C_{e_k}, because the invited users can already derive this information from what they learn from property IIP.

Attendee Identity Privacy (AIP)

For an event e_k, only a chosen set of users (e. g., U, I_{e_k}, C_{e_k} or only o_{e_k}) learns who is attending (i. e., sees all members of C_{e_k}).

Attendee Count Privacy (ACP)

For an event e_k, only a chosen set of users (e. g., U, I_{e_k}, C_{e_k} or only o_{e_k}) learns how many users are attending (i. e., learns $|C_{e_k}|$).

Similarly to properties IIP and ICP, these two properties specify who can see information about the users who committed to attend an event. Property AIP defines who can see the identities of the attendees while property ACP defines to whom the number of attendees is disclosed. The same relation, regarding the possible parameter choices, as described for properties IIP and ICP, also holds here.

Attendee-only Information Reliability (AIR)

An invited user u_j can only get access to the private description $d_{e_k}^S$ of the event e_k once committed and the organizer o_{e_k} can only claim the attendance of the user u_j once the private description $d_{e_k}^S$ is available to u_j.

This property has two sides. First, a user u_j can only get access to information exclusive to the attendees C_{e_k}, i. e., the private description $d_{e_k}^S$ from the organizer o_{e_k} for an event e_k, if she has committed to attend. Second, and conversely, the organizer o_{e_k} can only claim that user u_j has committed to attend if she has made it possible for u_j to access the private description $d_{e_k}^S$.

4   Implementation

We now propose an implementation of the event invitation feature described in Sect. 3 in a privacy-preserving DOSN. We assume that user identifiers u_i are public keys, and we will denote their corresponding private keys as u_i^S (where S stands for "secret").

4.1   System Components

The main components of the system are event objects, invitation objects and commitment objects as depicted in Fig. 2.

- **Event Object:** When a user wants to create a new event, she first generates a public/private keypair e_k/e_k^S. The public key will become the identifier for the event and the user will be denoted as organizer o_{e_k}. She then assembles the event object $event_k$: She writes a public event description d_{e_k} and a private description $d_{e_k}^S$ that will be encrypted with a symmetric key PDK. She creates one list to store the invitation objects (*invite-list*) encrypted with a symmetric key ILK, another list for the commitment objects (*commit-list*) and one for disclosing secret information to committed users (*disclose-list*).

The event object contains links ILL, CLL and DLL, pointing to the storage locations of these three lists. Additionally the organizer creates a list of public/private keypairs $rk_1/rk_1^S, \ldots, rk_n/rk_n^S$, to encrypt the entries on the commit-list, and includes the public keys in the event object. Moreover, the event object contains information about the chosen privacy settings.

The organizer signs the public key of the event with her own user key to confirm that she is the organizer and signs the whole event object $event_k$ with the event's private key e_k^S. Therefore, an event object is composed as follows:

$$event_k = Sign_{e_k^S}(Sign_{u_i^S}(e_k)||u_i||d_{e_k}||Enc_{PDK}(d_{e_k}^S)$$
$$||ILL||ILK||CLL||DLL||rk_1, \ldots, rk_n||\text{privacy settings})$$

Some of the elements of the event object might, however, be encrypted with additional keys or only be hashes (made with a cryptographic hash function H, e.g., SHA-2 [7]) of the actual values. This depends on the chosen privacy settings and will be explained in more detail later.

- **Invitation Object:** An invitation object is composed of the invitee's identifier u_j (her public key), signed by the organizer o_{e_k} with the event's private key e_k^S:

$$i_{e_k}^{u_j} = Sign_{e_k^S}(u_j)$$

- **Commitment Object:** A commitment object is composed of the invitation object $i_{e_k}^{u_j}$ and the cryptographic hash of the event object $event_k$, both signed by the attending user u_j with her private key u_j^S as follows,

$$c_{e_k}^{u_j} = Sign_{u_j^S}(H(event_k)||i_{e_k}^{u_j})$$

4.2   Privacy Enhancing Tools

Before describing the implementation, we introduce tools that we will use several times.

Storage Location Indirection and Controlled Ciphertext Inference. If we want to make the size of a list, i.e., the number of its elements, available to a subset of users, but not the content of the list elements (in our scenario because each element contains a user identifiers), we can use storage location indirection and ciphertext inference: The list will not be stored together with the event object, but at a secret location in the distributed storage such that it can only be reached if the link to it is known. Additionally, the elements of the list will be encrypted so that the stored content can only be accessed if the encryption key is known.

This provides the possibility of a controlled information disclosure depending on the knowledge of a user: Users who do not know the link, learn nothing, neither the size nor the content of the list. Making the link to the list but not

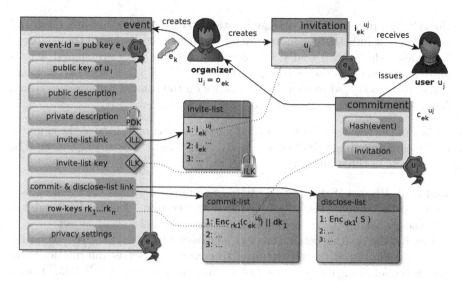

Fig. 2. Overview of the actors, system components and their relations.

the encryption key available to a subset of users, enables these users to learn the size of the list (assuming a constant ciphertext size for each entry), while it does not give them any details about the contents stored. Users that received both the link and the encryption key, learn the content and can act as verifiers, checking that there are no invalid entries that incorrectly increase the perceived number of elements as seen by those users holding only the link but not the key.

Commit-Disclose Protocol. The organizer may want to share some information only with users who have committed to attend the event (attendees). To ensure fairness, the invited users need some guarantee that they can expect to receive the promised information when they commit to attend.

While this is easy to solve if both parties, the organizer and the invited users, trust a neutral third party that can act as broker, it becomes more difficult in our setting where we do not assume the existence of any TTP. So we base our solution on a significantly weaker trust assumption: the availability of append-only storage objects as described in Sect. 3.1.

The aim of the protocol is to provide an invitee u_j who commits to the event e_k with a secret S held by the organizer o_{e_k}. It is composed of three main components, provided by the organizer of the event:

- **Commit-List**, a public and append-only storage object where invited users store their (encrypted) commitments.
- **Disclose-List**, a public readable, but only writeable by the organizer, append-only storage object where the organizer discloses (encrypted) secrets for the committed users.
- **Anchor Point**, a storage object (in our case the event object) serving as common entry point, referencing the commit-list and the disclose-list either

directly by providing their storage locations, i.e., a commit-list link CLL and a disclose-list link DLL or indirectly by holding salted hashes of these storage locations (where DLL and CLL together with the salts are shared with a subset of users in another way). Additionally, a list of public keys $rk_1, \ldots, rk_n$, called row-keys, used to encrypt the entries on the commit-list are also stored here. All this information is signed by the organizer.

Each key in the row-keys list is intended for encrypting one entry of the commit-list. The corresponding private keys $rk_1^S, \ldots, rk_n^S$, are held by the organizer. The protocol runs in three phases:

- **Commit Phase:** If the user u_j wants to commit to attend the event e_k, she looks up the commit-list and finds the next free row – let this have index l. She then looks up the corresponding row key rk_l in the event object.

  Finally, she crafts a commitment $c_{e_k}^{u_j}$, creates a fresh keypair dk_l^P/dk_l^S (disclose key, later used by the organizer to encrypt the secret information) and writes the following entry to row l of the commit-list: $Enc_{rk_l}(c_{e_k}^{u_j})||dk_l^P$ that is the commitment, encrypted with the row-key, together with the public disclose key in plain.

- **Disclose Phase:** When the organizer o_{e_k} sees that a new row l has been added to the commit-list, she tries to decrypt the first entry, using the secret row key rk_l^S. If this succeeds and the commitment is valid the organizer writes the secret information, encrypted with the provided disclose key to row l of the disclose-list, i.e., $Enc_{dk_l^P}(S)$. If the decryption fails or the commitment is invalid, the organizer publishes the secret row-key of row l in the disclose-list instead, i.e., rk_l^S, thus proving to everybody who can access the lists that she was not obliged to disclose the secret information to the creator of row l.

- **Blame Phase:** If the organizer misbehaves and does not provide a protocol-abiding user with the secret information after a reasonable amount of time, the user can blame the organizer. She does this by publishing a blame-entry in the commit-list, referring to the row l and disclosing the secret disclosure key dk_l^S. Thus everybody who can access the lists can see that she did not receive the secret information encrypted to the disclosure key she provided in row l. It can be assumed that the commitment (which cannot be decrypted by the verifying public) was correct, as otherwise the organizer would have published the secret row-key of row l.

In this way, the commit-disclose protocol does not keep the organizer from cheating, but it allows the user to reliably blame the organizer if it is the case.

4.3   Basic Security Properties

The basic security properties are fulfilled by the construction of an event, invitations and commitments described in Sect. 4.1 and the guarantees of the PKI. The first basic security property is fulfilled because an invitation $i_{e_k}^{u_j}$ for a user u_j is created by using the event's private key e_k^S, owned by the organizer o_{e_k} to sign the invited user's identifier. The invitee cannot forge the event's key and the organizer cannot deny having issued the invitation because the signature used to sign the invitation is publicly verifiable. The second basic security property is also fulfilled because an organizer o_{e_k} cannot forge a commitment $c_{e_k}^{u_j}$ as she is not able to forge another users' signature. A user u_j, having sent the commitment $c_{e_k}^{u_j}$ to the organizer o_{e_k}, cannot deny the commitment as her signature is again publicly verifiable and binding to the event e_k.

4.4   Invitee Identity Privacy and Invitee Count Privacy

In order to implement properties IIP and ICP, we let the organizer o_{e_k} store all invitation objects for the event in the invite-list. Retrieving the list requires knowledge of the invite-list link ILL, and in order to decrypt it, the symmetric invite-list key ILK must be known beforehand.

Knowledge of the link ILL is equivalent to learning the total number of invitations, even if the decryption key ILK is unknown because the number of invitations can be inferred from the size of the ciphertext in the list. Knowledge of the encryption key ILK allows learning the identities of the invited users I_{e_k} because the invitations $i_{e_k}^{u_j}$ store the user identifiers in plain text.

If the organizer o_{e_k} wants to make the identifiers of the invitees I_{e_k}, or the amount of them, i.e., $|I_{e_k}|$, available to all users U, she will publish ILL or ILK in plain text together with the event object $event_k$. Making this information available only for invitees I_{e_k} can be realized by the organizer privately sharing it with the invited users. In order to share the decryption key ILK only with the committed users C_{e_k}, the commit-disclose protocol can be used, while the link ILL is then either available publicly (i.e., choosing U for property ICP), shared only with the invitees (i.e., choosing I_{e_k} for ICP) or kept secret and only shared with the committed users together with ILK (i.e., choosing C_{e_k} for ICP).

It is also possible to avoid sharing any information about the invitations by keeping ILL and ILK secret, i.e., choosing o_{e_k} both for properties IIP and ICP. When the identities should not be known to anyone but the number of invitees should be made public to a subset of users (i.e., choosing o_{e_k} for property IIP), the link ILL will be shared with the respective users and a particular encryption scheme for the invite-list is employed: Instead of encrypting the invite-list as a whole, we encrypt its individual entries with the public keys of the recipient of the invitation stored at each entry. Thus, the invited users can verify that their own invitation is included in the list. However, this only allows for a weak verification of the correctness of the list, i.e., it provides an upper-bound of the size of the list, because the organizer o_{e_k} can add invalid or dummy entries (e.g., to artificially increase the perceived number of invitees to the event).

A summary of how ILL and ILK are shared depending on the choice of parameters for properties IIP and ICP is shown in Table 1. Note that the row describing the privacy settings IIP: C_{e_k}, ICP: I_{e_k} corresponds to the example mentioned in the introduction and Sect. 3.

Table 1. Sharing of ILL and ILK as per the IIP and ICP settings. P = publicly available in $event_k$, I = privately shared with I_{e_k}, C = shared only with C_{e_k} (via the commit-disclose protocol), S = fully secret (only o_{e_k} knows about it) and S* = special encryption scheme for the invite-list.

SETTINGS		IMPLEMENTATION	
IIP	ICP	ILL	ILK
U	U	P	P
I_{e_k}	U	P	I
	I_{e_k}	I	I
C_{e_k}	U	P	C
	I_{e_k}	I	C
	C_{e_k}	C	C
o_{e_k}	U	P	S*
	I_{e_k}	I	S*
	C_{e_k}	C	S*
	o_{e_k}	S	S

4.5   Attendee Identity Privacy and Attendee Count Privacy

To implement the AIP and ACP properties, we mainly use the commit-disclose protocol. The link to the commit-list CLL can be shared publicly in the event object $event_k$ except for those cases where the count of attendees $|C_{e_k}|$ must be kept private. In this situation, if the invitees I_{e_k} are allowed to learn $|C_{e_k}|$, CLL is shared privately with them. Alternatively, the organizer can add dummy entries in the list to hinder inferences from the number of (encrypted) entries. When not even attendees should learn how many other users are attending, dummy entries in the commit-list are the only solution as the CLL must always be shared with all invitees, so that they can commit if they want to attend.

Dummy entries follow the pattern of usual entries, i.e., random data with a specific size to fake an encrypted commitment object and a public key in the commit-list, and random data in the disclose-list to fake an encrypted secret. All users who hold the private row-keys can identify them because the first part of a dummy entry in the commit-list cannot be decrypted with the respective row-key, while those users without the private row-keys cannot distinguish dummy entries from real ones as the ciphertext structure looks the same for all of them.

When the link CLL should not be shared publicly in the event object $event_k$, a salted hash of the link will be stored instead so that the organizer o_{e_k} cannot cheat by sharing different links with different groups of users. As the event object is unique per event and group of invitees, the invited users can check they all got the same link from the organizer by comparing it with the hash value in $event_k$.

Otherwise the implementation varies only in how the private row-keys are disclosed, as they protect the commitments in the commit-list: If all users U are allowed to learn who is attending, the private row-keys will be public, i.e., the rows do not need to be encrypted. If only the invited users I_{e_k} should see the identities of the attendees, the private row-keys will be shared with the invitees directly. And if only the attending users should learn about the identities of other attendees, the private row-keys are disclosed using the commit-disclose protocol.

This way we are able to implement all possible parameter combinations of the AIP and ACP properties, except for the combination AIP: o_{e_k}, ACP: C_{e_k}. For this case, i.e., AIP: o_{e_k}, nobody except the organizer should learn the identities of the committed users, so the private row-keys have to be kept secret. And as not even invitees (who need to know CLL to be able to commit to the event) should learn the count of attendees, the organizer would need to add dummy entries on the commit-list to hide the count of attendees from the invitees. But this will also hide it from the attendees, as they do not have the private row-keys to tell apart dummy entries from normal entries, so ACP: C_{e_k} is not fulfilled.

A summary of how CLL and the private row-keys $rk_1^S \ldots rk_n^S$ are shared depending on the settings for properties AIP and ACP is shown in Table 2.

Table 2. Sharing of CLL and $rk_1^S \ldots rk_n^S$ as per the AIP and ACP settings. P = publicly available in $event_k$, I = privately shared with I_{e_k}, C = shared only with C_{e_k} (via the commit-disclose protocol), S = fully secret (only o_{e_k} knows about it).

SETTINGS		IMPLEMENTATION			
AIP	ACP	CLL	$rk_1^S \ldots rk_n^S$	dummies	notes
U	U	P	P	-	
I_{e_k}	U	P	I	-	
	I_{e_k}	P/I	I	if CLL public	
C_{e_k}	U	P	C	-	
	I_{e_k}	P/I	C	if CLL public	
	C_{e_k}	P	C	necessary	
o_{e_k}	U	P	S	-	
	I_{e_k}	I	S	-	
	C_{e_k}	-	-	-	not possible
	o_{e_k}	P	S	necessary	

4.6   Attendee-Only Information Reliability Property

To implement this property, we will again use the commit-disclose protocol. The organizer o_{e_k} shares a private description $d_{e_k}^S$, encrypted with the key PDK, with the committed users C_{e_k}. The key is shared with these users in the disclose-list as soon as they store a valid commitment $c_{e_k}^{u_j}$ in the commit-list. The organizer

o_{e_k} cannot have different private descriptions for groups of attendees of the same event e_k because they will all see the same ciphertext in the event object $event_k$. A cheating organizer o_{e_k} will be caught in the same manner as described above: if a user u_j commits and receives an invalid decryption key PDK, she will publish the private disclose key dk_i^S to prove that she did not receive the promised private description $d_{e_k}^S$.

5   Discussion

The implementation presented realizes the event invitation feature in a decentralized system and fulfills the requirements of all of the defined security and privacy properties. Except for one parameter combination of the attendee identity/count privacy properties we were able to present implementation solutions for all possible choices of the tunable properties IIP, ICP, AIP and ACP.

An honest but curious user does not learn anything more than what is specified by the privacy settings.

A general limitation of our approach is, however, that for all properties based on the commit-disclose protocol, a malicious organizer is still able to cheat. But it disincentives her to do so as it provides a reliable cheating detection mechanism and offers the affected users the possibility to blame a cheating organizer – either publicly or in front of a chosen set of users, e.g., only other invitees of the event. We consider this an effective protection in the social scenarios that we see as possible application contexts of the event invitation feature. User identifiers are long-lived there and costly to change (as all friends have to be informed about a new identity), so we assume users care about their reputation and will try to avoid being exposed as misbehaving. Another limitation of our approach is the general problem of information usage control, i.e., insiders can always leak information to parties that should not learn this information according to a chosen privacy setting. For example, if only the invitees should learn the identities of other invited users, this can be violated by an invitee simply publishing the invite-list.

Some of the privacy protections are not secure against very powerful adversaries. For example the link obfuscation technique described in Sect. 4.2 relies on the unlinkability of the encrypted list object and the event object. This will be decreased by access patterns of invited users (if they are known), the structure/size of the list object (if distinguishable from other storage objects) and the entropy of the addressing scheme for storage objects. An adversary with the capability to pervasively monitor a large fraction of network traffic might be able to correlate requests for a certain event object and related list objects.

Finally, depending on the choice of privacy settings, the protocols not only allow the participants, i.e., organizer, invitees and attendees, to verify each others' claims, but also, to show the proof to an outsider. Such a process can be implemented in a client and used as one of the inputs for a reputation system, although this is out of the scope of this work.

6   Conclusion and Future Work

We have described and formalized a set of security and privacy properties for the event invitations feature in DOSNs, such as invitee/attendee identity privacy (who learns the identities of the invitees/attendees), invitee/attendee count privacy (who learns the count of invitees/attendees), and attendee-only information reliability (availability of information exclusive to the attendees).

We described privacy enhancing tools, such as storage location indirection (to control not only who can decrypt an object but also who can see the ciphertext), controlled ciphertext inference (to allow a controlled information leak, e.g., about the size of an encrypted object to parties not able to decrypt the content) and a commit-disclose protocol to disclose a secret only to users who committed to attend an event and to detect a misbehaving party. Using these tools together with standard cryptographic primitives, we proposed a TTP-free architecture and decentralized protocols to implement the event invitation feature in a DOSN and analyzed the usability and privacy implications.

The results can be applied in the context of Privacy-Preserving DOSNs, but might also be useful in other domains such as Collaborative Working Environment and their corresponding collaborative-specific tools, i.e., groupware, for example, to perform tasks on shared documents. Another relevant domain is Massively Open Online Course, for example, when restricting the access to lecture material of an online course to the registered students.

Possible future work includes evaluation of the performance, extending the security and privacy properties to include plausible deniability, anonymity or revocation, and extending the functionality of the feature to consider transferable invitation-rights or multiple organizers. Plausible deniability properties can be important when organizing political events. At the same time, it will probably introduce trade-offs with respect to the authenticity guarantees provided by the properties presented in this paper, e.g., the correctness of the attendee-count. Transferable invitation-rights would allow the organizer to specify a set of initially invited users, who then in turn can invite their friends to the event as well (but maybe limited to a certain number of hops in the social graph).

Acknowledgments. This research has been funded by the Swedish Foundation for Strategic Research grant SSF FFL09-0086 and the Swedish Research Council grant VR 2009-3793.

References

1. Baden, R., Bender, A., Spring, N., Bhattacharjee, B., Starin, D.: Persona: an online social network with user-defined privacy. In: Rodriguez, P., Biersack, E.W., Papagiannaki, K., Rizzo, L. (eds.) SIGCOMM, pp. 135–146. ACM (2009)
2. Buszko, D., Lee, W.H.D., Helal, A.: Decentralized ad-hoc groupware API and framework for mobile collaboration. In: GROUP, pp. 5–14. ACM (2001)
3. Cutillo, L.A., Molva, R., Strufe, T.: Safebook: a privacy-preserving online social network leveraging on real-life trust. IEEE Commun. **47**(12), 94–101 (2009)

4. El-Saddik, A., Rahman, A.S.M.M., Abdala, S., Solomon, B.: PECOLE: P2P multimedia collaborative environment. Multimed. Tools Appl. **39**(3), 353–377 (2008)
5. Famulari, A., Hecker, A.: Mantle: a novel DOSN leveraging free storage and local software. In: Guyot, V. (ed.) ICAIT 2012. LNCS, vol. 7593, pp. 213–224. Springer, Heidelberg (2013)
6. Freitas, M.: twister - a P2P microblogging platform. CoRR abs/1312.7152 (2013)
7. Gilbert, H., Handschuh, H.: Security analysis of SHA-256 and sisters. In: Matsui, M., Zuccherato, R.J. (eds.) SAC 2003. LNCS, vol. 3006, pp. 175–193. Springer, Heidelberg (2004)
8. Greschbach, B., Kreitz, G., Buchegger, S.: The devil is in the metadata - new privacy challenges in decentralised online social networks. In: PerCom Workshops, pp. 333–339. IEEE (2012)
9. Greschbach, B., Kreitz, G., Buchegger, S.: User search with knowledge thresholds in decentralized online social networks. In: Hansen, M., Hoepman, J.-H., Leenes, R., Whitehouse, D. (eds.) Privacy and Identity 2014. IFIP AICT, vol. 421, pp. 188–202. Springer, Heidelberg (2014)
10. Johnson-Lenz, P., Johnson-Lenz, T.: Groupware: coining and defining it. SIGGROUP Bull. **19**(2), 34 (1998)
11. Kim, M.K., Kim, H.C.: Awareness and privacy in groupware systems. In: CSCWD, pp. 984–988. IEEE (2006)
12. Li, W.D., Ong, S.K., Fuh, J.Y.H., Wong, Y.S., Lu, Y.Q., Nee, A.Y.C.: Feature-based design in a distributed and collaborative environment. Comput. Aided Des. **36**(9), 775–797 (2004)
13. Lunden, I.: Facebook turns off facial recognition in the EU, gets the all-clear on several points from Ireland's data protection commissioner on its review, September 2012. http://techcrunch.com/2012/09/21/facebook-turns-off-facial-recognition-in-the-eu-gets-the-all-clear/
14. Nakamoto, S.: Bitcoin: A peer-to-peer electronic cash system (2009). http://www.bitcoin.org/bitcoin.pdf
15. Reinhard, W., Schweitzer, J., Völksen, G., Weber, M.: CSCW tools: concepts and architectures. IEEE Comput. **27**(5), 28–36 (1994)
16. Rodden, T., Blair, G.S.: CSCW and distributed systems: the problem of control. In: Bannon, L.J., Robinson, M., Schmidt, K. (eds.) ECSCW. Kluwer (1991)
17. Rowstron, A., Druschel, P.: Pastry: scalable, decentralized object location, and routing for large-scale peer-to-peer systems. In: Guerraoui, R. (ed.) Middleware 2001. LNCS, vol. 2218, pp. 329–350. Springer, Heidelberg (2001)
18. Shih, G.: Facebook admits year-long data breach exposed 6 million users, June 2013. http://www.reuters.com/article/2013/06/21/net-us-facebook-security-idUS BRE95K18Y20130621
19. Smith, C.: Reinventing social media: Deep learning, predictive marketing, and image recognition will change everything, March 2014. http://www.businessinsider.com/social-medias-big-data-future-2014-3
20. Trevor, J., Koch, T., Woetzel, G.: Metaweb: bringing synchronous groupware to the world wide web. In: ECSCW, pp. 65–80 (1997)
21. Zhang, G., Jin, Q.: Scalable information sharing utilizing decentralized p2p networking integrated with centralized personal and group media tools. In: AINA (2), pp. 707–711. IEEE Computer Society (2006)
22. Zurko, M.E.: IBM Lotus Notes/Domino: Embedding Security in Collaborative Applications, Chap. 30. O'Reilly Media, Inc., Sebastopol (2005)

Blank Digital Signatures: Optimization and Practical Experiences

David Derler[✉], Christian Hanser, and Daniel Slamanig

Institute for Applied Information Processing and Communications (IAIK),
Graz University of Technology (TUG), Inffeldgasse 16a, 8010 Graz, Austria
{david.derler,christian.hanser,daniel.slamanig}@tugraz.at

Abstract. Blank Digital Signatures (BDS) [18] enable an originator to delegate the signing rights for a template, containing fixed and exchangeable elements, to a proxy. The proxy is then able to choose one of the predefined values for each exchangeable element and issue a signature for such an instantiation of the template on behalf of the originator. In this paper, we propose optimizations for the BDS scheme from [18] and present a library, integrating this optimized version within the Java Cryptography Architecture and the keying material into X.509 certificates. To illustrate the flexibility of the proposed library, we introduce two proof-of-concept implementations building up on XML and PDF, respectively. Finally, we give a detailed insight in the performance of the protocol and our implementation.

1 Introduction

In contrast to conventional digital signatures, involving a signer and a verifier, proxy-type digital signature schemes are signature schemes involving three parties, namely an originator, a proxy and a verifier. Here, the originator delegates the signing power (for some particular well defined set of messages) to a proxy. The proxy can then sign messages on behalf of the originator. Any verifier, given a message and a corresponding signature, can check whether the proxy has produced the signature on behalf of the originator (authenticity), the integrity of the message and whether the given message is one of the "allowed" messages.

Blank Digital Signatures (BDS) [18] are a special instance of proxy-type digital signatures, allowing an originator to define and issue a signature on a template, containing fixed and exchangeable elements. A designated proxy can then produce signatures for instantiations of this template (messages). More precisely, given a template signature, the proxy creates an instantiation by choosing one of the predefined values for each of the exchangeable elements and issues a signature with respect to the template signature. When verifying this signature, only the message and the corresponding signature is needed, and it is required that the verifier

Part of this work has been supported by the European Commission through project FP7-FutureID, grant agreement number 318424. We thank the anonymous referees for their helpful comments.

J. Camenisch et al. (Eds.): Privacy and Identity 2014, IFIP AICT 457, pp. 201–215, 2015.
DOI: 10.1007/978-3-319-18621-4_14

does not learn anything about the unused choices in the exchangeable elements in the template (privacy property).

Blank Digital Signatures give rise to a lot of interesting applications, and, accordingly, the question arises how a BDS scheme would perform in a practical implementation, and to which extent it can be integrated into off-the-shelf cryptographic frameworks such as the Java Cryptography Architecture [26] and key infrastructures such as PKIX [8].

1.1 Our Contribution

In this paper, we propose optimizations for the BDS scheme in [18] and present a full-fledged implementation of this optimized version. Firstly, we briefly revisit the scheme and discuss possible practical applications. Then, we show how the scheme can be modified to use Type-3 pairings instead of the originally proposed Type-1 pairings and introduce optimizations for the encoding of templates. Subsequently, we show how the scheme can be integrated into the Java Cryptography Architecture and how the keying material can be encapsulated within X.509 certificates. Moreover, two possible signature formats, namely an XML and a PDF signature format, are proposed. Finally, timings of our implementation, showing the practical applicability of the BDS scheme, are provided and discussed.

2   Background

We use additive notation for groups, which are always of prime order p. A function $\epsilon : \mathbb{N} \to \mathbb{R}^+$ is called *negligible* if for all $c > 0$ there is a k_0 such that $\epsilon(k) < 1/k^c$ for all $k > k_0$. In the remainder of this paper, we use ϵ to denote such a negligible function.

Definition 1 (Bilinear Map:). *A bilinear map (pairing) is a map* $e : \mathbb{G}_1 \times \mathbb{G}_2 \to \mathbb{G}_T$, *where* $\mathbb{G}_1, \mathbb{G}_2$ *and* $\mathbb{G}_T$ *are cyclic groups of prime order* p. *Let* P *and* P' *generate* $\mathbb{G}_1$ *and* $\mathbb{G}_2$, *respectively. We require* e *to be efficiently computable and to satisfy:*

    Bilinearity: $e(aP, bP') = e(P, P')^{ab} = e(bP, aP') \quad \forall a, b \in \mathbb{Z}_p$
    Non-degeneracy: $e(P, P') \neq 1_{\mathbb{G}_T}$, *i.e.,* $e(P, P')$ *generates* $\mathbb{G}_T$.

If $\mathbb{G}_1 = \mathbb{G}_2$, e *is called* symmetric *and* asymmetric *otherwise. Asymmetric pairings can be either Type-2 or Type-3 pairings. The difference between Type-2 and Type-3 pairings is that an efficiently computable isomorphism* $\Psi : \mathbb{G}_2 \to \mathbb{G}_1$ *exists for Type-2 pairings, while for Type-3 pairings such an isomorphism is unknown.*

Definition 2 (t-SDH Assumption [5]). *Let* p *be a prime of bitlength* κ, $\mathbb{G}_1$ *and* $\mathbb{G}_2$ *be finite cyclic groups of order* p, *generated by* $P \in \mathbb{G}_1$ *and* $P' \in \mathbb{G}_2$, *respectively,* $P = \Psi(P')$, $\alpha \in_R \mathbb{Z}_p^*$ *and* $t > 0$. *Then, for all PPT adversaries* $\mathcal{A}$ *it holds that*

$$\Pr\left[\left(c, \frac{1}{\alpha + c}P\right) \leftarrow \mathcal{A}(P, (\alpha^i P')_{i=0}^t)\right] \leq \epsilon(\kappa), \text{ where } c \in \mathbb{Z}_p \setminus \{-\alpha\}.$$

In this paper, we concentrate on Type-3 pairings on Barreto-Naehrig curves [4] with embedding degree 12. Thus, elements in $\mathbb{G}_T$ have a bitlength of $12 \cdot$ bitlength(p). For our setting, we chose a bitlength of 256 bits, leading to a bitlength of 3072bit in $\mathbb{G}_T$. This choice is ideal w.r.t. the comparable strengths proposed by NIST [3], since the discrete logarithm problem should be equally hard in the additive groups $\mathbb{G}_1$, $\mathbb{G}_2$ and in the multiplicative group $\mathbb{G}_T$. In the Type-3 setting, we can use the natural counterpart of the t-SDH assumption, i.e., the co-t-SDH assumption [7,19].

Definition 3 (co-t-SDH Assumption [7,19]). *Let p be a prime of bitlength κ, $\mathbb{G}_1$ and $\mathbb{G}_2$ be finite cyclic groups of order p, generated by $P_1 \in \mathbb{G}_1$ and $P_2 \in \mathbb{G}_2$, respectively, $\alpha \in_R \mathbb{Z}_p^*$, $i \in \{1,2\}$ and $t > 0$. Then, for all PPT adversaries $\mathcal{A}$ it holds that*

$$\Pr\left[\left(c, \frac{1}{\alpha+c}P_i\right) \leftarrow \mathcal{A}((\alpha^i P_1)_{i=0}^t, (\alpha^i P_2)_{i=0}^t)\right] \leq \epsilon(\kappa), \text{ where } c \in \mathbb{Z}_p \setminus \{-\alpha\}.$$

2.1 Digital Signature Schemes

A *digital signature scheme* DSS is a triple (DKeyGen, DSign, DVerify) of PPT algorithms. Thereby, DKeyGen is a key generation algorithm that takes a security parameter $\kappa \in \mathbb{N}$ as input and outputs a secret (signing) key sk and a public (verification) key pk. Further, DSign is a (probabilistic) algorithm, which takes a message $M \in \{0,1\}^*$ and a secret key sk as input, and outputs a signature σ. Finally, DVerify is a deterministic algorithm, which takes a signature σ, a message $M \in \{0,1\}^*$ and a public key pk as input, and outputs a single bit $b \in \{\text{true}, \text{false}\}$ indicating whether σ is a valid signature for M under pk.

A digital signature scheme is required to be *correct*, i.e., for all security parameters κ, all (sk, pk) generated by DKeyGen and all $M \in \{0,1\}^*$ one requires DVerify(DSign(M, sk), M, pk) = true. Additionally, for security one requires existential unforgeability under adaptively chosen-message attacks (EUF-CMA) [16].

2.2 Java Cryptography Architecture

The Java Cryptography Architecture [26] (JCA) constitutes an API, providing standardized access to cryptographic algorithms. Each library that implements this API needs to implement a so-called cryptographic `Provider`, registering the provided algorithm implementations at the JCA. The desired `Provider` is then set by the user of the library, and instances of the algorithm implementations can be obtained using the JCA-provided factories. The primitives we use in this paper are implementations of the `Signature` interface, the `KeyPairGenerator` interface and the `KeyFactory` interface, respectively. The `Signature` interface resembles the DSign and DVerify functionality of a digital signature scheme as discussed above, whereas the `KeyPairGenerator` interface and the `KeyFactory` interface provide methods for conveniently generating and handling keys in general. Using the JCA, entire implementations can be easily exchanged by simply setting another `Provider`.

3   The Blank Digital Signature Scheme

In this section, we introduce the notion of BDS schemes in general, and then give a brief overview of the BDS scheme from [18] (further referred to as BDSS). We discuss the basic building blocks, as well as the principles underlying the signature generation and verification. Since this paper lays focus on the practical aspects of the BDSS, we keep this section quite informal and refer the reader to [18] for more formal definitions.

A BDS scheme allows an *originator* to designate the signing rights for a certain template to a *proxy*. A template $\mathcal{T}$, thereby, is a sequence of non-empty sets of bitstrings T_i. Depending on the cardinality of the respective set, such sets are either called fixed or exchangeable elements, i.e., fixed elements contain exactly one bitstring, whereas exchangeable elements contain $k > 1$ distinct bitstrings. More formally, we have:

$$\mathcal{T} = (T_1, T_2, \ldots, T_n), \ T_i = \{M_{i_1}, M_{i_2}, \ldots, M_{i_k}\}.$$

The template length is defined as the sequence length n of the template, while the template size $|\mathcal{T}|$ is defined as $|\mathcal{T}| = \sum_{i=1}^{n} |T_i|$. Furthermore, each template is assigned a unique identifier $id_{\mathcal{T}}$. Once the template is defined, the *originator* issues a signature on $\mathcal{T}$ for a particular *proxy*. Based on this so called template signature, the designated *proxy* can choose concrete values for each exchangeable element (fixed elements stay fixed) and compute a so called instance signature on this message $\mathcal{M} = (M_i)_{i=1}^{n}$. With the instance signature at hand, anyone is able to verify the validity of the instance signature and the designation.

Besides the usual *correctness* property, a BDS scheme provides *unforgeability*, *immutability* and *privacy*. Informally, these properties are defined as follows. *Unforgeability* requires that, without knowledge of the secret keys, it is intractable to (existentially) forge template or instance signatures. *Immutability* essentially models a stronger adversary in the unforgeability setting, i.e., additionally covers adversaries knowing the signing key of the proxy. Finally, *privacy* requires that it is intractable (for outsiders) to determine template elements (except the ones revealed by instantiations).

3.1   Applications

Basically, a BDS scheme enables an originator to hand over a signed form (template), containing fixed and exchangeable elements, to a proxy being designated to sign an arbitrary instance of this form, i.e., a filled in form, on behalf of the originator. Figure 1 illustrates a sample template running through a BDS protocol execution. As shown in this figure, it is also possible to encode yes-/no-choices within a template by simply encoding yes and no in an exchangeable element.

In particular, a BDS scheme is applicable to any contract, which requires to leave a few choices open to an intermediary party, while the rest of the content is fixed. For instance, it would be thinkable that a broker makes a business deal on behalf of a client, using a template, previously defined and signed by the client [18].

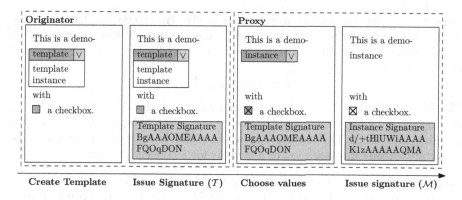

Fig. 1. Schematic view of the BDS scheme

Thereby, it can be of importance that the unused choices of the template do not get revealed upon verification of an instance signature, which is ensured by the *privacy property* of BDS schemes. Other applications cover various fields, among others, any types of digital reports like lab reports in healthcare, or authorized (public) tender forms, questionnaires and application forms in the eGovernment field.

3.2 The BDSS

From a technical point of view, the BDSS builds up on standard digital signature schemes and a modified version of the polynomial commitments proposed by Kate et al. [24].[1] Using these polynomial commitments necessitates a unique encoding, mapping templates and messages to polynomials in the polynomial ring $\mathbb{Z}_p[X]$. For the rest of this paper, let $H : \{0,1\}^* \to \mathbb{Z}_p$ be a secure cryptographic hash function. The BDSS uses the following (unique) encoding for a template $\mathcal{T}$, which is denoted by $t(X) \in \mathbb{Z}_p[X]$:

$$t(X) \leftarrow \prod_{i=1}^{n} \prod_{M \in T_i} (X - H(M\|id_{\mathcal{T}}\|i)).$$

An encoding $m(X) \in \mathbb{Z}_p[X]$ of a message $\mathcal{M}$ looks as follows:

$$m(X) \leftarrow \prod_{i=1}^{n} (X - H(M_i\|id_{\mathcal{T}}\|i)).$$

Finally, the so-called complementary message polynomial $\overline{m}(X)$ is defined such that $t(X) = m(X) \cdot \overline{m}(X)$ holds. More precisely, $\overline{m}(X)$ contains all factors which are contained in $t(X)$ but not in $m(X)$. For the rest of this paper, we use $\mathcal{C}_{\mathcal{T}}, \mathcal{C}_{\mathcal{M}}$ and $\mathcal{C}_{\overline{\mathcal{M}}}$ to denote the (polynomial) commitments to the encodings of templates,

---

[1] Note that this polynomial commitment variant has later been formalized in [19].

messages and complementary-messages, respectively. The commitments used in the BDSS are unconditionally hiding and computationally binding and due to the nature of the commitments (they are instantiated within bilinear groups), it holds that

$$e(\mathcal{C}_T, P) = e(\mathcal{C}_\mathcal{M}, \mathcal{C}_{\overline{\mathcal{M}}}).$$

The BDSS defines five algorithms, which we briefly introduce subsequently. We assume the public parameters pp generated in KeyGen to be an implicit input to all other algorithms. Furthermore, we assume that both, the originator and the proxy are already in possession of a keypair for a conventional DSS.

KeyGen: This algorithm takes a security parameter κ and an upper bound t for the template size. It chooses two groups $\mathbb{G}_1, \mathbb{G}_T$ of the same prime order p (with $\log_2 p = \kappa$), generated by P, having a bilinear map $e : \mathbb{G}_1 \times \mathbb{G}_1 \to \mathbb{G}_T$, a secure cryptographic hash function $H : \{0,1\}^* \to \mathbb{Z}_p$ and a random $\alpha \in \mathbb{Z}_p^*$. Finally, it outputs the public parameters $\mathsf{pp} = (H, \mathbb{G}_1, e, p, (\alpha^i P)_{i=0}^t)$.[2]

Sign: This algorithm takes a template T of length n, the signing key of the originator $\mathsf{sk_O}$ and the verification key of the proxy $\mathsf{pk_P}$. It computes the commitment $\mathcal{C}_T$ to T, $\mathcal{C} = e(\mathcal{C}_T, P)$ and $\tau = \mathsf{DSign}(id_T || \mathcal{C} || n || \mathsf{pk_P}, \mathsf{sk_O})$ and outputs $\sigma_T = (id_T, \mathcal{C}, n, \tau)$ together with a private instantiation key for the proxy $\mathsf{sk_P^T}$ (required for recomputing the commitment).

Verify$_T$: This algorithm takes a template T, a template signature σ_T, the verification keys of the originator ($\mathsf{pk_O}$) and the proxy ($\mathsf{pk_P}$), as well as $\mathsf{sk_P^T}$. It computes $\mathcal{C}_T$ and $\mathcal{C} = e(\mathcal{C}_T, P)$, and outputs the result of $\mathsf{DVerify}(\sigma_T, id_T || \mathcal{C} || n || \mathsf{pk_P}, \mathsf{pk_O})$.

Inst: This algorithm takes a template T with corresponding message $\mathcal{M}$, a template signature σ_T, the signing key of the proxy $\mathsf{sk_P}$ and the instantiation key $\mathsf{sk_P^T}$. It computes $\mathcal{C}_{\overline{\mathcal{M}}}$ and $\mu = \mathsf{DSign}(\tau || \mathcal{C}_{\overline{\mathcal{M}}} || \mathcal{M}, \mathsf{sk_P})$ and returns $\sigma_\mathcal{M} = (\mu, \mathcal{C}_{\overline{\mathcal{M}}}, \mathcal{M}, \sigma_T)$.

Verify$_\mathcal{M}$: This algorithm takes $\mathcal{M}$, $\sigma_\mathcal{M}$ and the verification keys of the originator ($\mathsf{pk_O}$) and the proxy ($\mathsf{pk_P}$) and computes $\mathcal{C}_\mathcal{M}$ from $\mathcal{M}$. Then, it checks whether $\mathsf{DVerify}(\tau, id_T || \mathcal{C} || n || \mathsf{pk_P}, \mathsf{pk_O}) = \mathtt{true}$ and $\mathsf{DVerify}(\mu, \tau || \mathcal{C}_{\overline{\mathcal{M}}} || \mathcal{M}, \mathsf{pk_P}) = \mathtt{true}$ holds. If so, it checks whether the number of elements in the message is equal to n, whether there is exactly one element at each position in the message and whether $e(\mathcal{C}_\mathcal{M}, \mathcal{C}_{\overline{\mathcal{M}}}) = \mathcal{C}$. On success it returns $\mathtt{true}$ and $\mathtt{false}$ otherwise.

4   Tweaks and Optimizations

Since the BDSS is designed for Type-1 pairings, we need to modify the scheme to make it compatible with much more efficient Type-3 pairings. In this section we discuss these modifications, together with an optimization regarding the encoding of templates and messages to reduce the degree of the encoding polynomials.

---

[2] Note that these parameters are required for computing the polynomial commitments.

4.1   Using Type-3 Pairings

The authors of [18] informally suggested that the scheme can be used with Type-3 pairings by duplicating some of the points in the system-wide parameters, i.e., some points in $\mathbb{G}_1$ also have to be mapped to points in $\mathbb{G}_2$. In the following, we discuss the necessary modifications in detail. For all these modifications it is crucial that the counterpart Q' in $\mathbb{G}_2$, of a point Q in $\mathbb{G}_1$, contains the same discrete logarithm as the point Q, i.e., $Q = aP$ and $Q' = aP'$ for $a \in \mathbb{Z}_p$.

Currently, the system-wide parameters pp of the BDS scheme contain a sequence $\mathcal{P} = (\alpha^i P)_{i=0}^t$ of multiples of a point P, with t being the maximal template size. For Type-3 pairings, the sequence has to be extended with the same multiples of a point $P' \in \mathbb{G}_2$, i.e., $\mathcal{P}' = ((\alpha^i P)_{i=0}^t, (\alpha^i P')_{i=0}^t)$.

In the subsequent protocol steps, one has to choose the appropriate representative of the required point, i.e., the representative in $\mathbb{G}_1$ or $\mathbb{G}_2$. Additionally, in the verification step of the message (Verify$_\mathcal{M}$) the pairing $e(\mathcal{C}_\mathcal{M}, \mathcal{C}_{\overline{\mathcal{M}}})$ is evaluated. Thus, in the instantiation step (Inst), the commitment to the complementary message polynomial $\mathcal{C}_{\overline{\mathcal{M}}}$ needs to be computed in $\mathbb{G}_2$.[3] Using this modification, the computation of $\mathcal{C}_{\overline{\mathcal{M}}}$ is the only remaining computation which requires operations in $\mathbb{G}_2$. Thus, it seems to be impossible to find further optimizations based on moving computations from one group to the other.

It is easy to see that switching to the Type-3 setting does not influence the security of the scheme. The original BDSS [18] was proven secure under the t-SDH assumption. Using the co-t-SDH assumption, the security proof of the modified BDSS is (up to the extended problem instance) equivalent to the original proof in [18], and, thus, using Type-3 pairings does not influence the security of the scheme.

4.2   Aggregating Fixed Elements

An important optimization can be based on the reduction of the degree of the encoding polynomials by aggregation. The idea behind the aggregation of the fixed elements is the observation that in the originally proposed BDSS encoding, each fixed element corresponds to one factor in the encoding polynomials. The scheme does, however, not require this separate encoding. Thus, we can simply aggregate the fixed elements within one factor of the encoding polynomials by concatenating the identifier of the template, the messages and the positions of the messages in the template as follows:

$$m_i = M_i||i, M = m_1||m_2||...||m_u$$
$$m_{\text{fixed}}(X) = X - H(id_\mathcal{T}||M).$$

This reduces the degree of the encoding polynomials, and, thus, also the computation times. Note that this optimization also enables the reduction of the size

---

[3] We note that it would also be possible to compute $\mathcal{C}_\mathcal{M}$ in $\mathbb{G}_2$ and evaluate the pairing $e(\mathcal{C}_{\overline{\mathcal{M}}}, \mathcal{C}_\mathcal{M})$ upon Verify$_\mathcal{M}$. Then, $\mathcal{C}_{\overline{\mathcal{M}}}$ would still be computed in $\mathbb{G}_1$. However, our goal is to make Verify$_\mathcal{M}$ as fast as possible, and, thus opt for the former option (observe that computations in $\mathbb{G}_2$ are more expensive than computations in $\mathbb{G}_1$).

of the system parameters pp, i.e., pp is no longer dependent on the number of fixed elements. Subsequently, we analyze the security of these modification.

Proof. In the original construction [18], every fixed element represents a factor in the template encoding polynomial and in further consequence in every message encoding polynomial. The modification proposed here integrates all fixed elements into a single factor, which reduces the degree of the respective polynomials. Now, we have to show that this has no impact on the security of the construction. Our argumentation is as follows. Using one factor for the fixed elements in the modified version can be seen as the original construction using only a single fixed element in the template. Therefore, the construction as such still remains secure. What remains to show, however, is that the modified encoding does not influence the correctness (signature soundness) and the unforgeability as well as immutability, respectively.

In this context, signature soundness essentially says that, given a template signature $\sigma_{\mathcal{T}}$ for some template $\mathcal{T}$, the probability that this signature will verify for any $\mathcal{T}' \neq \mathcal{T}$ is negligible in the security parameter κ. To achieve this (for fixed elements), one would need to find

$$H(id_{\mathcal{T}}\|m_{i_1}\|i_1\| \ldots \|m_{i_u}\|i_u) = H(id_{\mathcal{T}'}\|m'_{i'_1}\|i'_1\| \ldots \|m'_{i'_{u'}}\|i'_{u'}),$$

which is clearly intractable if H is collision resistant. The same argumentation holds for unforgeability and immutability (cases **T1, M1** [18]), where the problem is to find a second preimage for $H(id_{\mathcal{T}}\|m_{i_1}\|i_1\| \ldots \|m_{i_u}\|i_u)$.   □

5   Implementation in JAVA and Integration into the JCA

In this section, we provide an in-depth description of the implementation related aspects of the optimized BDSS. Our design is based on the observation that the signing and verification algorithms for both, templates and messages, can be interpreted as conventional signature algorithms with special types of messages. This means that one can use a standard signature API, such as the one provided by the Java Cryptography Architecture (JCA) [26], to obtain an easy to use implementation. Furthermore, X.509 provides, among others, a convenient and well-established method to ensure key authenticity and integrity. Besides, also methods for revocation checking are provided [8]. Thus, we follow this approach and integrate the keying material within X.509 certificates.

Finally, we propose two container formats, i.e., XML and PDF, encapsulating the templates and messages, respectively, together with their corresponding signatures.

5.1   Overview

Figure 2 links the BDSS algorithms to the parties performing the respective computations and provides an overview of the required interaction during a usual workflow (note that all algorithms are non-interactive). The gray boxes in

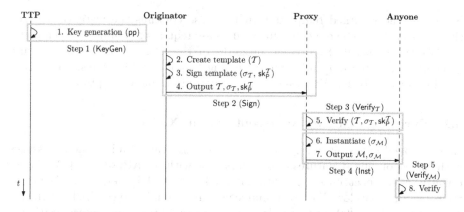

Fig. 2. BDS scheme computation steps

the figure logically group consecutive computation steps to units with defined input and output. For the sake of simplicity, we omitted the visualization of the distribution of the system parameters pp by the trusted third party (TTP). We, however, assume that the TTP provides means for retrieving pp in an authentic manner. For instance, our default implementation encapsulates pp within an X.509 certificate (cf. Sect. 5.2). To provide maximum flexibility, the library relies on a generic interface for accessing the TTP, and, consequently, our library is not bound to one fixed TTP implementation. From a JCA point of view, the generation of pp is wrapped in a `KeyPairGenerator` implementation and is, thus, conveniently usable by arbitrary TTP implementations.

The subsequent steps, i.e., Step 2–5 in Fig. 2, are packed into two JCA `Signature` implementations, namely the `BDSSTemplateSignature` (Step 2 and 3) and the `BDSSInstanceSignature` (Step 4 and 5). To be compatible with the JCA `Signature` interface, we override the `engineSetParameter` method. This way, it is possible to supply so called `AlgorithmParameterSpec` implementations containing the additionally required parameters for executing the protocol. Furthermore, the API assumes that the signing and verification algorithms operate on arrays of bytes. Thus, we (de-)serialize the respective inputs to preserve their structure (cf. Sect. 5.2). Listing 1 provides an example for obtaining a BDSS signature on a template. The `BDSSInstanceSignature` can be used in a similar way and is therefore omitted.

```java
1 Signature signature = Signature.getInstance("BDSSTemplateSignature");
2 TemplateSignParamSpec p = new TemplateSignParamSpec(pp, pkP);
3 signature.setParameter(p);
4 signature.initSign(skO); // set sign mode
5 signature.update(template.serialize()); // add data
6 byte[] templateSignature = signature.sign(); // sign
7
8 TemplateVerifyParamSpec pv = new TemplateVerifyParamSpec(pp, pkP);
9 signature.setParameter(pv);
10 signature.initVerify(pkO); // set verify mode
11 signature.update(template.serialize()); // add data
12 boolean success = signature.verify(templateSignature); // verify
```

Listing 1. Java code to obtain a BDS template signature

Note that the returned template signature also contains the instantiation key sk_P^T, which needs to be removed when a use case requires to publish the template.

Also note that if the privacy property of the BDSS is required, a secure transmission of the output of Step 2 in Fig. 2 is inevitable. Thus, our library provides means for ECIES (see e.g., [22]) encryption and decryption.

5.2   Encoding and Key Representation in X.509

As mentioned before, it is required to (de-)serialize the templates and messages with corresponding signatures to be compatible with the API of the JCA. Consequently, a compact encoding with minimal overhead is desired to keep the transmission times low. We use a unique encoding, similar to the BER/DER [21] encoding of ASN.1 [20] and provide means for serialization and deserialization.

It also turns out that this encoding is useful to integrate the keying material as public key info into X.509 certificates [8]. To (re-)extract the serialized keys from the public key info, our Java cryptographic provider provides the appropriate KeyFactory implementations (performing the deserialization).

To bring the (signed) templates and messages into a user friendly form, e.g., to support users to conveniently fill in a templates, we introduce two container formats in the remainder of this section. For both formats, we follow the approach that the templates and messages are included in a human readable form, whereas the signatures are serialized using our encoding from above.

5.3   Defining an XML Signature Format

To use XML, we added Java annotations for XML binding (JAXB), as defined in [13], to the classes serving as input-/output-containers. These annotations, together with the appropriate XML schema allow to conveniently marshal/unmarshal Java objects to/from XML using the routines provided by the Java platform. Listings 2 and 3 show the proposed signature format, with "?" and "+" denoting the multiplicity of the tags, i.e., "?" means at most once, whereas "+" means at least once.

```
1  <template id="...">
2    (<templateentry>
3      (<message type="exch"|"fix" length="[Integer]">
4        <text>[String]</text>
5      </message>)+
6    </templateentry>)+
7    (<signature>
8      <signaturevalue>[Base64 encoded string]</signaturevalue>
9      (<keyId>[String]</keyId>)?
10     (<ttpcert>[Base64 encoded string]</ttpcert>)?
11     (<originatorcert>[Base64 encoded string]</originatorcert>)?
12     (<proxycert>[Base64 encoded string]</proxycert>)?
13   </signature>)?
14 </template>
```

Listing 2. BDS template format

```
1  <instance id="...">
2    (<message type="exch"|"fix" length="[Integer]">
3       <text>[String]</text>
4    </message>)+
5    (<signature>
6       <signaturevalue>[Base64 encoded string]</signaturevalue>
7       (<keyId>[String]</keyId>)?
8       (<ttpcert>[Base64 encoded string]</ttpcert>)?
9       (<originatorcert>[Base64 encoded string]</originatorcert>)?
10      (<proxycert>[Base64 encoded string]</proxycert>)?
11   </signature>)?
12 </instance>
```

Listing 3. BDS message format

5.4 Using PDF as Signature Format

Signable PDF forms seem to be an essential application of BDSS. Thus, a proof-of-concept implementation using PDF as container format is introduced subsequently. Thereby, our library provides means to create, sign and verify templates and messages in PDF format. Furthermore, signed templates can directly be filled in in the same way as conventional PDF forms using a standard PDF reader. Figure 3 shows a sample template and a corresponding message, both containing a signature.

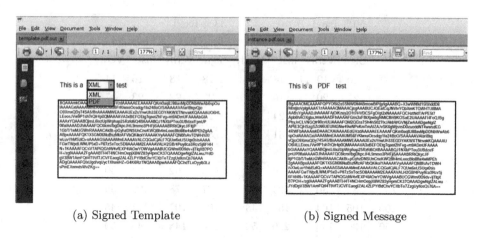

(a) Signed Template   (b) Signed Message

Fig. 3. BDS PDF signature format

6 Performance Evaluation

In this section, we provide an overview of the performance of our proof-of-concept implementation. For the timings, we use the BNPairings library [15] for computing the optimal Ate pairing [30] on BN curves [4] with 256 bit group size and an embedding degree of 12. As conventional digital signatures we use ECDSA [14,17] with the NIST P-224 curve [14]. The timings were performed using a *single* core on a *Lenovo ThinkPad T420s* with an *Intel Core i5 2540M* with 2.6/3.3 GHz and 8 GB of RAM. On the software side Java 1.7.0_55 was used on top of Ubuntu 14.04/amd64.

We measure the execution time of the four protocol steps (Step 2–5 in Fig. 2) for different template sizes and template compositions. To isolate timing-related influences, e.g., the garbage collector, each timing represents the mean of 100 consecutive runs. Figure 1 shows the computation times for template sizes ranging from 3 to 1000. To illustrate the influence of the distribution of the element types on the timing, we provide timings for two different element type distributions. Note that it does not make sense to choose a template with less than 50 % of exchangeable elements, since templates are always chosen minimal, i.e., there are no two fixed elements next to each other.[4] The used element type distribution is indicated by the percentage values in the top row of Table 1. Figure 4 gives an overview of the computation time with increasing template size. As expected, the computation times depend heavily on the degree of the encoding polynomials. Consequently, having more fixed elements, for the same size $|T|$, results in a lower degree polynomial – using our trick from Sect. 4.2 – and corresponding shorter computation times.

Table 1. Timings for various template sizes in milliseconds

	50 % fixed				33 % fixed			
	Template		Message		Template		Message	
$|T|$	Sign	Verify	Inst	Verify	Sign	Verify	Inst	Verify
3	20	19	18	17	18	18	16	14
5	21	20	16	17	23	22	23	17
10	23	23	24	17	28	27	31	19
15	28	27	31	19	31	30	38	20
30	38	37	48	23	43	42	59	24
50	56	55	79	29	63	62	94	30
70	82	80	124	40	77	78	122	35
100	105	104	164	48	105	107	171	45
150	136	135	220	56	150	148	248	59
300	279	277	469	103	289	289	483	103
500	400	395	666	137	490	489	811	163
1000	759	755	1219	241	1053	1050	1656	322

---

[4] For some applications it could make sense to place two or more exchangeable elements next to each other, which would allow to encode ranges. For instance, all three digit numbers could be modeled by three exchangeable elements, each containing the numbers from 0 to 9.

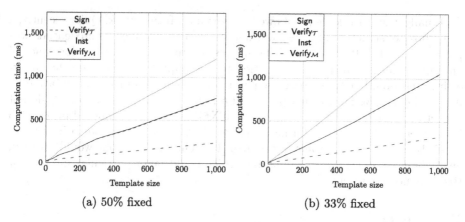

Fig. 4. Computation times in relation to the template-size and the element type distribution.

In practice, most forms will contain less than 100 elements, which leads to computation times of less than 180ms for each step. This is perfectly acceptable for practical use.

Finally, observe that BDS allow to quite straightforwardly define the template in a way, which enables similar functionalities as redactable/sanitizable signatures [2,6,23,25,29]. Although, such an application of BDS is not considered in this paper (it has been done in [28] as a replacement for redactable signatures as used in [31]), we conclude that – due to its good performance – our BDSS implementation might also be an alternative to implementations of redactable/sanitizable signatures (e.g., [27]) in certain settings.

7   Conclusion and Future Work

In this paper, we proposed an optimization regarding the template and message encoding of the BDSS and modified it to use much more efficient Type-3 pairings. We introduced a JCA-based interoperable framework for the BDSS, providing an easy to use API. To illustrate the capabilities, concerning the integration into other applications, two signature formats were proposed. Moreover, we gave an overview of the performance of the scheme and our implementation. Meanwhile, our implementation based on the XML signature format has been integrated into the *FutureID eSignServices* framework [1] – a flexible framework for signature generation and validation.

The execution times presented in Sect. 6 are totally practical, since in most scenarios it can be expected that templates will have a template-size of less than 100, leading to computation times of less than 180 ms for arbitrary template constellations. This shows that the BDSS is fully feasible for practical use. For further details on our BDSS implementation and optimization, we refer the reader to [9].

Finally, there are some points we leave open for future work. Quite recently, a black-box construction of BDS from non-interactive anonymous credentials was presented in [10]. It would, thus, be interesting to compare the performance of an implementation of this construction to our implementation. Another interesting step would be to increase the practical usability of our implementation by integrating the BDSS within a plug-in of a PDF reader. Furthermore, we do not expect any problems when integrating the XML signatures proposed in Sect. 5.3 into other XML signature formats such as XMLDSig [11] or the various types of XML Advanced Electronic Signatures [12]. The latter format would, in turn, enable long term signature validation, which could be of particular interest for BDSS signed contracts.

References

1. FutureID project. http://www.futureid.eu
2. Ateniese, G., Chou, D.H., de Medeiros, B., Tsudik, G.: Sanitizable signatures. In: di Vimercati, S.C., Syverson, P.F., Gollmann, D. (eds.) ESORICS 2005. LNCS, vol. 3679, pp. 159–177. Springer, Heidelberg (2005)
3. Barker, E., Barker, W., Burr, W., Polk, W., Smid, M.: Recommendation for key management - part 1: general (Revision 3). In: NIST. Special Publication (2012)
4. Barreto, P.S.L.M., Naehrig, M.: Pairing-friendly elliptic curves of prime order. In: Preneel, B., Tavares, S. (eds.) SAC 2005. LNCS, vol. 3897, pp. 319–331. Springer, Heidelberg (2006)
5. Boneh, D., Boyen, X.: Short signatures without random oracles. In: Cachin, C., Camenisch, J.L. (eds.) EUROCRYPT 2004. LNCS, vol. 3027, pp. 56–73. Springer, Heidelberg (2004)
6. Brzuska, C., Busch, H., Dagdelen, O., Fischlin, M., Franz, M., Katzenbeisser, S., Manulis, M., Onete, C., Peter, A., Poettering, B., Schröder, D.: Redactable signatures for tree-structured data: definitions and constructions. In: Zhou, J., Yung, M. (eds.) ACNS 2010. LNCS, vol. 6123, pp. 87–104. Springer, Heidelberg (2010)
7. Chatterjee, S., Menezes, A.: On cryptographic protocols employing asymmetric pairings - the role of ψ revisited. Discret. Appl. Math. **159**(13), 1311–1322 (2011)
8. Cooper, D., Santesson, S., Farrell, S., Boeyen, S., Housley, R., Polk, W.: Internet X.509 public key infrastructure certificate and certificate revocation list (CRL) profile. RFC 5280 (Proposed Standard), May 2008
9. Derler, D.: On the optimization of two recent proxy-type digital signature schemes and their efficient implementation in java. Master's thesis, Institute for Applied Information Processing and Communications (IAIK), Graz University of Technology (2013)
10. Derler, D., Hanser, C., Slamanig, D.: Privacy-enhancing proxy signatures from non-interactive anonymous credentials. In: Atluri, V., Pernul, G. (eds.) DBSec 2014. LNCS, vol. 8566, pp. 49–65. Springer, Heidelberg (2014)
11. Eastlake, D., Reagle, J., Solo, D.: XML-signature syntax and processing. W3C Recommendation (2002)
12. European Telecomunications Standards Institute: Electronic Signatures and Infrastructures (ESI); XML Advanced Electronic Signatures (XAdES); ETSI TS 101 903 (2010)
13. Fialli, J., Vajjhala, S.: Java Architecture for XML Binding (JAXB) 2.0: Java Specification Request (JSR) 222, October 2005

14. Gallagher, P., Foreword, D.D., Director, C.F.: FIPS PUB 186–3 FEDERAL INFORMATION PROCESSING STANDARDS PUBLICATION Digital Signature Standard (DSS) (2009)

15. Geovandro, C.C.F.P., Barreto, P.S.L.M.: bnpairings - a java implementation of efficient bilinear pairings and elliptic curve operations, 5 November 2012. Public Google code project at: https://code.google.com/p/bnpairings/

16. Goldwasser, S., Micali, S., Rivest, R.L.: A digital signature scheme secure against adaptive chosen-message attacks. SIAM J. Comput. **17**(2), 281–308 (1988)

17. Hanser, C.: IAIK ECCelerate SDK 2.51 (2014)

18. Hanser, C., Slamanig, D.: Blank digital signatures. In: 8th ACM SIGSAC Symposium on Information, Computer and Communications Security (AsiaCCS). Full Version: Cryptology ePrint Archive, Report 2013/130, pp. 95–106. ACM (2013)

19. Hanser, C., Slamanig, D.: Structure-preserving signatures on equivalence classes and their application to anonymous credentials. In: Sarkar, P., Iwata, T. (eds.) ASIACRYPT 2014. LNCS, vol. 8873, pp. 491–511. Springer, Heidelberg (2014)

20. International Telecommunication Union: Information Technology – Abstract Syntax Notation One (ASN.1): Specification of Basic Notation. ITU-T Recommendation X.680, July 2002

21. International Telecommunication Union: Information Technology – ASN.1 Encoding Rules – Specification of Basic Encoding Rules (BER), Canonical Encoding Rules (CER), and Distinguished Encoding Rules (DER). ITU-T Recommendation X.690, July 2002

22. Information Technology - Security Techniques - Encryption Algorithms - Part 2: Asymmetric Ciphers (2006)

23. Johnson, R., Molnar, D., Song, D., Wagner, D.: Homomorphic signature schemes. In: Preneel, B. (ed.) CT-RSA 2002. LNCS, vol. 2271, p. 244. Springer, Heidelberg (2002)

24. Kate, A., Zaverucha, G.M., Goldberg, I.: Constant-size commitments to polynomials and their applications. In: Abe, M. (ed.) ASIACRYPT 2010. LNCS, vol. 6477, pp. 177–194. Springer, Heidelberg (2010)

25. Miyazaki, K., Iwamura, M., Matsumoto, T., Sasaki, R., Yoshiura, H., Tezuka, S., Imai, H.: Digitally signed document sanitizing scheme with disclosure condition control. IEICE Trans. **88–A**(1), 239–246 (2005)

26. Oracle: Java^{TM} Cryptography Architecture (JCA) Reference Guide. http://docs.oracle.com/javase/7/docs/technotes/guides/security/crypto/CryptoSpec.html

27. Pöhls, H.C., Samelin, K., Posegga, J.: Sanitizable signatures in XML signature — performance, mixing properties, and revisiting the property of transparency. In: Lopez, J., Tsudik, G. (eds.) ACNS 2011. LNCS, vol. 6715, pp. 166–182. Springer, Heidelberg (2011)

28. Slamanig, D., Stranacher, K., Zwattendorfer, B.: User-centric identity as a service-architecture for eIDs with selective attribute disclosure. In: 19th ACM Symposium on Access Control Models and Technologies (SACMAT 2014), pp. 153–163. ACM (2014)

29. Steinfeld, R., Bull, L., Zheng, Y.: Content extraction signatures. In: Kim, K. (ed.) ICISC 2001. LNCS, vol. 2288, pp. 285–304. Springer, Heidelberg (2002)

30. Vercauteren, F.: Optimal pairings. IEEE Trans. Inf. Theory **56**(1), 455–461 (2010)

31. Zwattendorfer, B., Slamanig, D.: On privacy-preserving ways to porting the austrian eID system to the public cloud. In: Janczewski, L.J., Wolfe, H.B., Shenoi, S. (eds.) SEC 2013. IFIP AICT, vol. 405, pp. 300–314. Springer, Heidelberg (2013)

Project Workshops and Tutorial Papers

Tools for Cloud Accountability:
A4Cloud Tutorial

Carmen Fernandez-Gago[1]($\boxtimes$), Vasilis Tountopoulos[2],
Simone Fischer-Hübner[3], Rehab Alnemr[4], David Nuñez[1],
Julio Angulo[3], Tobias Pulls[3], and Theo Koulouris[4]

[1] Network, Information and Computer Security Lab,
University of Malaga, 29071 Malaga, Spain
{mcgago,dnunez}@lcc.uma.es
[2] Athens Technology Center S.A., Athens, Chalandri, Greece
v.tountopoulos@atc.gr
[3] Karlstad University, Karlstad, Sweden
{simone.fischer-huebner,julio.angulo,tobias.pulls}@kau.se
[4] HP Labs, Bristol, UK
{rehab.alnemr,theofrastos.koulouris}@hp.com

Abstract. Cloud computing is becoming a key IT infrastructure technology being adopted progressively by companies and users. Still, there are issues and uncertainties surrounding its adoption, such as security and how users data is dealt with that require attention from developers, researchers, providers and users. The A4Cloud project tries to help solving the problem of accountability in the cloud by providing tools that support the process of achieving accountability. This paper presents the contents of the first A4Cloud tutorial. These contents include basic concepts and tools developed within the project. In particular, we will review how metrics can aid the accountability process and some of the tools that the A4Cloud project will produce such as the Data Track Tool (DTT) and the Cloud Offering Advisory Tool (COAT).

1 Introduction

Cloud computing is becoming a key IT infrastructure technology being adopted progressively by companies and users. Still, there are issues and uncertainties surrounding its adoption, such as security and how users data is dealt with that require attention from developers, researchers, providers and users. It is essential that there are tools and mechanisms available that can help providing trust in the cloud. It is then when accountability can be useful. According to the definition provided by the A4Cloud project [3], *Accountability* consists of defining governance to comply in a responsible manner with internal and external criteria, ensuring

This work has been partially funded by the European Commission through the FP7/2007-2013 project A4Cloud under grant agreement number 317550. The fifth author is funded by a FPI fellowship from the Junta de Andalucía through the project PISCIS (P10-TIC-06334).

© IFIP International Federation for Information Processing 2015
J. Camenisch et al. (Eds.): Privacy and Identity 2014, IFIP AICT 457, pp. 219–236, 2015.
DOI: 10.1007/978-3-319-18621-4_15

implementation of appropriate actions, explaining and justifying those actions and remedying any failure to act properly. The A4Cloud project will then provide the tools and mechanisms needed in order to achieve accountability for cloud providers and users. The first step towards the development of these tools come from a conceptual level to go then into the development level. In this paper we will describe the problem of accountability and how the A4Cloud project is addressing it. In particular, it will be very useful to have some mechanisms that can help us determining in a quantitative or qualitative way how transparent a service provider. Thus, defining metrics can be useful for determining accountability. In order to elicit these metrics, we introduce the process that we follow. This process consists of a top-down approach for the identification of concepts that can be measured and, a bottom-up approach that serves as a way to provide evidence, based on existing controls [1,2,5].

The mechanisms that the A4Cloud project introduces are implemented through a set of tools that are introduced in this paper. These tools cover different aspects that include legal and regulatory aspects, socio-econmica or legal aspects. In this paper we will concentrate on two specific tools within the toolset of A4Cloud: The Data Track Tool (DTT) and the Cloud Offering Adviosry Tool (COAT). The DTT aims to provide information to the user about how their personal data is dealt with. The COAT tool helps users deciding about the best cloud service provider to use by conciling the users requirements on transparency, legal terms, privacy or security with those offered by the providers.

The structure of the paper is as follows. In Sect. 2 we introduce the problem of accountability and how the project A4Cloud can help solving it. Thus, Sect. 3 describes how defining metrics can be useful for aiding achieving accountability. Section 4 gives a general overview on the A4Cloud tools and the following sections describe two of them. In particular, Sect. 5 describes the Data Track Tool (DTT) and Sect. 6 the Cloud Offering Advisory Tool (COAT). Finally, Sect. 7 concludes the paper and outlines the future research within A4Cloud.

2   The Objectives of the A4Cloud Project

A4Cloud's goal, among others, is to understand what users need to trust a cloud provider with their personal data. A4Cloud focuses on the *accountability for cloud and other future internet services* as the most critical prerequisite for effective governance and control of corporate and private data processed by cloud-based IT services. The project goal is to increase trust in cloud computing by devising methods and tools, through which cloud stakeholders can be made accountable for the privacy and confidentiality of information held in the cloud. These methods and tools will combine risk analysis, policy enforcement, monitoring and compliance auditing. They will contribute to the governance of cloud activities, providing transparency and assisting legal, regulatory and socio-economic policy enforcement. The A4Cloud project has four interlocking objectives to bring users, providers, and regulators together in chains of accountability for data in the cloud, clarifying liability and providing greater transparency overall to[1]:

---

[1] Description is taken from the official documentation of the project.

1. Enable cloud service providers to give their users appropriate control and transparency over how their data is used.
2. Enable users to make choices about how cloud service providers may use and will protect data in the cloud.
3. Monitor and check compliance with users' expectations enforce business policies, and regulations.
4. Implement accountability ethically and effectively.

3   Accountability Metrics

One of the important aspects behind the accountability concept is the ability of an organization to demonstrate their conformity with required obligations [4]. The concept of Accountability goes beyond behaving in a responsible manner, and deals also with showing compliance and providing transparency to the internal process of accountability provision. One of the goals of the A4Cloud project is the demonstration of this through the measurement of the degree of such conformity and the provision of meaningful evidence. Thus, measurement becomes an important tool for assessing the accountability of an organization by external authorities (and organizations themselves, in the case of self-assessment).

It would be logical to think that if we are interested in assessing how accountable an organisation is we should be able to assess or provide techniques for measuring the attributes that influence accountability. How much or to what extent they should be measured is a key issue. One of the goals of A4Cloud is to develop a collection of metrics for performing meaningful measures on the attributes that influence accountability.

3.1   The Role of Metrics in Accountability

The definition of cloud computing given by NIST [9] includes as one of its main characteristics, measured service. This characteristic is defined as the capacity of cloud systems for measuring aspects related to the utilization of services, in order to provide automatic control and optimization of the usage of cloud resources, and ultimately, to support transparency and enhance trust of cloud consumers with regard to cloud providers. Metrics in cloud computing environments are also of paramount importance for other reasons. For instance, metrics can also be derived on the consumer side, enabling cloud consumers to monitor the quality of service of the cloud provider and to verify the compliance of agreed terms. Metrics are also a tool that facilitate the decision making process of cloud consumer organizations, as they can be used for making informed decisions with regard to the election and evaluation of cloud providers.

As for cloud service governance, metrics are very useful means for assessing performance of operational processes and for demonstrating the implementation of appropriate practices through the provision of quantifiable evidence of the application of such practices. Metrics also support accountability governance and can be used as an instrument for identifying strengths and weaknesses in the security and privacy mechanisms in place. From the perspective of the accountability framework, metrics are a means for demonstrating accountability, through the provision of quantifiable evidence of the application of proper practices and the performance of operational processes. This way, progress in the implementation of accountability practices can be justified in a quantitative way.

3.2   Eliciting Metrics for Accountability

In order to measure the accountability attributes we need to have a clear target of the aspects of the attributes that are to be measured. The definitions of the attributes are in some cases vague, subjective or ambiguous, thus it is difficult to measure specific aspects. We need a suitable model that allows us to identify measurable factors from the definitions of the attributes. Once these specific factors are identified we need to derive metrics for them based on the analysis of existing control frameworks. Thus, the process of eliciting accountability metrics consists of two complementary approaches:

- A top-down approach. This approach is based on the definition of a Metamodel for Accountability Metrics, to aid during the initial phases of the elicitation of metrics.
- A bottom-up approach. It is used for complementing the previous one, based on the analysis of relevant control frameworks.

Metrics Metamodel. The goal of the metamodel for eliciting accountability metrics [10] (see Fig. 1) is to serve as a language for describing accountability properties in terms of entities, evidence and actions, and metrics for measuring them. In this metamodel metrics are defined in two kinds of central inputs: evidence and criteria. We claim that any assessment or evaluation (i.e, a metric) can only be made using as input some tangible and empirical evidence, such as an observation, a system log, a certification asserted by a trusted party, a textual description of a procedure, etc. That is, a metric does not directly measure a property of a process, behaviour, or a system, but uses the evidence associated with them in order to derive a meaningful measure. On the other hand, criteria are all the elements that convey contextual input that may constrain what should be measured, such as stakeholder's preferences, regulations and policies.

This top-down approach is useful for reasoning about high-level concepts such as Accountability, however, it does not guarantee to reach measurable concepts. Actually, the value of the proposed metrics metamodel lays principally in aiding to correctly identify and specify the subconcepts that are relevant or influence the Accountability Attributes, rather than being a method for extracting relevant metrics. For this reason, we need a complementary strategy.

Besides evidence and criteria the metamodel includes other elements such as *property*, which refers to the accountability properties; *goal* that refers to a high-level description of the property that is modelled; *entity*, which is a physical or

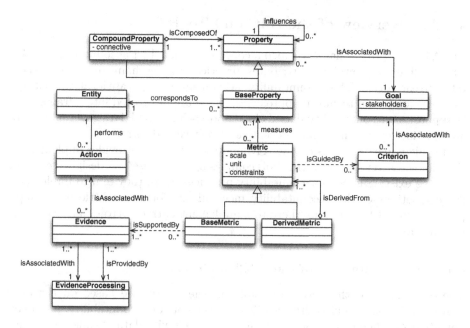

Fig. 1. Metrics metamodel

conceptual objects that performs an *action*; and *metric*, which is an evaluation method for assessing the level of satisfaction of a non-functional property in a quantitative or qualitative way, on the basis of evidence and contextual criteria.

Bottom-up Approach. Control frameworks that are relevant for account-ability, such as the Cloud Control Matrix [2], the Generally Accepted Privacy Principles [1], and NIST SP 500-83 [5], are specifically designed for covering the categories of mechanisms that implement security, privacy and information gov-ernance. For this reason, it is fair to assume that they can be used as sources of evidence from where metrics can be derived. Thus, we can use the application of these frameworks for audit records as evidence for deriving metrics. The steps of the bottom-up approach are as follows:

1. To analyse relevant control frameworks in the light of Accountability Attributes. The goal of this step is to select those controls that influence Accountability.
2. To study the nature of the control, in order to identify whether there is any quantifiable element in the description of the control that is susceptible to being measured. Qualitative elements may be identified too, if they have at least an ordinal nature.
3. To define a metric that measures the identified elements, using the qualitative or quantitative elements identified in the previous step.
4. To check that the metric supports the concept of Accountability and, in par-ticular, the Accountability Attribute to which is related to.

4   An Overview of the A4Cloud Tools

The A4Cloud project has developed a conceptual model for accountability in [7], which defines accountability attributes, practices and mechanisms and how they relate to each other. The accountability mechanisms incorporate legal, regulatory, socio-economic and technical approaches, which are integrated into a framework to support an accountability -based cloud approach to cloud data governance and are functionally classified into preventive, detective and corrective.

In this paper, we focus on the A4Cloud toolset, which provides implementations for these mechanisms. The tools comprising this toolset are designed considering the existing gaps in accountability practices, thus, they aim to implement those functions of the accountability mechanisms, for which little or no support was found to exist out there to complement current privacy and security mechanisms.

4.1   The Architecture of the A4Cloud Tools

The definition and the design principles of the toolset are based on the fact that each A4Cloud tool addresses different elements of accountability, and may operate over different time scales, while interacting with data at different stages of its life cycle. In that respect, the tools implementing preventive mechanisms investigate the potential risks in cloud data governance in order to form policies and decide on relevant mechanisms that should be enacted. The tools implementing detective mechanisms put in place detection and traceability measures to monitor misbehaviours, such as policy violations, in the normal operation of cloud processes. Finally, the tools implementing corrective mechanisms provide notification and remediation, as a response to detected abnormalities of the cloud service chains.

The A4Cloud toolset is composed of eleven tools, as shown in Fig. 2. The tools can be further classified into five functional areas, according to the scope of each tool and the functions provided in the three phases of the accountability framework. These areas are analysed in the following lines The Contract and Risk Management area addresses the need for support in managing risks and cloud service contract selection in the context of accountability for classified data in the cloud. The respective tools serve a preventive role, which is realised through two complementary mechanisms. The first one has to do with the assessment of the risks associated with various facets of the cloud service consumption process, involving personal and/or confidential data and elicitation of actionable information and guidance on how to mitigate them., which is implemented through the Data Protection Impact Assessment Tool (DPIAT). The evaluation of cloud offerings and contract terms complements this mechanism, which is performed through the Cloud Offerings Advisory Tool (COAT), with the goal of enabling a more educated decision making on which service to select.

The Policy Definition and Enforcement area hosts two tools that supplement the tools in the previous area as preventive mechanisms to support accountability. In this category, we introduce the Accountability Lab (AccLab), as a

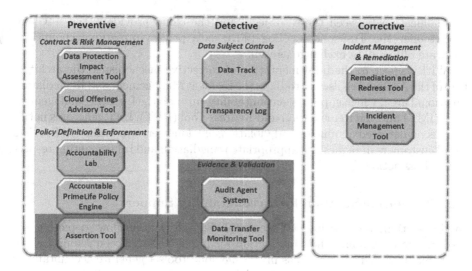

Fig. 2. The high level view of the A4Cloud toolset architecture

tool, which translates human readable accountability obligations expressed in Abstract Accountability Language (AAL) [13] into an A4Cloud specific lower level machine-readable accountability policy language, called Accountable Primelife Policy Language (A-PPL) language. On top of it, we provide the Accountable Primelife Policy Engine (A-PPL Engine), which enforces data handling policies and actions, as they are specified in A-PPL.

Moving to the implementation of the detective mechanisms, the Evidence and Validation category of tools offers accountability by implementing mechanisms for the monitoring of the appropriate software resources to control and verify the accountability policy-based operations occurred in complex cloud service provision chains. This is enabled through the Audit Agent System (AAS), which enables the automated audit of multi-tenant and multi-layer cloud applications and respective infrastructures for compliance with accountability policies, using software agents. Furthermore, we automate the collection of evidence, describing how data transfers comply with data handling policies within a cloud infrastructure through the Data Transfer Monitoring Tool (DTMT). In this category, we, also, include the Assertion Tool (AT) that ensures the validation of the A4Cloud tools through a test case-based methodology, during the development and deployment of accountability mechanisms.

In A4Cloud, we put particular emphasis on enabling individuals, whose personal data are collected and/or processed by cloud service providers, to take control over how these data are exploited along cloud service chains. To this direction, we introduce Data Track (DT), which is used by data subjects to get a user-friendly visualisation of all personal data they have disclosed to cloud service, with the additional capability to rectify data if necessary. DT embeds a Plug-in for Assessment of Policy Violation (PAPV) that provides an assessment on the criticality of previously detected policy violations. In order to secure the communication between these subjects and the cloud providers, the A4Cloud toolset offer the Transparency Log (TL), as a privacy-preserving channel to facilitate offline data exchange as well.

With respect to the implementation of corrective mechanisms, the architecture of the A4Cloud toolset introduces the Incident Management and Remediation functional area, which supports accountability through the Incident Management Tool (IMT) and the Remediation and Redress Tool (RRT). IMT generates notifications on detected anomalies and violations in cloud services, while RRT assists cloud customers in requesting appropriate remediation and implementing respective redress actions.

4.2   Tools Collaboration for Accountability Support

In this section, we describe the accountability information flow, depicting the tools dependencies and their interaction for implementing accountability along the three phases. Thus, the tools in the A4Cloud toolset generate accountability specific data objects, which are shared among them to accomplish the respective functions laid on the preventive, detective and corrective mechanisms. The flow of the accountability information among the tools is depicted in Fig. 3.

As shown there, the type of data that are collected from the data subjects drives the definition of specific accountability obligations identified for the respective cloud providers processing such data, which are analysed along with the privacy and security requirements of the end users and the organisational level policies for providing security in their services, such as access control and encryption. This information is exploited by the tools of the Contract and Risk Management category to reduce the risks of the loss of data governance in complex cloud service provision chains. The outcome of this tool category is the impact assessment report, which elaborates on the privacy risks and the proposed mitigation for a cloud service process chain, based on risk and trust models, and the cloud offering report, analysing the privacy and security guarantees for given functional features offered by cloud providers.

Given the outcome of the previous category, AccLab is used to compile the obligations into A-PPL policies, setting the legal and technical conditions, under which a cloud service that involves the processing of personal and/or business confidential data is operating. The enforcement of these policies is handled by the A-PPL Engine, which generates logs with respect to performed data handling actions against the rules of the A-PPL policies.

These policies are used in the Evidence and Validation functional area to configure the detection mechanisms applied in a cloud service chain. The functions in this tool category exploit the logs produced by the external cloud resources, which are aggregated in the form of evidence records, and produce an incident referring to an abnormal behaviour of the cloud service chain with respect to the A-PPL policies. This tool category, also, enables the cloud providers demonstrating their compliance to the policies by generating audit reports, based on a collection of evidence.

The incidents are utilised by IMT to alert the cloud stakeholders about detected violations and formulate a set of corrective actions that could be undertaken in response to the occurred incidents, through RRT. In parallel, the

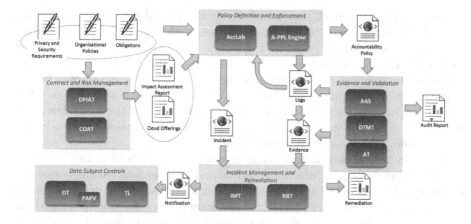

Fig. 3. The flow of the accountability information in the A4Cloud toolset

A4Cloud toolset enables verification of the followed data handling processes by the cloud providers, through a set of tools used to control the cloud subjects data disclosure in the cloud.

5   Data Track Tool

As part of the European FP6 and FP7 research projects PRIME[2] and PrimeLife[3], the Data Track tool was developed [8,11]. Initially, the PRIME Data Track comprised of a history function for keeping a log of each transaction in which a user discloses personal data. The log contained a record for the user about which personal data were disclosed to whom, for which purposes, which credentials and/or pseudonyms have been used in the context of the disclosure as well as the details of the agreed-upon privacy policy. These transaction records were stored at the user side in a secure manner (protected by the PRIME core). In the PrimeLife project and in the follow-up A4Cloud project, the Data Tack was extended to allow cloud subjects to exercise their data subjects' rights pursuant to Art. 12 EU Data Protection Directive 95/46/EC to access their data at the remote services sides online and to correct or delete their data online if the service provider allows it.

In its backend the architecture of the Data Track consists of four high-level components. First, the *user interface* component, which displays different visualizations of the data provided by the Data Track's *core*. Second, the *core* component is a backend to the UI with local encrypted storage. Through a RESTful API, the core is able to provide a uniform view to the UI of all users' data obtained from a service provider via *plugins*. Third, the *plugin* component provides the means for acquiring data disclosures from a source and parsing them into the internal format readable by the core. Fourth, the Data Track specifies

---

[2] EU FP6 project PRIME, https://www.prime-project.eu/.
[3] EU FP7 project PrimeLife http://primelife.ercim.eu/.

a generic *API* component that enables a service provider to support the Data Track by providing remote access, correction, and deletion of personal data. Based on the solution proposed by Pulls *et al.* [12], the transfer of data through a service's API can be done in a secure and privacy-friendly manner. By retrieving data from different services through their provided APIs users would be able to import their data immediately into the Data Track and visualize it in different ways. The possibility to immediately import data into the Data Track and visualize it is an important feature that can add instant value to the tool and provide users with immediate gratification.

Usability tests of early design iterations of the PrimeLife's Data Track revealed that many test users had problems to understand whether data records were stored in the Data Track client on the users side (under the users control) or on the remote service providers side. Therefore, in the A4Cloud project, we have developed and tested an alternative HCI concept consisting of graphical UI illustrations of where data is stored and to which entities data has even distributed (see [14,15]). One motivation for this new UI concept of so-called trace view illustrations is that graphical illustrations of data storage and data flows have a potential to display data traces more naturally, like in real world networks.

The Trace View Visualization. After several rounds of paper sketches and lo-fi mockups, which were discussed and refined with the help of domain and HCI experts[4], an interactive prototype of the Data Track's graphical user interface, the trace view, was implemented using HTML5 and jQuery libraries (shown in Fig. 4). In the trace view the user is represented by a profile picture in the middle of the screen, motivated by design experts suggesting that users focus most of their attention in the middle of the screen after gazing at the top left corner. In particular, we wanted to give users the feeling that this interface is a *place* that focuses on them (i.e. data about them and services that they have contacted).

The interface is then separated into two main panels, following the design guidelines which advice that clearly separating different regions in the screen diminishes the users' cognitive demands. The services to which the user has released information appear in the bottom panel and the information attributes that have been released by the user to these services appear in the top panel. By clicking in one (or many) of the services at the bottom, the interface shows a *trace* from the service to the user, and then from the user to the data items that she has released to that specific service. If the user clicks instead on a data item at the top, the trace shows which online services have that particular item. The traces are coloured to easily differentiate between them.

The services in the bottom panel contain a button with an icon from which users can also access the data about them stored on the services' sides (as seen in Fig. 5). Clicking this button opens a modal dialog where users can review

---

[4] Early versions of lo-fi mockups with a trace view visualization were developed within the scope of a Google Research Award project in discussion with technical and HCI specialists from Google.

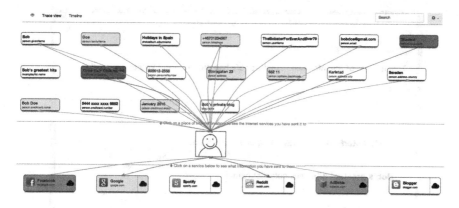

Fig. 4. The trace view interface of the Data Track tool

the data concerning them that the selected service has stored in their databases (Fig. 6). Contrasting colours, an explicit headline and adequate spacing are used to differentiate between data that was explicitly submitted by the user from data that has been implicitly collected or derived by the service provider. In this view users can also exercise their rights to correct or remove data about them.

Evaluation. The Data Track trace view was evaluated in two iteration cycles with 14 and 17 volunteering test participants between 19 and 40 years, which were recruited from the region of Karlstad. 16 of them were students and 15 had other professional background. For the evaluations, the test participants were first introduced to an eShopping scenario, where they had to conduct a purchase transaction for an eBook with fictitious personal data that was claimed to be send to an online bookshop. Then, they were asked to used the Data Track tool to complete different tasks in regard to tracking the data that they previously released.

Both test rounds confirmed that participants easily understood and appreciated having an overview of the data that they have sent to different service providers using coloured tracing lines. However, the test of the first design iteration showed that the controls to access their data remotely on the services side did not provide enough *affordance*, and it was still hard for them to grasp the distinction between data logged locally by the Data Track program and data about them stored remotely in the services' databases. Therefore we included an introduction tour in the second design iteration that illustrated the different

Fig. 5. A node representing a service provider, from where users can also access their data located at the services' side.

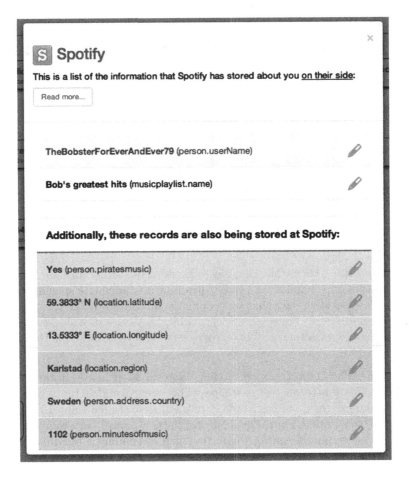

Fig. 6. Information about a user stored at the services' side.

aspects of the interface and explained the distinction of the view showing data stored by the Data Track under the users' control and the dialog that showed data stored remotely at the service provider. The tour does not only explain the difference between these views, but also how to access them. We also included timely tooltips to explain interface elements that were deemed important when users moved the mouse over them. The tests of the second design iteration showed that in general the interface evoked the right mental model in 13 out 17 participants, who understood that the records shown in the trace view were under their control. When asked to identify where would they click to access their personal data that the bookstore had stored about them in their servers, only 4 participants did not complete the task successfully, but they understood the idea after getting assistance from the moderator. Once the modal dialog opened, all participants correctly identified that more data than they have explicitly submitted was collected and stored on the service's servers. Eye-tracking analysis of the results revealed that participants paid a lot of attention to the section of the dialog on the right side on the bottom displaying the implicitly collected data, which allows us to assume that the test users found especially the functionality of the Data Track allowing users to access also implicitly disclosed data as valuable.

In A4Cloud, the Data Track is combined with the transparency logging tool by Pulls *et al.* [12], from which the Data Track receives information about the flow of the 2 user's personal data along chains of cloud providers. These data flows along cloud chains can also be visualised by the Data Track trace view user interface that we are currently implementing within the A4Cloud project (see also [15] for further discussion and illustrations).

6   Cloud Offerings Advisory Tool

Finding a trustworthy cloud provider among the abundance of available offerings is not an easy task particularly for individuals or small and medium enterprises (SMEs) who do not have the professional advisors available to large enterprsies. Cloud brokers aim to match users' requirements with the offerings but only with a focus on functional requirements and rarely on non-functional ones. In A4Cloud we have developed a brokerage tool, Cloud Offerings Advisor Tool (COAT), that matches the users' non-functional requirements - such as transparency, legal terms, court of choice, privacy and security, etc.- with the contract terms in cloud providers' service offerings. The tool, has several benefits for both cloud customers and providers. For the customers, it will provide an easy comparison for alternative cloud offerings based on customers' requirements, hence increasing transparency and in the process easing the public concern about the security and privacy risks of moving to the cloud. The tool will help customers in understanding the risks involved and help them make appropriate decisions. If a cloud provider is offering unique terms in their offers, COAT can highlight these unique terms in the offer giving the provider a competitive advantage in such a vast market. COAT can then increase market exposure for some cloud providers. The tool is unique in giving the users the option to state their security and privacy requirements so they get matches based on them. It is also unique in the categorization and structuring of the contractual terms to make it easy for users to understand these terms and the security and privacy requirements they are choosing. In the next subsection we elaborate on the tool design and development and how we analysed the requirements to be included in the tool. More details on the tool can be found in [6].

6.1   COAT Design and Architecture

COAT filters the variety of offers being presented to customers based largely on the security and privacy attributes of the cloud service. It is aimed primarily at individuals and SMEs. The tool acts as an independent web-based broker

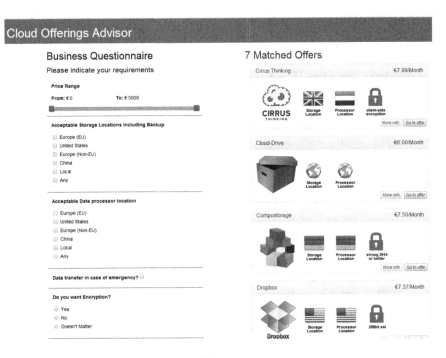

Fig. 7. COAT interface

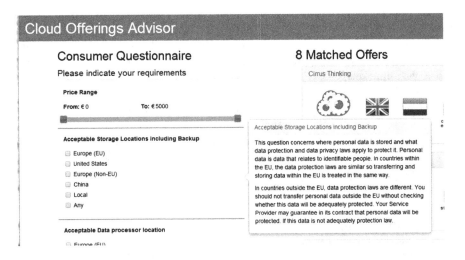

Fig. 8. COAT: information and guidance text for the user-requirements

that: checks user requirements; matches offers by cloud service providers; compares these offers; explains the terms of offerings; suggests best offerings that match the user requirement; gives general guidance to customers on service offerings. The tool also educates the user on the meaning of the requirements being selected via an explanation text associated with each requirement as shown in Fig. 8.

The web-based interface lands on a page which asks the user about their: *Location* (anticipates it first based on the IP address) and their *Role* (whether they are a business SME or an end-user). The tool proceeds by asking the user about the type of service they are searching for, shown in Fig. 9 (for SME and non-expert end-users). The tool then uses *dynamic filtering*:

- After selecting the service type. It shows the users the initial list of service offerings filtered only by the type of service they offer.
- During filling/answering the requirements questionnaire the list is updated after answering each requirement, filtering the service offerings based on the values of these answers.

Figures 7, 8 and 9 are some snapshots of the tool. The **inputs** to the tool are: User information (location and role), user needs and requirements (answers to the requirement questionnaire), structured service offerings (contract details), and a model of cloud contracts and points of attention. The **outputs** are: matching results of service offerings, guidance on things to pay attention to when exploring and comparing the terms of service offerings, overview of comparable service offerings along with links to their contract details (organized by attributes to facilitate easy understanding of contract terms), a requirement list to give to the Cloud Service Provider (CSP), and SME guidance. The main internal processes are: Matching offers to requirements, Assessment of a cloud service provider offering from a privacy and security perspective, Comparison of offerings (from a

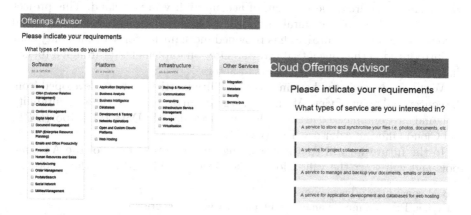

Fig. 9. COAT: service-types question shown to expert (left) and non-expert (right) end-users

data protection compliance and provider accountability point of view), Guidance on the meaning of the comparison attributes and education of users on security, and Logging of the offered advice and the user's decision.

The tool connects to a database of predefined questions regarding the user's requirements and a database of service offerings (MySQL). The *server-side application* and the *webservice layer* that provide access to the questionnaire management and matchmaker are written in Java. The *Matchmaker component* along with the *Questionnaire management* (logic) are implemented in Java as well. The *client-side application* is implemented using HTML5 and JavaScript and is backed by Backbone[5] for a client-side MVC structure. The offers management and associated webservices are written in Python[6]. The Search Index used to find the matched service offerings is done by SOLR. We use RESTful API as a transport layer and JSON[7] as the data-interchange format.

We evaluated the tool by testing it in two workshops: one for cloud service providers and one for cloud customers. The overall feedback was positive. One of the feedback resulted in creating a new service-types page for the customer (Fig. 9, right handside) to make it simpler for the non-expert users to select the type of services they want. Another feedback was a concern that some cloud service providers will not cooperate in entering their contract details in the tool service-offerings side (populating the tool with offers). However, our argument is that the tool provides good exposure for them and more specifically an exposure to the unique terms that they can offer to their users; this would give small(er) businesses a competitive advantage over large cloud providers. The participants in the cloud customers' workshop evaluated the tool as easy to use and that it has useful functionalities.

7   Conclusion

In this paper, we have provided a general description of the A4Cloud project, which aims to address the problem of accountability in the cloud. This project tackles the problem of accountability from different perspectives: technical, legal or socio-economic. The project has provided mechanisms for accountability that are introduced in the conceptual way and later on implemented through a toolset that can be used for the different cloud actors.

We have concentrated here in accountability metrics that are developed from the conceptual point of view. We have also given an overview on the accountability tools and have emphasized in two of them in particular: the Data Track Tool (DTT) and Cloud Offering Advisory Tool (COAT).

In the future we will continue working on the development of the A4Cloud tools and will start the validation of the DTT, COAT and the other tools. As

---

[5] Backbone: http://backbonejs.org/.

[6] Python Programming Language: https://www.python.org.

[7] JSON: http://json.org/.

for the work on metrics we will apply it on the development of an Accountability Maturity Model (AAM) and contribute to some consolidated standards on metrics (NIST, ISO) b including the ones that we have defined for accountability.

References

1. AICPA/CICA privacy task force. generally accepted privacy principles. http://www.aicpa.org/INTERESTAREAS/INFORMATIONTECHNOLOGY/ RESOURCES/PRIVACY/GENERALLYACCEPTEDPRIVACYPRINCIPLES/ Pages/default.aspx
2. Cloud security alliance. cloud control matrix (ccm) v3. https:// cloudsecurityalliance.org/research/ccm/
3. The cloud accountability project. http://www.a4cloud.eu/
4. Implementing accountability in the marketplace - a discussion document, accountability phase iii - the madrid project. Centre for Information Policy Leadership (CIPL), November 2011
5. National institute of standards and technology, nist sp 800–53 - security and privacy controls for federal information systems and organizations. revision 4 (2013)
6. Alnemr, R., Pearson, S., Leenes, R., Mhungu, R: Coat: cloud offerings advisory tool. In: IEEE 6th International Conference on Cloud Computing Technology and Science, CloudCom 2014, Singapore, December 2014, pp. 15–18 (2014)
7. Felici, M., Koulouris, T., Pearson, S: Accountability for data governance in cloud ecosystems. In: IEEE 5th International Conference on Cloud Computing Technology and Science, CloudCom 2013, Bristol, United Kingdom, 2–5 December, 2013, vol. 2, pp. 327–332 (2013)
8. Fischer-Hübner, S., Hedbom, H., Wästlund, E.: Trust and assurance HCI. In: Camenisch, J., Fischer-Hübner, S., Rannenberg, K. (eds.) PrimeLife - Privacy and Identity Management for Life in Europe, p. 261. Springer, Heidelberg (2011)
9. Mell, P., Grance, T.: The NIST definition of cloud computing. Technical report SP 800-145 (2011)
10. Nuñez, D., Fernandez-Gago, C., Pearson, S., Felici, M.: A metamodel for measuring accountability attributes in the cloud. In: 2013 IEEE 5th International Conference on Cloud Computing Technology and Science (CloudCom), vol. 1, pp. 355–362. IEEE (2013)
11. Pettersson, J.S., Fischer-Hübner, S., Bergmann, M.: Outlining "Data Track": privacy-friendly data maintenance for end-users. In: Wojtkowski, W., Wojtkowski, W.G., Zupancic, J., Magyar, G., Knapp, G. (eds.) Advances in Information Systems Development, pp. 215–226. Springer, Heidelberg (2007)
12. Pulls, T., Peeters, R., Wouters, K.: Distributed privacy-preserving transparency logging. In: Workshop on Privacy in the Electronic Society (WPES), Heidelberg, Germany, November 2013, pp. 83–94 (2013)
13. Benghabrit, W., Grall, H., Royer, J-C., Sellami, M., Azraoui, M., Elkhiyaoui, K., Önen, M., Santana De Oliveira, A., Bernsmed, K.: A cloud accountability policy representation framework. In: CLOSER 2014, 4th International Conference on Cloud Computing and Services Science, 3–5 April 2014, Barcelona, Spain (2014). http://www.eurecom.fr/publication/4222
14. Fischer-Hübner, S., Angulo, J., Pulls, T.: How can cloud users be supported in deciding on, tracking and controlling how their data are used? In: Hansen, M., Hoepman, J.-H., Leenes, R., Whitehouse, D. (eds.) Privacy and

Identity 2013. IFIP AICT, vol. 421, pp. 77–92. Springer, Heidelberg (2014). http://dx.doi.org/10.1007/978-3-642-55137-6_6

15. Angulo, J., Fischer-Hübner, S., Pulls, T., Wästlund, E.: Usable transparency with the "Data Track" - a tool for visualising data disclosures. In: SIGCHI Conference on Human Factors in Computing Systems (CHI 2015), Seoul, South Korea (2015). (Work-in-progress track)

Privacy for Peer Profiling
in Collective Adaptive Systems

Mark Hartswood[1], Marina Jirotka[1], Ronald Chenu-Abente[2(✉)],
Alethia Hume[2(✉)], Fausto Giunchiglia[2], Leonardo A. Martucci[3(✉)],
and Simone Fischer-Hübner[3]

[1] Oxford University, Oxford, UK
{mark.hartswood,marina.jirotka}@cs.ox.ac.uk
[2] Trento University, Trento, Italy
{chenu,hume,giunchiglia}@disi.unitn.it
[3] Karlstad University, Karlstad, Sweden
{leonardo.martucci,simone.fischer-hubner}@kau.se

Abstract. In this paper, we introduce a privacy-enhanced Peer Manager, which is a fundamental building block for the implementation of a privacy-preserving collective adaptive systems computing platform. The Peer Manager is a user-centered identity management platform that keeps information owned by a user private and is built upon an attribute-based privacy policy. Furthermore, this paper explores the ethical, privacy and social values aspects of collective adaptive systems and their extensive capacity to transform lives. We discuss the privacy, social and ethical issues around profiles and present their legal privacy requirements from the European legislation perspective.

1 Introduction

Smart Society, an EU FP7 FET integrated project, explores how Collective Adaptive System (CAS) comprised of people and machines may help solve problems of urban living. Smart Society aims to capture how contemporary techno-social trends can be harnessed towards solving challenges facing modern society. The Smart alludes to how innovative, social, mobile and sensor based technologies can support powerful collectives of people and machines that are capable of utilizing constrained shared resources, such as, such as transport networks, in more effective and therefore sustainable ways.

Smart Society is partly inspired by the idea of the 'Smart City', a multifaceted concept that recognizes the benefits of urban living but also the strains that are developing on existing infrastructures and resources due to urban growth. According to this vision, cities made 'smart' will be more productive, more sustainable, and pleasanter places to live. One aspect of Smart Cities concerns augmenting service infrastructures, such as transport, energy and health,

S. Fischer-Hübner—This research was funded by SMARTSOCIETY, a project of the Seventh Framework Programme for Research of the European Community under grant agreement no. 600854.

© IFIP International Federation for Information Processing 2015
J. Camenisch et al. (Eds.): Privacy and Identity 2014, IFIP AICT 457, pp. 237–252, 2015.
DOI: 10.1007/978-3-319-18621-4_16

with sensor-based digital technologies that are able to visualize patterns of service delivery and use stretching across space and time and with a high degree of fidelity. The idea is that service operators can utilize this information to make efficiency savings by tailoring provision to match demand, and by shaping demand through use of incentives or other motivating feedback mechanisms. At the same time, users of shared resources can use those resources more effectively if they are aware of the global state of the resource and able to coordinate between themselves about how the resource might be used.

An objective of Smart Society is to identify problems related to CAS and design solutions to preempt them. In the case of protection of personal data, Smart Society identified a set of potential problems in CAS, including: user profiling, 'big data' analysis of personal data acquired from mobile devices, and the use of analytic technologies that reveal user actions, such as activity recognition–all of which resonate strongly contemporary ICT-based privacy challenges. We aim to explore how far state-of-the-art privacy enhancing technologies, such as privacy policy languages, anonymous credentials, and data anonymization techniques, may find an application within Smart Society, focusing particularly on practical implementation issues and how their use trades-off against other important social values, such as accountability and security.

1.1 Smart Society and Collectives

A key principle in Smart Society is founded on the idea of 'collectives'–a collection of humans and/or machines that identify themselves as a group. In Smart Society, collectives are seen as a source of expertise and discoverable via peer profiles. At the same time they are consumers of resources whose patterns of consumption can be shaped by appropriate interventions such as incentives. Diversity within collectives provides a resource pool to enable the development of a range of responses to a situation, but can also be a source of friction and contention. All together, the socio-technical entity powering the Smart Society vision is referred to as a Hybrid and Diversity Aware Collective Adaptive System (HDA-CAS).

Since collective adaptive systems comprise people and machines that seamlessly collaborate to solve problems and execute tasks, a computing platform that supports a CAS has as input two sets of data about:

1. problems and tasks,
2. peers, i.e., people and/or machines.

The objective of a CAS computing platform is to match these two sets in a way that the specific problems are re-directed to the group of peers that are most capable, interested and/or efficient in solving them. Thus, a CAS computing platform needs access to the attributes of all peers stored in peer profiles. However, unlimited access to the peers' attributes in the peer profiles is not desirable because they may include personal data in the case of peers that are people. The collection, storage and processing of personal data is subject to legislation. The CAS computing platform therefore has to accommodate requirements and should be designed upon a privacy-preserving framework.

1.2   Contributions

This paper summarizes the presentations and discussion results of a workshop by the Smart Society project that was held at the IFIP Summer School on Privacy and Identity Management in September 2014. We first discuss the ethical and legal aspects and requirements in regard to peer profiling in Smart Society. Then we outline the first steps for realizing a privacy-preserving CAS computing platform. We present a *semantic schema* for the representation of peers' personal data and *Peer Manager*, which is a distributed database that stores the peers' personal data. Our contribution sets the minimum requirements for the design and implementation of an attribute-based access control privacy policy for a privacy-preserving CAS computing platform.

In the remainder of this paper, we begin by describing the contextual background and ethical and privacy aspects of CAS computing platform that are introduced in Sect. 2. Section 3 outlines the privacy requirements taken into account in our research work. The semantic schema and the Peer Manager are presented in Sect. 4. Section 5 summarizes our work and findings as well as the results of the workshop discussions during the summer school.

2   Ethical and Privacy Issues

In this section we explore how the Smart Society project pays attention to issues of privacy, ethics and social values, and expands upon issues associated more generally with 'big data' and profiling driven approaches. In particular, we draw attention to the extensive scope of the Smart Society vision and its extensive capacity to transform our lives to highlight the importance of these issues. To do this we draw on existing literature detailing the ethical challenge that now confront us from increasing levels of digital mediation within our everyday lives.

The reference to 'Society' in the Smart Society name underlines the extensive ambition of the project. Examples and scenarios generated within the project encompass Tourism, Care, Health, Policing and span from grand aims of solving problems of sustainability to assisting the mundane practicalities of finding somewhere to eat in an unfamiliar town. This breadth and depth underlines the vast scope and everyday pervasiveness implied by the ambition of a 'Smart Society' that aims to address 'societal challenges' and operate at 'internet scale' whilst at the same time penetrating into the mundane aspects of many of our everyday routines and activities. The aim is not to leave these activities unaltered, but rather to supercharge them by linking individuals into collectives to access collectives' problem solving and self-organizing abilities, and to draw upon portable devices, sensors, data and algorithms to assist in 'orchestrating' these newly collectivized activities. Part of the motivation for Smart Society stems from the perception that the existing accumulations of digital mediation for everyday activities have until now been technically untidy, due to a lack of appropriate engineering principles, and ethically haphazard, as a consequence of being unplanned and undirected. Hence Smart Society's twin foci on engineering and ethics. Improved engineering is seen to address the problem of ethics by providing a structured and therefore more considered process for creating such systems. Ethics helps solve engineering problems by guiding the engineers towards solutions that preserve certain important social values, such as privacy.

In the context of an increasingly digitally augmented lives, the performance of everyday activities now involves numerous data streams leading to vast accumulations of data. This data is viewed as a resource towards solving a wide array of social problems, but its misuse is also seen as threatening our privacy and autonomy. Goodman analyzes ethical issues in the era of personal 'big data' draws attention to the following attributes that carry these types of risk: [11]:

- *"The sensor infused world"*. The shear array of sensors, devices and increasingly everyday objects interconnected via online infrastructures passively generating increasing quantities of data from an ever wider range of activities.
- *"Data as commodity"*. As data has become valuable in its own right beyond the services which generated leading to important questions as to who gets to realize value from data and for what purposes? Nissenbaum's concept of 'data integrity' maintains that use of data should be consistent with the values attached to the activities producing the data [17]. The privacy principle of purpose limitation has a role to play here too as an a-priori contractual determination of the sorts of value that may be derived from data - although there are issues with this approach in making it sensitive to context.
- *"Opacity of back-end information exchange"*. The many ways by which data circulates and are traded are hidden from view, as are the ultimate purposes to which those data may be put. So the ways that such data are subsequently used to filter or shape our experience of the world are often concealed.
- *"Mass scale"*. How this is happening on an unprecedented scale and in ways that do not differentiate between diverse cultural expectations about privacy and data use.

Smart Society could be prone to the hazards described by Goodman for social platforms if data is similarly centralized and its stewardship remains in the hands of platform operators. Extending control of data to users and that bind operators to principles of transparency are important challenges for Smart Society - particularly where this creates technical and operational inconveniences. But also, as Goodman points out, 'big data' may be prone to bias and present an unfair representation of a population, which may be further compounded by the opt outs and obscurification of privacy enhancing technologies.

In the era of personal 'big data' it is common to use data to profile individuals and stratify populations as a means to tailoring or individualizing experience, e.g. by targeting advertising, creating recommendations or tailoring services. Profiles are used within Smart Society to involve peers in collectives, perhaps to solve problems, based upon their experience, skills and reputation. We describe below the importance of profiles for Smart Society but first we enumerate some of the hazards of profiling already identified in the literature.

2.1   Social and Ethical Issues of Profiles

- *Social sorting.* Social Sorting refers to how profiling technologies sorts individuals into categories in order to affect their experiences and opportunities. Examples include banks routing calls from wealthier customers deliver speedier service at the expense of less well off customers or internet service providers giving priority to certain traffic or favored customers. Negative effects of sorting include reinforcing existing social divisions and creating new yet invisible hierarchies of access and privilege [16].
- *Autonomy and self-determination.* Often profiles are created and used without our knowledge or consent, and the ways that our experience of services is modified by this is invisible. Where profiles are computed from data about us, then we are subject the values embedded in the algorithms used to sift that information, but not given a voice in the creation of those algorithms. When we create profiles (e.g. on Linkedin or Facebook) then we are still constrained by what we can express and have little control over how much a flat partial identity may be read by others as a literal depiction of who we are.
- *Diminishing diversity.* "With commercial personalization services, the myriad of individual differences is reduced to one or a few consuming categories, on the basis of which their preferences, character, life-style and so forth are determined for a specific context. Because of its tendency to generalize, personalization may lead to diminishing preferences, differences and values..." [12]. A question raised during the Patras workshop underlines this point. The questioner characterized our experience of city life as in turns vivid, serendipitous, frustrating and pleasurable and questioned how city life mediated through Smart Society 'apps' may lead to a dulling, standardisation and impoverishment of these sorts of experience. It is important for Smart Society to retain elements of fun, chance, discovery and provide an experience that is enriching to and complementary to existing beneficial forms of city life, avoiding to frame problems narrowly in terms of optimization.

Profiles are a crucial component within the Smart Society platform and it is the Peer Profile which gives participants their identity within the system and thereby governs the relationship between individuals and the collectives in which they may become involved. The Smart Society Peer Profile codifies the participant's reputation, interests, expertise and actions. The system uses this information to work out if it can recruit the 'peer' to contribute to solving a problem. In this way the peer profile plays a role in determining participants' opportunities within the system. Given the extent of Smart Society vision then this could imply significant advantages or deficits in life-chances where profiles govern participants' access to culture, education, healthcare and their ability to engage in economic activity. In the context of Smart Society then peoples' very participation in civil society may be at stake.

Some risks of privacy profiling within Smart Society are being addressed in Smart Society, as it is presented in the following sections of this paper. In particular, risks to autonomy are addressed by creating mechanisms that give the participant ownership of their profile by hosting it on their device; allowing the user to edit or amend any aspect; and in specifying policies describing in what circumstances the data may be shared across the platform.

2.2 Privacy Issues of Profiles

Peer profiling may affect privacy in different respects. As the Council of Europe has discussed in its recommendation CM/REC(2010)13 on profiling [4], the collection, linking, calculation, comparison and statistical correction of data with the objective to create profiles may have significant privacy impacts, as profiling enables a person's personality, behavior, interests and habits to be determined, analyzed and/or predicted. Often such profiling is even happening without the knowledge of the individuals concerned. While profiling may offer benefits for users and society at large, e.g. by providing users with targeted and better services addressing personal and societal interests or by permitting an analysis of risks and fraud, profiling techniques can also have the impact on the individuals concerned by placing them in predetermined categories and may unjustifiably deprive them from accessing certain services and by this discriminate individuals [4].

Moreover, profiling techniques do not only allow to analyze data that are actually recorded, but also allow to statistically predict or implicitly derive information from such records. For instance, sensitive data including about political opinions, religious beliefs, intelligence or sexual orientation can be automatically predicted from Facebook Likes (see e.g., [13]).

During the workshop at Patras, the following more specific privacy questions were raised and discussed but not finally answered, which implies that they still largely remain challenges to be addressed within Smart Society:

– How can privacy interests of "collectives" (consisting of several individuals and/or machines) be protected? How can collectives be formed in an anonymous manner, i.e. in a way that it does not relate to any identified or identifiable person? Can privacy policy languages (to be discussed in the next section) be extended to define privacy preferences of Collectives and negotiate privacy policies for Collectives? Is it a challenge to define/jointly agree on privacy preferences for Collectives in regard to personal data that they have in common/share, or can group decisions and crowdsourcing on privacy preference settings enable/motivate users to spend more efforts on privacy preference management?
– In hybrid systems, peer profiles of machines could include personal data of one or even several data subjects. For instance, in the application of Smart Society to a care scenario, sensors may capture data about when and for how long health care professionals and patients have met. This implies that the sensor readings may reveal both personal information about health care professionals and the patients. Under which conditions can data subjects of data relating also to other data subjects can exercise their data subject rights (if for example the data is only intended for the health care professionals to organise their work, the patient (or their relatives) may still have the right to

access data items that relate to them (e.g., to check whether the patient gets the right treatment)?).

- Are anonymous credentials suitable PETs (privacy-enhancing technologies) for enhancing the privacy of passengers and drivers participating in a Smart Society enabled 'ride sharing' platform that is currently under implementation? Both drivers and passengers could be pseudonymously be registered by the platform and prove only certain properties (e.g., passion of driving license for more than five years, reputation scores). Will the use of anonymous credentials in this context be practically feasible and socially accepted?

Privacy-related questions concerning privacy on sensor data collection [3], trust and reputation [15], and provenance [5] were also raised. These topics are being addressed by Smart Society and are not discussed in this paper.

3 Legal Privacy Requirements in Regard to Profiling

In this section we present the requirements for a CAS computing platform that accommodate data protection and it is designed upon a privacy preserving framework. Basic legal privacy principles, especially those enacted by the EU Data Protection Directive 95/46/EC [7], need to be enforced when profiles that include personal data are created and processed.

These basic principles comprise the following:

- **Legitimacy & Informed Consent:** The collection and processing of personal data in profiles needs to be *legitimate*, which usually implies that the data subjects[1] have given their informed consent (Art. 7).
- **Purpose Specification & Binding:** Personal data used in the context of profiling must be collected for specified and legitimate purposes and may later only be used for those purposes (Art. 6 Ib).
- **Data Minimization:** The amount of personal data and the extent to which they are collected and processed in profiles should be minimized (Art. 6 Ic), i.e., if possible data in profiles should be anonymised or pseudonymised.
- **No Sensitive Data:** The collection and processing of so-called special categories of data in the context of profiling should in principle be prohibited (Art. 8 I), unless the exceptions of Art. 8 II apply.
- **Transparency & Data Subject Rights:** Data controllers[2] have to provide the data subjects with sufficient privacy policy information pursuant to Art. 10 when personal data are collected in the context of profiling. Data subjects have the right to obtain information about their personal data, to be informed about the logic underpinning the processing of their data, to correction, deletion and blocking of their data, and not to be subject to a "decision which produces legal effects concerning him or significantly affects him and

---

[1] A data subject is a natural person about whom personal data are processed. We use the terms data subjects, users, and individuals concerned interchangeably.

[2] According to EU Directive 95/5/EC, a data controller is an entity that alone or jointly with others determines the purposes and means of personal data processing.

which that is based solely on automated processing of data intended to evaluate certain personal aspects relating to him, such as his performance at work, creditworthiness, reliability, conduct, etc."

- **Security:** The data controller has to implement proper technical and organizational security measures for the protection of personal profile data.

The Council of Europe proposed more specific privacy principles that should further strengthen the data subject's protection in an appendix to its recommendation CM/REC(2010)13.

In the context of the EU data protection reform, the proposed General EU Data Protection Regulation (GDPR) [8] introduced with its Art. 20 "Measures based on Profiling". This was however criticized by the Art. 29 Data Protection Working Party on focusing merely on the outcome of profiling rather than on the profiling as such [1].

The compromise amendment to the proposed EU Data Protection Regulation [6], which was passed by the LIBE Committee (Committee on Civil Liberties, Justice and Home Affairs) of the European Parliament on October 21, 2013, has taken up this proposal by providing greater transparency and control for data subjects. According to the amended Art. 14 (ga), data controllers should provide "information about the existence of profiling, of measures based on profiling, and the envisaged effects of profiling on the data subject". In addition, the amended proposal includes the right for data subjects to object to profiling (Art. 20 I). Furthermore, pursuant to Art. 20 III, "profiling that has the effect of discriminating against individuals on the basis of race or ethnic origin, political opinions, religion or beliefs, trade union membership, sexual orientation or gender identity, or that results in measures which have such effect, shall be prohibited". Pursuant to Art. 20 V, "Profiling which leads to measures producing legal effects concerning the data subject or does similarly significantly affect the interests, rights or freedoms of the concerned data subject shall not be based solely or predominantly on automated processing and shall include human assessment, including an explanation of the decision reached after such an assessment."

The amendment text to the GDPR also introduced in Art. 4 (2a) the concept of "pseudonymous data", which it defines as "personal data that cannot be attributed to a specific data subject without the use of additional information, as long as such additional information is kept separately and subject to technical and organisational measures to ensure non-attribution". Recital 58a of the amendment, further states that profiling based solely on the processing of pseudonymous data that cannot be attributed to a specific person should be presumed not to significantly affect the interests, rights or freedoms of the data subject.

4 Concept for a Privacy-Enhanced Peer Manager

We define *information peers* as equally privileged participants in an information exchange. Subjects (i.e., humans, machines and services) are represented by informational peers, which interact under a common set of rules, and can be both providers and subscribers of different information exchanges at different times. They are equally privileged with regard to the decision of engaging or not in the information exchange given the set of rules that apply to such interaction.

Personal data protection is embedded in the design of the Peer Manager and its implementation, the Peer Manager Platform. To address the privacy issues raised in previous sections, the Peer Manager follows three core guiding principles for technically protecting privacy:

1. *Well-defined information separation between information owned by different subjects.* For guaranteeing that the subjects control their own data, the Peer Manager creates distributed environments that host the knowledge container of each subject. Therefore, as the knowledge containers can be physically and logically distributed, the personal information of a subject is isolated from the personal information of other subjects.
2. *User-centred identity management.* The Peer Manager gives to each subject the control of the flow over personally identifying information. Furthermore, the identity management system allows subjects the definition and use of pseudonyms for different interactions as part of their partial identities.
3. *A deconstruction and re-imagining of information profiling.* While the high-level objective of the Peer Manager's Profiles is in general the same as the one of traditional profiles (i.e. an information-holding structure that is maintained and updated separately from the subject to which it refers), we have focused on turning around the regular profiling practices by making them transparent and controllable by the subjects that they refer to.

For enhancing management of information and enforcing the privacy requirements of purpose specification and binding, we define the Peer Manager on top of the entity-centric semantic-enhanced model presented in the next subsection.

4.1 Preliminaries

In the Peer Manager, the representation of information related to peers builds upon the notion of a *semantic schema* defining an attribute-based representation of peers' characteristics. The semantic schema we adopt follows an entity-centric approach that uses the notion of entity to refer to a "thing" that exists in the real world. Within the peer manger we formalize this notion of entity and use it, as the basic element representing information about peers. We distinguish between a *schema level* that defines the "format" to represent information and a *instance level* that defines how to instantiate the schema into actual knowledge [10, 14].

A Knowledge Base (KB) stores data from the schema level. The Schema.org[3] initiative defines schemas as "a set of types, each associated with a set of properties and where the types are arranged in a hierarchy". We adopt an approach that is aligned with this idea and allows the definition of templates for each type of entity used in the system. These templates allows to establish restrictions on the set of attributes that can be used to describe a given type of entity.

---

[3] http://schema.org/.

The meaning is further specified by mapping single elements from the schema (i.e., types of entities, the names of attributes and their values) to concepts from the underlying ontology that is also part of the same knowledge base.

- A **concept** is "an idea of what something is or how it works."[4] In the area of knowledge representation, concepts are used to formalize and represent the meaning of words in a language independent manner. Concepts can be mapped to an underlying ontology that greatly helps identifying purposes (for purpose binding) and other hard to manage limitations for the shared information (e.g., alignment between different data sources). It also provides the basis for more accurate access control methodologies as introduced in [2,9].
- An **entity type** ET provides a template for the creation of entities by establishing a set of constraints about the metadata (i.e., attributes) that entities of that type can instantiate. The template for attributes are defined by mean of the so-called attribute definitions. An *attribute definition AD* imposes an explicit constraint about the name and the quantitative or qualitative values of a certain attribute that can be associated to an entity.

An *entity base* (EB) is defined to store information corresponding to the instance level. It includes concrete information about abstract and physical entities that exist in the real world and is represented by the following elements.

- An **entity** (E) is defined as an abstract or physical object, it can be of different types defined at the knowledge level (e.g., person, location, event, etc.) and is described by attributes (e.g., name, birth date, latitude-longitude, size, duration, etc.), which can be different for different types of entities.
- An **attribute** (A) instantiates an attribute definition AD to represent a particular characteristic of the entity. Some attributes may have multiple values, its values may be mapped to a meaning in some knowledge base (i.e., semantic values) or can represent a relation to another entity when the value is a reference to another E (i.e., relational attribute).

4.2 Privacy-Enhancing Structures

The three main structures used in the Peer Manager to protect personal data are: the peer, the user, and the profile structures.

Peers as Distributed Storage Providers. Peer structures are units of storage under the control of the Peer Manager Platform and of the subjects that participate in it. The Peer Manager keeps an entity's data and knowledge base. Every user has a its own Peer Manager and defines the access control policies related to their data. An entity's data is kept isolated from the rest, thus helping to promote the privacy principle of *informational self-determination*.

When an entity registers to the platform, it is assigned a peer structure defined as the tuple $P = \langle ID, KB, EB, ME, \{U\} \rangle$ where:

---

[4] Merriam-Webster (http://www.merriam-webster.com/dictionary/concept).

- *ID* is a unique identifier and a reference number to a peer;
- *KB* is the id of the Knowledge Base owned by the peer that will be used to store all of the concepts and Etypes that belong to the peer;
- *EB* is the id of the Entity Base owned by the peer that will be used to store all of the Entities that belong to the peer;
- *ME* is the id of the Main Entity of the peer and it is stored in *EB*. In the case of a person, the main entity is a person entity. There are other types of main entity, such as for service peers and collective peers; and
- $\{U\}$ is a non-empty set of user structures, which is defined below.

The peer structure allows each subject in the system to have its own dedicated storages (to which then they can apply their own policies and AC directives) as shown in Fig. 1.

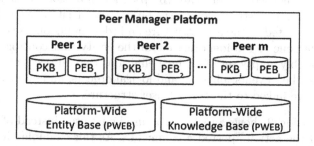

Fig. 1. A Platform handled by the Peer Manager. Each subject its assigned its own peer storage, while the platform itself offers a shared Knowledge and Entity storages for different interactions.

Figure 1 shows that each Peer has its own PKB (Peer Knowledge Base) and PEB (Peer Entity Base) assigned and clearly separated from the other peers and the platform. The design of the Peer Manager infrastructure also states that only the subject in control of Peer structure has access to it by default and allows for each of these Peers to be stored either in the same server or in different machines altogether. Through this, the platform guarantees that each subject will be always in control of the information stored in his/her assigned peer and that nobody (not even the platform holders) would be able to access this information unless given access by the same subject.

Users Structures as Subject Pseudonyms. When interacting with other peers registered in the platform, entities have the option to control the amount of personal data they reveal. User structures (corresponding to pseudonyms that a subject can act under) are introduced to enhance the privacy of all the subjects that participate in actions/interactions in the Smart Society platform. Entities are able to define N user structures (corresponding to N different pseudonyms) defined as tuples $U = \langle UN, AUTH, P, MPD, \{PD\}\rangle$, where:

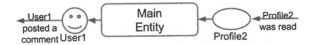

Fig. 2. User structures are used instead of the Main Entity when it acts as a subject and profile structures are used for when the Main Entity is read as an object.

- UN is an alphanumeric string used as the unique identifier to the user structure. This string is a pseudonym for the entity that controls the peer;
- $AUTH$ is an authentication token that is issued by the platform as a proof of peer's identity;
- P is the id of the peer to which a user structure corresponds.
- MPD is the id of the Main profile definition structure that is applied to the peer's ME. It is used to obfuscate (by pseudonymization or anonymization) the link between user structure and the peer that owns it. The resulting Entity Profile is associated to the user structure and (depending on its configuration) may provide none to full identification of the entity that controls it;
- $\{PD\}$ a possibly empty set of profile definitions that subjects create for their entities (e.g. their events, physical and logical objects, and other partial identities) that are linked to the current user structure.

The left side of Fig. 2 shows an user structure being used instead of the ME as the subject of the action "posted a comment". As this example illustrates, the user structure corresponds to a pseudonym for the peer. For achieving a high degree of privacy/unlinkability, different user structures (i.e. different transaction pseudonyms) could be used for different actions.

More in general, Fig. 2 shows how user structures and profiles enhance privacy by providing indirect and partial access to the information from the Peer and its Main Entity, which may contain personal data.

Profiles as Object Indirections. Instead of directly allowing access to the information contained in the peer's entities, *Profile* structures are created to reply to queries that are sent to the peer (normally only revealing partial or obfuscated information about these entities). The right side of Fig. 2 shows an example where, upon receiving a read query, the peer allows the requester to access the Profile named "Profile2", which contains partial and obfuscated information from ME but not ME, which may contain personal data that the subject may not want to disclose. Profile structures, when they refer to ME, may represent partial identities of the subject controlling the Peer.

The profile structure definition PD is used to define the subset of information to be included in the profile from the ME. A profile definition is defined as the tuple $PD = \langle ID, PE, \{PP\}, \{GP\}, \{NR\} \rangle$ where:

- ID is a numeric unique identifier. It is a reference to the PD;
- PE is the id of the Profiled Entity, the entity to which this profile refers to;

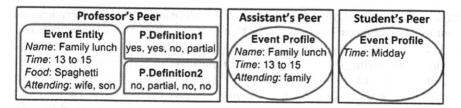

Fig. 3. An example containing Entities, simplified profile definitions and profile materializations for sharing an Event Entity.

- $\{PP\}$ is a non-empty set that specifies the different parameters that feed the algorithms that are to be applied to the profiled entity to obtain the profile, both this set of parameters and the algorithms are entity type-dependent (although future versions may consider its generalization);
- $\{GP\}$ is a possibly empty set that contains the id of all Generated Profiles obtained from the current definition, and;
- $\{NR\}$ represent the Negotiation Requirements that need to be complied by the parties wanting to have access to the information that this profile definition will generate.

Applying a profile definition to the Entity it refers to materializes the actual Profile into an *Entity Profile* structure. An Entity Profile is defined as the tuple $EP = \langle ID, U, S, \{A\}, \{R\}, \{AR\} \rangle$ where:

- ID is a numeric unique identifier.
- U is the id of the user structure that was the source of this profile.
- $\{A\}$ is a set of attributes defined as before but the specific attribute definitions and values may be different from the ones in the entity.
- $\{R\}$ is a set of relations defined as before but the specific relation definitions and values may be different from the ones in the entity.
- $\{AR\}$ is the possibly empty set of Agreed Requirements set between source user structure of the profile (U) and the owner of this entity instance, this property can be checked to make sure that the terms or agreements are not breached.

The profile definition structure (i.e., the filter to apply to the original information before sharing it) is stored at the source peer's storage while the materialized Profile structure (containing the shared partial and/or obfuscated information) is stored at the destination peer's storage, as shown in the example from Fig. 3.

The left part of Fig. 3 shows an Event (family lunch) that belongs to a professor's Peer. The professor created two profile definition structures, which are presented here in a simplified manner, to define how this event is shared to assistants and students. The rest of the figure shows the peer structures that belong to the subjects with the materialized profiles created from applying the restrictions from the profile definition. These materializations include examples of omitted pieces of information (e.g. the 'food' attribute is not shared in neither profile) and partial/obfuscated information (e.g. the time of the event becomes

'Midday'). It is important to note that the realisation of these materializations requires the formalisation of functions that can provide different levels of abstractions for the original information, subjects should be able then to select a particular level during the creation of a profile definition. However, such formal definition is out of the scope of this paper and is left as part of our future work.

The use of the information in the materialized Profiles is restricted by the Agreed Requirements, which are agreed upon a privacy policy based on PPL [18]. Policy enforcement at the platform-level guarantees that the shared information is only used for the stated purposes. For example, if profiles are used to share contact information, e.g. the professor gives her telephone number to her assistant, the professor may restrict its use to "call over phone only". Therefore, any other operation over the data, such as reading or copying the telephone number is not allowed, i.e., the assistant may call the professor but the actual phone number is not revealed to the assistant.

5   Conclusions

This paper provides an initial discussion of privacy and other ethical issues of peer profiling within the scope of the Smart Society project. It also presents the concept of a privacy-enhanced Peer Manager, which is a fundamental building block for the implementation of a privacy-preserving CAS computing platform. As presented in Sect. 4, the Peer Manager allows people and other actors, such as sensors and actuators, to store their information in a secure and preserving framework. The design and development of the Peer Manager followed the following three core guiding principles for enforcing legal privacy principles including the principles of data minimisation, purpose binding, transparency and user control:

1. Separation of information among peers.
2. A user-centered identity management.
3. A user-controlled approach to peer profiling.

The information stored by the Peer Manager follows a semantic schema that defines an attribute-based representation of a peer's characteristics. The Peer Manager allows people (i.e. users) to define profiles that contain and reveal only partial or obfuscated information that are used for replying to information requests and is thus enforcing data minimisation. In addition, the purposes and use of personal data are specified and limited by a PPL privacy policy.

The Peer Manager addresses the presented challenges of information profiling, such as the lack of information and feedback about how profile data is collected and traded, by giving transparency and control of this process to the actual subject that the profile refers to. Hence, subjects can create their own profiles with the minimal amount of information needed and share this information with the promise that their requirements will be enforced by the platform and that the shared data will not be misused or traded against their will. Other features of the platform partially reduce the influence of issues like social sorting (profiled users may not consent giving information for these purposes or create a new pseudonyms to avoid them altogether), diminishing diversity (the greater expressiveness of the semantic schema provides more diversity to data and its representation) and improve self-determination (for the same reasons as the previous two).

It is important to emphasize that the current version of the approach does not completely solve the issues raised in the workshop and that it also introduces potential new issues such information management complexity for users and going against some of the popular business models related to data management.

Management complexity refers to the fact that giving full control of the information could become overwhelming to it owners; specially at the scale in which personal information is produced. For this reason, it is key for the future adoption and practicability of this approach to present itself as an extension of existing identity management systems. While some people may not be interested in fine-grained privacy settings, we plan to provide the possibility to individuals to review and change their privacy settings in a usable way.

It is also worth considering that companies and platforms that base their revenue on the harvesting, processing and reselling customer information may initially be reluctant to give back to their customers more control over their information. There are however, other organizations (e.g. public utilities, health organizations) that value much highly the trust that their customers have in them. Moreover, this higher-degree of customer trust and sense of being in control may also make setting partial limits and transparency settings beneficial to some of the applications that do use this information as source of revenue.

The close attention we pay to privacy and social values for profiles within Smart Society does not mean that all difficulties are circumvented - there are a host of future challenges too. We have to be continually vigilant over whether autonomy and self-determination are indeed preserved by the envisaged technical measures are implementing to protect profiles within Smart Society. For example, despite having the tools to control circulation of their data, a participant may still feel compelled to disclose an item to the system if refusing to do so leaves them materially disadvantaged. This means that we have to keep sight of the wider governance of Smart Society at the same time as we focus at specific technical means that preserve privacy locally.

References

1. Art.29 Data Protection Working Party: Advise paper on essential elements of a definition and a provision on profiling within the EU General Data Protection Regulation. http://ec.europa.eu/justice/data-protection/article-29/documentation/other-document/files/2013/20130513_advice-paper-on-profiling_en.pdf (13052013)
2. Chenu-Abente, R., Zaihrayeu, I., Giunchiglia, F.: A semantic-enabled engine for mobile social networks. In: Cimiano, P., Fernández, M., Lopez, V., Schlobach, S., Völker, J. (eds.) ESWC 2013. LNCS, vol. 7955, pp. 298–299. Springer, Heidelberg (2013)

3. Christin, D., Roßkopf, C., Hollick, M., Martucci, L.A., Kanhere, S.S.: IncogniSense: an anonymity-preserving reputation framework for participatory sensing applications. Pervasive and Mobile Computing, vol. 9(3), pp. 353–371 (2013). http://dx.doi.org/10.1016/j.pmcj.2013.01.003
4. Council of Europe: Recommendation CM/Rec(2010) 13 of the Committee of Ministers to member states on the protection of individuals with regard to automatic processing of personal data in the context of profiling, November 2010. https://wcd.coe.int/ViewDoc.jsp?id=1710949
5. Davidson, S.B., Khanna, S., Roy, S., Stoyanovich, J., Tannen, V., Chen, Y.: On provenance and privacy. In: Proceedings of the 14th International Conference on Database Theory - ICDT, pp. 3–10 (2011). http://doi.acm.org/10.1145/1938551.1938554
6. European Commission: Proposal for a regulation of the European Parliament and of the Council on the protection of individual with regard to the processing of personal data and on the free movement of such data (General Data Protection Regulation) (COM(2012) 0011—C7 0025/2012—2012/0011(COD)) Compromise amendments on Articles 1–29. http://www.europarl.europa.eu/meetdocs/2009_2014/documents/libe/dv/comp_am_art_01-29/comp_am_art_01-29en.pdf (21102013)
7. European Commission: Directive 95/46/EC of the European Parliament and of the Council of 24 October 1995 on the protection of individuals with regard to the processing of personal data and on the free movement of such data. http://eur-lex.europa.eu/LexUriServ/LexUriServ.do?uri=CELEX:31995L0046:en:HTML (23111995)
8. European Commission: Proposal for a REGULATION OF THE EUROPEAN PARLIAMENT AND OF THE COUNCIL on the protection of individuals with regard to the processing of personal data and on the free movement of such data (General Data Protection Regulation), COM(2012) 11 final 2012/0011 (COD). http://ec.europa.eu/justice/data-protection/document/review2012/com_2012_11_en.pdf (2512012)
9. Giunchiglia, F., Crispo, B., Zhang, R.: Access control via lightweight ontologies. In: 2011 5th IEEE International Conference on Semantic Computing (ICSC), pp. 352–355, September 2011
10. Giunchiglia, F., Dutta, B., Maltese, V.: From knowledge organization to knowledge representation. In: ISKO UK Conference (2013)
11. Goodman, E.: Design and ethics in the era of big data. Interactions 21(3), 22–24 (2014). http://doi.acm.org/10.1145/2598902
12. van der Hof, S., Prins, C.: Personalisation and its inuence on identities. In: Behaviour and Social Values. chap. 6, pp. 111–127. Springer, New York (2008). http://opac.inria.fr/record=b1126046
13. Kosinski, M., Stillwell, D., Graepel, T.: Private traits and attributes are predictable from digital records of human behavior. Proc. Natl. Acad. Sci. 110(15), 5802–5805 (2013)
14. Maltese, V., Giunchiglia, F., Dutta, B.: Domains and context: first steps towards managing diversity in knowledge. Web Semant.: Sci. Serv. Agents World Wide Web 12, 53–63 (2012)
15. Martucci, L.A., Ries, S., Mühlhäuser, M.: Sybil-free pseudonyms, privacy and trust: identity management in the internet of services. J. Inf. Process. 19, 317–331 (2011)
16. Monahan, T.: Surveillance and inequality. Surveill. Soc. 5(3), 217–226 (2002)
17. Nissenbaum, H.: Privacy as contextual integrity. Wash. L. Rev. 79, 119 (2004)
18. Trabelsi, S., Neven, G., Raggett, D. (eds.): PrimeLife Public Deliverable D5.3.4 - Report on design and implementation, 20 May 2011

ABC4Trust Workshop on Core Features of Privacy-ABCs, Practical Use, and Legal Issues

Felix Bieker[1], Marit Hansen[1(✉)], Gert Læssøe Mikkelsen[2], and Hannah Obersteller[1]

[1] Unabhängiges Landeszentrum für Datenschutz Schleswig-Holstein, Kiel, Germany
{fbieker,marit.hansen, hobersteller}@datenschutzzentrum.de
[2] Alexandra Institute AS, Aarhus, Denmark
gert.l.mikkelsen@alexandra.dk

Abstract. The project "ABC4Trust – Attribute-based Credentials for Trust" presented its two pilot trials in a workshop and engaged participants in discussions on the two existing as well as potential future application scenarios. Participants were asked to assess several different scenarios in order to determine when an inspection could be carried out without jeopardizing the potential of Privacy-ABCs to protect users' rights. Their findings have been incorporated in a model inspection process that can be adapted to arbitrary scenarios.

Keywords: ABC4Trust · Identity management · Attribute-based credentials · Privacy-ABCs · Conditional identification · Privacy · Data protection

1 Introduction

During the 9th IFIP Summer School on Privacy and Identity Management for the Future Internet in the Age of Globalisation the EC-funded project "ABC4Trust – Attribute-based Credentials for Trust" [1] organized a workshop. Core topics discussed in the workshop were technical, organizational, and legal aspects for using privacy-preserving attribute-based credentials (Privacy-ABCs) in practice.

The workshop took place after two invited talks on Privacy-ABCs and the ABC4Trust project: Professor Kai Rannenberg from Goethe University Frankfurt/Main held a presentation entitled "Identity Management – who is managing what?" (cf. [2]). Dr. Gregory Neven from IBM Zurich introduced "Privacy-preserving authentication: Concepts and policy languages from the ABC4Trust project".

In addition to further familiarizing participants with the instrument of privacy-preserving attribute-based credentials, the workshop served to discuss the existing, as

The research leading to these results has received funding from the European Community's Seventh Framework Programme (FP7/2007-2013) under Grant Agreement no. 257782 for the project Attribute-based Credentials for Trust (ABC4Trust).

J. Camenisch et al. (Eds.): Privacy and Identity 2014, IFIP AICT 457, pp. 253–266, 2015.
DOI: 10.1007/978-3-319-18621-4_17

well as potential future application scenarios for Privacy-ABCs and their implementation in a users' rights-centered approach.

The workshop was organized in three parallel sessions and an additional hands-on session:

- Session I: New Application Scenarios and Storage Devices
  Jonas Lindstrøm Jensen and Michael Bladt Stausholm,
  Alexandra Institute (ALX), Denmark;
  this session was followed by the hands-on session, moderated by the same speakers.
- Session II: Optional Features – Inspection and Revocation
  Yannis Stamatiou,
  Computer Technology Institute & Press – "DIOPHANTUS" (CTI), Greece.
- Session III: Data Protection and Privacy Requirements for Privacy-ABCs
  Felix Bieker and Hannah Obersteller,
  Unabhängiges Landeszentrum für Datenschutz (ULD), Germany.

The remainder of this text is structured as follows: Sect. 2 describes the pilot trial applications of Privacy-ABCs as conducted in the ABC4Trust project. This information served as a basis for the discussions on application scenarios (elaborated in session I, see Sect. 3) and on legal and organizational issues with a focus on inspection and revocation (debated in sessions II and II, see Sect. 4). The conclusions are summarized in the final Sect. 5.

2 Privacy-ABCs in the Pilots of the ABC4 Trust Project

The ABC4Trust workshop primarily addressed issues of Privacy-ABCs in practice. Therefore, starting point of the interactive discussions were the experiences gained from the pilots: In the ABC4Trust project privacy-preserving attribute-based credentials (Privacy-ABCs) were implemented in pilot trial applications to protect users' privacy. Privacy-ABCs provide options for attribute selection and attribute aggregation by the user. They can be used either fully anonymously or allow for conditional identification (so-called inspection) in order to support accountability. However, all these features can only be used to their best potential when they are implemented in a rights-centered way. The workflow of a Privacy-ABC authentication and Privacy-ABC features as well as their benefits are described in more detail elsewhere in this book (cf. [2]).

In the two pilots of the ABC4Trust project, Privacy-ABCs were used as means of authentication for an online communication platform of a Swedish school, where students, teachers and other stakeholders could securely and privately discuss matters of school life [3–5]. Some of the chat rooms were used fully anonymously, while in others a user's identity could be revealed under predefined conditions via an inspection process. In the other use case, the Greek University of Patras implemented an online platform for course evaluations [6–8]. There, students could rate their courses fully anonymously; the inspection feature was not implemented. However, in the second round of the pilot, students who participated in the course evaluation could obtain an additional credential which was inspectable. With this credential they could enter a tombola and be selected to win a prize. In order to reveal the winning student's identity, the inspection process was implemented.

As with any authentication technology, there may be instances where the credentials issued through Privacy-ABCs have to be invalidated. In the ABC4Trust pilot trials this is for instance the case when a student leaves school or university. This can be realized through revocation of the respective credentials (for implementation in the pilots see [4] pp. 38 et sqq.; [7], pp. 18, 20; [8], pp. 77, 123).

Especially with regard to the school pilot, it is very clear that the inspection feature must not be used as a "backdoor" to reveal a user's identity at will. Instead, the full potential of Privacy-ABCs can only be achieved if inspection is an exception, rather than the rule. Similarly, a user loses all access to the respective service when her credentials are revoked. Therefore, revocation also has a users' rights dimension and should occur only in justified and limited instances. In order to safeguard this aim, a model process for inspection and guidelines for revocation were developed within the ABC4Trust project [9, 10].

3 Workshop Sessions on New Application Scenarios and Storage Devices

In session I, aspects of applying Privacy-ABC systems to new application scenarios were discussed based on the project partners' experiences with the project and from the pilots. Applying Privacy-ABCs to new application scenarios is not always a straight forward process, and despite being a technology with many features, Privacy-ABCs are sometimes not the most appropriate tool for a given scenario. Participants investigated potential new application scenarios (based on the scenarios tackled in sessions II and III). Moreover, they pondered how to validate whether Privacy-ABCs actually are the right tool for a given application, and – if so – how to map the entities of the scenario to the entities of Privacy-ABCs. Furthermore, the participants dealt with the process of developing policies and some related topics such as efficiency expectations etc.

As far as security tokens are concerned, the use of a storage device was suggested. In the workshop the participants assessed different options for tamper-proof devices (smartcards, mobile phones, USB sticks, etc.) which offer security and are ideal hardware tokens for storing the user's device key. The technical aspects for choosing a storage device as well as how the choice of the storage device could influence the user's confidence and trust to the system were explored. Also, it was found that the choice of the storage device could influence the usability of the system since the user has to carry the device with her every time she wants to use it.

Following up on this session, the participants had the opportunity to attend the additional hands-on session where they were tutored how to integrate ABC4Trust technology in future own applications. Instructions for developers as presented in these sessions are available at [11]. This encompasses the source code of the Privacy-preserving Attribute-based Credential Engine as well as further explanations on concepts and features of Privacy-ABCs, the reference architecture, and the integration into an application.

4   Workshop Sessions on Inspection, Revocation, and Legal Issues

Two sessions tackled inspection and revocation, especially how to set up appropriate procedures with checks and balances: session II "Optional Features – Inspection and Revocation" and session III "Data Protection and Privacy Requirements for Privacy-ABCs". These sessions' primary goal was to improve and validate the model processes developed in the ABC4Trust project [9, 10].

4.1   Organization of the Sessions

In session II the focus lay on the inspection and revocation features of Privacy-ABCs as they have been implemented in practice within the Patras University pilot trial. Technical requirements and practical problems were explained in detail. The adaptability of the inspection and revocation tools to various needs and systems as well as device requirements were demonstrated. From the practical experiences the responsible partners had gained with developing and piloting the application, guidelines for an optimal inspection and revocation process were given. This was illustrated with an in-depth look at the implementation of Privacy-ABCs in the ABC4Trust university pilot.

During session III participants were given an introduction to the European legal framework for data protection and privacy. This brief lecture addressed the bases in primary law for data protection legislation, including the fundamental rights to privacy and data protection. It focused on the obligations of data processors under the Data Protection Directive 95/46/EC and on data protection principles.

After this short presentation, participants were split into groups of four to five people. Based on their own knowledge and what had been taught in the beginning of the session, the participants' task was to assess one of five fictitious scenarios (see full descriptions in Appendix A), which dealt with a variety of existing and potential future Privacy-ABCs use cases. In each case, there were escalating levels of conflicts, which were to be resolved by finding an appropriate way of employing the inspection and revocation features.

In another step, the participants of the parallel sessions II and III joined. The scenarios, including their resolution by the participants of session III, as well as the model process for inspection [9] were discussed in the plenary. Participants of session II could comment on the findings from their practical background experience.

4.2   Discussions Among the Participants

While each group was provided a different scenario description, similarities could be identified in the composition of the use cases: The group members were asked to act as if they were the people in charge of deciding on a conflict between various parties. The objective was to think of measures to remedy the situation while achieving a balanced result. This may or may not mean to identify a Privacy-ABC user via inspection under specific circumstances; other measures also had to be contemplated. For deciding on a potential inspection, a list of inspection grounds was presented: Apart from possible internal policy demands as this was the case in the Swedish school pilot, these grounds covered:

- Situations implying a severe threat to the life, or the physical/mental integrity of a person.
- An existing court order or other valid administrative request because of criminal proceedings.
- Damage compensation (protection of third people's rights claims).

The examples provided in the scenarios (cf. Appendix A) gradually escalated, e.g. from a conflict which could be remedied without the need for inspection (even if the anger shown may well be understandable in human terms) to a situation as severe as a threat to people's life. The fact that all examples contained the possibility of inspection did not mislead the participants into always choosing this instrument for achieving remedy. Interestingly enough, the legally trained persons among the groups did not dominate the discussions – it seemed that they did not have an advantage in answering the questions because they would have liked to first analyze all applicable national regulation which may have given further guidance. While that procedure is excellent for a thorough check of legal compliance, we focused in this exercise on the gut feeling of mainly laypeople, being no legal specialists.

4.3   Results

The discussions of the Summer School participants showed that they were very much aware of the privacy implications of revealing a user's identity through inspection. As the examples provided in the scenarios gradually escalated, every group adapted to each case by also escalating their responses. All of the groups found that in *variation 1* inspection was not a feasible option, as there were lower level solutions available, which were less invasive to the user's privacy (see Appendix A, "Situations to be discussed", no. 1). These included for instance deletion of offending posts in a forum. Additionally, the importance of properly defined inspection grounds was stressed, in order to facilitate the finding of a decision whether inspection even was an option.

In *variation 2* (see Appendix A, "Situations to be discussed", no. 2), the participants had to weigh the conflicting interests and rights of the user and the service provider to reach a nuanced solution for the problem. With respect to this balancing exercise, participants stressed the importance of the separation between the entity performing the weighing and the entity to reveal the identity. Ideally, the entity deciding on a solution should consist of all relevant stakeholders in the use case, i.e. not only representatives of the service provider, but also users. Additionally, it is desirable to incorporate an element of external supervision to this decision entity, in the form of an external expert focused on ethical or legal implications of the decision. It was further discussed that the service provider's Data Protection Officer could partake in the deliberations, as he or she is an expert with a certain level of autonomy. Alternatively the Data Protection Officer could be involved in reviewing and auditing the process. This review is enabled by an audit trail that logs any activity within the process on all its stages, comprising e.g. technical access log entries as well as manually generated reasoning for inspection decisions. This could be supported by an automated ticketing system, which can provide check lists and assist the various entities in the execution of the process.

When participants were asked to outline a model for an inspection process, almost all of the groups suggested that this entity should be independent from the service provider in finding a solution for a problem.

As *variation 3* (see Appendix A, "Situations to be discussed", no. 3) included instances of emergencies, such as threats to the life or physical integrity of persons, participants agreed that there was a need to ensure a quick response, which can be realized through break glass procedures. This could include fast-tracking decisions of the entity deciding whether an inspection should take place. However, as the levels of emergency in the various scenarios differed to an extent, the concept of what constitutes an emergency was discussed controversially. It was concluded that just as the inspection grounds themselves emergency situations should be clearly defined in advance in order to use the full potential of Privacy-ABCs.

The additional questions in some of the scenarios, e.g. concerning the timing for proving that a customer in an e-commerce setting is over 18, stimulated further discussions in the individual groups. In the case of ordering alcohol or cigarettes it was discussed that the proof would be necessary only at check-out time, but the customers should be made aware of such requirements from the beginning. If adult content may not even be displayed to customers younger than 18, proof would be required before showing the content, similar to realizing a separated room with special access control.

4.4   The Model Inspection Process

In the group discussions a few ideas emerged on a structured workflow, defined entities, and assigned tasks for the inspection process, and similarly for any unplanned revocation. While many papers on inspection only focus on technical issues such as the process of decrypting inspectable tokens by an entity (i.e. the *Inspector*) that has access to the inspection key, the organizational and legal setting would be relevant, too. For this purpose, a model inspection process was developed [9, 10] that contains several roles and looks a bit more complex than simply adding the *Inspector* component (see Fig. 1). However, it is de facto quite similar to other workflows where a service provider is notified about a conflict and has to react accordingly. Also, it is important to understand that inspection should be the exception rather than the rule. This is the reason for separating the access to the inspection key and to the encrypted inspectable tokens as long as no inspection has to be performed.

The process starts with an inspection request, sent by the *Inspection Request Sender* to the *Inspection Request Recipient* within the *Service Provider's Domain* (step 1). This could be a user who thinks a policy rule has been violated, or it could be the police demanding inspection in an investigation, potentially with a warrant issued by the competent judicial authorities. The *Inspection Request Recipient* has to check the inspection request (step 2). In some cases, actions independent from inspection could be taken (step 3), e.g. removal of an insulting posting. Note that such an intervention could mean an infringement of users' rights and needs a balancing approach, too.

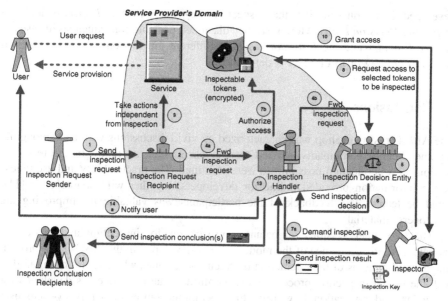

Fig. 1. A model inspection process [9]

The *Inspection Request Recipient* forwards the inspection request to the *Inspection Handler* (step 4a) where the entire inspection process is being orchestrated. The first action of the *Inspection Handler* is a further forwarding of the inspection request to the *Inspection Decision Entity* (step 4b). This could be a board of different stakeholders where difficult conflicts may be discussed to achieve a balanced solution. The decision on whether to inspect or not (step 5) is documented and sent back to the *Inspection Handler* (step 6).

In case inspection should be performed, the *Inspection Handler* orders the *Inspector* to inspect specific inspectable tokens (step 7a) and authorizes access for the *Inspector* to those tokens stored within the *Service Provider's Domain* (step 7b). The *Inspector* requests access to selected tokens to be inspected (step 8). This request is checked against the authorization (step 9). In case of a match access is granted (step 10), otherwise this attempted access would be logged, and the process would end.

The *Inspector* who possesses the inspection key decrypts the tokens (step 11) and sends the inspection results to the *Inspection Handler* (step 12). The *Inspection Handler* takes action based on the inspection results, e.g. notifying the *User* whose identity has been revealed (step 14a), generating target-specific inspection conclusions, and informing the *Inspection Conclusion Recipient(s)* (step 14b). This recipient could be identical with the *Inspection Request Sender*, but may also be different. Again, further steps may be taken by the *Inspection Conclusion Recipients* (step 15).

Further details, e.g. on the legal relation between *Inspector* and *Service Provider*, on the composition and tasks of *Inspection Decision Entity*, on demanded logging of decisions for accountability purposes, and on possible short cuts in the process (e.g. in case of a valid warrant that has to be obeyed, or in cases of emergency), have been discussed in [9]. Looking at the model process, the participants of the session developed ideas on splitting the inspection key between the *Inspector* and the *Inspection Decision Entity*. Moreover, they discussed possible consequences in case the *Service Provider* and the *Inspector* reside in different jurisdictions and governmental access to the key or to the data is demanded.

5   Conclusions

The ABC4Trust workshop was characterized by vivid discussions with and among the Summer School participants and led to a much appreciated input. In the technical sessions new application possibilities were identified. The practicability and usefulness of the information provided online for developers, together with source code [11], could be tested. The feedback of the participants was valuable for improving the developers' material.

The two other sessions on balanced procedures for inspection and revocation showed a broad acceptance of the model process developed in the ABC4Trust project. The general patterns of the interaction between participants, who had not been familiar with the model inspection process before, confirmed that the processes developed for inspection and revocation flow from the operationalization of a privacy- and user rights-centered approach. Participants generally concluded that specific implementations have their own factual and legal requirements and thus implementation always has to be use case specific. Nevertheless, the model inspection process as it was presented to the participants after the discussions was appraised as a way to enhance transparency and make the best use of the privacy-friendly technology employed in the ABC4Trust project pilots.

A   Appendix

This appendix contains the five scenario descriptions that were handed out to the participants of the workshop. Each group had to assess one of the scenarios (school, e-commerce, casino, car rental, e-petitions) and think of solutions for different escalating situations.

School Scenario. *Task:* You are the people in charge of deciding on the case detailed below. Which measures can you adopt to remedy the situation while achieving a balanced result? How can this process of revealing a user's identity best be implemented in practice to ensure a system of checks and balances?

The *N School* runs a Privacy-ABC based communication system. All pupils of the school can use the communication system, inter alia for chatting with each other, sharing documents and seeking advice from the school's counsellors. The pupils act under pseudonyms they can choose anew any time.

Inspection grounds:

To guarantee the physical and mental safety of each participating pupil, the School Communication System foresees in all restricted areas except those for political discussions the revelation of the pupil's identity (called inspection) in certain predefined emergency situations (called inspection grounds).

Inspection grounds:

- Situations implying a severe threat to the life, or the physical/mental integrity of a person.
- Situations demanding an intervention according to the school policy against discrimination and degrading treatment. It strives to prevent discrimination based on gender, sexual orientation, ethnic background, religion. The policy also sanctions harassment and other threats to the safety of students, including offensive language. It is a legal requirement to report such behavior and the names of the perpetrators to the school authority.
- An existing court order or other valid administrative request.
- Damage compensation (protection of third people's rights claims).

Class 9b has opened a chat room "9B Only", their own restricted area, accessible only to pupils and teachers of class 9b. The class and its teachers use this chat room especially for exchanging information on class activities – for instance a boat trip to the small rock islands along the shoreline.

Situations to be discussed:

1. The boat trip was fun. The pupils took hundreds of photos. *Pupil A* shares several photos she took in the restricted area of class 9b. One of the photos is a portrait picture of B. B is not happy with the photo visible for the whole class. She recently has decided to be a punk and therefore dyed her hair green. But on the picture, taken two days ago, she is still naturally blonde. She demands deletion, first via chat and then in front of the class. A thinks that B has simply gone bonkers and decides neither to say that it was her who uploaded the picture nor to delete it. B thinks she has the right to deletion of the picture and to know who uploaded it. She demands inspection. She wants to confront the "photographer" personally.

2. Finally, B found out that it was A who uploaded the picture. She is extremely disappointed, since she had thought A was her friend. B writes a chat message to all: "I never thought A would not respect other people's feelings. I think everyone has the right to express her own personality. I am very disappointed that A did not delete the picture. I am not her friend anymore." A feels offended – she is sure that it was B who wrote this. Since she is kind of clever, she decides not to answer in a way that would identify her as A. She writes: "I think what A did was alright. B is always exaggerating – she is such a wannabe and a drama queen and just silly." A lively discussion is initiated. *X1, X2,* and *X3* agree with what A wrote and call B "birdbrained", "dumb blonde" and "insane".

3. B is devastated. No one understands her or even seems to take her seriously. Furthermore, everyone is making fun of her because of her new style. Former friends seem to stay away from her. So, late at night, after a day full of frustration, B writes the following chat message to "9B Only": "I will kill you all. I got a reason, I got the means – tomorrow I will use the opportunity!"

E-Commerce Scenario. *Task:* You are the people in charge of deciding on the case detailed below. Which measures can you adopt to remedy the situation while achieving a balanced result? How can this process of revealing a user's identity best be implemented in practice to ensure a system of checks and balances?

The e-commerce platform *E-Buy* offers traders to sell their goods via its portal. It is based on Privacy-ABC technologies. Users/potential customers do not reveal their identity to *E-Buy* nor to the sellers when registering to *E-Buy* and going shopping. They act under pseudonyms they can choose anew any time. Users can also rate the products they bought. The rating is visible to everyone who visits the platform. A user can have her products delivered to a central store, and pick them up there by identifying herself using the credential she gets from *E-Buy* when buying the respective products.

Customer C is looking for a mosquito blind. He makes a find among the products provided by *D* who mainly sells pesticides and other means to control pests. *C* buys the mosquito blind. When unpacking the mosquito blind, *C* finds a manual how to fix the mosquito blind on windows. One has to cut it to the proper size. *C* reads the manual carefully. But, however, he comes to the conclusion that one has to measure the internal side of the window's frame. In fact, one has to measure the outer dimensions. Consequently, the mosquito blind is too small for the window and *C* cannot make use of it like this. *C* tries to call the seller *D*. *D* just says the product and manual were fine.

Inspection grounds:

- Situations implying a severe threat to the life, or the physical/mental integrity of a person.
- An existing court order or other valid administrative request because of criminal proceedings.
- Damage compensation (protection of third people's rights claims).

Situations to be discussed:

1. *C* feels his problems were treated as a joke or something. He is angry and rates the mosquito blind with only one of five possible stars. Additionally he states, "In my opinion, the instruction manual provided by the seller was inadequate. Like this it is de facto impossible to fix this mosquito blind. The manual clearly states that in order to find the right size one has to measure the internal side of the window's frame. In fact, one has to measure the outer dimensions. Otherwise the mosquito blind is too small." *D* does not want this comment to ruin his impeccable reputation. In fact, he does not sell any mosquito blind during the following week. *D* is convinced that *C*'s rating irritates other customers. He demands the revelation of this customer's identity, in order to claim compensation from *C*.

2. *C* is furious. His rating of *D* is gone! Fortunately *D* still sells goods on *E-Buy*. *C* picks a nice rat trap. Actually *C* just wanted to have another possibility to rate *D* on *E-Buy*. So, after the trap was delivered, *C* writes, "No rat trap is big enough to trap the biggest rat on *E-Buy*: Its seller. *D* is a fraudster and sells inferior crap." *D* thinks this is a severe offence and wants to make a complaint.

3. Alternative: *C* is really furious. His rating is gone. Fortunately *D* still sells goods on *E-Buy*. *C* picks some poisonous gas (meant to be used for parasite prevention). After the gas was delivered, *C* writes, "Caution you pest! I got the gas and I know where you live. You will not live through this night!"

4. Additional question: On the *E-Buy* platform some traders sell alcohol and cigarettes. According to the self-imposed rules of *E-Buy* such products may not be sold to persons under age 18. At which point should the potential customer have to prove that she is over 18?

Casino Scenario. *Task:* You are the people in charge of deciding on the case detailed below. Which measures can you adopt to remedy the situation while achieving a balanced result? How can this process of revealing a user's identity best be implemented in practice to ensure a system of checks and balances?

J has is addicted to gambling. Since *J* is a junkie, but has a sense of style he only visits casinos of the *LB Group*. Admission only to members. *LB* casinos have a Privacy-ABC based access control system. This means, members can prove their membership (and access permission) via their smartphones when entering the casinos. The membership credentials also contain information about how much money is stored on a member's account, since one cannot pay in cash at *LB* casinos. The *LB Group* only learns that a member has entered one of their casinos, but not which member. It cannot analyze the member's usage behavior.

In the past five years, it got worse and worse. *J* lost his friends, because he borrowed money from them and never gave it back and lost his job because he repeatedly was gone for days without permission. Finally, his girlfriend threatens to move out if *J* does not stop gambling, because she cannot stand it anymore. Sitting on his mount of debt – round about EUR 250,000 – *J* comes to the conclusion that something has to change.

Inspection grounds:

- Situations implying a severe threat to the life, or the physical/mental integrity of a person.
- An existing court order or other valid administrative request because of criminal proceedings.
- Damage compensation (protection of third people's rights claims).

Situations to be discussed:

1. Via the Privacy-ABC based *LB* communication system for members, *J* resigns his *LB* casino membership contract. *LB Group* accepts the notice, but denies releasing *J* from the membership contract immediately. It insists on the notice period of 3 months. *J* is devastated. Once committed to get rid of his gambling addiction by just keeping himself from going to the casino, he wants to make sure that he cannot access *LB* casinos anymore. Even though for the next 3 months he still will be a member. His girlfriend does not believe him that he will not go to the casino anymore although he still could.

2. Although *J* managed not to gamble anymore for 4 weeks, his girlfriend left him for a professional poker player. *J* does not see any reason why he should not start gambling again. He wants to have access to the *LB* casinos again. In the end, he might still make a fortune … The *LB Group* is very generous and accepts the withdrawal of the notice. *J* will stay a member. But his membership credential is not valid anymore. He does not want a whole new membership credential, because there is still money stored on his original one.

3. Believe it or not – *J* won 2 million Euros in one night. Boosted by such a success, *J* visits several *LB* casinos in the following days. Now that he is rich he can travel. And he keeps winning. The *LB Group* – due to Privacy-ABCs – does not know that it is always the same member who is winning tons of money. But the management is suspicious. In statistics, this is more than the standard deviation. *LB Group's* lawyers suspect fraud. All the money is won in Black Jack. *LB Group* wants to know if it is the same person who is winning all the time.

Car Rental Scenario. *Task:* You are the people in charge of deciding on the case detailed below. Which measures can you adopt to remedy the situation while achieving a balanced result? How can this process of revealing a user's identity best be implemented in practice to ensure a system of checks and balances?

Ride Ltd. runs a conventional car rental via an online platform. The platform is Privacy-ABC based. Users do not reveal their identity to *Ride Ltd.* when registering to the platform and renting cars. They act under pseudonyms they can choose anew any time. Users can pick up the car keys and the car from a central parking lot by identifying themselves using the credential they get from *Ride Ltd.* when renting a car. *Ride Ltd.* terms and conditions of business determine that in case of damages up to an amount of EUR 100, it is entitled to just debit the amount from the customer's account. Such damages include minor accident damages, reimbursement of costs related to inappropriate use of the car, and giving back the car in a non-contractual condition. Customers are required to give back the car refueled.

N rents a car for a nice weekend trip to the sea side.

Inspection grounds:

- Situations implying a severe threat to the life, or the physical/mental integrity of a person.
- An existing court order or other valid administrative request because of criminal proceedings.
- Damage compensation (protection of third people's rights claims).

Situations to be discussed:

1. *N* is back from the seaside. It has been a long day and he just wants to go home. The tank is really empty and *N* hardly makes it to the parking lot. Whatever – *N* just parks the car on the parking lot of *Ride Ltd.* and places the keys in the letter-box. The next morning, *E* – an employee of *Ride Ltd.* – checks the car and finds the empty tank. He cannot even drive the car to the gas station. *E* has to haul the gasoline canister to the car … thank you very much, dear customer …
2. After refueling the car, *E* checks the interior. What the …? The whole backseat is full of blood. Indeed, *N* went fishing and made a pretty good catch. Unfortunately, the fish obviously had not had properly bled when *N* threw it on the back seat. Put briefly, the back seat is ruined and cannot be cleaned. The replacement will cost about EUR 3,000. *Ride Ltd.* contacts the customer – *N* – but of course *Ride Ltd.* only knows the pseudonym of the customer who had rented the car via the internal communication system. *N* does not answer. *Ride Ltd.* wants to claim compensation from him.

3. While the lawyers of *Ride Ltd.* are preparing the civil proceedings against *N*, there is an incoming call. It is the police. A witness alleges that a man has just forced a girl into a car of *Ride Ltd.* The police suspect a crime – kidnapping or abduction – and want to know who has currently rented the car.

E-Petitions Scenario. *Task:* You are the people in charge of deciding on the case detailed below. Which measures can you adopt to remedy the situation while achieving a balanced result? How can this process of revealing a user's identity best be implemented in practice to ensure a system of checks and balances?

In country *X* everyone has the right to petition to the parliament. It is a fundamental right which guarantees that the public authorities at least have to file the petition. If the public authority lacks competence concerning a petition's content, it may dismiss the petition as inadmissible. Within the parliament there is a petition committee which is competent to decide on and answer petitions. Petitions offer the possibility to raise an issue and oblige the democratically elected representatives to address this issue. They can be filed in writing (via post) or electronically, via an online form which is provided on the petition committee's website. The website employs Privacy-ABCs. This means, users can petition anonymously. Petitions are published automatically online if the petitioner does not object when filing the petition. Since the petitions are not manually checked before they are published online, you sometimes find interesting howlers inside ...

Inspection grounds:

- Situations implying a severe threat to the life, or the physical/mental integrity of a person.
- An existing court order or other valid administrative request because of criminal proceedings.
- Damage compensation (protection of third people's rights claims).

Situations to be discussed:

1. "After almost 10 years of female rule of *President M* we are only inches away from the abyss. Everything will run down the drain if we do not stop them. We need to take a step back, back to the days when the world was still governed by worthy men – and only by men. Reasonable, reliable, and down-to-earth. Women are nothing but a victim of their genes and hormones. We cannot let them govern our homeland any longer. Abolish women's suffrage!!!"
2. "The killing of male chicks is a blatant injustice which cannot be accepted anymore! We, the *National Chicken Liberation Forces*, demand satisfaction! The killing must be stopped immediately. If the parliament does not adopt an anti-male-chicken-killing law within the next 48 h, we will free all chicken farms!"
3. In country *X* all armament deals are subject to the approval of a supervisory board. In general, weapons from *X* may not be sold and delivered to countries which are currently considered as "region in crisis". *Y* owns an arms company. Business is going pretty bad since, due to all those crises in the world, the supervisory board does not easily give the green light to all deals anymore. *Y* panics a bit. So he petitions the parliament: "If you do not drop the prior approval, I will give you a

product presentation right in the middle of the parliament! Our tanks will break your walls and make you approve them!"

4. Additional question: Assumed, someone is petitioning all the time – say, twice a day. What to do?

References

1. Rannenberg, K., Camenisch, J., Sabouri, A. (eds.): Attribute-based Credentials for Trust – Identity in the Information Society. Springer, Heidelberg (2015)
2. Sabouri, A., Rannenberg, K.: ABC4Trust: protecting privacy in identity management by bringing privacy-ABCs into real-life. In: Camenisch, J., Fischer-Hübner, S., Hansen, M. (eds.) Privacy and Identity 2014. IFIP AICT, vol. 457, pp. xx–yy (2015)
3. Bcheri, S., Goetze, N., Orski, M., Zwingelberg, H.: Application description for the school deployment. deliverable D6.1 of the ABC4Trust Project (2012). https://abc4trust.eu/download/ABC4Trust-D6.1-Application-Description-School.pdf. Accessed 22 March 2015
4. Abendroth, J., Bcheri, S., Damgaard K., Ghani, H., Luna, J., Mikkelsen, G.L., Moneta, M., Orski, M., Suri, N., Zwingelberg, H.: Necessary hardware and software package for the school pilot deployment. Deliverable D6.2 of the ABC4Trust project (2013). https://abc4trust.eu/download/ABC4Trust-D6.2.Hard-and-Software-Package-for-School-Pilot.pdf. Accessed 22 March 2015
5. Bcheri, S., Björk, E., Deibler, D., Hånell, G., Lerch, J., Moneta, M., Orski, M., Schlehahn, E., Tesfay, W.: Evaluation of the school pilot. Deliverable D6.3 of the ABC4Trust Project (2014). https://abc4trust.eu/download/Deliverable%20D6.3.pdf. Accessed 22 March 2015
6. Abendroth, J., Liagkou, V., Pyrgelis, A., Raptopoulos, C., Sabouri, A., Schlehahn, E., Stamatiou, Y., Zwingelberg, H.: Application description for students. Deliverable D7.1 of the ABC4Trust project (2012). https://abc4trust.eu/download/ABC4Trust-D7.1-Application-Description-Students.pdf. Accessed 22 March 2015
7. Damgaard, K, Ghani, H., Goetze, N., Lehmann, A., Liagkou, V., Luna, J., Mikkelsen, G.L., Pyrgelis, A., Stamatiou, Y.: Necessary hardware and software package for the student pilot deployment. Deliverable D7.2 of the ABC4Trust project (2012). https://abc4trust.eu/download/ABC4Trust-D7.2.Hard-and-Software-Package-for-Student-Pilot.pdf. Accessed 22 March 2015
8. Deibler, D., Engeler, M., Krontiris, I., Liagkou, V., Pyrgelis, A., Schlehahn, E., Stamatiou, Y., Tesfay, W., Zwingelberg, H.: Evaluation of the student pilot. Deliverable D7.3 of the ABC4Trust Project (2014). https://abc4trust.eu/download/Deliverable%20D7.3.pdf. Accessed 22 March 2015
9. Bieker, F., Hansen, M., Zwingelberg, H.: Towards a privacy-preserving inspection process for authentication solutions with conditional identification. In: Hühnlein, D., Roßnagel, H. (eds.) Proceedings of Open Identity Summit 2014. LNI, vol. P-237, pp. 85–96. Gesellschaft für Informatik, Bonn (2014)
10. Bieker, F., Hansen, M.: Modelling the inspection process considerations concerning the revocation process. In: Rannenberg, K., Camenisch, J., Sabouri, A. (eds.) Attribute-Based Credentials for Trust Identity in the Information Society, pp. 155–161. Springer, Heidelberg (2015)
11. Alexandra Institute, Miracle, and IBM Research – Zurich: Privacy-Preserving Attribute-Based Credential Engine (p2abcengine). Repository on GitHub (2015). https://github.com/p2abcengine/p2abcengine. Accessed 22 March 2015

Author Index

Printed in the United States
By Bookmasters